OXFORD
Illustrated
Children's
Thesaurus

footprints

butterfly

OXFORD
UNIVERSITY PRESS

Great Clarendon Street, Oxford OX2 6DP

Oxford University Press is a department of the University of Oxford.
It furthers the University's objective of excellence in research, scholarship,
and education by publishing worldwide in

Oxford   New York

Auckland   Cape Town   Dar es Salaam   Hong Kong   Karachi
Kuala Lumpur   Madrid   Melbourne   Mexico City   Nairobi
New Delhi   Shanghai   Taipei   Toronto

With offices in

Argentina   Austria   Brazil   Chile   Czech Republic   France   Greece
Guatemala   Hungary   Italy   Japan   Poland   Portugal   Singapore
South Korea   Switzerland   Thailand   Turkey   Ukraine   Vietnam

Oxford is a registered trade mark of Oxford University Press
in the UK and in certain other countries

treasure chest

owl

scorpion

British Library Cataloguing in Publication Data

Data available

ISBN: 9780-19-911994-3

5 7 9 10 8 6 4

Printed in China

balls

core

feet

starfish

lion

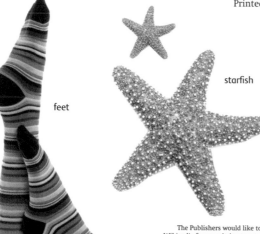

The Publishers would like to thank Shutterstock and
Wikipedia for permission to use their material. Every care has
been taken to trace copyright holders. However, if there have
been unintentional omissions or failure to trace copyright
holders, we apologize, and will, if informed, endeavour to
make corrections in any future edition.

How to Use your Thesaurus

numbered senses
show you when a word has more than one meaning

example sentences
show how you might use a word, each meaning has a separate example sentence

headwords
are words you look up, they are in alphabetical order

guide words
give the first and last word on the page

better ▷ bird

word class
tells you whether a word is a *noun*, *verb*, *adjective*, *adverb*, or *preposition*

alphabet tab
shows the letter of the alphabet

synonyms
words that mean the same, or nearly the same, as the headword

word web panels
give lists of words related to a topic, useful for project work and story writing

labels
tell you that certain synonyms are formal or informal

opposites
words that are opposite in meaning to the headword

overused word panels
offer more interesting words for common words like *nice*, *good*, or *bad*

writing tips panels
help you create more colourful descriptions

---

2 *The look in her eyes betrayed her true feelings.*
reveal, show, indicate, disclose, divulge, expose, tell
better *adjective*
1 *Which of these songs do you think is better?*
superior, finer, preferable
2 *I had a cold, but I'm better now.*
recovered, cured, healed, improved, well
beware *verb*
Beware! There are thieves about.
be careful! watch out! look out! take care! be on your guard!
beware of
Beware of the bull.
watch out for, avoid, mind, heed, keep clear of
biased *adjective*
A referee should not make a biased decision.
prejudiced, partial, one-sided, partisan, unfair
OPPOSITE impartial
big *adjective*
The giant owned three pairs of big boots.
large, huge, great, massive, enormous, gigantic, colossal, mammoth
(*informal*) whopping, ginormous, humungous
OPPOSITE small, little, tiny

! OVERUSED WORD
Try to vary the words you use for **big**. Here are some other words you could use.
FOR A **big person** OR **big creature**:
burly, giant, hefty, hulking, mighty, monstrous, towering *The mighty robot clanked as it moved.*
FOR A **big object**:
bulky, heavy, hefty, weighty *What could be inside that bulky envelope?*
FOR A **big room** OR **big box**:
roomy, sizeable, spacious *Inside, the spaceship was surprisingly roomy.*
OPPOSITE cramped
FOR A **big distance**:
immense, infinite, vast *A vast stretch of ocean lay before them.*
FOR A **big amount** OR **big helping**:
ample, considerable, substantial *We each got an ample helping of porridge.*
OPPOSITE meagre, paltry
FOR A **big decision** OR **big moment**:
grave, important, serious, significant *Yesterday was the most significant day in my short life.*
OPPOSITE unimportant, minor

★ WORD WEB

bird *noun*
A female bird is a **hen**.
A male bird is a **cock**.
A young bird is a **chick**, **fledgling**, or **nestling**.
A family of chicks is a **brood**.
A group of birds is a **colony** or **flock**.
A group of flying birds is a **flight** or **skein**.
A person who studies birds is an **ornithologist**.

SOME COMMON BRITISH BIRDS
blackbird, blue tit, bullfinch, bunting, chaffinch, crow, cuckoo, dove, greenfinch, jackdaw, jay, linnet, magpie, martin, nightingale, pigeon, raven, robin, rook, skylark, sparrow, starling, swallow, swift, thrush, tit, wagtail, waxwing, woodpecker, wren, yellowhammer

BIRDS OF PREY
buzzard, eagle, falcon, hawk, kestrel, kite, merlin, osprey, owl, sparrowhawk, vulture

FARM AND GAME BIRDS
chicken, duck, goose, grouse, partridge, pheasant, quail, turkey

Birds kept by farmers are called *poultry*.

SEA AND WATER BIRDS
albatross, auk, bittern, coot, cormorant, crane, curlew, duck, gannet, goose, guillemot, gull, heron, kingfisher, kittiwake, lapwing, mallard, moorhen, oystercatcher, peewit, pelican, penguin, puffin, seagull, snipe, stork, swan, teal

BIRDS FROM OTHER COUNTRIES
bird of paradise, budgerigar, canary, cockatoo, flamingo, humming bird, ibis, kookaburra, lovebirds, macaw, mynah bird, parakeet, parrot, toucan

lovebirds

BIRDS WHICH CANNOT FLY
emu, kiwi, ostrich, peacock, penguin

eagle

PARTS OF A BIRD'S BODY
beak, bill, claw, talon, breast, crown, throat, crest, feather, down, plumage, plume, wing

SOME TYPES OF BIRD HOME
nest, nesting box, aviary, coop, roost

SOUNDS MADE BY BIRDS
cackle, caw, cheep, chirp, chirrup, cluck, coo, crow, gabble, honk, peep, pipe, quack, screech, squawk, trill, tweet, twitter, warble
A turkey *gobbles*.
An owl *hoots*.

SPECIAL NAMES
A female peacock is a *peahen*.
A young duck is a *duckling*.
A young goose is a *gosling*.
A young swan is a *cygnet*.
An eagle's nest is an *eyrie*.
A place where rooks nest is a *rookery*.

flamingo

✎ WRITING TIPS
You can use these words to describe a **bird**.
1 TO DESCRIBE *how a bird moves*
circle, dart, flit, flutter, fly, glide, hop, hover, peck, perch, preen, skim, soar, swoop, waddle, wheel *A pair of swallows flitted among the rooftops.*
2 TO DESCRIBE *a bird's feathers*
bedraggled, downy, drab, fluffy, gleaming, iridescent, ruffled, smooth, speckled *The peacock displayed its iridescent tail.*

ostrich

owl

a
b
c
d
e
f
g
h
i
j
k
l
m
n
o
p
q
r
s
t
u
v
w
x
y
z

17

What is a thesaurus for?

Here are three good reasons to use your thesaurus:

✓ **to find a more interesting word**
What words can you use besides *fly* for how a bird moves? Look up **bird** to find some other ways of describing how birds fly.

✓ **to find the right word**
What do you call a line of mountains? Look up **mountain** to find the answer.

✓ **to give you ideas for writing**
Imagine you are describing outer space. Look up **space** and **planet** for some ideas for the setting, and then look up **alien** for some ideas on what might be out there!

In this book you will find the following special panels:

Overused Words ❗
bad
big
good
nice
say

Word Webs 🕸
aircraft
alien
animal
armour
artist
astronaut
bird
boat
body
building
clothes
cook
dance
detective
dinosaur
dragon
expression
fairy
family
farm
food
football

fruit
ghost
house
insect
knight
moon
mountain
music
pirate
planet
reptile
sea
shop
sound
space
sport
spy
transport
travel
weather
writing

Writing Tips ✏
animal
bird
colour
clothes
face
hair
light
sea
smell
surprise
teeth
water

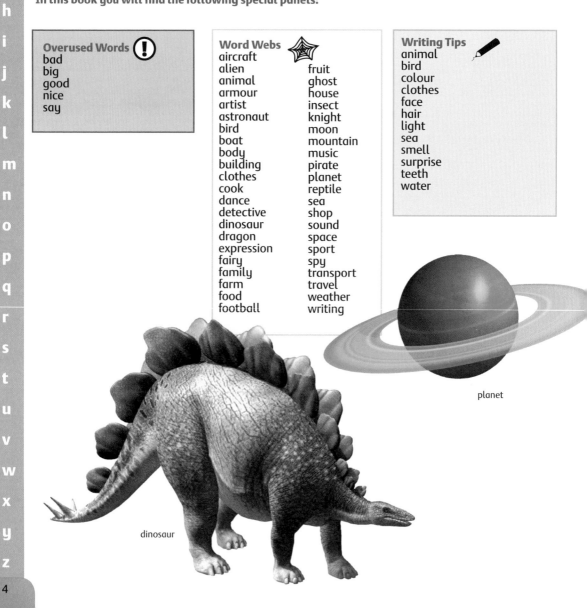

planet

dinosaur

Aa

abandon verb
1 *The robbers abandoned the stolen car.*
leave, desert, forsake, leave behind, strand
(*informal*) dump, ditch
2 *We abandoned our picnic because of the rain.*
cancel, give up, scrap, drop, abort, discard

ability noun
Skin has a natural ability to heal itself.
capability, competence, aptitude, talent, expertise, skill

able adjective
1 *Will you be able to come to my party?*
allowed, permitted, free, willing
OPPOSITE unable
2 *Penguins are very able swimmers.*
competent, capable, accomplished, expert, skilful, proficient, talented, gifted
OPPOSITE incompetent

abolish verb
I wish someone would abolish homework!
get rid of, do away with, put an end to, eliminate
OPPOSITE create

about preposition
There are about two hundred children in the school.
approximately, roughly, close to, around
to be about something
The film is about a dog called Scruff.
concern, deal with, involve

abrupt adjective
1 *The book came to a very abrupt end.*
sudden, hurried, hasty, quick, unexpected
OPPOSITE gradual
2 *The sales assistant had a very abrupt manner.*
blunt, curt, sharp, rude, gruff, impolite, tactless, unfriendly
OPPOSITE polite

absent adjective
Why were you absent from school yesterday?
away, missing
To be absent from school without a good reason is to *play truant*.
OPPOSITE present

absolute adjective
The hypnotist asked for absolute silence.
complete, total, utter, perfect

absolutely adverb
This floor is absolutely filthy!
completely, thoroughly, totally, utterly, wholly, entirely

abuse verb
1 *The rescued dog had been abused by its owners.*
mistreat, maltreat, hurt, injure, damage, harm, misuse
2 *The referee was abused by players from both teams.*
be rude to, insult, swear at
(*informal*) call someone names

abuse noun
1 *They campaigned against the abuse of animals.*
mistreatment, misuse, damage, harm, injury
2 *A spectator yelled abuse at the referee.*
insults, name-calling, swear words

accelerate verb
The bus accelerated when it reached the motorway.
go faster, speed up, pick up speed
OPPOSITE slow down

accept verb
1 *I accepted the offer of a lift to the station.*
take, receive, welcome
OPPOSITE reject
2 *The club accepted my application for membership.*
approve, agree to, consent to
OPPOSITE reject
3 *Do you accept responsibility for the damage?*
admit, acknowledge, recognize, face up to
OPPOSITE deny
4 *They had to accept the umpire's decision.*
agree to, go along with, tolerate, put up with, resign yourself to

acceptable adjective
1 *Would a pound be acceptable as a tip?*
welcome, agreeable, appreciated, pleasant, pleasing, worthwhile
2 *She said my handwriting was not acceptable.*
satisfactory, adequate, appropriate, permissible, suitable, tolerable, passable
OPPOSITE unacceptable

accident noun
1 *There has been an accident at a fireworks display.*
misfortune, mishap, disaster, calamity, catastrophe
A person who is always having accidents is *accident-prone*.
2 *A motorway accident is causing traffic delays.*
collision, crash, smash
An accident involving a lot of vehicles is a *pile-up*.
A railway accident may involve a *derailment*.
3 *It was pure accident that led us to the secret passage.*
chance, luck, a fluke

accidental adjective
1 *The damage to the building was accidental.*
unintentional, unfortunate, unlucky
2 *The professor made an accidental discovery.*
unexpected, unforeseen, unplanned, fortunate, lucky, chance
OPPOSITE deliberate

account noun
1 *I wrote an account of our camping trip in my diary.*
report, record, description, history, narrative, story, chronicle, log
(*informal*) write-up
2 *Money was of no account to him.*
importance, significance, consequence, interest, value

accurate adjective
1 *The detective took accurate measurements of the room.*
careful, correct, exact, meticulous, minute, precise
OPPOSITE inexact, rough
2 *Is this an accurate account of what happened?*
faithful, true, reliable, truthful, factual
OPPOSITE inaccurate, false

accuse verb
accuse of
Miss Sharp accused her opponent of cheating.
charge with, blame for, condemn for, denounce for
OPPOSITE defend

ache noun
The ache in my tooth is getting worse.
pain, soreness, throbbing, discomfort, pang, twinge

achieve verb
1 *He achieved his ambition to play rugby for Wales.*
accomplish, attain, succeed in, carry out, fulfil
2 *The singer achieved success with her first CD.*
acquire, win, gain, earn, get, score

achievement noun
To climb Mount Everest would be an achievement.
accomplishment, attainment, success, feat, triumph

act noun
1 *Rescuing the boy from the river was a brave act.*
action, deed, feat, exploit, operation

2 *The best act at the circus involved three clowns.*
performance, sketch, item, turn

act verb
1 *We must act as soon as we hear the signal.*
do something, take action
2 *Give the medicine time to act.*
work, take effect, have an effect, function
3 *Stop acting like a baby!*
behave, carry on
4 *I acted the part of a pirate in the play.*
perform, play, portray, represent, appear as

action noun
1 *The driver's action prevented an accident.*
act, deed, effort, measure, feat
2 *The fruit ripens through the action of the sun.*
working, effect, mechanism
3 *The film was packed with action.*
drama, excitement, activity, liveliness, energy, vigour, vitality

active adjective
1 *Mr Aziz is very active for his age.*
energetic, lively, dynamic, vigorous, busy
2 *My uncle is an active member of the football club.*
enthusiastic, devoted, committed, dedicated, hard-working
OPPOSITE inactive

activity noun
1 *The town centre was full of activity.*
action, life, busyness, liveliness, excitement, movement, animation
2 *My mum's favourite activity is gardening.*
hobby, interest, pastime, pursuit, job, occupation, task

actual adjective
Did you see the actual crime?
real, true, genuine, authentic
OPPOSITE imaginary, supposed

actually adverb
What did the teacher actually say to you?
really, truly, definitely, certainly, genuinely, in fact

adapt verb
1 *I'll adapt the goggles so that they fit you.*
alter, change, modify, convert, reorganize, transform
2 *Our family adapted quickly to life in the country.*
become accustomed, adjust, acclimatize

add verb
The poet added an extra line in the last verse.
join on, attach, append, insert

to add to
The herbs add to the flavour of the stew.
improve, enhance, increase

to add up
1 *Can you add up these figures for me?*
count up, find the sum of, find the total of, (informal) tot up
2 *(informal) Her story just doesn't add up.*
be convincing, make sense

additional adjective
There are additional toilets downstairs.
extra, further, more, supplementary

adequate adjective
1 *A sandwich will be adequate, thank you.*
enough, sufficient, ample
2 *Your work is adequate, but I'm sure you can do better.*
satisfactory, acceptable, tolerable, competent, passable, respectable

adjust verb
1 *You need to adjust the TV picture.*
correct, modify, put right, improve, tune
2 *She adjusted the central heating thermostat.*
alter, change, set, vary, regulate

admire verb
1 *I admire her skill with words.*
think highly of, look up to, value, have a high opinion of, respect, applaud, approve of, esteem
OPPOSITE despise
2 *The travellers stopped to admire the view.*
enjoy, appreciate, be delighted by

admit verb
Did he admit that he told a lie?
acknowledge, agree, accept, confess, grant, own up
OPPOSITE deny

adopt verb
1 *Our school has adopted a healthy eating policy.*
take up, accept, choose, follow, embrace
2 *We have adopted a stray kitten.*
foster, take in

adore verb
1 *Rosie adores her big sister.*
love, worship, idolize, dote on
2 *(informal) I adore chocolate milk shakes!*
love, like, enjoy
OPPOSITE hate, detest

adult adjective
An adult zebra can run at 80km an hour.
grown-up, mature, full-size, fully grown
OPPOSITE young, immature

advance verb
1 *As the army advanced, the enemy fled.*
move forward, go forward, proceed, approach, come near, press on, progress, forge ahead, gain ground, make headway, make progress
OPPOSITE retreat
2 *Mobile phones have advanced in the last few years.*
develop, grow, improve, evolve, progress

advantage noun
We had the advantage of the wind behind us.
assistance, benefit, help, aid, asset
OPPOSITE disadvantage, drawback

adventure noun
1 *He told us about his latest adventure.*
enterprise, exploit, venture, escapade
2 *They travelled the world in search of adventure.*
excitement, danger, risk, thrills

advertise verb
We made a poster to advertise the cake sale.
publicize, promote, announce, make known, (informal) plug

advice noun
The website gives advice on building a bird table.
guidance, help, directions, recommendations, suggestions, tips, pointers

advise verb
1 *What did the doctor advise?*
recommend, suggest, advocate, prescribe
2 *He advised me to rest.*
counsel, encourage, urge

affect verb
1 *Global warming will affect our climate.*
have an effect or impact on, influence, change, modify, alter
2 *The bad news affected us deeply.*
disturb, upset, concern, trouble, worry

afford verb
I can't afford a new bike just now.
have enough money for, pay for, manage, spare

afraid adjective
1 *We felt afraid as we approached the haunted house.*
frightened, scared, terrified, petrified, alarmed, fearful, anxious, apprehensive
OPPOSITE brave
2 *Don't be afraid to ask questions.*
hesitant, reluctant, shy

age noun
The book is set in the age of the Vikings.
period, time, era, epoch, days

aggressive *adjective*
*Bats are not **aggressive** creatures.*
hostile, violent, provocative, quarrelsome, bullying, warlike
OPPOSITE **friendly**

agile *adjective*
*Mountain goats are extremely **agile**.*
nimble, graceful, sure-footed, sprightly, acrobatic, supple, swift
OPPOSITE **clumsy, stiff**

agony *noun*
*He screamed in **agony** when he broke his leg.*
pain, suffering, torture, torment, anguish, distress

agree *verb*
1 *I'm glad that we **agree**.*
be united, think the same, concur
OPPOSITE **disagree**
2 *I **agree** that you are right.*
accept, acknowledge, admit, grant, allow
OPPOSITE **disagree**
3 *I **agree** to pay my share.*
consent, promise, be willing, undertake
OPPOSITE **refuse**

agreement *noun*
1 *There was **agreement** on the need for longer holidays.*
consensus, unanimity, unity, consent, harmony, sympathy, conformity
OPPOSITE **disagreement**
2 *The two sides signed an **agreement**.*
alliance, treaty
An agreement to end fighting is an **armistice** or **truce**.
A business agreement is a **bargain**, **contract**, or **deal**.

aid *noun*
1 *We can climb out with the **aid** of this rope.*
help, support, assistance, backing, cooperation
2 *They agreed to send more **aid** to the poorer countries.*
donations, subsidies, contributions

aid *verb*
*The local people **aided** the police in their investigation.*
help, assist, support, back, collaborate with, cooperate with, contribute to, lend a hand to, further, promote, subsidize

aim *noun*
*What was the **aim** of the experiment?*
ambition, desire, dream, goal, hope, intention, objective, purpose, target, wish

aim *verb*
1 *She **aims** to be a professional dancer.*
intend, mean, plan, propose,

★ **WORD WEB**

aircraft *noun*

aeroplane

SOME TYPES OF AIRCRAFT
aeroplane, airliner, airship, biplane, bomber, fighter, glider, helicopter, hot-air balloon, jet, jumbo jet, seaplane

PARTS OF AIRCRAFT
cabin, cargo hold, cockpit, engine, fin, flap, flight deck, fuselage, joystick, passenger cabin, propeller, rotor, rudder, tail, tailplane, undercarriage, wing

PLACES WHERE AIRCRAFT TAKE OFF AND LAND
aerodrome, airfield, airport, airstrip, helipad, heliport, landing strip, runway

PEOPLE WHO FLY IN AIRCRAFT
pilot, aviator, balloonist, co-pilot, cabin crew, flight attendant, passengers

airship

helicopter

want, wish, seek
2 *He **aimed** his bow and arrow at the target.*
point, direct, take aim with, line up, level, train, focus

air *noun*
1 *We shouldn't pollute the **air** we breathe.*
atmosphere
2 *This room needs some **air**.*
fresh air, ventilation
3 *There was an **air** of mystery about the place.*
feeling, mood, look, appearance, sense

aircraft *noun see panel above*

alarm *verb*
*The barking dog **alarmed** the sheep.*
frighten, startle, scare, panic, agitate, distress, shock, surprise, upset, worry
OPPOSITE **reassure**

alarm *noun*
1 *Did you hear the **alarm**?*
signal, alert, warning, siren
2 *The sudden noise filled me with **alarm**.*
fright, fear, panic, anxiety, apprehension, distress, nervousness, terror, uneasiness

alien *adjective*
1 *The desert landscape looked **alien** to us.*
strange, foreign, unfamiliar, different, exotic

OPPOSITE **familiar**
2 *They saw the lights of an **alien** spaceship.*
extraterrestrial

★ **WORD WEB**

alien *noun*
*I wrote a story about **aliens** from Mars.*
extraterrestrial, alien life-form, spaceman or spacewoman, starman or starwoman

AN ALIEN FROM ANOTHER PLANET MIGHT BE
humanoid, insect-like, lizard-like, reptilian, intelligent, primitive, super-intelligent, telepathic

alien

BODY PARTS AN ALIEN MIGHT HAVE
antenna, blotches, scales, slime, sucker, tentacle, webbing

TRANSPORT AN ALIEN MIGHT USE
alien vessel, flying saucer, mothership, pod, spacecraft, spaceship, starship, time-machine, transporter beam

An alien might call someone from Earth an *Earthling*.

alive adjective
Fortunately, my goldfish was still **alive**.
living, live, existing, in existence, surviving, breathing, flourishing
OPPOSITE **dead**

allow verb
1 *They don't* **allow** *skateboards in the playground.*
permit, let, authorize, approve of, agree to, consent to, give permission for, license, put up with, stand, support, tolerate
OPPOSITE **forbid**
2 *Have you* **allowed** *enough time for the journey?*
allocate, set aside, assign, grant, earmark

all right adjective
1 *The survivors appeared to be* **all right**.
well, unhurt, unharmed, uninjured, safe
2 *The food in the hotel was* **all right**.
satisfactory, acceptable, adequate, reasonable, passable
3 *Is it* **all right** *to play music in here?*
acceptable, permissable

almost adverb
1 *I have* **almost** *finished the crossword.*
nearly, practically, just about, virtually, all but, as good as, not quite
2 **Almost** *a hundred people came to the concert.*
about, approximately, around

alone adjective, adverb
1 *Did you go to the party* **alone**?
on your own, by yourself, unaccompanied
2 *Zoe had no friends and felt very* **alone**.
lonely, friendless, isolated, solitary, lonesome, desolate

also adverb
We need some bread, and **also** *more butter.*
in addition, besides, additionally, too, furthermore, moreover

alter verb
They have **altered** *the route for the cycle race.*
change, adjust, adapt, modify, transform, amend, make different, revise, vary

always adverb
1 *The sea is* **always** *in motion.*
constantly, continuously, endlessly, eternally, for ever, perpetually, unceasingly
2 *This bus is* **always** *late.*
consistently, continually, invariably, persistently, regularly, repeatedly

amaze verb
It **amazes** *me to think that the*

Earth is billions of years old.
astonish, astound, startle, surprise, stun, shock, stagger, dumbfound
(*informal*) flabbergast

amazed adjective
I was **amazed** *by the number of emails I received.*
astonished, astounded, stunned, surprised, dumbfounded, speechless, staggered
(*informal*) flabbergasted

amazing adjective
The Northern Lights are an **amazing** *sight.*
astonishing, astounding, staggering, remarkable, surprising, extraordinary, incredible, breathtaking, phenomenal, sensational, stupendous, tremendous, wonderful, mind-boggling

ambition noun
1 *She had great* **ambition** *when she was young.*
drive, enthusiasm, enterprise, push, zeal
2 *My* **ambition** *is to play tennis at Wimbledon.*
goal, aim, intention, objective, target, desire, dream, wish, hope, aspiration

ambitious adjective
1 *If you're* **ambitious**, *you will probably succeed.*
enterprising, enthusiastic, committed, go-ahead, keen
OPPOSITE **unambitious**
2 *I think your plan is too* **ambitious**.
grand, big, large-scale

amount noun
1 *Mum wrote a cheque for the correct* **amount**.
sum, total, whole
2 *There's a large* **amount** *of paper in the cupboard.*
quantity, measure, supply, volume, mass, bulk

amuse verb
I think this joke will **amuse** *you.*
make you laugh, entertain, cheer up, divert
(*informal*) tickle

amusing adjective
I didn't find his jokes very **amusing**.
funny, witty, humorous, comic, comical, hilarious, diverting, entertaining
OPPOSITE **unamusing, serious**

ancient adjective
1 *Does that* **ancient** *car still go?*
old, old-fashioned, antiquated, out of date, obsolete
2 *In* **ancient** *times, our ancestors were hunters.*
early, primitive, prehistoric, remote, long past, olden

The times before written records were kept are **prehistoric** *times. The ancient Greeks and Romans lived in* **classical** *times.*
OPPOSITE **modern**

anger noun
I was filled with **anger** *when I read her letter.*
rage, fury, indignation
(*old use*) wrath, ire
An outburst of anger is a **tantrum** *or a* **temper**.

anger verb
His cruelty towards his dog **angered** *me.*
enrage, infuriate, incense, madden, annoy, irritate, exasperate, antagonize, provoke
(*informal*) make your blood boil, make you see red
OPPOSITE **pacify**

angry adjective
Miss Potts turns purple when she gets **angry**.
cross, furious, enraged, infuriated, irate, livid, annoyed, incensed, exasperated, fuming, indignant, raging, seething
(*informal*) mad
To become angry is to **lose your temper**.
OPPOSITE **calm**

animal noun
see panel opposite

announce verb
1 *The head* **announced** *that sports day was cancelled.*
declare, state, proclaim, report
2 *The DJ* **announced** *the next record.*
present, introduce, lead into

announcement noun
1 *The head reads the* **announcements** *in assembly.*
notice
2 *The prime minister issued an* **announcement**.
statement, declaration, proclamation, pronouncement
3 *I heard the* **announcement** *on TV.*
report, bulletin, news flash

annoy verb
1 *I was* **annoyed** *that I missed the bus.*
irritate, bother, displease, exasperate, anger, upset, vex, trouble, worry
OPPOSITE **please**
2 *Please don't* **annoy** *me while I'm working.*
pester, bother, harass, badger, nag, plague, trouble, try
(*informal*) bug

annoying adjective
My brother has a lot of **annoying** *habits.*
irritating, exasperating, maddening, provoking, tiresome, trying, vexing, troublesome

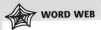

animal *noun*
*Wild **animals** roam freely in the safari park.*
creature, beast, brute
A word for wild animals in general is *wildlife*.
A scientific word for animals is *fauna*.

VARIOUS KINDS OF ANIMAL
amphibian, arachnid, bird, fish, insect, invertebrate, mammal, marsupial, mollusc, reptile, rodent, vertebrate

An animal that eats meat is a *carnivore*.
An animal that eats plants is a *herbivore*.
An animal that eats many things is an *omnivore*.
Animals that sleep most of the winter are *hibernating animals*.
Animals that are active at night are *nocturnal animals*.

SOME ANIMALS THAT LIVE ON LAND
aardvark, antelope, ape, armadillo, baboon, badger, bat, bear, beaver, bison, buffalo, camel, cheetah, chimpanzee, chinchilla, chipmunk, deer, dormouse, elephant, elk, fox, gazelle, gibbon, giraffe, gnu, gorilla, grizzly bear, hare, hedgehog, hippopotamus, hyena, jackal, jaguar, kangaroo, koala, lemming, lemur, leopard, lion, llama, lynx, mongoose, monkey, moose, mouse, ocelot, opossum, orang-utan, otter, panda, panther, platypus, polar bear, porcupine, rabbit, rat, reindeer, rhinoceros, skunk, squirrel, stoat, tapir, tiger, vole, wallaby, weasel, wildebeest, wolf, wolverine, wombat, yak, zebra

SOME ANIMALS THAT LIVE IN THE SEA
dolphin, porpoise, seal, sea lion, walrus, whale

SOME EXTINCT ANIMALS
dinosaur, dodo, quagga

PARTS OF AN ANIMAL'S BODY
antler, claw, fang, foreleg, hind leg, hoof, horn, jaws, mane, muzzle, paw, snout, tail, trotter, tusk, whisker, fur, coat, fleece, hide, pelt

MALE AND FEMALE ANIMALS
A male elephant or whale is a *bull* and a female is a *cow*.
A male fox is a *dog* and a female is a *vixen*.
A male goat is a *billy goat* and a female is a *nanny goat*.
A male hare or rabbit is a *buck* and a female is a *doe*.
A male horse is a *stallion* and a female is a *mare*.
A female lion is a *lioness*.
A female pig is a *sow*.
A male sheep is a *ram* and a female is a *ewe*.
A female tiger is a *tigress*.
A male wolf is a *dog* and a female is a *bitch*.

✏️ **WRITING TIPS**

You can use these words to describe an **animal**.
TO DESCRIBE *how an animal moves*
bound, creep, crouch, dart, gallop, gambol, leap, lumber, nuzzle, pad, paw, pounce, roam, scuttle, skip, slink, slither, spring, stamp, stampede, trot, waddle
*The jaguar **padded** along silently.*
TO DESCRIBE *an animal's body*
agile, nimble, sinewy, wiry; lumbering, majestic, mighty, muscular, powerful *The cheetah stretched its long, **sinewy** body.*
TO DESCRIBE *an animal's skin or coat*
coarse, fluffy, furry, glistening, glossy, hairy, leathery, matted, prickly, scaly, shaggy, shiny, silky, sleek, slimy, slippery, smooth, spiky, thick, thorny, tough, wiry, woolly; mottled, piebald, spotted, striped *The otters' coats were **smooth** and **silky**.*

YOUNG ANIMALS
A young beaver is a *kit*.
A young fox or lion is a *cub*.
A young goat is a *kid*.
A young hare is a *leveret*.
A young horse is a *foal*, *colt* (male), or *filly* (female).
A young pig is a *piglet*.
A young otter or seal is a *pup*.
A young sheep is a *lamb*.

lemur

HOMES OF WILD ANIMALS
den, lair
A badger lives in a *sett*.
A beaver or otter lives in a *lodge*.
A fox lives in an *earth*.
A rabbit lives in a *burrow* or *warren*.
A squirrel lives in a *drey*.

SOUNDS MADE BY ANIMALS
bark, bay, bellow, buzz, gnash, growl, grunt, hiss, howl, jabber, purr, roar, snap, snarl, snort, snuffle, squeak, trumpet, whimper, whine, yap, yelp, yowl

A sheep *bleats*.
A donkey *brays*.
A frog *croaks*.
Cattle *low* or *moo*.
A cat *mews* or *miaows*.
A horse *neighs* or *whinnies*.

giraffe

zebra

gorilla

lion

skunk

tortoise

answer noun
1 *Did you get an **answer** to your letter?*
reply, response, acknowledgement, reaction
A quick or angry answer is a *retort*.
2 *The **answers** to the quiz are on the next page.*
solution, explanation
answer verb
1 *You haven't **answered** my question.*
give an answer to, reply to, respond to, react to, acknowledge
2 *'I'm quite well,' I **answered**.*
reply, respond, return
To answer quickly or angrily is to *retort*.
anxious adjective
1 *Are you **anxious** about your exams?*
nervous, worried, apprehensive, concerned, uneasy, fearful, edgy, fraught, tense, troubled
(*informal*) uptight, jittery
OPPOSITE calm
2 *I'm **anxious** to do my best.*
eager, keen, impatient, enthusiastic, willing
apologize verb
*The ogre **apologized** for being rude.*
make an apology, say sorry, express regret, repent, be penitent
apparent adjective
*There was no **apparent** reason for the crash.*
obvious, evident, clear, noticeable, detectable, perceptible, recognizable, conspicuous, visible
OPPOSITE concealed
appeal verb
to appeal for
*The prisoners **appealed for** our help.*
request, beg for, plead for, cry out for, entreat, ask earnestly for, pray for
to appeal to
*That kind of music doesn't **appeal** to me.*
attract, interest, fascinate, tempt
appear verb
1 *Snowdrops **appear** in the spring.*
come out, emerge, become visible, come into view, develop, occur, show, crop up, spring up, surface
2 *Our visitors didn't **appear** until midnight.*
arrive, come, turn up
(*informal*) show up
3 *It **appears** that the baby is asleep.*
seem, look

4 *I once **appeared** in a musical.*
act, perform, take part, feature
appearance noun
1 *They were startled by the **appearance** of the ghost.*
approach, arrival, entrance, entry
2 *Mr Hogweed had a grim **appearance**.*
air, aspect, bearing, look
appetite noun
1 *When I was ill, I completely lost my **appetite**.*
hunger
2 *Explorers have a great **appetite** for adventure.*
desire, eagerness, enthusiasm, passion, keenness, wish, urge, taste, thirst, longing, yearning, craving, lust, zest
apply verb
1 *The nurse told me to **apply** the ointment generously.*
administer, put on, lay on, spread
2 *My brother has **applied** for a new job.*
make an application for, ask for, request
3 *The rules **apply** to all our members.*
be relevant, relate, refer
4 *The vet **applied** all her skill to save the animal's life.*
use, employ, exercise, utilize
appreciate verb
1 *He **appreciates** good music.*
enjoy, like, love
2 *I **appreciate** her good qualities.*
admire, respect, regard highly, approve of, value, esteem
OPPOSITE despise
3 *I **appreciate** that you can't afford much.*
realize, recognize, understand, comprehend, know, see
4 *Dad hopes that the value of our house will **appreciate**.*
grow, increase, go up, mount, rise
approach verb
1 *The lioness **approached** her prey.*
draw near to, move towards, come near to, advance on
2 *I **approached** the head to ask if we could have a party.*
speak to, contact, go to
3 *The volunteers **approached** their work cheerfully.*
begin, undertake, embark on, set about
approach noun
1 *We could hear the **approach** of heavy footsteps.*
arrival, advance, coming
2 *Dad made an **approach** to the bank manager for a loan.*
application, appeal, proposal

3 *I like her positive **approach**.*
attitude, manner, style, way
4 *The easiest **approach** to the castle is from the west.*
access, entry, entrance, way in
appropriate adjective
*It's not **appropriate** to wear jeans to a wedding.*
suitable, proper, fitting, apt, right, tactful, tasteful, well-judged
OPPOSITE inappropriate
approval noun
1 *We cheered to show our **approval**.*
appreciation, admiration, praise, high regard, acclaim, respect, support
OPPOSITE disapproval
2 *The head gave her **approval** to our plan.*
agreement, consent, authorization, assent, go-ahead, permission, support, blessing
OPPOSITE refusal
approve verb
*The head **approved** my request for a day off school.*
agree to, consent to, authorize, allow, accept, pass, permit, support, back
OPPOSITE refuse
approximate adjective
*What is the **approximate** length of the journey?*
estimated, rough, nexact, near
OPPOSITE exact
approximately adverb
*The film will finish at **approximately** five o'clock.*
roughly, about, around, round about, close to, nearly, more or less
area noun
1 *From the plane we saw a big **area** of desert.*
expanse, stretch, tract
A small area is a *patch*.
An area of water or ice is a *sheet*.
2 *I live in an urban **area**.*
district, locality, neighbourhood, region, zone, vicinity
argue verb
1 *You two are always **arguing** over something.*
quarrel, disagree, differ, fall out, fight, have an argument, squabble, wrangle, bicker
OPPOSITE agree
2 *We **argued** over the price of the cloth.*
bargain, haggle
3 *He **argued** that it was my turn to walk the dog.*
claim, assert, try to prove, maintain, reason, suggest
argument noun
1 *They was an **argument** over*

who should pay for the meal.
disagreement, quarrel, dispute, row, clash, controversy, debate, difference, fight, squabble, altercation
2 *Did you follow the **argument** of the book?*
line of reasoning, theme, outline, gist

⭐ WORD WEB

armour *noun*
PARTS OF A MEDIEVAL KNIGHT'S ARMOUR
breastplate, cuirass (breast and back plate), gauntlet, greave (shin guard), habergeon (sleeveless coat), helmet, visor

Armour made of linked rings is *chain mail*.
An outfit of armour is a *suit of armour*.

---

arrange *verb*
1 *The books are **arranged** in alphabetical order.*
sort, order, put in order, group, organize, categorize, classify, collate, display, sort out, set out, lay out, line up
2 *Do you need any help **arranging** the party?*
plan, organize, prepare, set up, see to

arrangement *noun*
1 *They have improved the **arrangement** of the garden.*
layout, organization, design, planning
2 *Did you change the **arrangement** of my CDs?*
order, grouping, display, distribution, spacing
3 *We have an **arrangement** to use the swimming pool.*
agreement, deal, bargain, contract, scheme

arrive *verb*
*When is the train due to **arrive**?*
appear, come, turn up, show up, get in
*When a plane arrives it **lands** or **touches down**.*
to arrive at
*We **arrived at** the castle before midnight.*
get to, reach

arrogant *adjective*
*His **arrogant** manner annoys me.*
boastful, conceited, proud, haughty, self-important, bumptious, pompous, snobbish, superior, vain
(*informal*) cocky, snooty, stuck-up
OPPOSITE modest

art *noun*
see panel below

article *noun*
1 *Have you any **articles** for the jumble sale?*
item, object, thing
2 *Did you read my **article** in the magazine?*
essay, report, piece of writing

artificial *adjective*
1 *Organic gardeners don't use **artificial** fertilizers.*
man-made, synthetic, unnatural, manufactured
OPPOSITE natural
2 *She had an **artificial** flower in her buttonhole.*
fake, false, imitation, unreal, bogus, counterfeit
OPPOSITE genuine, real

ashamed *adjective*
*He was **ashamed** because of what he had done.*
sorry, remorseful, repentant, embarrassed, shamefaced, abashed, mortified, apologetic, penitent
(*informal*) red-faced
OPPOSITE unashamed, unrepentant

ask *verb*
1 *I **asked** them to be careful with the parcel.*
beg, entreat, appeal to, implore, plead with
2 *'Are you ready?' I **asked**.*
demand, enquire, inquire, query, question
3 *I'm going to **ask** you to my party.*
invite (*formal*) request the pleasure of your company

asleep *adjective*
*I didn't hear the phone because I was **asleep**.*
sleeping, dozing, having a nap,

⭐ WORD WEB

art *noun* and **artist** *noun*
SOME ARTISTS AND CRAFTSPEOPLE
animator, blacksmith, carpenter, cartoonist, designer, draughtsman, draughtswoman, embroiderer, engraver, goldsmith, graphic designer, illustrator, knitter, mason, painter, photographer, potter, printer, quilter, sculptor, silversmith, weaver

SOME ARTS AND CRAFTS
animation, basketry, batik, beadwork, carpentry, carving, collage, crochet, cross-stitch, decoupage, drawing, embroidery, enamelling, engraving, etching, graphics, illustration, jewellery, knitting, metalwork, modelling, mosaics, needlework, origami, painting, patchwork, photography, pottery, printing, quilting, screen printing, sculpture, sewing, sketching, spinning, stained glass, stamping, stencilling, tapestry, weaving, woodwork

artistic *adjective*
*Mum's flower arrangements are very **artistic**.*
creative, imaginative, aesthetic, attractive, beautiful, tasteful
OPPOSITE ugly

potter

photographer

napping
(*formal*) slumbering
A patient asleep for an operation
is **anaesthetized** or **under
sedation**.
An animal asleep for the winter
is **hibernating**.
OPPOSITE awake
to fall asleep *We waited until the
giant fell asleep.*
drop off, doze, nod off
To fall asleep quickly is **to go out
like a light**.

assemble *verb*
1 *A crowd assembled to watch the
rescue.*
gather, come together, converge,
accumulate, crowd together,
flock together, meet, convene
OPPOSITE disperse
2 *We assembled our luggage at
the front door.*
collect, gather, bring together,
pile up, put together
3 *The general assembled his
troops.*
round up, rally, muster

assembly *noun*
*There was a large assembly of
people in the market square.*
gathering, meeting, crowd,
throng
An assembly for worship is a
service.
A large assembly to show
support for something, often
out of doors, is a **rally**.
An assembly to discuss
political matters is a **council** or
parliament.
An assembly to discuss and learn
about a particular topic is a
conference or **congress**.

assistance *noun*
1 *Do you need assistance with
your luggage?*
help, aid, support,
encouragement
2 *We bought new sports
equipment with the assistance
of a local firm.*
backing, collaboration,
cooperation, sponsorship,
subsidy, support

assistant *noun*
*The magician was training a new
assistant.*
helper, partner, colleague,
associate, supporter

assorted *adjective*
*I bought a bag of sweets with
assorted flavours.*
various, different, mixed,
diverse, miscellaneous, several

assortment *noun*
*There was an assortment of
sandwiches to choose from.*
variety, mixture, selection, array,
choice, collection, diversity

assume *verb*
1 *I assume you'd like some
chocolate.*
suppose, presume, imagine,
believe, guess, expect, gather,
suspect, think
2 *The bandit assumed a disguise.*
put on, adopt, dress up in, wear

assure *verb*
*I assure you that I will take
care of your dog.*
promise, give your word to

astonish *verb*
*It astonished us to learn that the
house was haunted.*
amaze, astound, surprise,
stagger, shock, dumbfound,
leave speechless, startle, stun,
take aback, take by surprise
(*informal*) flabbergast, take your
breath away

astonishing *adjective*
*The volcano was an astonishing
sight.*
amazing, astounding,
staggering, remarkable,
surprising, extraordinary,
incredible, breathtaking,
phenomenal, sensational,
stupendous, tremendous,
wonderful

✦ WORD WEB

astronaut *noun*
*The astronauts
climbed aboard
the space shuttle.*
spaceman or
spacewoman

THINGS AN ASTRONAUT
MIGHT USE OR WEAR
spacesuit, jet pack, oxygen
tank;, gloves, helmet,
moonboots or spaceboots,
visor

PLACES AN ASTRONAUT MIGHT VISIT
alien planet, moonbase,
spacelab, space shuttle,
space station,
starbase

athletic *adjective*
*You need to be athletic to run
in a marathon.*
fit, active, energetic, strong,
muscular, powerful, robust,
sturdy, vigorous, well-built
(*informal*) sporty
OPPOSITE feeble, puny

atrocious *adjective*
*Everyone was shocked by the
atrocious crime.*
wicked, terrible, dreadful,
abominable, brutal, savage,
barbaric, bloodthirsty,
callous, cruel, diabolical, evil,
fiendish, horrifying, merciless,
outrageous, sadistic, terrible,
vicious, villainous

attach *verb*
Attach this label to the parcel.
fasten, fix, join, tie, bind, secure,
connect, link, couple, stick, affix,
add, append
OPPOSITE detach

satellite

attack noun
1 *The pirates' **attack** took us by surprise.*
assault, strike, charge, rush, raid, ambush, invasion, onslaught
An attack with big guns or bombs is a *blitz* or *bombardment*.
An attack by planes is an *air raid*.
2 *The newspaper published an **attack** on his character.*
criticism, outburst, abuse, tirade
3 *I had a sneezing **attack** in assembly.*
bout, fit, spasm (*informal*) turn

attack verb
1 *The travellers were **attacked** by highwaymen.*
assault, beat up, mug, set on, assail
To attack someone else's territory is to *invade* or *raid* it.
To attack someone from a hidden place is to *ambush* them.
To attack the enemy with bombs or heavy guns is to *bombard* them.
To attack by rushing at the enemy is to *charge*.
To attack a place suddenly is to *storm* it.
If an animal attacks you, it might *savage* you.
2 *He **attacked** her reputation.*
abuse, criticize, denounce
OPPOSITE defend

attempt verb
*They will **attempt** to reconstruct a Viking ship.*
try, endeavour, strive, seek, aim, make an effort

attend verb
*Are you going to **attend** the end-of-term concert?*
go to, appear at, be present at
to attend to
1 *Please **attend** carefully **to** my instructions.*
listen to, pay attention to, follow carefully, heed, mark, mind, note, notice, observe, think about
2 *Who will **attend to** the washing up?*
deal with, see to
3 *The nurses **attended to** the wounded.*
take care of, care for, look after, help, mind, tend

attitude noun
*I'm trying to take a more positive **attitude** to life.*
outlook, approach, behaviour, stance, frame of mind, disposition, view, position, manner, mood

attract verb
1 *Do you think our exhibition will **attract** people?*
interest, appeal to, fascinate, tempt, entice
2 *Baby animals **attract** big crowds at the zoo.*
draw, pull in

attractive adjective
1 *Miranda was a very **attractive** young woman.*
beautiful, pretty, good-looking, handsome, gorgeous, glamorous, striking, fetching, charming, lovely, delightful, pleasing, fascinating, captivating, enchanting
OPPOSITE unattractive, repulsive
2 *There are some **attractive** bargains in the sale.*
appealing, agreeable, interesting, desirable, tempting, irresistible

authority noun
1 *I have the head's **authority** to go home early.*
permission, consent, approval
2 *The king had the **authority** to execute the prisoners.*
power, right, influence
3 *My uncle is an **authority** on steam trains.*
expert, specialist

automatic adjective
1 *We took our car through the **automatic** car wash.*
automated, mechanical, programmed, computerized
2 *My sneezing was an **automatic** response to the pepper.*
instinctive, involuntary, impulsive, spontaneous, reflex, natural, unconscious, unthinking

available adjective
1 *There are no more seats **available**.*
obtainable, free
2 *Is there a phone **available** in the library?*
accessible, ready, usable, at hand, handy, within reach, convenient

average adjective
*It was an **average** kind of day at school.*
everyday, ordinary, normal, typical, usual, regular, commonplace, familiar
OPPOSITE unusual, extraordinary

avoid verb
1 *The driver tried hard to **avoid** the collision.*
get out of the way of, avert, dodge, keep clear of, steer clear of, fend off, shun
2 *The outlaws **avoided** capture for months.*
elude, evade, run away from, escape from
3 *How did you manage to **avoid** the washing up?*
get out of, shirk

awake adjective
*Hester lay **awake** all night worrying.*
wide awake, restless, sleepless, conscious, astir
Not being able to sleep is to be suffering from *insomnia*.
OPPOSITE asleep

award noun
*Kirsty got a national **award** for gymnastics.*
prize, trophy, medal

aware adjective
aware of
*The spy was **aware of** the dangers of the mission.*
acquainted with, conscious of, familiar with, informed about
OPPOSITE ignorant of

awful adjective
1 *The weather was **awful** last weekend.*
bad, dreadful, terrible, appalling, dire, abysmal (*informal*) rubbish, lousy
2 *The teacher complained about our **awful** behaviour.*
disgraceful, shameful, disobedient, naughty
3 *Cinderella's stepmother was an **awful** woman.*
unpleasant, disagreeable, nasty, horrid, detestable, unkind, unfriendly
4 *The country was shocked by the **awful** crime.*
horrifying, shocking, atrocious, abominable, outrageous
5 *I feel **awful** about forgetting your birthday.*
sorry, ashamed, embarrassed, guilty, remorseful

awkward adjective
1 *The parcel was an **awkward** shape.*
bulky, inconvenient, unmanageable, unwieldy
OPPOSITE convenient
2 *The giant was very **awkward** with his knife and fork.*
clumsy, unskilful, bungling
OPPOSITE skilful
3 *We found ourselves in a very **awkward** situation.*
difficult, troublesome, trying, perplexing, tough
OPPOSITE straightforward, easy
4 *Are you trying to be **awkward**?*
obstinate, stubborn, uncooperative, unhelpful, exasperating
OPPOSITE cooperative
5 *I felt **awkward** as I didn't know anyone at the party.*
embarrassed, uncomfortable, uneasy, out of place
OPPOSITE comfortable, at ease

a
b
c
d
e
f
g
h
i
j
k
l
m
n
o
p
q
r
s
t
u
v
w
x
y
z

Bb

baby noun
infant, child
A baby who has just been born is
a *newborn*.
A baby just learning to walk is
a *toddler*.
The time when someone is a
baby is their *babyhood*.

babyish adjective
*My brother thinks that dolls are
babyish.*
childish, immature, infantile
OPPOSITE grown-up, mature

back noun
*We always sit at the back of the
bus.*
end, rear, tail end
OPPOSITE front

back adjective
*The back door of the cabin was
locked.*
end, rear, tail
The back
legs of an
animal are
its *hind*
legs.
OPPOSITE
front

back verb
1 *A big lorry
was backing
into our driveway.*
go backwards, reverse
2 *I'm backing the blue team to
win the race.*
bet on, put money on
3 *The council is backing the plan
to build a skate park.*
support, sponsor, endorse

background noun
1 *I drew a mermaid with the sea
in the background.*
OPPOSITE foreground
2 *The first chapter deals with
the background to the war.*
circumstances of, history
of, lead-up to
3 *My mother's family has a
Swedish background.*
tradition,
upbringing,
ancestry

bad
adjective
*This has been a
bad week for all
of us.*
awful,
horrible,
terrible
OPPOSITE
good, fine,
excellent

! **OVERUSED WORD**

bad adjective
Try to vary the words you use for
bad. Here are some other words
you could use.

FOR A *bad person*
wicked, evil, cruel, malevolent,
malicious, vicious, villainous,
mean, nasty, beastly,
monstrous, corrupt, deplorable,
detestable, immoral, infamous,
shameful, sinful *Gobo was a
detestable king who was loathed
by his subjects.*
A bad person is a *scoundrel*,
rogue, or *rascal*.
A bad character in a story or film
is a *villain* or (*informal*) *baddy*.
OPPOSITE good, virtuous
FOR A *bad accident* OR *bad illness*
serious, severe, grave,
distressing, acute *Ingrid has a
severe case of chickenpox.*
OPPOSITE minor
FOR *bad behaviour*
naughty, mischievous,
disobedient, disgraceful, wrong
*That mischievous kitten drank my
milk!*
OPPOSITE exemplary, angelic
FOR A *bad experience* OR *bad news*
unpleasant, unwelcome,
disagreeable, horrible, awful,
terrible, dreadful, horrific,
appalling, shocking, hideous,
disastrous, ghastly, frightful,
abominable, diabolical
*The letter contained disagreeable
news.*
Another word for a bad
experience is an *ordeal*.
OPPOSITE good, excellent
FOR A *bad habit* OR SOMETHING
THAT IS *bad for you*
harmful, damaging, dangerous,
undesirable, detrimental,
injurious *Fizzy drinks can be
harmful to your teeth.*
FOR *bad weather*
harsh, hostile, unfavourable,
adverse, miserable
(*informal*) lousy *Penguins face
hostile weather in the Antarctic.*
OPPOSITE fine, favourable
FOR FOOD THAT HAS *gone bad*
mouldy, rotten, off, decayed,
sour, spoiled, rancid *The
strawberries have started to
go mouldy.*
OPPOSITE fresh
TO *feel bad* ABOUT SOMETHING
guilty, ashamed, sorry,
remorseful, repentant *Scrooge
feels repentant by the end of
the story.*
OPPOSITE unashamed,
unrepentant

---

bad-tempered adjective
*Trolls are always bad-tempered
before breakfast.*
cross, grumpy, irritable, moody,
quarrelsome, fractious, ill-
tempered, short-tempered,
cantankerous, crotchety,
snappy, testy, sullen
OPPOSITE good-
tempered, cheerful

bag noun
*I put my wet clothes in
a plastic bag.*
sack, carrier,
holdall, satchel,
handbag, shoulder
bag
A bag you carry on
your back is a *backpack*
or *rucksack*.

ball noun
*Wind the string into
a ball.*
sphere, globe, orb
A small ball of something is
a *pellet* or *globule*.

ban verb
*Rollerblades are
banned from the
playground.*
forbid, prohibit, bar,
exclude, outlaw
OPPOSITE allow, permit

band noun
1 *The king was surrounded by a
band of courtiers.*
company, group, gang, party,
troop, crew
2 *I play piano in the
junior jazz band.*
group,
ensemble,
orchestra
3 *The team
captain
wears a
red arm
band.*
strip, stripe, ring, line,
belt, hoop

bang noun
1 *There was a loud bang as the
balloon burst.*
blast, boom, crash, thud, thump,
pop, explosion, report
2 *He got a bang on the head from
the low ceiling.*
bump, blow, hit,
knock, thump,
punch, smack, whack,
clout
(*informal*) wallop

bang *verb*
*Miss Crabbit **banged** her fist on the desk and scowled.*
hit, thump, strike, bash, slam, wham

banish *verb*
*The king's brother was **banished** forever.*
exile, expel, deport, send away, eject

bank *noun*
1 *The temple was built on the **banks** of the River Nile.*
edge, side, shore, margin, brink
2 *We rolled our Easter eggs down a grassy **bank**.*
slope, mound, ridge, embankment

banquet *noun*
*There was a **banquet** on the queen's birthday.*
dinner, feast

bar *noun*
1 *Did you eat the whole **bar** of chocolate?*
block, slab, chunk, wedge
A bar of gold or silver is an **ingot**.
A bar of soap is a **cake**.
2 *The window had iron **bars** across it.*
rod, pole, rail, stake, beam, girder

bar *verb*
1 *Two athletes were **barred** from competing in the race.*
ban, prohibit, exclude, keep out
2 *A fallen tree **barred** our way.*
block, hinder, impede, obstruct, stop, check

bare *adjective*
1 *I put suncream on my **bare** arms and legs.*
naked, nude, exposed, uncovered, unclothed, undressed
2 *The wolf had a **bare** patch on its back.*
bald, hairless
3 *We slept outside on the **bare** mountain.*
barren, bleak, treeless
4 *Inside, the dungeon was cold and **bare**.*
empty, unfurnished, vacant
5 *There wasn't a **bare** patch of wall left.*
blank, plain, clear, empty
6 *There is only room to pack the **bare** essentials.*
basic, minimum

barely *adverb*
*We **barely** had time to get dressed.*
hardly, scarcely, only just

bargain *noun*
1 *We made a **bargain** with the captain to take us ashore.*
deal, agreement, promise, pact
2 *That camera you bought was a **bargain**.*
good buy, special offer
(*informal*) snip, steal

bargain *verb*
*He refused to **bargain** with the pirates for his life.*
argue, do a deal, haggle, negotiate

bark *verb*
*The guard dog began to **bark** fiercely.*
woof, yap, yelp, growl

barrel *noun*
*The smugglers carried **barrels** of gunpowder.*
cask, drum, tub, keg, butt

barrier *noun*
1 *Spectators were asked to stay behind the **barrier**.*
wall, fence, railing, barricade
A barrier across a road is a **roadblock**.
2 *His shyness was a **barrier** to making friends.*
obstacle, hurdle, drawback, handicap, hindrance, stumbling block

base *noun*
1 *The footprints stop at the **base** of the pyramid.*
bottom, foot
2 *The dolls' house comes with a wooden **base**.*
foundation, support
A base under a statue is a **pedestal** or **plinth**.
3 *The mountaineers returned to their **base**.*
headquarters, camp, depot

basic *adjective*
1 *These are the **basic** moves in ice-skating.*
main, chief, principal, key, central, essential, fundamental, crucial
2 *My knowledge of French is very **basic**.*
elementary, simple
OPPOSITE advanced

bathe *verb*
1 *It was too cold to **bathe** in the sea.*
swim, go swimming, splash about, take a dip
To walk about in shallow water is to **paddle**.
To walk through deep water is to **wade**.
2 *The nurse gently **bathed** the wound.*
clean, cleanse, wash, rinse

battle *noun*
*The **battle** between our countries raged for many years.*
fight, clash, conflict, action, engagement, hostilities, struggle

beach *noun*
*We found these shells on the **beach**.*
sands, seashore, seaside, shore

beam *noun*
1 *Wooden **beams** ran across the ceiling.*
bar, timber, joist, plank, post, rafter, boom, spar, strut, support
2 *A **beam** of sunlight entered the cave.*
ray, shaft, stream, gleam
A strong narrow beam of light used in various devices is a **laser**.

bear *verb*
1 *The rope won't **bear** my weight.*
carry, support, hold, take
2 *The messenger **bore** a letter from the king.*
bring, carry, convey, transport, take, transfer
3 *The gravestone **bears** an old inscription.*
display, show, have
4 *The stench in the cave was too much to **bear**.*
put up with, cope with, stand, suffer, tolerate, endure, abide
5 *The lioness has **borne** three cubs.*
give birth to

beast *noun*
*In the darkness, they heard a wild **beast** howl.*
animal, creature
You might call a large or frightening beast a **brute** or **monster**.

beat *verb*
1 *It's cruel to **beat** an animal with a stick.*
hit, strike, thrash, batter, whip, lash, flog
(*informal*) whack, wallop
2 *I **beat** my brother at chess for the first time.*
defeat, conquer, vanquish, win against, get the better of, overcome, overwhelm, rout, thrash, trounce
(*informal*) hammer
3 ***Beat** the eggs, milk, and sugar together.*
whisk, whip, blend, mix, stir
4 *Can you feel your heart **beating**?*
pound, thump, palpitate

to beat someone up
*The bully threatened to **beat me up**.*
assault, attack

a
b
c
d
e
f
g
h
i
j
k
l
m
n
o
p
q
r
s
t
u
v
w
x
y
z

beat noun
1 *Can you feel the **beat** of your heart?*
pulse, throb
2 *Reggae music has a strong **beat**.*
rhythm, accent, stress

beautiful adjective
1 *The fairy queen looked **beautiful** by moonlight.*
attractive, good-looking, pretty, gorgeous, glamorous, radiant, elegant, enchanting, dazzling, stunning, magnificent, resplendent
A man who is pleasing to look at is *good-looking* or *handsome*.
OPPOSITE ugly, unattractive
2 *It was a **beautiful** day for a bicycle trip.*
fine, excellent, glorious, marvellous, sunny, superb, splendid, wonderful
OPPOSITE dull, gloomy, drab
3 *The Northern Lights are a **beautiful** sight.*
glorious, magnificent, picturesque, scenic, spectacular, splendid
4 *The nightingale has a **beautiful** song.*
harmonious, mellifluous, melodious, sweet-sounding
OPPOSITE grating

beckon verb
*The guard was **beckoning** me to approach.*
signal, gesture, motion, gesticulate

become verb
1 *I soon **became** frustrated with the video game.*
begin to be, turn, get
2 *Eventually, the tadpoles will **become** frogs.*
grow into, change into, develop into, turn into
3 *That style of hat **becomes** you.*
look good on, suit, flatter

bed noun
1 *The children slept on hard, wooden **beds**.*
bunk, mattress
A bed for a baby is a *cot*, *cradle*, or *crib*.
Two single beds one above the other are *bunk beds*.
A bed on a ship or train is a *berth*.
A bed made of net or cloth hung up above the ground is a *hammock*.
2 *We planted daffodils in the flower **beds**.*
plot, patch, border
3 *These creatures feed on the **bed** of the ocean.*
bottom, floor
OPPOSITE surface

beg verb
*He **begged** me not to let go of the rope.*

ask, plead with, entreat, implore, beseech

begin verb
1 *The hunters **began** their search at dawn.*
start, commence, embark on, set about
OPPOSITE end, finish, conclude
2 *When did the trouble **begin**?*
start, commence, arise, emerge, appear, originate, spring up
OPPOSITE end, stop, cease

beginning noun
*The house was built at the **beginning** of last century.*
start, opening, commencement, introduction, establishment, foundation, initiation, launch, dawn
The beginning of the day is *dawn* or *daybreak*.
The beginning of a journey is the *starting point*.
The beginning of a stream or river is the *origin* or *source*.
A piece of writing at the beginning of a book is an *introduction*, *preface*, or *prologue*.
A piece of music at the beginning of a musical or opera is a *prelude* or *overture*.
OPPOSITE end, conclusion

behave verb
*Our neighbour is **behaving** very strangely.*
act, react, perform
to behave yourself
*We promised to **behave ourselves** in the car.*
be good, be on your best behaviour

behaviour noun
*I give my puppy treats for good **behaviour**.*
actions, conduct, manners, attitude

belief noun
1 *She was a woman of strong religious **beliefs**.*
faith, principle, creed, doctrine
2 *It is my **belief** is that he stole the money.*
opinion, view, conviction, feeling, notion, theory

believable adjective
*None of the characters in the book are **believable**.*
credible, plausible
OPPOSITE unbelievable, implausible

believe verb
1 *I don't **believe** anything he says.*
accept, have faith in, rely on, trust
OPPOSITE disbelieve, doubt

2 *I **believe** they used to live in Canada.*
assume, feel, know, presume, reckon, suppose, think

belong verb
1 *This ring **belonged** to my grandmother.*
be owned by
2 *Do you **belong** to the sports club?*
be a member of, be connected with

belongings plural noun
*Don't leave any **belongings** on the bus.*
possessions, property, goods, things

bend verb
*This drinking straw **bends** in the middle.*
curve, turn, twist, curl, coil, loop, arch, warp, wind
A word for things which bend easily is *flexible* or (*informal*) *bendy*.
OPPOSITE straighten
to bend down
*I **bent down** to tie my shoelaces.*
stoop, bow, crouch, duck, kneel

bend noun
*Watch out for the sharp **bend** in the road.*
curve, turn, angle, corner, twist, zigzag

bent adjective
1 *After the crash, the car was a mass of **bent** metal.*
curved, twisted, coiled, looped, buckled, crooked, arched, folded, warped
(*informal*) wonky
2 *The witch had a **bent** back and walked with a stick.*
crooked, hunched, curved, arched, bowed

best adjective
1 *She is our **best** goalkeeper.*
top, leading, finest, foremost, supreme, star, outstanding, unequalled, unrivalled
OPPOSITE worst
2 *We did what we thought was **best**.*
most suitable, most appropriate

betray verb
1 *He **betrayed** us by telling the enemy our plan.*
be disloyal to, be a traitor to, cheat, conspire against, double-cross
Someone who betrays you is a *traitor*.
To betray your country is to commit *treason*.

bend

2 *The look in her eyes betrayed her true feelings.*
reveal, show, indicate, disclose, divulge, expose, tell

better adjective
1 *Which of these songs do you think is better?*
superior, finer, preferable
2 *I had a cold, but I'm better now.*
recovered, cured, healed, improved, well

beware verb
Beware! There are thieves about.
be careful! watch out! look out! take care! be on your guard!
beware of
Beware of the bull.
watch out for, avoid, mind, heed, keep clear of

biased adjective
A referee should not make a biased decision.
prejudiced, partial, one-sided, partisan, unfair
OPPOSITE impartial

big adjective
The giant owned three pairs of big boots.
large, huge, great, massive, enormous, gigantic, colossal, mammoth
(*informal*) whopping, ginormous, humungous
OPPOSITE small, little, tiny

(!) OVERUSED WORD

Try to vary the words you use for **big**. Here are some other words you could use.

FOR A **big person** OR **big creature**
burly, giant, hefty, hulking, mighty, monstrous, towering
The mighty robot clanked as it moved.

FOR A **big object**:
bulky, heavy, hefty, weighty
What could be inside that bulky envelope?

FOR A **big room** OR **big box**
roomy, sizeable, spacious *Inside, the spaceship was surprisingly roomy.*
OPPOSITE cramped

FOR A **big distance**
immense, infinite, vast *A vast stretch of ocean lay before them.*

FOR A **big amount** OR **big helping**
ample, considerable, substantial
We each got an ample helping of porridge.
OPPOSITE meagre, paltry

FOR A **big decision** OR **big moment**
grave, important, serious, significant *Yesterday was the most significant day in my short life.*
OPPOSITE unimportant, minor

🕸 WORD WEB

bird noun
A female bird is a *hen*.
A male bird is a *cock*.
A young bird is a *chick*, *fledgling*, or *nestling*.
A family of chicks is a *brood*.
A group of birds is a *colony* or *flock*.
A group of flying birds is a *flight* or *skein*.
A person who studies birds is an *ornithologist*.

flamingo

SOME COMMON BRITISH BIRDS
blackbird, blue tit, bullfinch, bunting, chaffinch, crow, cuckoo, dove, greenfinch, jackdaw, jay, linnet, magpie, martin, nightingale, pigeon, raven, robin, rook, skylark, sparrow, starling, swallow, swift, thrush, tit, wagtail, waxwing, woodpecker, wren, yellowhammer

BIRDS OF PREY
buzzard, eagle, falcon, hawk, kestrel, kite, merlin, osprey, owl, sparrowhawk, vulture

FARM AND GAME BIRDS
chicken, duck, goose, grouse, partridge, pheasant, quail, turkey

Birds kept by farmers are called *poultry*.

SEA AND WATER BIRDS
albatross, auk, bittern, coot, cormorant, crane, curlew, duck, gannet, goose, guillemot, gull, heron, kingfisher, kittiwake, lapwing, mallard, moorhen, oystercatcher, peewit, pelican, penguin, puffin, seagull, snipe, stork, swan, teal

BIRDS FROM OTHER COUNTRIES
bird of paradise, budgerigar, canary, cockatoo, flamingo, humming bird, ibis, kookaburra, lovebirds, macaw, mynah bird, parakeet, parrot, toucan

lovebirds

BIRDS WHICH CANNOT FLY
emu, kiwi, ostrich, peacock, penguin

eagle

PARTS OF A BIRD'S BODY
beak, bill, claw, talon, breast, crown, throat, crest, feather, down, plumage, plume, wing

SOME TYPES OF BIRD HOME
nest, nesting box, aviary, coop, roost

SOUNDS MADE BY BIRDS
cackle, caw, cheep, chirp, chirrup, cluck, coo, crow, gabble, honk, peep, pipe, quack, screech, squawk, trill, tweet, twitter, warble
A turkey *gobbles*.
An owl *hoots*.

SPECIAL NAMES
A female peacock is a *peahen*.
A young duck is a *duckling*.
A young goose is a *gosling*.
A young swan is a *cygnet*.
An eagle's nest is an *eyrie*.
A place where rooks nest is a *rookery*.

✏ WRITING TIPS

You can use these words to describe a **bird**.
1 TO DESCRIBE *how a bird moves*
circle, dart, flit, flutter, fly, glide, hop, hover, peck, perch, preen, skim, soar, swoop, waddle, wheel *A pair of swallows flitted among the rooftops.*
2 TO DESCRIBE *a bird's feathers*
bedraggled, downy, drab, fluffy, gleaming, iridescent, ruffled, smooth, speckled *The peacock displayed its iridescent tail.*

ostrich

owl

bit *noun*
1 *Mum divided the cake into eight bits.*
piece, portion, part, section, segment, share, slice
2 *These jeans are a bit long for me.*
a little, slightly, rather, fairly, somewhat, quite

bite *verb*
1 *I bit a chunk out of my apple.*
munch, nibble, chew, crunch, gnaw, (*informal*) chomp
2 *Take care. These animals can bite.*
nip, pinch, pierce, wound
When an animal tries to bite you it *snaps* at you.
When an insect bites you it *stings* you.
A fierce animal *mauls* or *savages* its prey.

bitter *adjective*
1 *The medicine had a bitter taste.*
sour, sharp, acid, acrid, tart
OPPOSITE **sweet**
2 *His brother was still bitter about the quarrel.*
resentful, embittered, disgruntled, aggrieved
OPPOSITE **contented**
3 *The wind blowing in from the sea was bitter.*
biting, cold, freezing, icy, piercing, raw, wintry, (*informal*) perishing
OPPOSITE **mild**

black *adjective, noun*
The pony had a shiny black coat.
coal-black, jet-black, pitch-black, ebony, raven
You can also describe a black night as *pitch-dark*.
Someone in a bad mood is said to look *as black as thunder*.
Common similes are *as black as coal* and *as black as night*.

blame *verb*
Don't blame me if you miss the bus.
accuse, criticize, condemn, reproach, scold

blank *adjective*
1 *There are no blank pages left in my jotter.*
empty, bare, clean, plain, unmarked, unused
2 *The old woman gave us a blank look.*
expressionless, faceless, vacant

blaze *noun*
Firefighters fought the blaze for hours.
fire, flames, inferno

blaze *verb*
Within a few minutes the campfire was blazing.
burn brightly, flare up

bleak *adjective*
1 *The countryside was bleak and barren.*
bare, barren, desolate, empty, exposed, stark

2 *The future looks bleak for the club.*
gloomy, hopeless, depressing, dismal, grim, miserable
OPPOSITE **promising**

blend *verb*
1 *Blend the flour with a tablespoon of water.*
beat together, mix, stir together, whip, whisk
2 *The paint colours blend well with each other.*
go together, match, fit, harmonize
OPPOSITE **clash**

blind *adjective*
Polar bear cubs are born blind.
sightless, unsighted, unseeing
A common simile is *as blind as a bat*.
OPPOSITE **sighted, seeing**

blind to
The captain was blind to his own faults.
ignorant of, unaware of, oblivious to
OPPOSITE **aware of**

bliss *noun*
Having a whole day off school was sheer bliss.
joy, delight, pleasure, happiness, heaven, ecstasy
OPPOSITE **misery**

blob *noun*
The alien left blobs of green slime on the carpet.
drop, lump, spot, dollop, daub, globule

block *noun*
1 *A block of ice fell from the glacier.*
chunk, hunk, lump, piece
2 *There must be a block in the drainpipe.*
blockage, jam, obstacle, obstruction

block *verb*
1 *A tall hedge blocked our view of the house.*
obstruct, hamper, hinder, interfere with
2 *A mass of leaves had blocked the drain.*
clog, choke, jam, plug, stop up, congest
(*informal*) bung up

bloodthirsty *adjective*
The bloodthirsty pirates rattled their swords.
brutal, cruel, barbaric, murderous, inhuman, pitiless, ruthless, savage, vicious

bloom *noun*
The pear tree was covered in white blooms.
flower, blossom, bud

bloom *verb*
The daffodils bloomed early this year.
blossom, flower, open
OPPOSITE **fade**

blot *noun*
The old map was covered with ink blots.
spot, blotch, mark, blob, splodge, smudge, smear, stain

blot *verb*
to blot something out
The new tower block blots out the view.
conceal, hide, mask, obliterate, obscure

blow *noun*
1 *He was knocked out by a blow on the head.*
knock, bang, bash, hit, punch, clout, slap, smack, swipe, thump
(*informal*) wallop, whack
2 *Losing the hockey match was a terrible blow.*
shock, upset, setback, disappointment, catastrophe, misfortune, disaster, calamity

blow *verb*
The wind was blowing from the east.
blast, gust, puff, fan
To make a shrill sound by blowing is to *whistle*.

blunder *noun*
Forgetting her birthday was a terrible blunder.
mistake, error, fault, slip, slip-up, gaffe
(*informal*) howler

blunt *adjective*
1 *This pencil is blunt.*
dull, worn, unsharpened
OPPOSITE **sharp, pointed**
2 *Her reply to my question was very blunt.*
abrupt, frank, direct, outspoken, plain, tactless
OPPOSITE **tactful**

blurred *adjective*
The background of the photograph is all blurred.
indistinct, vague, blurry, fuzzy, hazy, out of focus
OPPOSITE **clear, distinct**

blush *verb*
The actor blushed with embarrassment.
flush, go red, colour

boast *verb*
The knight was always boasting about his fencing skills.
brag, show off, crow, gloat, swagger
(*informal*) blow your own trumpet

boastful *adjective*
Giants are boastful creatures and brag about everything.
arrogant, big-headed, conceited, vain, bumptious
(*informal*) cocky, swanky
OPPOSITE **modest, humble**

WORD WEB

boat *noun*
*Several fishing **boats** were moored in the harbour.*
ship, craft, vessel

SOME TYPES OF BOAT OR SHIP
barge, canoe, catamaran, cruise liner, dhow, dinghy, dugout, ferry, freighter, gondola, hovercraft, hydrofoil, junk, launch, lifeboat, motor boat, oil tanker, paper boat, punt, raft, rowing boat, schooner, skiff, speedboat, steamship, tanker, trawler, tug, yacht

MILITARY BOATS OR SHIPS
aircraft carrier, battleship, destroyer, frigate, gunboat, minesweeper, submarine, warship

SOME BOATS USED IN THE PAST
brigantine, clipper, coracle, cutter, galleon, galley, man-of-war, paddle steamer, schooner, trireme, windjammer

kayak

WORDS FOR PARTS OF A BOAT OR SHIP
boom, bridge, bulwark, cabin, crow's nest, deck, engine room, fo'c'sle or forecastle, funnel, galley, helm, hull, keel, mast, poop, porthole, propeller, quarterdeck, rigging, rudder, sail, tiller

SPECIAL NAMES
The front part of a boat is the *bow* or *prow*. The back part of a boat is the *stern*.

The left-hand side of a boat is called *port*. The right-hand side of a boat is called *starboard*. A shed where boats are stored is a *boathouse*.

canoe

lifeboat

yacht

cruise liner

dinghy

a
b
c
d
e
f
g
h
i
j
k
l
m
n
o
p
q
r
s
t
u
v
w
x
y
z

 WORD WEB

body noun
The study of the human body is *anatomy*.
The main part of your body except your head, arms, and legs is your *trunk* or *torso*.
The shape of your body is your *build*, *figure*, or *physique*.
A person's dead body is a *corpse*.
The dead body of an animal is a *carcass*.

OUTER PARTS OF THE HUMAN BODY
abdomen, ankle, arm, armpit, breast, buttocks, calf, cheek, chest, chin, ear, elbow, eye, finger, foot, forehead, genitals, groin, hand, head, heel, hip, instep, jaw, knee, kneecap, knuckle, leg, lip, mouth, navel, neck, nipple, nose, pores, shin, shoulder, skin, stomach, temple, thigh, throat, waist, wrist

INNER PARTS OF THE HUMAN BODY
arteries, bladder, bowels, brain, eardrum, glands, gullet, gums, guts, heart, intestines, kidneys, larynx, liver, lung, muscles, nerves, ovaries, pancreas, prostate, sinews, stomach, tendons, tongue, tonsil, tooth, uterus, veins, windpipe, womb

bog noun
We felt our boots sinking into the *bog*.
swamp, quagmire, quicksand, fen

boisterous adjective
Baby dragons can be loud and *boisterous*.
lively, noisy, rowdy, unruly, wild, disorderly
OPPOSITE restrained, calm

bold adjective
1 It was a *bold* move to attack the fortress.
brave, courageous, daring, adventurous, audacious, confident, enterprising, fearless, heroic, valiant, intrepid, plucky
OPPOSITE cowardly
2 The poster uses large letters in *bold* colours.
striking, strong, bright, loud, showy, conspicuous, eye-catching, noticeable, prominent
OPPOSITE inconspicuous, subtle

bolt verb
1 Did you remember to *bolt* the door?
fasten, latch, lock, secure, bar
2 The horses *bolted* when they heard the thunder.
dash away, dart, flee, sprint, run away, rush off

3 Don't *bolt* your food.
gobble, gulp, guzzle, wolf down

book verb
1 Have you *booked* a seat on the train?
order, reserve
2 I've *booked* the disco for the party.
arrange, engage, organize

border noun
1 The town is on the *border* between France and Germany.
boundary, frontier
2 I drew a thin line around the *border* of the picture.
edge, margin, perimeter
A decorative border round the top of a wall is a *frieze*.
A border round the bottom of a skirt is a *hem*.
A decorative border on fabric is a *frill*, *fringe*, or *trimming*.

boring adjective
The film was so *boring* I fell asleep.
dull, dreary, tedious, tiresome, unexciting, uninteresting, dry, monotonous, uninspiring, insipid, unimaginative, uneventful, humdrum
OPPOSITE interesting, exciting

bossy adjective
Stop being so *bossy* towards your sister.
domineering, bullying, dictatorial, officious, tyrannical
An informal name for a bossy person is *bossy boots*.

bother verb
1 Would it *bother* you if I played some music?
disturb, trouble, upset, annoy, irritate, pester, worry, vex, exasperate, (*informal*) bug, hassle
2 Don't *bother* to phone tonight.
make an effort, take trouble, concern yourself, care, mind

bother noun
It's such a *bother* to remember the password.
nuisance, annoyance, irritation, inconvenience, pest, trouble, difficulty, problem
(*informal*) hassle

bottom noun
1 We camped at the *bottom* of the mountain.
foot, base
OPPOSITE top, peak
2 The wreck sank to the *bottom* of the sea.
bed, floor
OPPOSITE surface
3 A wasp stung me on the *bottom*.
backside, behind, buttocks, rear, rump, seat, (*informal*) bum

bottom adjective
I got the *bottom* mark in the test.
least, lowest
OPPOSITE top

bounce verb
The ball *bounced* twice before it reached the net.
rebound, ricochet, spring, leap

bound verb
The puppies *bounded* across the lawn.
leap, bounce, jump, spring, skip, gambol, caper, frisk

box noun
case, chest, crate, carton, packet
A small box for jewellery or treasure is a *casket*.
A large box for luggage is a *trunk*.

boy noun
lad, youngster, youth
(*informal*) kid

brain noun
You'll need to use your *brain* to solve this riddle.
intelligence, intellect, mind, reason, sense, wit

branch noun
1 A robin perched on a *branch* of the tree.
bough, limb
2 I've joined the local *branch* of the Kennel Club.
section, division, department, wing

branch verb
Follow the track until it *branches* into two.
divide, fork

brand noun
Which *brand* of ice cream do you like?
make, kind, sort, type, variety, label
The sign of a particular brand of goods is a *trademark*.

brave adjective
It was *brave* of you to save the cat from drowning.
courageous, heroic, valiant, fearless, daring, gallant, intrepid, plucky
A common simile is *as brave as a lion*.
OPPOSITE cowardly

bravery noun
The police dog was awarded a medal for *bravery*.
courage, heroism, valour, fearlessness, daring, nerve, gallantry, grit, pluck
(*informal*) guts, bottle
OPPOSITE cowardice

break noun
1 Can you see any *breaks* in the chain?
breach, crack, hole, gap, opening, split, rift, puncture, rupture, fracture, fissure
2 Let's take a *break* for coffee.
interval, pause, rest, lull, time-out
(*informal*) breather

break verb
1 *The vase fell off the shelf and broke.*
smash, shatter, fracture, chip, crack, split, snap, splinter
(*informal*) bust
2 *The burglar was arrested for breaking the law.*
disobey, disregard, violate, flout
3 *In her last race, she broke the world record.*
beat, better, exceed, surpass, outdo

breathe verb
To breathe in is to *inhale*.
To breathe out is to *exhale*.
To breathe heavily when you have been running is to *pant* or *puff*.
The formal word for breathing is *respiration*.

breed verb
1 *Salmon swim upstream to breed every year.*
reproduce, have young, multiply, procreate, spawn
2 *Bad hygiene breeds disease.*
cause, produce, generate, encourage, promote, cultivate, induce

breed noun
What breed of dog is that?
kind, sort, type, variety
The evidence of how a dog has been bred is its *pedigree*.

breezy adjective
This morning the weather was bright and breezy.
windy, blowy, blustery, gusty, fresh, draughty

bridge noun
A bridge you can walk over is a *footbridge*.
A bridge to carry water is an *aqueduct*.
A long bridge carrying a road or railway is a *viaduct*.

brief adjective
1 *We paid a brief visit to our cousins on the way home.*
short, quick, hasty, fleeting, temporary
2 *Give me a brief account of what happened.*
short, concise, abbreviated, condensed, compact, succinct

bright adjective
1 *We saw the bright lights of the town in the distance.*
shining, brilliant, blazing, dazzling, glaring, gleaming
OPPOSITE dull, dim, weak
2 *Bright colours will make the poster stand out.*
strong, intense, vivid
Colours that shine in the dark are *luminous* colours.
OPPOSITE dull, faded, muted

3 *Her teachers thought she was very bright.*
clever, intelligent, gifted, sharp, quick-witted
(*informal*) brainy
A common simile is **as bright as a button**.
OPPOSITE stupid, dull-witted
4 *Miranda gave me a bright smile.*
cheerful, happy, lively, merry, jolly, radiant
OPPOSITE sad, gloomy
5 *The day was cold, but bright.*
sunny, fine, fair, clear, cloudless
OPPOSITE dull, cloudy, overcast

brilliant adjective
1 *The fireworks gave off a brilliant light.*
bright, blazing, dazzling, glaring, gleaming, glittering, glorious, shining, splendid, vivid
OPPOSITE dim, dull
2 *Brunel was a brilliant engineer.*
clever, exceptional, outstanding, gifted, talented
OPPOSITE incompetent, talentless
3 (*informal*) *I saw a brilliant film last week.*
excellent, marvellous, outstanding, wonderful, superb
(*informal*) fantastic, fabulous

bring verb
1 *Can you bring the shopping in from the car?*
carry, fetch, deliver, bear, transport
2 *You can bring a friend to the party.*
invite, conduct, escort, guide, lead
3 *The war has brought great sorrow to our people.*
cause, produce, lead to, result in, generate
to bring something about
The new coach brought about some changes.
cause, effect, create, introduce, be responsible for
to bring someone up
In the story, Tarzan is brought up by apes.
rear, raise, care for, foster, look after, nurture, educate, train
to bring something up
I wish you hadn't brought up the subject of money.
mention, talk about, raise, broach

brisk adjective
1 *Mr Hastie went for a brisk walk every evening.*
lively, fast-paced, energetic, invigorating, vigorous, refreshing, bracing
OPPOSITE slow, leisurely
2 *The flower shop does a brisk trade around Easter.*
busy, lively, bustling, hectic

OPPOSITE quiet, slack, slow

broad adjective
1 *The streets in the city were broad and straight.*
wide, open, large, roomy, spacious, vast, extensive
OPPOSITE narrow
2 *Just give me a broad outline of what happened.*
general, rough, vague, loose, indefinite, imprecise
OPPOSITE specific, detailed

broken adjective
1 *Don't use that computer—it's broken.*
faulty, defective, damaged, out of order
OPPOSITE working
2 *After losing all his money, Forbes was a broken man.*
crushed, defeated, beaten, spiritless

brush verb
1 *Jill spent ages brushing her hair for the party.*
groom, comb, tidy
2 *A bird brushed against my cheek as it flew past.*
touch, contact, rub, scrape

brutal adjective
The bandits launched a brutal attack.
savage, vicious, cruel, barbaric, bloodthirsty, callous, ferocious, inhuman, merciless, pitiless, ruthless, sadistic
OPPOSITE gentle, humane

bubble verb
A green liquid bubbled in the witch's cauldron.
boil, seethe, gurgle, froth, foam

bubbly adjective
1 *Bubbly drinks get up my nose.*
fizzy, sparkling, effervescent
2 *Sophie has a bright and bubbly personality.*
cheerful, lively, vivacious, spirited, animated

buckle noun
The pirate wore a belt with a large silver buckle.
clasp, fastener, fastening, clip, catch

buckle verb
1 *Please buckle your seat belts.*
fasten, secure, clasp, clip, do up, hook up
2 *The bridge buckled when the giant stepped onto it.*
bend, warp, twist, crumple, cave in, collapse

budge verb
The window was stuck and wouldn't budge.
give way, move, shift, stir

bug noun
1 *Birds help to control bugs in the garden.*

a
b
c
d
e
f
g
h
i
j
k
l
m
n
o
p
q
r
s
t
u
v
w
x
y
z

insect, pest
2 (*informal*) *I can't get rid of this stomach bug.*
infection, virus, germ, disease, illness
3 *There are a few bugs in the computer program.*
fault, error, defect, flaw
(*informal*) gremlin

build *verb*
Dad is going to build a shed in the garden.
construct, erect, put together, put up, set up, assemble
to build up
1 *I'm building up a collection of DVDs.*
accumulate, assemble, collect, put together
2 *We felt the tension building up in the crowd.*
increase, intensify, rise, grow, mount up, escalate

build *noun*
Charlotte was a girl of slender build.
body, form, frame, figure, physique

WORD WEB

building *noun*
The new building will have seven storeys.
construction, structure, dwelling
A person who designs buildings is an **architect**.

lighthouse

BUILDINGS WHERE PEOPLE LIVE
apartment, barracks, bungalow, castle, cottage, farmhouse, flat, fort, fortress, house, mansion, palace, skyscraper, tenement, terrace, tower, villa

BUILDINGS WHERE PEOPLE WORK
factory, garage, lighthouse, mill, shop, store, warehouse

BUILDINGS WHERE PEOPLE WORSHIP
abbey, cathedral, chapel, church, monastery, mosque, pagoda, shrine, synagogue, temple

OTHER TYPES OF BUILDING
cabin, cafe, cinema, college, gallery, hotel, inn, library, museum, observatory, police station, post office, power station, prison, pub or public house, restaurant, school, shed, theatre

---

bulge *noun*
There was a large bulge in the robber's sack.
bump, hump, lump, swelling, protuberance

bulge *verb*
The creature had eyes which bulged out of its head.
stick out, swell, puff out, protrude

bulky *adjective*
The parcel is too bulky to go through the letterbox.
big, large, hefty, substantial, sizeable, cumbersome, unwieldy
OPPOSITE small, compact

bully *verb*
Some of the children were afraid of being bullied.
persecute, torment, intimidate, terrorize, push around

bump *verb*
1 *The baby bumped his head on the table.*
hit, strike, knock, bang
2 *My bicycle bumped up and down over the cobbles.*
bounce, shake, jerk, jolt
to bump into
1 *The taxi bumped into the car in front of it.*
collide with, bang into, run into, crash into

PARTS YOU MIGHT FIND INSIDE A BUILDING
balcony, basement, cellar, conservatory, corridor, courtyard, crypt, dungeon, foyer, gallery, lobby, porch, quadrangle, room, staircase, veranda

PARTS YOU MIGHT FIND OUTSIDE A BUILDING
arch, balustrade, bay window, bow window, buttress, chimney, colonnade, column, dome, dormer window, drainpipe, eaves, foundations, gable, gutter, masonry, parapet, pediment, pillar, pipes, roof, tower, turret, vault, wall, window, windowsill

CASTLES AND FORTIFIED BUILDINGS
château, citadel, fort, fortress, motte and bailey, palace, stronghold, tower

PARTS OF A CASTLE
bailey, barbican, battlement, buttress, courtyard, donjon, drawbridge, dungeon, gate, gateway, keep, magazine, moat, motte, parapet, portcullis, postern, rampart, tower, turret, wall, watchtower

skyscraper

---

2 *I bumped into one of my friends in the bookshop.*
meet, come across, run into

bump *noun*
1 *We felt a bump as the plane landed.*
thud, thump, bang, blow, knock
2 *How did you get that bump on your head?*
lump, swelling, bulge

bumpy *adjective*
1 *The car jolted up and down on the bumpy road.*
rough, uneven, irregular, lumpy
OPPOSITE smooth, even
2 *We had a bumpy ride in a jeep over muddy tracks.*
bouncy, jerky, jolting, lurching, choppy

bunch *noun*
1 *The jailer jangled a bunch of keys.*
bundle, cluster, collection, set
2 *She picked a bunch of flowers.*
bouquet, posy, spray
3 (*informal*) *They're a friendly bunch of people.*
group, set, circle, band, gang, crowd

bundle *noun*
I found a bundle of old newspapers.
bunch, batch, pile, stack, collection, pack, bale

burn *verb*
1 *We could see the campfire burning in the distance.*
be alight, be on fire, blaze, flame, flare, flicker
To burn without flames is to *glow* or *smoulder*.
2 *The captain ordered them to burn the enemy ship.*
set fire to, incinerate, reduce to ashes
To start something burning is to *ignite*, *kindle*, or *light* it.
To burn something slightly is to *char*, *scorch*, or *singe* it.
To hurt someone with boiling liquid or steam is to *scald* them.
To burn a dead body is to *cremate* it.
To burn a mark on an animal is to *brand* it.

burst *verb*
The balloon burst when my brother sat on it.
puncture, rupture, break, give way, split, tear

bury *verb*
1 *The document was buried under a pile of old letters.*
cover, conceal, hide, secrete

2 *They say the old witch was*
buried in that graveyard.
inter, entomb

bushy *adjective*
*The troll had **bushy** green eyebrows.*
hairy, thick, dense, shaggy, bristly

business *noun*
1 *My uncle runs a restaurant*
business.
company, firm, organization
2 *The new bookshop does a lot*
of business.
trade, trading, buying and
selling, commerce
3 *What sort of business do you*
want to go into?
work, job, career, employment,
industry, occupation, profession,
trade
4 *He left early to attend to some*
urgent business.
matter, issue, affair, problem,
point, concern, question

bustle *verb*
*Miss Flyte **bustled** about the*
kitchen making tea.
rush, dash, hurry, scurry,
scuttle, fuss

busy *adjective*
1 *Mum is busy making my*
birthday cake just now.
occupied, engaged, employed,
working, slaving away,
beavering away
(*informal*) hard at it, up to your
eyes
A common simile is *as busy as*
a bee.
OPPOSITE idle
2 *Christmas is a very busy time*
for shops.
active, hectic, frantic, lively
OPPOSITE quiet, restful
3 *Is the town always this busy*
on Saturdays?
crowded, bustling, hectic, lively,
teeming
OPPOSITE quiet, peaceful

buy *verb*
I'm saving up to buy a skateboard.
get, pay for, purchase, acquire
OPPOSITE sell

cabin *noun*
The outlaws hid in a cabin in the
woods.
hut, shack, shed, lodge, chalet,
shelter

cafe *noun*
We had lunch in a cafe overlooking
the river.
cafeteria, coffee shop, tearoom,

snack bar, buffet, canteen, bistro,
brasserie

cage *noun*
A large cage or enclosure for birds
is an *aviary*.
A cage or enclosure for poultry is
a *coop*.
A cage or enclosure for animals
is a *pen*.
A cage or box for a pet rabbit is a
hutch.

calculate *verb*
I calculated that it would take an
hour to walk home.
work out, compute, figure out,
reckon, add up, count, total
To calculate something roughly
is to *estimate*.

call *noun*
1 *We heard a call for help from*
inside the cave.
cry, exclamation, scream, shout,
yell
2 *Grandad made an unexpected*
call.
visit, stop, stay
3 *There's not much call for*
suncream in winter.
demand, need

call *verb*
1 *'Stop that racket!' called the*
janitor.
cry out, exclaim, shout, yell
2 *It was too late at night to call*
my friends.
phone, ring, telephone
3 *The headteacher called me to*
her office.
summon, invite, send for, order
4 *The doctor called to see if I was*
feeling better.
visit, pay a visit, drop in, drop by
5 *They called the baby Jessica.*
name, baptize, christen, dub
6 *What is your new book going to*
be called?
name, title, entitle

calm *adjective*
1 *The weather was too calm to*
fly our kites.
still, quiet, peaceful, tranquil,
serene, windless
OPPOSITE stormy, windy
2 *The sea was calm, and we had a*
pleasant voyage.
smooth, still, flat, motionless,
tranquil
OPPOSITE rough, choppy
3 *I tried to stay calm before my*
judo exam.
cool, level-headed, patient,
relaxed, sedate, unemotional,
unexcitable, untroubled
OPPOSITE anxious, nervous

cancel *verb*
We had to cancel the race because
of the weather.
abandon, call off, scrap, drop
(*informal*) scrub, ditch, axe

To cancel something after it has
already begun is to *abort* it.
To put something off until later is
to *postpone* it.
To cancel items on a list is to
cross out, *delete*, or *erase* them.

capture *verb*
1 *The bank robbers were captured*
by police this morning.
catch, arrest, apprehend, seize,
take prisoner
(*informal*) nab, nick
2 *The castle has never been*
captured by enemy forces.
occupy, seize, take, take over, win

care *noun*
1 *The old wizard's face was full of*
care.
worry, anxiety, trouble, concern,
burden, responsibility, sorrow,
stress
2 *I took great care with my*
handwriting.
attention, concentration,
thoroughness, thought,
meticulousness
OPPOSITE carelessness
3 *Jake left his pet hamster in my care.*
charge, keeping, protection,
safe keeping, supervision
to take care
Please take care crossing the road.
be careful, be on your guard, look
out, watch out
to take care of someone or
something
My granny takes care of me after
school.
care for, look after, mind, watch
over, attend to, tend

care *verb*
Do you care which team wins the
World Cup?
mind, bother, worry, be
interested, be troubled, be
bothered, be worried
to care for someone or **something**
1 *The veterinary hospital cares for*
sick animals.
take care of, look after, attend to,
tend, nurse
2 *I don't really care for broccoli.*
like, be fond of, be keen on, love

career *noun*
Max had a successful career as a
racing driver.
job, occupation, profession, trade,
business, employment, calling

careful *adjective*
1 *You must be more careful with*
your spelling.
accurate, conscientious,
thorough, thoughtful,
meticulous, painstaking, precise
OPPOSITE careless, inaccurate
2 *Dad kept a careful watch on the*
bonfire.
attentive, cautious, watchful,
alert, wary, vigilant

a
b
c
d
e
f
g
h
i
j
k
l
m
n
o
p
q
r
s
t
u
v
w
x
y
z

OPPOSITE careless, inattentive
to be careful *Please* **be careful** *with those scissors.*
take care, be on your guard, look out, watch out

careless *adjective*
1 *This is a very* **careless** *piece of work.*
messy, untidy, thoughtless, inaccurate, slapdash, shoddy, scrappy, sloppy, slovenly
OPPOSITE careful, accurate
2 *I was* **careless** *and cut my finger.*
inattentive, thoughtless, absent-minded, heedless, irresponsible, negligent, reckless
OPPOSITE careful, attentive

carnival *noun*
The whole village comes out for the annual **carnival**.
fair, festival, fête, gala, parade, procession, show, celebration, pageant

carry *verb*
1 *I helped Mum to* **carry** *the shopping to the car.*
take, transfer, lift, fetch, bring, lug
2 *Aircraft* **carry** *passengers and goods.*
transport, convey
3 *The rear axle* **carries** *the greatest weight.*
bear, support, hold up
to carry on *We* **carried on** *in spite of the rain.*
continue, go on, persevere, persist, keep on, remain, stay, survive
to carry something out
The soldiers **carried out** *the captain's orders.*
perform, do, execute, accomplish, achieve, complete, finish

carve *verb*
1 *The statue was* **carved** *out of stone.*
sculpt, chisel, hew
2 *Mum* **carved** *the chicken for Sunday dinner.*
cut, slice

case *noun*
1 *I loaded my* **case** *into the boot of the car.*
suitcase, trunk
A number of suitcases that you take on holiday is your *baggage* or *luggage*.
2 *What's in those* **cases** *in the attic?*
box, chest, crate, carton, casket
3 *This has been a clear* **case** *of mistaken identity.*
instance, occurrence, example, illustration
4 *It was one of Sherlock Holmes's most famous* **cases**.
inquiry, investigation
5 *She presented a good* **case** *for abolishing hunting.*
argument, line of reasoning

casual *adjective*
1 *It was just a* **casual** *remark, so don't take it too seriously.*
accidental, chance, unexpected, unintentional, unplanned
OPPOSITE deliberate
2 *The restaurant had a* **casual** *atmosphere.*
easy-going, informal, relaxed
OPPOSITE formal
3 *The teacher complained about our* **casual** *attitude.*
apathetic, careless, slack, unenthusiastic
OPPOSITE enthusiastic

catastrophe *noun*
The drought is a **catastrophe** *for the farmers.*
disaster, calamity, misfortune, mishap, tragedy

catch *verb*
1 *My friends yelled at me to* **catch** *the ball.*
clutch, grab, grasp, grip, hang on to, hold, seize, snatch, take
2 *One of the anglers* **caught** *a fish.*
hook, net, trap
3 *The police hoped to* **catch** *the thief red-handed.*
arrest, capture, corner
(*informal*) nab
4 *I hope you don't* **catch** *my cold.*
become infected by, contract, get
(*informal*) go down with
5 *You must hurry if you want to* **catch** *the bus.*
be in time for, get on

catch *noun*
1 *The angler got a large* **catch** *of salmon.*
haul
2 *The car is so cheap that there must be a* **catch**.
problem, obstacle, snag, difficulty, disadvantage, drawback, trap, trick
3 *All the windows are fitted with safety* **catches**.
fastening, latch, lock, bolt, hook

cause *noun*
1 *What was the* **cause** *of the trouble?*
origin, source, start
You can also talk about the *reasons* for the trouble.
2 *You've got no* **cause** *to complain.*
grounds, basis, motive
3 *The sponsored walk is for a good* **cause**.
purpose, object

cause *verb*
A single spark from the fire could **cause** *an explosion.*
bring about, create, generate, lead to, give rise to, result in, provoke, arouse

caution *noun*
1 *We decided to proceed with* **caution**.
care, attention, watchfulness, wariness, vigilance
2 *The traffic warden let him off with a* **caution**.
warning, reprimand, telling-off
(*informal*) ticking-off

cautious *adjective*
My grandad is a **cautious** *driver.*
careful, attentive, watchful, wary, vigilant, hesitant
OPPOSITE reckless

cease *verb*
The fighting **ceased** *at midnight.*
come to an end, end, finish, stop, halt
OPPOSITE begin

celebrate *verb*
1 *Let's* **celebrate**!
enjoy yourself, have a good time, be happy, rejoice
2 *What shall we do to* **celebrate** *Granny's birthday?*
commemorate, observe, keep

celebration *noun*
We had a big **celebration** *for my cousin's wedding.*
festivity, party, feast, festival, banquet, jamboree

celebrity *noun*
The awards were handed out by a TV **celebrity**.
famous person, personality, public figure, VIP, star, idol

cemetery *noun*
A famous author is buried in the local **cemetery**.
graveyard, burial ground, churchyard
A place where dead people are cremated is a *crematorium*.

central *adjective*
1 *We are now in the* **central** *part of the building.*
middle, core, inner, interior
OPPOSITE outer
2 *Who are the* **central** *characters in the story?*
chief, crucial, essential, fundamental, important, main, major, principal, vital
OPPOSITE unimportant

centre *noun*
The library is in the **centre** *of the town. The burial chamber is in the* **centre** *of the pyramid.*
middle, heart, core, inside, interior
The centre of a planet or a piece of fruit is the *core*.
The centre of an atom or a living cell is the *nucleus*.
The centre of a wheel is the *hub*.
The point at the centre of a see-saw is the *pivot*.
The edible part in the centre of a nut is the *kernel*.
OPPOSITE edge, outside, surface

ceremony *noun*
1 *We watched the **ceremony** of the opening of parliament.*
rite, ritual, formalities
A ceremony where someone is given a prize is a *presentation*.
A ceremony where someone is given a special honour is an *investiture*.
A ceremony to celebrate something new is an *inauguration* or *opening*.
A ceremony where someone becomes a member of a society is an *initiation*.
A ceremony to make a church or other building sacred is a *dedication*.
A ceremony to remember a dead person or a past event is a *commemoration*.
A ceremony held in a church is a *service*.
2 *They had a quiet wedding without a lot of **ceremony**.*
formality, pomp, pageantry, spectacle

certain *adjective*
1 *My mum was **certain** she would win the cookery competition.*
confident, convinced, positive, sure, determined
OPPOSITE uncertain
2 *We have **certain** proof that the painting is a forgery.*
definite, clear, convincing, absolute, unquestionable, reliable, trustworthy, undeniable, infallible, genuine, valid
OPPOSITE unreliable
3 *The damaged plane faced **certain** disaster.*
inevitable, unavoidable
OPPOSITE possible
4 *Her new book is **certain** to be a best-seller.*
bound, sure

chain *noun*
1 *The anchor was attached to a **chain**.*
One ring in a chain is a *link*.
A chain used to link railway wagons together is a *coupling*.
2 *The police formed a **chain** to keep the crowd back.*
line, row, cordon
3 *Holmes described the **chain** of events that led to the murder.*
series, sequence, succession, string

champion *noun*
1 *She is the current world **champion** at ice-skating.*
title-holder, prizewinner, victor, winner, conqueror
2 *Martin Luther King was a **champion** of civil rights.*
supporter, advocate, defender,

upholder, patron, backer

championship *noun*
*Fifteen schools took part in the karate **championship**.*
competition, contest, tournament

chance *noun*
1 *They say there's a **chance** of rain later.*
possibility, likelihood, probability, prospect, danger, risk
2 *I haven't had a **chance** to reply yet.*
opportunity, time, occasion
3 *The director took a **chance** in hiring an unknown actor.*
gamble, risk
by chance
*I found the house quite **by chance**.*
by accident, accidentally, by coincidence
An unfortunate chance is *bad luck* or a *misfortune*.
A fortunate chance is *good luck* or a *fluke*.

change *verb*
1 *They've **changed** the programme for the concert.*
alter, modify, rearrange, reorganize, adjust, adapt, vary
2 *The town has **changed** a lot since Victorian times.*
alter, become different, develop, grow, move on
3 *Can I **change** these jeans for a bigger size, please?*
exchange, replace, switch, substitute
(*informal*) swap
to change into
*Tadpoles **change into** frogs.*
become, turn into, be transformed into

change *noun*
*There has been a slight **change** of plan.*
alteration, modification, variation, difference, break
A change to something worse is a *deterioration*.
A change to something better is an *improvement* or a *reform*.
A very big change is a *revolution* or *transformation* or *U-turn*.
A change in which one person or thing is replaced by another is a *substitution*.

chaos *noun*
*After the earthquake, the city was in **chaos**.*
confusion, disorder, mayhem, uproar, tumult, pandemonium, anarchy, bedlam, muddle, shambles
OPPOSITE order

chaotic *adjective*
*Alice finds that life in Wonderland is **chaotic**.*

confused, disorderly, disorganized, muddled, topsy-turvy, untidy, unruly, riotous
OPPOSITE orderly, organized

chapter *noun*
*I read a **chapter** of my book last night.*
part, section, division
One section of a play is an *act* or *scene*.
One part of a serial is an *episode* or *instalment*.

character *noun*
1 *Her **character** is quite different from her sister's.*
personality, temperament, nature, disposition, make-up, manner
2 *Our neighbour is a well-known **character** in our street.*
figure, personality, individual, person
3 *Which **character** would you like to play in Peter Pan?*
part, role

charge *noun*
1 *The admission **charge** is five euros.*
price, rate
The charge made for a ride on public transport is the *fare*.
The charge made to post a letter or parcel is the *postage*.
A charge made to join a club is a *fee* or *subscription*.
A charge made for certain things by the government is a *duty* or a *tax*.
A charge made to use a private road, bridge, or tunnel is a *toll*.
2 *The robbers face several criminal **charges**.*
accusation, allegation
3 *Many soldiers were killed in the **charge**.*
assault, attack, onslaught, raid
4 *My best friend left her hamster in my **charge**.*
care, keeping, protection, custody, trust
to be in charge of something
*An experienced sailor was in **charge** of the crew.*
manage, lead, command, direct, supervise, run

charge *verb*
1 *The library **charges** ten pence for a photocopy.*
ask for, make you pay
2 *A man has been **charged** with attempted robbery.*
accuse (of)
3 *The cavalry **charged** the enemy line.*
attack, assault, storm, rush

charm *verb*
*Winnie the Pooh has **charmed** readers all over the world.*

a
b
c
d
e
f
g
h
i
j
k
l
m
n
o
p
q
r
s
t
u
v
w
x
y
z

bewitch, captivate, delight, enchant, entrance, fascinate, please

charming *adjective*
We drove through some charming scenery.
delightful, attractive, pleasant, pleasing, likeable, appealing

chart *noun*
1 *The explorer stopped to consult his chart.*
map
2 *This chart shows the average rainfall for each month.*
diagram, graph, table

chase *verb*
The wolves chased a deer through the forest.
pursue, run after, follow, track, trail, hunt

chatty *adjective*
Frank is usually shy, but today he's quite chatty.
talkative, communicative
OPPOSITE silent

cheap *adjective*
1 *We got a cheap flight to London.*
inexpensive, affordable, bargain, cut-price, discount, reasonable
2 *These tyres are made from cheap rubber.*
inferior, shoddy, second-rate, worthless, trashy
(*informal*) tacky, tatty
OPPOSITE superior, good-quality

cheat *verb*
1 *She was cheated into buying a fake diamond ring.*
deceive, trick, swindle, double-cross, hoax
(*informal*) con, diddle, fleece, fool, rip off
2 *Anyone who cheats in the quiz will be disqualified.*
copy, crib

cheat *noun*
Don't trust him—he's a cheat.
cheater, deceiver, swindler, fraud, impostor, hoaxer

check *verb*
1 *Have you checked your work carefully?*
examine, inspect, look over, scrutinize
2 *The heavy snow checked their progress towards the Pole.*
hamper, hinder, block, obstruct, delay, hold back, slow, slow down, halt, stop

check *noun*
I need to run some checks on your computer.
test, examination, inspection, check-up

cheeky *adjective*
Don't be so cheeky!
disrespectful, facetious, flippant, impertinent, impolite, impudent, insolent, insulting, irreverent, mocking, rude, saucy, shameless
OPPOSITE respectful

cheer *verb*
1 *We cheered when our team scored a goal.*
clap, applaud, shout, yell
OPPOSITE jeer
2 *The good news cheered us.*
comfort, console, gladden, delight, please, encourage, uplift
OPPOSITE sadden

cheerful *adjective*
The sun was shining, and we set out in a cheerful mood.
happy, good-humoured, light-hearted, merry, jolly, joyful, joyous, glad, pleased, optimistic, lively, elated, animated, bright, buoyant, jovial, gleeful, chirpy
OPPOSITE sad

chest *noun*
I found some old books in a chest in the attic.
box, crate, case, trunk

chew *verb*
Are you still chewing that toffee?
eat, gnaw, munch

chief *noun*
The pirates chose Redbeard as their chief.
leader, ruler, head, commander, captain, chieftain, master, governor, president, principal
(*informal*) boss

chief *adjective*
1 *The chief ingredients in a trifle are jelly, custard, and cream.*
main, central, key, principal, crucial, basic, essential, important, vital, major, primary, foremost, fundamental, indispensable, necessary, significant, predominant, prominent
OPPOSITE unimportant, minor, trivial
2 *Albert was Queen Victoria's chief advisor.*
head, senior

child *noun*
1 *The book festival is aimed especially at children.*
boy or girl, infant, juvenile, youngster, youth, lad or lass
(*informal*) kid, tot, nipper
2 *How many children do you have?*
son or daughter, descendant, offspring
A child who expects to inherit a title or fortune from parents is an *heir* or *heiress*.
A child whose parents are dead is an *orphan*.
A child looked after by a guardian is a *ward*.

childish *adjective*
It's childish to make rude noises.
babyish, immature, juvenile, infantile
OPPOSITE mature

chilly *adjective*
1 *It's a chilly evening, so wrap up well.*
cold, cool, frosty, icy, crisp, fresh, raw, wintry
(*informal*) nippy
OPPOSITE warm
2 *The librarian gave me a very chilly look.*
unfriendly, hostile, unwelcoming, unsympathetic
OPPOSITE friendly

chip *noun*
1 *There were chips of broken glass on the pavement.*
bit, piece, fragment, scrap, sliver, splinter, flake, shaving
2 *This mug's got a chip in it.*
crack, nick, notch, flaw

chip *verb*
I chipped a cup while I was washing up.
crack, nick, notch, damage

choice *noun*
1 *My bike had a flat tyre, so I had no choice but to walk.*
alternative, option
2 *She wouldn't be my choice as team captain.*
preference, selection, pick, vote
3 *The greengrocer has a good choice of vegetables.*
range, selection, assortment, array, mixture, variety, diversity

choke *verb*
1 *This tie is so tight it's choking me.*
strangle, suffocate, stifle, throttle
2 *Thick fumes made the firefighters choke.*
cough, gasp

choose *verb*
1 *We had a show of hands to choose a winner.*
select, appoint, elect, vote for
2 *I chose the blue shoes to go with my dress.*
decide on, select, pick out, opt for, plump for, settle on, single out
3 *Lola chose to stay at home.*
decide, make a decision, determine, prefer, resolve

chop *verb*
1 *Chop the celery into large chunks.*
cut, split
2 *They chopped down the undergrowth to make a path.*
hack, slash
To chop down a tree is to *fell* it.
To chop off an arm or leg is to *amputate* it.
To chop a branch off a tree is

to *lop* it.
To chop food into small pieces
is to *dice* or *mince* it.

chunk *noun*
I bit a chunk out of my apple.
piece, portion, lump, block,
hunk, slab, wedge

circle *noun*
1 *We arranged the chairs in a
circle.*
ring, round, hoop, loop, band
A flat, solid circle is a *disc*.
A three-dimensional round shape
is a *sphere*.
An egg shape is an *oval* or
ellipse.
The distance round a circle is the
circumference.
The distance across a circle is the
diameter.
The distance from the centre to
the circumference is the *radius*.
A circular movement is a
revolution or *rotation*.
A circular trip round the world is
a *circumnavigation*.
A circular trip of a satellite round
a planet is an *orbit*.
2 *She has a wide circle of friends.*
group, set, crowd

city *noun*
The chief city of a country or
region is the *metropolis*.
An area of houses outside the
central part of a city is the
suburbs.
A word meaning 'to do with a
town or city' is *urban*.
A word meaning 'to do with
a city and its suburbs' is
metropolitan.

claim *verb*
1 *You can claim your prize for the
raffle here.*
ask for, request, collect, demand,
insist on
2 *The professor claims to be an
expert on dinosaurs.*
declare, assert, allege, maintain,
argue, insist

clap *verb*
1 *The audience clapped loudly at
the end of the concert.*
applaud, cheer
2 *Suddenly, a hand clapped me
on the shoulder.*
slap, hit, pat, smack

class *noun*
1 *There are 26 children in our
class.*
form, set, stream
The other pupils in your class are
your *classmates*.
2 *There are many different
classes of plants.*
category, group,
classification, division, set,
sort, type, kind, species
3 *The ancient Romans*

divided people into social classes.
level, rank, status

clean *adjective*
1 *Can you bring me a clean cup,
please?*
spotless, washed, scrubbed,
swept, tidy, immaculate,
hygienic, sanitary
An informal word meaning
'very clean' is *squeaky-clean*.
A common simile is *as clean as
a whistle*.
OPPOSITE **dirty**
2 *I began my diary on a clean
piece of paper.*
blank, unused, unmarked,
empty, bare, fresh, new
OPPOSITE **used**
3 *This plaster will keep the wound
clean.*
sterile, sterilized, uninfected
4 *You can get clean water from
this tap.*
pure, clear, fresh, unpolluted,
uncontaminated
5 *The referee said he wanted a
clean fight.*
fair, honest, honourable,
sporting, sportsmanlike
OPPOSITE **dishonourable**

clean *verb*
1 *We cleaned the house from top
to bottom. I tried to clean the mud
off my boots.*
wash, wipe, mop, scour, scrub,
polish, dust, sweep, vacuum,
rinse, wring out, hose down,
sponge, shampoo, swill
To clean clothes is to *launder*
them.
OPPOSITE **dirty, mess up**
2 *The nurse cleaned the wound
with an antiseptic wipe.*
cleanse, bathe, disinfect,
sanitize, sterilize
OPPOSITE **infect, contaminate**

clear *adjective*
1 *We saw fish swimming in the
clear pool.*
clean, pure, colourless,
transparent
A common simile is *as clear
as crystal*.
A simile which means the
opposite is *as clear as mud*.
OPPOSITE **opaque**
2 *It was a beautiful clear day.*

bright, sunny, cloudless,
unclouded
A clear night is a *moonlit* or
starlit night.
OPPOSITE **cloudy, overcast**
3 *The instructions on the map
were quite clear.*
plain, understandable,
intelligible, lucid, unambiguous
OPPOSITE **ambiguous, confusing**
4 *The actor spoke his words with a
clear voice.*
distinct, audible
A common simile is *as clear as
a bell*.
OPPOSITE **muffled**
5 *The signature on this letter is
not clear.*
legible, recognizable, visible
OPPOSITE **illegible**
6 *My camera takes nice clear
pictures.*
sharp, well defined, focused
OPPOSITE **unfocused**
7 *Are you sure that your
conscience is clear?*
innocent, untroubled, blameless
OPPOSITE **guilty**
8 *There's a clear difference
between a male blackbird and
a female.*
obvious, definite, noticeable,
conspicuous, perceptible,
pronounced
OPPOSITE **imperceptible**
9 *They made sure the road was
clear for the ambulance.*
open, empty, free, passable,
uncrowded, unobstructed
OPPOSITE **congested**

clear *verb*
1 *I cleared the weeds from the
flower bed.*
get rid of, remove, eliminate,
strip
2 *The plumber cleared the blocked
drain.*
unblock, unclog, clean out, open
up
To clear a channel is to *dredge* it.
3 *I cleared the misty windows.*
clean, wipe, polish
4 *If the fire alarm goes, clear the
building.*
empty, evacuate
5 *The fog cleared slowly.*
disappear, vanish, disperse,
evaporate, melt away
6 *The forecast said that the
weather will clear.*
become clear, brighten,
fair up

climb

7 *He was **cleared** of all the charges against him.*
acquit, free, release
8 *The runners **cleared** the first hurdle.*
go over, get over, jump over, pass over, vault
to clear up
*Please **clear up** this mess before you go.*
clean up, tidy up, put right, put straight
clever *adjective*
1 *Dr Hafiz is very **clever** and can read hieroglyphics.*
intelligent, bright, gifted, able, knowledgeable
(*informal*) brainy, smart
OPPOSITE unintelligent
An informal name for a clever person is a *brainbox*.
An uncomplimentary synonym is *clever clogs* or *smartypants*.
2 *The elves were very **clever** with their fingers.*
accomplished, capable, gifted, skilful, talented
If you are clever at a lot of things, you are *versatile*.
OPPOSITE unskilful
3 *They are **clever** enough to get away with it.*
quick, sharp, shrewd, smart
Uncomplimentary synonyms are *artful*, *crafty*, *cunning*, *wily*.
OPPOSITE stupid
climax *noun*
*The **climax** of the film is a stunning car chase.*
high point, highlight, peak, crisis
OPPOSITE anticlimax
climb *verb*
1 *It took us several hours to **climb** the mountain.*
ascend, clamber up, go up, scale
2 *The plane **climbed** into the clouds.*
lift off, soar, take off
3 *The road **climbs** steeply up to the castle.*
rise, slope
to climb down
3 *It's harder to **climb down** rock than to get up.*
descend, get down from
*We all told him he was wrong, so he had to **climb down**.*
admit defeat, give in, surrender

---

clothes *plural noun*
*What **clothes** are you taking on holiday?*
clothing, garments, outfits, dress, attire, garb, finery
(*informal*) gear, togs, get-up
A set of clothes to wear is a *costume*, *outfit*, or *suit*.
An official set of clothes worn for school or work is a *uniform*.

SOME ITEMS OF CLOTHING
blouse, caftan, camisole, chador or chuddar, dhoti, dress, dungarees, frock, gown, jeans, jersey, jodhpurs, jumper, kilt, kimono, leggings, miniskirt, pinafore, polo shirt, pullover, robe, sari, sarong, shirt, shorts, skirt, slacks, smock, suit, sweater, sweatshirt, trousers, trunks, T-shirt, tunic, waistcoat

OUTER CLOTHES
anorak, apron, blazer, cagoule, cape, cardigan, cloak, coat, dressing gown, duffel coat, fleece, gilet, hoodie, greatcoat, jacket, mackintosh, oilskins, overalls, overcoat, parka, poncho, raincoat, shawl, stole, tracksuit, windcheater
UNDERWEAR
boxer shorts, bra, briefs, crop top, drawers, knickers, pants, petticoat, slip, socks, stockings, tights, underpants, vest

CLOTHES FOR SLEEPING IN
nightdress or (*informal*) nightie, pyjamas

CLOTHES WORN IN THE PAST
corset, doublet, frock coat, gauntlet, ruff, toga

ACCESSORIES WORN WITH CLOTHES
belt, braces, cravat, earmuffs, glove, sash, scarf, shawl, tie

PARTS OF A GARMENT
bodice, button, buttonhole, collar, cuff, hem, lapel, pocket, seam, sleeve, waistband, zip

THINGS USED TO DECORATE CLOTHES
beads, frills, fringes, lace, ruffles, sequins, tassels

SOME KINDS OF HAT
balaclava, baseball cap, bearskin, beret, boater, bonnet, bowler, cap, deerstalker, fez, helmet, mitre, mortarboard, panama hat, skull cap, sombrero, sou'wester, stetson, sun-hat, tam-o'shanter, top hat, trilby, turban

---

✏️ **WRITING TIPS**

You can use these words to describe **clothes**:
baggy, casual, chic, dowdy, drab, fashionable, fine, flashy, flattering, frilly, frumpy, glamorous, ill-fitting, loose, luxurious, old-fashioned, ornate, ragged, roomy, shabby, skimpy, smart, sporty, stylish, tattered or in tatters, threadbare, tight-fitting, trendy, worn

---

cling *verb*
to cling to someone or **something**
1 *The baby koala **clung to** its mother.*
clasp, grasp, clutch, embrace, hug
2 *Ivy **clings to** the wall.*
adhere to, fasten on to, stick to
clip *verb*
1 *The sheets of paper were **clipped** together.*
pin, staple
2 *Dad **clipped** the hedges in the back garden.*
cut, trim
To cut unwanted twigs off a tree or bush is to *prune* it.
close *adjective*
1 *Our house is **close** to the shops.*
near, nearby, not far
To be actually by the side of something is to be *adjacent*.
OPPOSITE far, distant
2 *Anisha and I are **close** friends.*
intimate, dear, devoted,

fond, affectionate
3 *The police made a **close** examination of the stolen car.*
careful, detailed, painstaking, minute, thorough
OPPOSITE casual
4 *It was an exciting race because it was so **close**.*
equal, even, level, well-matched
5 *Open the window—it's very **close** in here.*
humid, muggy, stuffy, clammy, airless, stifling, suffocating
OPPOSITE airy
close *verb*
1 *Don't forget to **close** the lid.*
shut, fasten, seal, secure
2 *The road has been **closed** to traffic for the parade.*
barricade, block, obstruct, stop up
3 *The band **closed** the concert with my favourite song.*
finish, end, complete, conclude, stop, terminate
(*informal*) wind up

clothes noun see panel opposite

cloudy adjective
1 The day was cold and **cloudy**.
dull, overcast, grey, dark, dismal, gloomy, sunless
OPPOSITE cloudless
2 We couldn't see any fish in the **cloudy** water.
muddy, murky, hazy, milky
OPPOSITE clear, transparent

club noun
1 The warrior brandished a wooden **club**.
stick, baton, truncheon
2 Would you like to join our book **club**?
group, society, association, organization, circle, union

clue noun
1 I don't know the answer. Can you give me a **clue**?
hint, suggestion, indication, pointer, tip, idea
2 'This footprint is an important **clue**,' said the detective.
piece of evidence, lead

clumsy adjective
The **clumsy** gnome was always breaking things.
careless, awkward, ungainly, inept
An informal name for a clumsy person is **butterfingers**.
OPPOSITE graceful

clutter noun
Clear up all this **clutter**.
mess, muddle, junk, litter, rubbish, odds and ends

coach verb
He was **coached** by a former champion.
train, teach, instruct

coarse adjective
1 The blanket was made of **coarse** woollen material.
rough, harsh, scratchy, bristly, hairy
OPPOSITE soft
2 We were shocked by their **coarse** table manners.
rude, offensive, impolite, improper, indecent, crude, vulgar
OPPOSITE polite, refined

coat noun
1 The detective was wearing a thick winter **coat**.
see clothes panel opposite
2 The fox had a reddish brown **coat**.
hide, pelt, skin, fur, hair
A sheep's coat is a **fleece**.
3 The front door needs a **coat** of paint.
layer, coating, covering

coat verb
We ate marshmallows **coated** with chocolate.
cover, spread, smear, glaze

coax verb
Sam **coaxed** the hamster back into its cage.
persuade, tempt, entice

coil noun
The snake twisted itself into a **coil**.
spiral, twist, curl, twirl, screw, corkscrew, whirl, whorl, roll, scroll A coil of wool or thread is a **skein**.

coil verb
The snake **coiled** itself round a branch.
curl, loop, roll, spiral, turn, twist, twirl, wind, writhe

cold adjective
1 Wrap up warm in this **cold** weather.
freezing, chilly, frosty, icy, raw, arctic, bitter, cool, crisp, snowy, wintry, (informal) perishing
A common simile is **as cold as ice**.
OPPOSITE hot, warm
2 I tried to shelter from the **cold** wind.
biting, bitter, keen, penetrating, piercing
3 I was **cold** in spite of my woolly hat.
freezing, frozen, chilly, chilled, shivering, shivery
To be so cold that you become ill is to suffer from **hypothermia**.
OPPOSITE hot, warm
4 The cyclops gave us a **cold** stare from his one eye.
unfriendly, unkind, unfeeling, distant, cool, heartless, indifferent, reserved, stony, uncaring, unemotional, unsympathetic
OPPOSITE warm, friendly

collapse verb
1 Many buildings **collapsed** in the earthquake.
fall down, fall in, cave in, give way, crumple, buckle, disintegrate, tumble down
2 Some of the runners **collapsed** in the heat.
faint, pass out, fall over, keel over

collect verb
1 Squirrels **collect** nuts for the winter.
gather, accumulate, hoard, heap, pile up, store up, stockpile, amass
2 A crowd **collected** to watch the fire.
assemble, gather, come together, converge
OPPOSITE scatter, disperse
3 We **collected** a large sum for charity.
raise, take in
4 She **collected** the car from the garage.
fetch, get, obtain, bring

OPPOSITE drop off, hand in

collection noun
Would you like to see my fossil **collection**?
assortment, set, accumulation, array, hoard, pile
A collection of books is a **library**.
A collection of poems or short stories is an **anthology**.

collide verb
to collide with The runaway trolley **collided with** a wall.
bump into, crash into, run into, smash into, hit, strike

collision noun
The **collision** dented the front wheel of my bike.
bump, crash, smash, knock, accident
A collision involving a lot of vehicles is a **pile-up**.

colossal adjective
A **colossal** statue towered above us.
huge, enormous, gigantic, immense, massive, giant, mammoth, monumental, towering, vast
OPPOSITE small, tiny

✎ **WRITING TIPS**

colour noun
You can use these words to describe a **colour**.
TO DESCRIBE **a pale colour**
delicate, faded, light, muted, neutral, pastel, washed-out
TO DESCRIBE **a strong colour**
bright, fluorescent, garish, loud, neon, vibrant, zingy

---

colourful adjective
1 The rose garden is **colourful** in the summer.
multicoloured, showy, vibrant, bright, brilliant, gaudy
OPPOSITE colourless
2 The book gives a **colourful** account of life on an island.
exciting, interesting, lively, vivid, striking, rich, picturesque
OPPOSITE dull

column noun
1 The roof of the temple was supported by stone **columns**.
pillar, post, support, shaft
2 A **column** of soldiers wound its way across the desert.
line, file, procession, row, string
3 I sometimes read the sports **column** in the newspaper.
article, piece, report, feature

combine verb
1 We **combined** our pocket money to buy a kite.

put together, add together, join, merge, unite, amalgamate
OPPOSITE **divide**
2 Combine the mixture with water to make a paste.
mix, stir together, blend, mingle, bind
OPPOSITE **separate**

come verb
1 We expect our guests to **come** in the afternoon.
arrive, appear, visit
OPPOSITE **go**
2 When you hear a cuckoo, you know that summer is **coming**.
advance, draw near
to come about
Can you tell me how the accident **came about**?
happen, occur, take place, result
to come across
I **came across** an old friend of mine.
find, discover, chance upon, meet, bump into
to come to
1 Tell me when you **come to** the last chapter.
reach, get to, arrive at
2 What did the repair bill **come to**?
add up to, amount to, total

comfort noun
1 My teddy bear was a **comfort** to me when I was ill.
reassurance, consolation, encouragement, support, relief
2 If I had a million pounds, I could live in **comfort**.
ease, luxury, contentment, well-being, prosperity, luxury, affluence

comfort verb
The coach tried to **comfort** the team after they lost.
cheer up, console, reassure, encourage, hearten, sympathize with, soothe

comfortable adjective
1 The bed was so **comfortable** that Goldilocks fell fast asleep.
cosy, snug, relaxing, easy, soft, warm, roomy, padded, plush (informal) comfy
OPPOSITE **uncomfortable**
2 We'll need **comfortable** clothes for travelling.
casual, informal, loose-fitting
3 Our cat leads a **comfortable** life.
contented, happy, pleasant, agreeable, well-off, prosperous, luxurious, affluent

command noun
1 The general gave the **command** to attack.
order, instruction, commandment, edict
2 Captain Nemo has **command** of the whole crew.
charge, control, authority (over), power (over),

management, supervision
3 My sister has a good **command** of Spanish.
knowledge, mastery, grasp, understanding, ability (in), skill (in)

command verb
1 The officer **commanded** his troops to fire.
order, instruct, direct, tell, bid
2 The captain **commands** the ship.
control, direct, be in charge of, govern, head, lead, manage, administer, supervise

comment noun
He made some nasty **comments** about his boss.
remark, statement, observation, opinion, mention, reference
A hostile comment is a **criticism**.

commit verb
The thieves were planning to **commit** another robbery.
carry out, do, perform, execute

common adjective
1 Colds are a **common** complaint in winter.
commonplace, everyday, frequent, normal, ordinary, familiar, well known, widespread
OPPOSITE **rare**
2 'Good morning' is a **common** way to greet people.
typical, usual, regular, routine, standard, customary, conventional, habitual, traditional
OPPOSITE **uncommon**
3 My friends and I have a **common** interest in music.
shared, mutual, joint

commotion noun
Football supporters were causing a **commotion** outside.
disturbance, row, fuss, trouble, disorder, unrest, agitation, turmoil, uproar, racket, rumpus, upheaval, riot, fracas, furore, hullabaloo, brouhaha, pandemonium, bedlam

communicate verb
1 Steve **communicated** his boredom with a yawn.
express, make known, indicate, convey, disclose, announce, pass on, proclaim, publish, report
2 Nowadays, we **communicate** by email.
contact each other, correspond, be in touch

company noun
1 My cousin works for a computer **company**.
business, firm, corporation, organization, establishment
2 Shrek shunned the **company** of other ogres.
fellowship, companionship, friendship, society

compare verb
Can you **compare** these sets of figures?
contrast, juxtapose, relate, set side by side
to compare with
This copy can't **compare with** the original painting.
compete with, rival, emulate, equal, match

compete verb
Five schools will be **competing** in the hockey tournament.
participate, perform, take part, enter
to compete against
We are **competing against** a strong team this week.
oppose, play against, contend with

competent adjective
You have to be a **competent** swimmer to join the club.
able, capable, skilful, skilled, accomplished, proficient, experienced, expert, qualified, trained
OPPOSITE **incompetent**

competitor noun
The **competitors** lined up for the start of the race.
contestant, contender, challenger, participant, opponent, rival
People who take part in an exam are **candidates** or **entrants**.

complain verb
Miss Grouch spent most of her life **complaining**.
moan, protest, grumble, grouse, gripe, whinge, make a fuss
to complain about
I wrote a letter **complaining about** the noise.
protest about, object to, criticize, find fault with
OPPOSITE **praise**

complaint noun
1 They received hundreds of **complaints** about the film.
criticism, objection, protest, moan, grumble
2 You have a nasty stomach **complaint**.
disease, illness, ailment, sickness, infection (informal) upset

complete adjective
1 Your training as a witch is not yet **complete**.
completed, ended, finished, accomplished, concluded
OPPOSITE **unfinished**
2 Have you got a **complete** set of cards?
whole, entire, full, intact
OPPOSITE **incomplete**
3 My birthday party was a **complete** disaster.

total, utter, sheer, absolute, thorough, downright, perfect, pure

complete verb
*We have **completed** all the tasks on the sheet.*
finish, end, conclude, carry out, perform

complex adjective
*Defusing a bomb is a **complex** task.*
complicated, difficult, elaborate, detailed, intricate, involved (*informal*) fiddly
OPPOSITE simple

complicated adjective
*The plot of the film is very **complicated**.*
complex, intricate, involved, difficult, elaborate, convoluted
OPPOSITE simple, straightforward

compliments plural noun
*It was nice to get **compliments** about my cooking.*
praise, appreciation, approval, congratulations, tribute
*Compliments which you don't deserve are **flattery**.*
OPPOSITE insults

compose verb
*Beethoven **composed** nine symphonies.*
create, devise, produce, make up, think up, write
to be composed of
*This quilt is **composed of** pieces of patchwork.*
be made of, consist of, comprise

compulsory adjective
*The wearing of seat belts is **compulsory**.*
required, obligatory, necessary
OPPOSITE optional

conceal verb
1 *The dog tried to **conceal** its bone.*
hide, cover up, bury
2 *We tried to **conceal** our hiding place.*
disguise, mask, screen, camouflage, make invisible
3 *Don't **conceal** the truth.*
keep quiet about, keep secret, hush up, suppress

conceited adjective
*He was so **conceited** when he won first prize!*
boastful, arrogant, proud, vain, self-satisfied
(*informal*) big-headed, cocky
OPPOSITE modest

concentrate verb
*I had to **concentrate** to hear what she was saying.*
be attentive, think hard, focus

concern verb
1 *This conversation doesn't **concern** you.*
affect, involve, be important to, matter to, be relevant to, relate to

2 *It **concerns** me that we are destroying the rain forests.*
bother, distress, trouble, upset, worry

concern noun
1 *My private life is no **concern** of theirs.*
affair, business
2 *Global warming is a great **concern** to us all.*
worry, anxiety, fear
3 *She's the head of a business **concern**.*
company, firm, enterprise, establishment

concerned adjective
1 *After waiting an hour, Julia began to feel **concerned**.*
worried, bothered, troubled, anxious, upset, distressed
2 *We're writing a letter to all those **concerned**.*
involved, connected, related, affected

conclusion noun
1 *The **conclusion** of the film was a bit puzzling.*
close, end, finale, finish, completion, culmination
2 *'What is your **conclusion**, Inspector?'*
decision, judgement, opinion, verdict, deduction

condemn verb
1 *The manager **condemned** the behaviour of the players.*
criticize, disapprove of, denounce, deplore, reproach
OPPOSITE praise
2 *The judge **condemned** the men to death.*
sentence
OPPOSITE acquit

condition noun
1 *Is your bike in good **condition**?*
state, order, repair
2 *A dog needs exercise to stay in good **condition**.*
fitness, health, shape
3 *It's a **condition** of membership that you pay a subscription.*
requirement, obligation, term

confess verb
*The goblin **confessed** that he had stolen the gold.*
admit, own up to, acknowledge, reveal

confidence noun
1 *We can face the future with **confidence**.*
hope, optimism, faith
OPPOSITE doubt
2 *I wish I had her **confidence**.*
self-confidence, assurance, boldness, conviction

confident adjective
1 *I am **confident** that we will win.*
certain, sure, positive, optimistic

OPPOSITE doubtful
2 *She is a **confident** sort of person.*
self-confident, assertive, bold, fearless, unafraid

confirm verb
1 *The strange events **confirmed** his belief in ghosts.*
prove, justify, support, back up, reinforce
OPPOSITE disprove
2 *I phoned to **confirm** my appointment at the dentist.*
verify, make official
OPPOSITE cancel

confront verb
*I decided to **confront** her and demand an apology.*
challenge, stand up to, face up to
OPPOSITE avoid

confuse verb
1 *I was **confused** by the directions on the map.*
puzzle, bewilder, mystify, baffle, perplex
2 *You must be **confusing** me with someone else.*
mix up, muddle

confusion noun
1 *There was great **confusion** when the lights went out.*
chaos, commotion, fuss, uproar, turmoil, pandemonium, bedlam, hullabaloo
2 *There was a look of **confusion** on her face.*
bewilderment, puzzlement, perplexity

congratulate verb
*We **congratulated** the winners.*
praise, applaud, compliment
OPPOSITE criticize

connect verb
1 *What's the best way to **connect** these wires?*
join, attach, fasten, link, couple, fix together, tie together
OPPOSITE separate
2 *The fingerprints **connected** him with the crime.*
make a connection between, associate, relate

connection noun
*There is a close **connection** between our two families.*
association, relationship, link

conquer verb
1 *Extra troops were sent to **conquer** the enemy forces.*
beat, defeat, overcome, vanquish, get the better of, overwhelm, crush, rout, thrash
2 *Gaul was **conquered** by Julius Caesar.*
seize, capture, take, win, occupy, possess

conscientious adjective
*Elves are very **conscientious** workers.*

a
b
c
d
e
f
g
h
i
j
k
l
m
n
o
p
q
r
s
t
u
v
w
x
y
z

hard working, careful, dependable, reliable, responsible, dutiful, meticulous, painstaking, thorough
OPPOSITE careless

conscious adjective
1 *The patient was* **conscious** *throughout the operation.*
awake, alert, aware
OPPOSITE unconscious
2 *She made a* **conscious** *effort to improve her work.*
deliberate, intentional, planned
OPPOSITE accidental

consequence noun
1 *He drank the potion without thinking of the* **consequences***.*
effect, result, outcome, sequel, upshot
2 *The loss of a few pence is of no* **consequence***.*
importance, significance

consider verb
1 *The detective* **considered** *the problem carefully.*
think about, examine, contemplate, ponder on, reflect on, study, weigh up, meditate about
2 *I* **consider** *this to be my best work.*
believe, judge, reckon

considerate adjective
It was **considerate** *of you to lend me your umbrella.*
kind, kind-hearted, helpful, obliging, sympathetic, thoughtful, unselfish, caring, charitable, neighbourly
OPPOSITE selfish

consist verb
to consist of
1 *The planet* **consists** *largely of craters.*
be made of, be composed of, comprise, contain, include, incorporate
2 *His job* **consists** *mostly of answering the phone.*
involve

consistent adjective
1 *These plants need to be kept at a* **consistent** *temperature.*
steady, constant, regular, stable, unchanging
2 *Fortunately, our goalkeeper is a* **consistent** *player.*
predictable, dependable, reliable

console verb
He did his best to **console** *me when my dog died.*
comfort, soothe, sympathize with, support

conspicuous adjective
1 *The clock tower is a* **conspicuous** *landmark.*
prominent, notable, obvious, eye-catching, unmistakable, visible

2 *I had made some* **conspicuous** *mistakes.*
clear, noticeable, obvious, evident, glaring

constant adjective
1 *There is a* **constant** *noise of traffic on the motorway.*
continual, continuous, never-ending, non-stop, ceaseless, incessant, interminable, endless, everlasting, permanent, perpetual, unending, persistent, relentless
OPPOSITE changeable
2 *My dog has been my* **constant** *friend for many years.*
faithful, loyal, dependable, reliable, firm, true, trustworthy, devoted
OPPOSITE unreliable

construct verb
We **constructed** *a tree-house in the back garden.*
build, erect, assemble, make, put together, put up, set up
OPPOSITE demolish

consult verb
1 *You should* **consult** *the dentist about your sore tooth.*
ask, get advice from, speak to
2 *If you don't know how to spell a word,* **consult** *your dictionary.*
refer to

contact verb
I'll **contact** *you when I have some news.*
call, call on, get in touch with, communicate with, notify, speak to, talk to, correspond with, phone, ring, write to

contain verb
1 *This box* **contains** *various odds and ends.*
hold
2 *A dictionary* **contains** *words and definitions.*
include, incorporate, comprise, consist of

contemplate verb
1 *The princess* **contemplated** *herself in the mirror.*
look at, view, observe, survey, watch, stare at, gaze at
2 *The robbers* **contemplated** *what to do next.*
think about, consider, ponder, study, reflect on, weigh up, meditate about

contempt noun
The knight stared at his enemy with

a look of **contempt***.*
hatred, scorn, loathing, disgust, dislike, distaste
OPPOSITE admiration

contented adjective
After her meal, the cat looked very **contented***.*
happy, pleased, content, satisfied, fulfilled, serene, peaceful, relaxed, comfortable, tranquil, untroubled
OPPOSITE discontented

contest noun
The tennis final was an exciting **contest***.*
competition, challenge, fight, bout, encounter, struggle, game, match, tournament

contestant noun
There are twenty **contestants** *in the spelling competition.*
competitor, participant, player, contender

continual adjective
I get sick of their **continual** *arguing.*
constant, persistent, perpetual, repeated, frequent, recurrent, eternal, unending
OPPOSITE occasional

continue verb
1 *We* **continued** *our search until it got dark.*
keep up, prolong, sustain, persevere with, pursue
(*informal*) stick at
2 *This rain can't* **continue** *for long.*
carry on, last, persist, endure, keep on, go on, linger
3 *We'll* **continue** *our meeting after lunch.*
resume, proceed with, pick up

continuous adjective
We had **continuous** *rain all through our holiday.*
never-ending, non-stop, ceaseless, everlasting, incessant, unbroken, unceasing, uninterrupted
An illness which continues for a long time is a **chronic** *illness.*
OPPOSITE intermittent

contract noun
The actress has signed a **contract** *for a new film.*
agreement, deal, undertaking
A contract between two countries is an **alliance** *or* **treaty***.*
A contract to end a dispute about money is a **settlement***.*

contract verb
1 *Metal* **contracts** *when it gets colder.*
reduce, lessen, shrink, tighten
OPPOSITE expand
2 *The crew* **contracted** *a mysterious illness.*
catch, develop, get

contrast verb
1 *We were asked to contrast two of our favourite poems.*
compare, juxtapose, distinguish between
2 *Her handwriting contrasts with mine.*
clash, differ (from)

contrast noun
There is a sharp contrast between the two paintings.
difference, distinction, opposition
OPPOSITE similarity

contribute verb
Will you contribute something to our charity collection?
donate, give, provide
(*informal*) chip in
to contribute to
The sunny weather contributed to our enjoyment.
add to, help, aid, encourage, enhance

control noun
The captain had complete control over the crew.
authority, power, command, government, management, direction, leadership, guidance

control verb
1 *The government controls the country's affairs.*
be in control of, be in charge of, manage, run, command, direct, lead, guide, govern, administer, regulate, rule, superintend, supervise
2 *Can't you control that dog?*
manage, handle, restrain
3 *They built a dam to control the floods.*
check, curb, hold back, contain

convenient adjective
1 *Is there a convenient place to put my umbrella?*
suitable, appropriate, available, nearby, accessible
OPPOSITE inconvenient
2 *Mum has a convenient tool for opening jars.*
handy, helpful, useful, labour-saving, neat

conventional adjective
The conventional way to greet someone is to shake hands.
customary, traditional, usual, accepted, common, normal, ordinary, everyday, routine, standard, regular, habitual
OPPOSITE unconventional

conversation noun
An informal conversation is a *chat* or *gossip*.
A more formal conversation is a *discussion*.
A very formal conversation is a *conference*.
Conversation in a play or novel is *dialogue*.

WORD WEB

cook verb
To cook food for guests or customers is to *cater* for them.
Cooking as a business is *catering*.
The art or skill of cooking is *cookery*.

SOME WAYS TO COOK FOOD
bake, barbecue, boil, braise, brew, broil, casserole, deep-fry, fry, grill, poach, roast, sauté, simmer, steam, stew, toast

OTHER WAYS TO PREPARE FOOD
baste, blend, chop, dice, grate, grind, infuse, knead, liquidize, marinade, mince, mix, peel, purée, sieve, sift, stir, whisk

SOME ITEMS THAT ARE USED FOR COOKING
baking tin or tray, barbecue, blender, bowl, carving knife, casserole, cauldron, chopping board, colander, cooker, dish, food processor, frying pan, grill, ladle, liquidizer, microwave, mincer, oven, pan, pot, rolling pin, saucepan, skewer, spatula, spit, strainer, toaster, whisk, wok, wooden spoon

blender

---

convert verb
1 *We have converted our attic into a games room.*
change, adapt, alter, transform
2 *I never used to like football, but my cousin converted me.*
change someone's mind, persuade, convince, win over

convince verb
The prisoner convinced them that he was innocent.
persuade, assure, satisfy, make believe, win round

convincing adjective
I tried to think of a convincing excuse.
persuasive, believable, credible, plausible

cook verb *see panel above*

cool adjective
1 *The weather is cool for the time of year.*
chilly, coldish
OPPOSITE hot, warm
2 *Would you like a cool glass of lemonade?*
chilled, iced, refreshing
OPPOSITE hot
3 *Clifford remained cool when everyone else panicked.*
calm, level-headed, relaxed, unexcitable, unflustered
(*informal*) laid-back
A common simile is *as cool as a cucumber*.
OPPOSITE frantic
4 (*informal*) *Those rollerskates are really cool!*
chic, fashionable, smart
(*informal*) trendy

cooperate verb
to cooperate with
The scouts cooperated with each other to build a fire.
work with or together with,
collaborate with, aid, assist, support

cope verb
Shall I help you, or can you cope on your own?
manage, carry on, get by, make do, survive
to cope with
I can't cope with all this homework!
deal with, handle, manage, get through

copy noun
That isn't the original painting—it's a copy.
replica, reproduction, duplicate, imitation, likeness
A copy made to deceive someone is a *fake* or a *forgery*.
A living organism which is identical to another is a *clone*.

copy verb
1 *I copied the poem into my jotter.*
duplicate, reproduce, write out
To copy something in order to deceive is to *fake* or *forge* it.
2 *My parrot can copy my voice.*
imitate, impersonate, mimic

core noun
It is very hot at the earth's core.
centre, inside, middle, heart, nucleus

corner noun
1 *I'll meet you at the corner of the road.*
turn, turning, junction, crossroads, intersection
The place where

core

two lines meet is an *angle*.
2 *I sat in a quiet* **corner** *and read her letter.*
alcove, recess, nook

correct *adjective*
1 *Your answers are all* **correct.**
right, accurate, exact, faultless
2 *I hope he has given us* **correct** *information.*
true, genuine, authentic, precise, reliable, factual
3 *What is the* **correct** *way to address this letter?*
proper, acceptable, regular, appropriate, suitable
OPPOSITE wrong

correct *verb*
1 *I have to* **correct** *my spelling mistakes.*
alter, put right, make better, improve
2 *Miss Nicol spent the day* **correcting** *exam papers.*
mark

correspond *verb*
to correspond with
1 *Her version of the story doesn't* **correspond with** *mine.*
agree with, match, be similar to, be consistent with, tally with
2 *Carol* **corresponds with** *a friend in Paris.*
write to, communicate with, send letters to

corrupt *adjective*
Corrupt *officials had accepted millions of pounds in bribes.*
dishonest, criminal, untrustworthy
(*informal*) bent, crooked
OPPOSITE honest

cost *noun*
The bill shows the total **cost.**
price, charge, amount, payment, fee, figure, expense, expenditure, tariff
The cost of travelling on public transport is the **fare.**

costume *noun*
The Irish dancers were wearing national **costumes.**
outfit, dress, clothing, suit, attire, garment, garb
(*informal*) get-up
A costume you dress up in for a party is **fancy dress.**
A set of clothes worn by soldiers or members of an organization is a **uniform.**

cosy *adjective*
It's good to feel **cosy** *in bed when it's cold outside.*
comfortable, snug, soft, warm, secure
OPPOSITE uncomfortable

count *verb*
1 *I'm* **counting** *the days until my birthday.*
add up, calculate, compute,

estimate, reckon, figure out, work out, total
2 *It's playing well that* **counts,** *not winning.*
be important, be significant, matter

to count on
You can **count on** *me to support you.*
depend on, rely on, trust, bank on

country *noun*
1 *England and Wales are separate* **countries.**
nation, state, land, territory
A country ruled by a king or queen is a **kingdom, monarchy,** *or* **realm.**
A country governed by leaders elected by the people is a **democracy.**
A democratic country with a President is a **republic.**
2 *We went for a picnic in the* **country.**
countryside, landscape, outdoors, scenery
A word meaning 'to do with the country' is **rural** *and its opposite is* **urban.**
OPPOSITE town, city

courage *noun*
The rescue dogs showed great **courage.**
bravery, boldness, daring, fearlessness, nerve, pluck, valour, heroism, grit
(*informal*) guts
OPPOSITE cowardice

course *noun*
1 *The hot-air balloon was drifting off its* **course.**
direction, path, route, way, progress, passage
2 *The war changed the* **course** *of history.*
development, progression, sequence, succession

cover *verb*
1 *A coat of paint will* **cover** *the graffiti.*
conceal, disguise, hide, obscure, mask, blot out
2 *She* **covered** *her face with her hands.*
shield, screen, protect, shade, veil
3 *An encyclopedia* **covers** *many subjects.*
deal with, include, contain, incorporate

cover *noun*
1 *The* **cover** *of the book was torn.*
wrapper
A cover for a letter is an **envelope.**
A cover for a book is a **jacket.**
A cover to keep papers in is a **file** *or* **folder.**

2 *On the bare hillside, there was no* **cover** *from the storm.*
shelter, protection, defence, shield, refuge, sanctuary

covering *noun*
There was a light **covering** *of snow on the hills.*
coating, coat, layer, blanket, carpet, film, sheet, skin, veil

cowardly *adjective*
It was **cowardly** *to run away.*
timid, faint-hearted, spineless, gutless
(*informal*) yellow, chicken
OPPOSITE brave

cower *verb*
A frightened creature was **cowering** *in the corner.*
cringe, shrink, crouch, flinch, quail

crack *noun*
1 *There's a* **crack** *in this cup.*
break, chip, fracture, flaw, chink, split
2 *The outlaw hid in a* **crack** *between two rocks.*
gap, opening, crevice, rift, cranny
3 *The detective heard the* **crack** *of a pistol shot.*
bang, fire, explosion, snap, pop
4 *She gave the robber a* **crack** *on the head.*
blow, bang, knock, smack, whack
5 *I had a* **crack** *at writing a poem.*
try, attempt, shot, go

crack *verb*
A brick fell down and **cracked** *the pavement.*
break, fracture, chip, split, shatter, splinter

craft *noun*
1 *I'd like to learn the* **craft** *of weaving.*
art, skill, technique, expertise, handicraft
2 *All sorts of* **craft** *were in the harbour.*
boats, ships, vessels

crafty *adjective*
The evil sorceress had a **crafty** *plan.*
cunning, clever, shrewd, scheming, sneaky, sly, tricky, wily, artful

cram *verb*
1 *We can't* **cram** *any more people in—the car is full.*
pack, squeeze, crush, force, jam, compress
2 *My sister is* **cramming** *for her maths exam.*
revise, study
(*informal*) swot

cramped *adjective*
The seating on the train was a bit **cramped.**
confined, narrow, restricted, tight, uncomfortable, crowded

(*informal*) poky
OPPOSITE roomy

crash *noun*
1 *I heard a loud* **crash** *from the kitchen.*
bang, smash
2 *We saw a nasty* **crash** *on the motorway.*
accident, collision, smash, bump
A crash involving a lot of vehicles is a **pile-up**.
A train crash may involve a **derailment**.

crash *verb*
The car **crashed** *into a lamp-post.*
bump, smash, collide, knock

crawl *verb*
I saw a caterpillar **crawling** *along a leaf.*
creep, edge, inch,
slither, clamber

crawl

craze *noun*
This game is the latest **craze** *in the playground.*
fad, trend, vogue, fashion,
enthusiasm, obsession, passion

crazy *adjective*
1 *The dog went* **crazy** *when it was stung by a wasp.*
mad, insane, frenzied, hysterical,
frantic, berserk, delirious, wild
(*informal*) loopy, nuts
2 *It was a* **crazy** *idea to try to build a space rocket!*
absurd, ridiculous, ludicrous,
daft, idiotic, senseless, silly,
stupid, foolhardy, preposterous
(*informal*) bonkers, barmy, wacky
OPPOSITE sensible

create *verb*
1 *The cats were* **creating** *a racket outside.*
make, cause, produce
2 *We have* **created** *a website for our chess club.*
set up, start up, bring about,
bring into existence, originate
You **write** *a poem or story.*
You **compose** *music.*
You **draw** *or* **paint** *a picture.*
You **carve** *a statue.*
You **invent** *or* **think up** *a new idea.*
You **design** *a new product.*
You **devise** *a plan.*
You **found** *a new club or organization.*
You **manufacture** *goods.*
You **generate** *electricity.*
You **build** *or* **construct** *a model or a building.*

creative *adjective*
My aunt is a very **creative** *person.*
artistic, imaginative, inventive,
original, inspired
OPPOSITE unimaginative

creator *noun*
Walt Disney was the **creator** *of Mickey Mouse.*
inventor, maker, originator,
producer, deviser
The creator of a design is an **architect** *or* **designer**.
The creator of goods for sale is a **manufacturer**.

creature *noun*
A wild-looking **creature** *emerged from the swamp.*
animal, beast, being

creep *verb*
1 *I watched the lizard* **creep** *back into its hiding place.*
crawl, edge, inch, slither, wriggle
2 *I* **crept** *out of bed without waking the others.*
move quietly, sneak, tiptoe, slip,
slink, steal

creepy *adjective*
There were **creepy** *noises coming from the cellar.*
scary, frightening, eerie,
ghostly, weird, sinister, uncanny,
unearthly
(*informal*) spooky

crisis *noun*
The election result caused a **crisis** *in the country.*
emergency, problem, difficulty,
predicament

crisp *adjective*
1 *Fry the bacon until it's* **crisp**.
crispy, crunchy, brittle
OPPOSITE soft, soggy, limp
2 *It was a* **crisp** *winter morning.*
cold, fresh, frosty

critical *adjective*
1 *Some people made* **critical** *comments about my hairstyle.*
negative, disapproving,
derogatory, uncomplimentary,
unfavourable
OPPOSITE complimentary
2 *This match is* **critical** *for our team's chances of success.*
crucial, important, vital, serious,
decisive
OPPOSITE unimportant

criticize *verb*
She **criticized** *us for being so careless.*
blame, condemn, disapprove
of, find fault with, reprimand,
reproach, scold, berate
OPPOSITE praise

crooked *adjective*
1 *The wizard bent his wand into a* **crooked** *shape.*
bent, twisted, warped, knarled
OPPOSITE straight
2 (*informal*) *The* **crooked**

salesman was selling fake diamonds.
criminal, dishonest, corrupt,
illegal, unlawful
(*informal*) bent
OPPOSITE honest

cross *verb*
1 *There is a bus stop where the two roads* **cross**.
criss-cross, intersect
2 *You can* **cross** *the river at the footbridge.*
go across, pass over, traverse,
ford, span

cross *adjective*
My mum will be **cross** *if we're late.*
angry, annoyed, upset, vexed,
bad-tempered, ill-tempered,
irritable, grumpy, testy, irate
OPPOSITE pleased

crouch *verb*
The outlaws **crouched** *silently in the bushes.*
squat, kneel, stoop, bend, duck,
bob down, hunch, huddle

crowd *noun*
1 *A* **crowd** *of people waited outside the theatre.*
gathering, group, assembly,
bunch, cluster, throng, mob,
multitude, crush, horde, swarm
2 *There was a huge* **crowd** *for the tennis final.*
audience, spectators, gate,
attendance

crowd *verb*
1 *People* **crowded** *on the pavement to watch the parade.*
gather, collect, assemble,
congregate, mass, flock, muster
2 *Hundreds of people* **crowded** *into the hall.*
push, pile, squeeze, pack, cram,
crush, jam, bundle, herd

crowd

crowded *adjective*
The shops are always **crowded** *at Christmas time.*
full, packed, teeming, swarming,
overflowing, jammed, congested
OPPOSITE empty

crude *adjective*
1 *The refinery processes* **crude** *oil.*
raw, natural, unprocessed,
unrefined
OPPOSITE refined
2 *We made a* **crude** *shelter out of twigs.*

a
b
c
d
e
f
g
h
i
j
k
l
m
n
o
p
q
r
s
t
u
v
w
x
y
z

rough, clumsy, makeshift, primitive
OPPOSITE **skilful**
3 *The teacher told them to stop using* ***crude*** *language.*
rude, obscene, coarse, dirty, foul, impolite, indecent, vulgar
OPPOSITE **polite**
cruel *adjective*
I think hunting is a ***cruel*** *way to kill animals.*
brutal, savage, vicious, fierce, barbaric, bloodthirsty, barbarous, heartless, ruthless, merciless, inhuman, sadistic, uncivilized, beastly
OPPOSITE **kind, humane, gentle**
crumb *noun*
We put out some ***crumbs*** *of bread for the birds.*
bit, fragment, scrap, morsel
crumble *verb*
1 *The walls of the castle were beginning to* ***crumble***.
disintegrate, break up, collapse, fall apart, decay, decompose
2 *The farmer* ***crumbled*** *some bread into his soup.*
crush, grind, pound, pulverize
crunch *verb*
1 *The dog was* ***crunching*** *on a bone.*
chew, munch, chomp, grind
2 *I heard heavy footsteps* ***crunching*** *up the path.*
crush, grind, pound, smash
crush *verb*
1 *He* ***crushed*** *his anorak into his schoolbag.*
squash, squeeze, mangle, pound, press, bruise, crunch, scrunch
To crush something into a soft mess is to *mash* or *pulp* it.
To crush something into a powder is to *grind* or *pulverize* it.
To crush something out of shape is to *crumple* or *smash* it.
2 *Our soldiers* ***crushed*** *the attacking army.*
defeat, conquer, vanquish, overcome, overwhelm, quash, trounce, rout
crush *noun*
There was a ***crush*** *of people at the front gates.*
crowd, press, mob, throng, jam, congestion
cry *verb*
1 *Someone was* ***crying*** *for help from the burning house.*
call, shout, yell, exclaim, roar, bawl, bellow, scream, screech, shriek
2 *The baby started to* ***cry*** *when she dropped her toy.*
sob, weep, bawl, blubber, wail, shed tears, snivel
When someone starts to cry, their eyes *well up with tears*.

cry *noun*
The wounded man let out a ***cry*** *of pain.*
call, shout, yell, roar, howl, exclamation, bellow, scream, screech, shriek, yelp
cuddle *verb*
My baby brother ***cuddles*** *a teddy bear in bed.*
hug, hold closely, clasp, embrace, caress, nestle against, snuggle against
cunning *adjective*
The pirates had a ***cunning*** *plan to seize the ship.*
clever, crafty, devious, wily, ingenious, shrewd, artful, scheming, sly, tricky
cup *noun*
A tall cup with straight sides is a *mug*.
A tall cup without a handle is a *beaker* or *tumbler*.
A decorative drinking cup is a *goblet*.
cure *verb*
1 *These pills will* ***cure*** *your headache.*
ease, heal, help, improve, make better, relieve
OPPOSITE **aggravate**
2 *No-one can* ***cure*** *the problem with my computer.*
correct, mend, sort, repair, fix, put an end to, put right
cure *noun*
I wish they could find a ***cure*** *for colds.*
remedy, treatment, antidote, medicine, therapy
curious *adjective*
1 *We were all very* ***curious*** *about the secret chamber.*
inquisitive, inquiring, interested (in), intrigued, agog
An uncomplimentary word is *nosy*.
OPPOSITE **uninterested, indifferent**
2 *What is that* ***curious*** *smell?*
odd, strange, peculiar, abnormal, queer, unusual, extraordinary, funny, mysterious, puzzling, weird
curl *verb*
1 *The snake* ***curled*** *itself around a branch.*
wind, twist, loop, coil, wrap, curve, turn, twine
2 *Steam* ***curled*** *upwards from the cauldron.*
coil, spiral, twirl, swirl, furl, snake, writhe, ripple
curl *noun*
The girl's hair was a mass of golden ***curls***.
wave, ringlet, coil, loop, twist, roll, scroll, spiral
curly *adjective*
My new doll has ***curly*** *black hair.*

curled, curling, wavy, frizzy, crinkly, ringletted
OPPOSITE **straight**
current *noun*
The wooden raft drifted along with the ***current***.
flow, tide, stream
A current of air is a *draught*.
current *adjective*
1 *The shop sells all the* ***current*** *teenage fashions.*
modern, contemporary, present-day, up to date, topical, prevailing, prevalent
OPPOSITE **past, old-fashioned**
2 *Have you got a* ***current*** *passport?*
valid, usable, up to date
OPPOSITE **out of date**
3 *Who is the* ***current*** *prime minister?*
present, existing
OPPOSITE **past, former**
curse *noun*
1 *Long ago, a wizard put a* ***curse*** *on the family.*
jinx, hex
2 *When the gardener hit his finger, he let out a* ***curse***.
swear word, oath
curve *noun*
Try to draw a straight line without any ***curves***.
bend, curl, loop, turn, twist, arch, arc, bow, bulge, wave
A curve in the shape of a new moon is a *crescent*.
A curve on a road surface is a *camber*.
curve *verb*
The road ahead ***curves*** *round to the right.*
bend, wind, turn, twist, curl, loop, swerve, veer, snake, meander
curved *adjective*
The wall was painted with a series of ***curved*** *lines.*
curving, curvy, curled, looped, coiled, rounded, bulging, bent, arched, bowed, twisted, crooked, spiral, winding, meandering, serpentine, snaking, undulating
A surface which is curved like the inside of a circle is *concave*.
A surface which is curved like the outside of a circle is *convex*.
custom *noun*
1 *It's our* ***custom*** *to give presents at Christmas.*
tradition, practice, habit, convention, fashion, routine, way
2 *The shop is having a sale to attract more* ***custom***.
customers, buyers, trade, business
cut *verb*
1 *The woodcutter* ***cut*** *the tree trunk to make logs.*

chop, slit, split, chip, notch, axe, hack, hew, cleave
To cut off a limb is to *amputate* or *sever* it.
To cut down a tree is to *fell* it.
To cut branches off a tree is to *lop* them.
To cut twigs off a growing plant is to *prune* it.
To cut something up to examine it is to *dissect* it.
To cut stone to make a statue is to *carve* it.
To cut an inscription in stone is to *engrave* it.
2 *The cook **cut** the apples into small pieces.*
chop, slice, dice, grate, mince, shred
3 *I'm going to get my hair **cut** in the holidays.*
trim, clip, crop, snip, shave
To cut wool off a sheep is to *shear* it.
To cut grass is to *mow* it.
To cut corn is to *harvest* or *reap* it.
4 *Josh **cut** his foot on a sharp stone.*
gash, slash, nick, stab, pierce, wound
5 *This letter is too long—I'll need to **cut** it.*
shorten, condense, edit
6 *The shop has **cut** its prices by 10%.*
lower, reduce, decrease
If you cut something by half, you *halve* it.

cut *noun*
*I got a nasty **cut** when I was slicing bread.*
gash, wound, injury, nick, slash, scratch, slit, snip

Dd

damage *verb*
*Many books were **damaged** in the fire.*
harm, spoil, mar, break, impair, weaken, disfigure, deface, mutilate, scar
To damage something beyond repair is to *destroy*, *ruin*, or *wreck* it.
To damage something deliberately is to *sabotage* or *vandalize* it.

damp *adjective*
1 *Don't wear those clothes if they are **damp**.*
moist, soggy, clammy, dank
2 *I don't like this **damp** weather.*
drizzly, foggy, misty, rainy, wet

WORD WEB

dance *noun*
SOME KINDS OF DANCE OR DANCING
ballet, ballroom dancing, barn dance, belly-dancing, bolero, break-dancing, cancan, disco, flamenco, folk dance, Highland dancing, hornpipe, jazz dance, jig, jive dancing, limbo dancing, line-dancing, mazurka, morris dance, quadrille, reel, rumba, samba, Scottish country dancing, square dance, step dancing, street dance, tap dancing, tarantella

breakdancing

ballet

A person who writes the steps for a dance is a *choreographer*.

SOME BALLROOM DANCES
foxtrot, minuet, polka, quickstep, tango, waltz

GATHERINGS WHERE PEOPLE DANCE
ball, ceilidh, disco

flamenco

ballroom dancing

Weather which is both damp and warm is *humid* or *muggy* weather.
OPPOSITE **dry**

dance *verb*
*I could have **danced** for joy.*
caper, cavort, frisk, frolic, gambol, hop about, jig about, jump about, leap, prance, skip, whirl

danger *noun*
1 *Who knows what **dangers** lie ahead?*
peril, jeopardy, trouble, crisis, hazard, menace, pitfall, threat, trap
OPPOSITE **safety**
2 *The forecast says there's a **danger** of frost.*
chance, possibility, risk

dangerous *adjective*
1 *We were in a **dangerous** situation.*
hazardous, perilous, risky, precarious, treacherous, unsafe, alarming, menacing
(*informal*) hairy
2 *The police arrested him for **dangerous** driving.*
careless, reckless
3 *A **dangerous** criminal had escaped from prison.*
violent, desperate, ruthless, treacherous
4 *It's wicked to empty **dangerous** chemicals into the river.*

harmful, poisonous, deadly, toxic
OPPOSITE **harmless, safe**

dangle *verb*
*There was a bunch of keys **dangling** from the chain.*
hang, swing, sway, droop, wave about, flap, trail

dare *verb*
1 *I wouldn't **dare** to make a parachute jump.*
have the courage, take the risk
2 *They **dared** me to climb the tree.*
challenge, defy

daring *adjective*
*It was a very **daring** plan.*
bold, brave, adventurous, courageous, fearless, intrepid, plucky, valiant
A daring person is a *daredevil*.
OPPOSITE **timid**

dark *adjective*
1 *It was a very **dark** night.*
black, dim, murky, shadowy, gloomy, dingy
OPPOSITE **bright**
2 *She wore a **dark** green coat.*
OPPOSITE **pale, light**

dash *verb*
1 *We **dashed** home because it was raining.*
hurry, run, rush, race, hasten, sprint, speed, tear, zoom
2 *She **dashed** her cup against the wall.*
throw, hurl, knock, smash

a b c d e f g h i j k l m n o p q r s t u v w x y z

data *plural noun*
*I entered all the **data** into the computer.*
information, details, facts
Data can be in the form of *figures*, *numbers*, or *statistics*.

dawn *noun*
1 *I was woken at **dawn** by the birds singing outside.*
daybreak, sunrise, first light
OPPOSITE dusk, sunset
2 *It was the **dawn** of the modern age.*
beginning, start, birth, origin

day *noun*
1 *Badgers sleep during the **day**.*
daytime
OPPOSITE night
2 *Things were different in my grandfather's **day**.*
age, time, era, epoch, period

dazed *adjective*
*He had a **dazed** expression on his face.*
confused, bewildered, muddled, perplexed

dazzle *verb*
1 *My eyes were **dazzled** by the bright lights.*
daze, blind
2 *The acrobats **dazzled** the audience with their skill.*
amaze, astonish, impress, fascinate, awe

dead *adjective*
1 *A **dead** fish floated by the side of the river.*
deceased, lifeless
Instead of 'the king who has just died', you can say 'the *late* king'.
A dead body is a *carcass* or *corpse*.
A common simile is *as dead as a doornail*.
OPPOSITE alive
2 *This battery is **dead**.*
flat, not working, worn out
3 *The town centre is **dead** at this time of night.*
dull, boring, uninteresting, slow
OPPOSITE lively

deadly *adjective*
*The witch gave her a **deadly** dose of poison.*
lethal, fatal, harmful, dangerous, destructive
OPPOSITE harmless

deafening *adjective*
*We complained about the **deafening** noise.*
loud, blaring, booming, thunderous, penetrating

deal *verb*
1 *Who is going to **deal** the cards?*
give out, distribute, share out
2 *My uncle used to **deal** in second-hand cars.*
do business, trade
to deal with something
1 *I can **deal with** this problem.*

cope with, sort out, attend to, see to, handle, manage, control, grapple with, look after, solve
2 *The book **deals with** the history of Rome.*
be concerned with, cover, explain about

deal *noun*
*She made a **deal** with the garage for her new car.*
arrangement, agreement, contract, bargain

dear *adjective*
1 *She is a very **dear** friend.*
close, loved, valued, beloved
OPPOSITE distant
2 *I didn't buy the watch because it was too **dear**.*
expensive, costly
(*informal*) pricey
OPPOSITE cheap

debate *noun*
*We had a **debate** about animal rights.*
discussion, argument, dispute
Something which people argue about a lot is a *controversy*.

debate *verb*
1 *We **debated** whether it is right to kill animals for food.*
discuss, argue
2 *I **debated** what to do next.*
consider, ponder, deliberate, weigh up, reflect on

decay *verb*
*Dead leaves fall to the ground and **decay**.*
decompose, rot, disintegrate, break down

decay

deceitful *adjective*
*Don't trust him—he's a **deceitful** person.*
dishonest, underhand, insincere, duplicitous, false, cheating, hypocritical, lying, treacherous, two-faced, sneaky
OPPOSITE honest

deceive *verb*
*The spy had been **deceiving** them for years.*
fool, trick, delude, dupe, hoodwink, cheat, double-cross, mislead, swindle, take in
(*informal*) con, diddle

decent *adjective*
1 *I did the **decent** thing and owned up.*
honest, honourable
2 *My friend's jokes were not **decent**.*
polite, proper, respectable, acceptable, appropriate, suitable, fitting
OPPOSITE indecent
3 *I haven't had a **decent** meal for ages!*
satisfactory, agreeable, good, nice
OPPOSITE bad

decide *verb*
1 *We **decided** to finish our work instead of going out to play.*
choose, make a decision, make up your mind, opt, elect, resolve
2 *The referee **decided** that the player was offside.*
conclude, judge, rule
3 *The last lap **decided** the result of the race.*
determine, settle

decision *noun*
1 *Can you tell me what your **decision** is?*
choice, preference
2 *The judge announced his **decision**.*
conclusion, judgement, verdict, findings

decisive *adjective*
1 *A **decisive** piece of evidence proved that he was innocent.*
crucial, convincing, definite
OPPOSITE uncertain
2 *A referee needs to be **decisive**.*
firm, forceful, strong-minded, resolute, quick-thinking
OPPOSITE hesitant

declare *verb*
*He **declared** that he was innocent.*
announce, state, assert, make known, pronounce, proclaim, swear

decline *verb*
1 *Our enthusiasm **declined** as the day went on.*
become less, decrease, diminish, lessen, weaken, dwindle, flag, wane, tail off
OPPOSITE increase
2 *Why did you **decline** my invitation to lunch?*
refuse, reject, turn down
OPPOSITE accept

decorate *verb*
1 *We **decorated** the Christmas tree with tinsel.*
ornament, adorn, beautify, prettify, deck, festoon
To decorate a dish of food is to *garnish* it.
To decorate clothes with lace or ribbon is to *trim* them.
2 *Dad is going to **decorate** my bedroom next weekend.*

paint, paper, or wallpaper
(*informal*) do up, make over
3 *The firefighters were decorated for their bravery.*
award or give a medal to, honour, reward

decrease *verb*
1 *We decreased speed.*
reduce, cut, lower, slacken
2 *Our enthusiasm decreased as the day went on.*
become less, decline, decrease, diminish, lessen, weaken, dwindle, flag, wane, tail off, shrink, subside
OPPOSITE increase

dedicate *verb*
He dedicates himself entirely to his art.
commit, devote

deed *noun*
They thanked the rescue team for their heroic deed.
act, action, feat, exploit, effort, achievement

deep *adjective*
1 *The pond is quite deep in the middle.*
OPPOSITE shallow
2 *The letter expressed his deep regret.*
intense, earnest, genuine, sincere
OPPOSITE insincere
3 *Veronica fell into a deep sleep.*
heavy, sound
OPPOSITE light
4 *The actor spoke in a deep and sombre voice.*
low, bass
OPPOSITE high

defeat *verb*
The Greeks attacked and defeated the Trojans.
beat, conquer, vanquish, triumph over, win a victory over, overcome, overpower, crush, rout, trounce
To defeat someone in chess is to *checkmate* them.
To be defeated is to *lose*.

defeat *noun*
The team suffered a humiliating defeat.
failure, humiliation, rout, trouncing
OPPOSITE victory

defect *noun*
Cars are tested for defects before they leave the factory.
fault, flaw, imperfection, shortcoming, failure, weakness
A defect in a computer program is a *bug*.

defence *noun*
1 *What was the accused woman's defence?*
justification, excuse, explanation, argument, case
2 *The castle was built as a defence*

against enemy attack.
protection, guard, safeguard, fortification, barricade, shield

defend *verb*
1 *They tried to defend themselves against the enemy.*
protect, guard, keep safe
OPPOSITE attack
2 *He gave a speech defending his actions.*
justify, support, stand up for, make a case for
OPPOSITE accuse

defiant *adjective*
The prisoner cursed with a defiant look in his eye.
rebellious, insolent, aggressive, challenging, disobedient, obstinate, quarrelsome, uncooperative, stubborn, mutinous
OPPOSITE submissive, compliant

definite *adjective*
1 *Is it definite that we're going to move?*
certain, sure, fixed, settled, decided
2 *The doctor saw definite signs of improvement.*
clear, distinct, noticeable, obvious, marked, positive, pronounced, unmistakable
OPPOSITE indefinite

definitely *adverb*
I'll definitely phone you tomorrow.
certainly, for certain, positively, surely, unquestionably, without doubt, without fail
OPPOSITE perhaps

defy *verb*
1 *The rebel army decided to defy the king.*
disobey, refuse to obey, resist, stand up to, confront
OPPOSITE obey
2 *I defy you to come up with a better idea.*
challenge, dare
3 *The jammed door defied our efforts to open it.*
resist, withstand, defeat, frustrate, beat

delay *verb*
1 *Don't let me delay you.*
detain, hold up, keep waiting, make late, hinder, slow down
2 *They delayed the race because of bad weather.*
postpone, put off, defer
3 *You'll miss the bus if you delay.*
hesitate, linger, pause, wait, dawdle, loiter
(*informal*) hang about or around, drag your feet

delay *noun*
There has been a delay with the building work.
hold-up, wait, pause

deliberate *adjective*
1 *That remark was a deliberate insult.*
intentional, planned, calculated, conscious, premeditated
OPPOSITE accidental, unintentional
2 *He walked with deliberate steps across the room.*
careful, steady, cautious, slow, unhurried
OPPOSITE hasty, careless

deliberately *verb*
Did you say that deliberately to hurt my feelings?
on purpose, intentionally
OPPOSITE accidentally, unintentionally

delicate *adjective*
1 *The blouse has delicate embroidery on the cuffs.*
dainty, exquisite, intricate, neat
2 *Take care not to damage the delicate material.*
fragile, fine, flimsy, thin
3 *Delicate plants should be protected from frost.*
sensitive, tender
OPPOSITE tough, hardy
4 *The child was born with a delicate constitution.*
frail, weak, feeble, sickly, unhealthy
OPPOSITE strong
5 *The pianist's fingers had a delicate touch.*
gentle, light, soft

delicious *adjective*
The food at the banquet was delicious.
tasty, appetizing, mouth-watering, delectable
(*informal*) scrumptious, yummy
OPPOSITE horrible, disgusting

delight *noun*
Imagine my delight when I saw my friend again!
happiness, joy, pleasure, enjoyment, bliss, ecstasy

delight *verb*
The puppet show delighted the children.
please, charm, entertain, amuse, divert, enchant, entrance, fascinate, thrill
OPPOSITE dismay

delighted *adjective*
The delighted crowd cheered the winners.
pleased, happy, joyful, thrilled, ecstatic, elated, exultant

deliver *verb*
1 *Does anyone deliver mail to the island?*
convey, bring, hand over, distribute, present, supply, take round
2 *The head delivered a lecture on good behaviour.*
give, make, read out

demand verb
1 *I demanded a refund for my train fare.*
insist on, claim, call for, require, want
2 *'What do you want?' demanded a voice inside.*
ask, enquire, inquire

demand noun
1 *The king refused the demands of his people.*
request, claim, requirement
2 *There is not much demand for ice lollies in winter.*
need, call

demolish verb
They demolished a building to make way for the road.
destroy, flatten, knock down, level, pull down, tear down, bulldoze
OPPOSITE build, construct

demonstrate verb
1 *The teacher demonstrated how warm air rises.*
show, exhibit, illustrate
2 *Animal rights campaigners were demonstrating in the street.*
protest, march, parade

demonstration noun
1 *I watched a demonstration of the new computer game.*
show, display, presentation
2 *Everyone joined the demonstration against world poverty.*
protest, rally, march, parade
(*informal*) demo

den noun
We built a den in the garden.
hideout, shelter, hiding place, secret place
The den of a wild animal is its *lair*.

dense adjective
1 *The accident happened in dense fog.*
thick, heavy
2 *A dense crowd waited in the square.*
compact, packed, solid
3 *I'm being rather dense today!*
stupid, slow

dent noun
There was a large dent in the car door.
indentation, depression, hollow, dip, dimple

deny verb
1 *The boy denied that he had stolen the money.*
reject, dispute, disagree with, contradict, dismiss, oppose
OPPOSITE admit, accept
2 *Her parents don't deny her anything.*
refuse, deprive of, withhold
OPPOSITE give

depart verb
1 *What time is the train due to depart?*
leave, set off, get going, set out, start, begin a journey
OPPOSITE arrive, get in
2 *It looks as if the robbers departed in a hurry.*
leave, exit, go away, retreat, withdraw, make off
(*informal*) clear off, scram, scarper
OPPOSITE arrive

depend verb
to depend on someone
I depend on you to help me.
rely on, count on, bank on, trust
to depend on something
My success will depend on good luck.
be decided by, rest on, hinge on

dependable adjective
Are these friends of yours dependable?
reliable, trustworthy, loyal, faithful, trusty, honest, sound, steady
OPPOSITE unreliable

depressed adjective
After his friends left, he began to feel depressed.
disheartened, dejected, discouraged, downcast, downhearted, unhappy, sad, low, gloomy, glum, melancholy, miserable, despondent, desolate, in despair
(*informal*) down
OPPOSITE cheerful

derelict adjective
They plan to pull down those derelict buildings.
dilapidated, crumbling, decrepit, neglected, deserted, abandoned, ruined

descend verb
1 *After admiring the view, we began to descend the mountain.*
climb down, come down, go down, move down
To descend through the air is to *drop* or *fall*.
To descend through water is to *sink*.
2 *The road descends gradually into the valley.*
drop, fall, slope, dip, incline
OPPOSITE ascend
to be descended from someone
She's descended from a French family.
come from, originate from

describe verb
1 *An eyewitness described how the accident happened.*
report, tell about, depict, explain, outline
2 *Friends described him as a quiet, shy man.*
portray, characterize, represent, present

description noun
1 *I wrote a description of our day at the seaside.*
report, account, story
2 *Write a description of your favourite character in the play.*
portrait, representation, sketch

descriptive adjective
The author writes in a very descriptive style.
expressive, colourful, detailed, graphic, vivid

desert verb
He deserted his friends when they needed him most.
abandon, leave, forsake, betray
(*informal*) walk out on
To desert someone in a place they can't get away from is to *maroon* or *strand* them.

deserted adjective
By midnight, the streets of the town were deserted.
empty, unoccupied, uninhabited, vacant
OPPOSITE crowded

deserve verb
You deserve a break after all your hard work.
be worthy of, be entitled to, have earned, merit, warrant

design noun
1 *This is the winning design for the new art gallery.*
plan, drawing, outline, blueprint, sketch
A first example of something, used as a model for making others, is a *prototype*.
2 *Do you like the design of this wallpaper?*
style, pattern, arrangement, composition

design verb
She designs all her own clothes.
create, develop, invent, devise, conceive, think up

desire verb
The magic mirror will show you what you most desire.
wish for, long for, want, crave, fancy, hanker after, yearn for, pine for, set your heart on, have a yen for

desire noun
My greatest desire is to swim with dolphins.
wish, want, longing, ambition, craving, fancy, hankering, urge, yearning
A desire for food is *appetite* or *hunger*.
A desire for drink is *thirst*.
Excessive desire for money or other things is *greed*.

desolate *adjective*
1 *Jamie felt* **desolate** *when his goldfish died.*
depressed, dejected, miserable, sad, melancholy, hopeless, wretched, forlorn
OPPOSITE cheerful
2 *No-one wants to live in that* **desolate** *place.*
bleak, depressing, dreary, gloomy, dismal, cheerless, inhospitable, deserted, uninhabited, abandoned, godforsaken
OPPOSITE pleasant

despair *noun*
The defeated knight was overcome by **despair**.
depression, desperation, gloom, hopelessness, misery, anguish, dejection, melancholy, pessimism, wretchedness
OPPOSITE hope

desperate *adjective*
1 *The shipwrecked crew were in a* **desperate** *situation.*
difficult, critical, grave, serious, severe, drastic, dire, urgent, extreme
2 *The hills were home to a band of* **desperate** *outlaws.*
dangerous, violent, reckless

despise *verb*
I **despise** *people who cheat at cards.*
hate, loathe, feel contempt for, deride, have a low opinion of, look down on, scorn, sneer at
OPPOSITE admire

destiny *noun*
Was it **destiny** *that brought us together?*
fate, fortune

destroy *verb*
1 *An avalanche* **destroyed** *the village.*
demolish, devastate, crush, flatten, knock down, level, pull down, shatter, smash, sweep away
2 *He tried to* **destroy** *the good work we had done.*
ruin, wreck, sabotage, undo

destruction *noun*
1 *The hurricane caused* **destruction** *all along the coast.*
devastation, damage, demolition, ruin, wrecking
OPPOSITE creation
2 *Global warming may cause the* **destruction** *of many animal species.*
elimination, annihilation, obliteration, extermination, extinction
OPPOSITE conservation

detach *verb*
The camera lens can be **detached** *for cleaning.*
remove, separate,
disconnect, take off, release, undo, unfasten, part
To detach a caravan from a vehicle is to **unhitch** it.
To detach railway wagons from a locomotive is to **uncouple** them.
To detach something by cutting it off is to **sever** it.
OPPOSITE attach

detail *noun*
Her account of what happened was accurate in every **detail**.
fact, feature, particular, aspect, item, point, respect

WORD WEB

CRIME SCENE DO NOT CROSS

detective *noun*
Detective *Dewar solved the case of the stolen tiara.*
investigator, sleuth
(*informal*) private eye

THINGS A DETECTIVE MIGHT LOOK FOR
clues, evidence, eyewitness, fingerprints, footprints, murder weapon, tracks; criminal, crook, culprit, felon, suspect

THINGS A DETECTIVE MIGHT DO
analyse, comb (an area), deduce, deduct, detect, dig up, ferret out, follow a hunch, follow a lead or a tip-off, interrogate or question (a witness), investigate, pursue, shadow, solve (a case), stake out (a hiding place), tail or track down (a suspect)

An informal name for a story in which a detective solves a crime is a **whodunnit**.

deteriorate *verb*
1 *The queen's health had begun to* **deteriorate**.
worsen, decline, degenerate, get worse, go downhill
2 *The walls will* **deteriorate** *if we don't maintain them.*
decay, disintegrate, crumble
OPPOSITE improve

determination *noun*
Marathon runners show great **determination**.
resolve, commitment, will-power, courage, dedication, drive, grit, perseverance, persistence, spirit
(*informal*) guts

determined *adjective*
1 *Boudicca must have been a* **determined** *woman.*
resolute, decisive, firm, strong-minded, assertive, persistent, tough
OPPOSITE weak-minded
2 *I'm* **determined** *to finish the race.*
committed, resolved

detest *verb*
I **detest** *the smell of boiled cabbage.*
dislike, hate, loathe
Informal expressions are **can't bear** and **can't stand**.
OPPOSITE love

develop *verb*
1 *The zoo is* **developing** *its education programme.*
expand, extend, enlarge, build up, diversify
2 *Her piano playing has* **developed** *this year.*
improve, progress, evolve, advance, get better
3 *The plants will* **develop** *quickly in the spring.*
grow, flourish
4 *How did he* **develop** *that posh accent?*
get, acquire, pick up, cultivate

device *noun*
The TV comes with a remote control **device**.
tool, implement, instrument, appliance, apparatus, gadget, contraption
(*informal*) gizmo

devious *adjective*
1 *The mad professor had a* **devious** *plan to take over the world.*
cunning, deceitful, dishonest, furtive, scheming, sly, sneaky, treacherous, wily
2 *Because of the roadworks, we took a* **devious** *route home.*
indirect, roundabout, winding, meandering
OPPOSITE direct

devoted *adjective*
She's a **devoted** *supporter of our team.*

a
b
c
d
e
f
g
h
i
j
k
l
m
n
o
p
q
r
s
t
u
v
w
x
y
z

41

loyal, faithful, dedicated,
enthusiastic, committed
OPPOSITE apathetic

devour *verb*
*He **devoured** a whole plateful of sandwiches.*
eat, consume, guzzle, gobble up, gulp down, swallow
(*informal*) scoff, wolf down

diagram *noun*
*We drew a **diagram** of the life cycle of a frog.*
chart, plan, sketch, outline

diary *noun*
*I write all about my birthday party in my **diary**.*
journal, daily record
A diary describing a voyage or mission is a *log* or *logbook*.
A diary in which you insert pictures and souvenirs is a *scrapbook*.
A diary published on a website is a *blog*.

die *verb*
1 *My sister's hamster **died** last week.*
expire, pass away, perish
(*informal*) snuff it, kick the bucket, croak
To die of hunger is to *starve*.
2 *The flowers will **die** if they don't have water.*
wither, wilt, droop, fade
to die out
*When did the dinosaurs **die out**?*
become extinct, cease to exist, come to an end, disappear, vanish

differ *verb*
*The two men **differed** in their beliefs.*
disagree, conflict, argue, clash, contradict each other, oppose each other, quarrel
OPPOSITE agree
to differ from
*My style of painting **differs from** hers.*
be different from, contrast with

difference *noun*
1 *Can you see any **difference** between these two colours?*

contrast, distinction
OPPOSITE similarity
2 *This money will make a **difference** to their lives.*
change, alteration, modification, variation

different *adjective*
1 *We have **different** views about global warming.*
differing, contradictory, opposite, clashing, conflicting
2 *It's important that the teams wear **different** colours.*
contrasting, dissimilar, distinguishable
3 *The packet contains sweets of **different** flavours.*
various, assorted, mixed, several, diverse, numerous, miscellaneous
4 *Let's go somewhere **different** on holiday this year.*
new, original, fresh
5 *Everyone's handwriting is **different**.*
distinct, distinctive, individual, special, unique

difficult *adjective*
1 *This crossword is really **difficult**. We were faced with a **difficult** problem.*
hard, complicated, complex, involved, intricate, baffling, perplexing, puzzling
(*informal*) tricky, thorny, knotty
OPPOSITE simple
2 *It is a **difficult** climb to the top of the hill.*
challenging, arduous, demanding, taxing, exhausting, formidable, gruelling, laborious, strenuous, tough
OPPOSITE easy
3 *Mum says I was a **difficult** child when I was little.*
troublesome, awkward, trying, tiresome, annoying, disruptive, obstinate, stubborn, uncooperative, unhelpful
OPPOSITE cooperative

difficulty *noun*
1 *The explorers were used to facing **difficulty**.*
trouble, adversity, challenges, hardship
2 *There are some **difficulties** with your application.*
problem, complication, hitch, obstacle, snag

dig *verb*
1 *We spent the afternoon **digging** the garden.*
cultivate, fork over, turn over
2 *Rabbits **dig** holes in the ground.*
burrow, excavate, tunnel, gouge out, hollow out, scoop out

3 *Did you **dig** me in the back?*
poke, prod, jab

dignified *adjective*
*Lady Snodgrass was a very **dignified** old lady.*
refined, stately, distinguished, noble, sedate, solemn, proper, grave, grand, august
OPPOSITE undignified

dim *adjective*
1 *I could see the **dim** outline of a figure in the mist.*
indistinct, faint, blurred, fuzzy, hazy, shadowy, vague
OPPOSITE clear
2 *The light in the cave was rather **dim**.*
dark, dull, dingy, murky, gloomy
OPPOSITE bright

din *noun*
*I can't hear you because of that awful **din**!*
noise, racket, row, clatter, hullabaloo

dingy *adjective*
*How can we brighten up this **dingy** room?*
dull, drab, dreary, dowdy, colourless, dismal, gloomy, murky
OPPOSITE bright

WORD WEB

dinosaur *noun*
SOME TYPES OF DINOSAUR
apatosaurus, archaeopteryx, brachiosaurus, diplodocus, gallimimus, iguanodon, megalosaurus, pterodactylus, stegosaurus, triceratops, tyrannosaurus rex, velociraptor

BODY PARTS WHICH A DINOSAUR MAY HAVE
dorsal plates, bony frill, fleshy fin, horn, wings, crest

A person who studies dinosaurs and other fossils is a *palaeontologist*.

dip *verb*
*I **dipped** my hand in the water.*
immerse, lower, plunge, submerge, dunk

dip *noun*
1 *There was a **dip** in the road ahead.*
hollow, hole, depression, slope
2 *It was so hot we decided to have a **dip** in the sea.*
swim, bathe

direct *adjective*
1 *It would be quicker to take the **direct** route.*
straight, shortest
OPPOSITE indirect
2 *Please give me a **direct** answer.*
straightforward, frank, honest, sincere, blunt, plain, outspoken, candid, unambiguous
OPPOSITE evasive

direct *verb*
1 *Can you **direct** me to the station?*
guide, point, show the way, give directions to
2 *A new manager has been apppointed to **direct** the company.*
manage, run, be in charge of, control, administer, superintend, supervise, take charge of
To direct an orchestra is to **conduct** it.
3 *The conductor **directed** us to begin playing.*
instruct, command, order, tell

dirt *noun*
1 *The floor was covered in **dirt**.*
filth, grime, mess, muck, mud, dust
2 *Chickens scratched about in the **dirt**.*
earth, soil, clay, loam, mud

dirty *adjective*
1 *Those **dirty** clothes need to be washed.*
unclean, filthy, grimy, grubby, soiled, stained, messy, mucky, muddy, sooty, foul (*informal*) manky, grotty
OPPOSITE clean
2 *We refused to drink the **dirty** water.*
impure, polluted, murky, cloudy
OPPOSITE pure

3 *The other team used **dirty** tactics.*
unfair, dishonest, illegal, mean, unsporting
OPPOSITE honest
4 *The comedian used a lot of **dirty** words.*
rude, offensive, coarse, crude, improper, indecent, obscene
OPPOSITE decent

disadvantage *noun*
*It's a **disadvantage** to be small if you play basketball.*
drawback, handicap, hindrance, inconvenience, downside, snag

disagree *verb*
*My sister and I often **disagree** about music.*
argue, differ, clash, quarrel, squabble, bicker, fall out
OPPOSITE agree
to disagree with
*He **disagrees with** everything I say.*
argue with, contradict, oppose, object to

disagreement *noun*
*We had a **disagreement** over who should pay for the meal.*
argument, dispute, difference of opinion, quarrel, row, clash, squabble, conflict
OPPOSITE agreement

disappear *verb*
1 *The markings will **disappear** as the chicks grow older.*
become invisible, vanish, fade, clear, disperse, dissolve
2 *The thief **disappeared** around the corner.*
run away, escape, flee, go away, withdraw
OPPOSITE appear

disappoint *verb*
*She didn't want to **disappoint** her fans by cancelling the show.*
let down, fail, dissatisfy, displease, upset
OPPOSITE please, satisfy

disappointed *adjective*
*I'm **disappointed** that you can't come to my party.*
saddened, unhappy, upset, let down, unsatisfied, displeased
OPPOSITE pleased, satisfied

disapprove *verb*
to disapprove of
*My aunt **disapproves of** watching television.*
object to, take exception to, dislike, deplore, condemn, criticize, denounce, frown on (*informal*) take a dim view of
OPPOSITE approve of

discipline *noun*
Discipline is important in the army.
order, control

discourage *verb*
1 *Don't let her criticism **discourage** you.*
demoralize, depress (*informal*) put you off
2 *The burglar alarm will **discourage** thieves.*
deter, dissuade, prevent, restrain, stop, hinder

discover *verb*
*I **discovered** some old toys in the attic.*
find, come across, spot, stumble across, uncover
To discover something that has been buried is to **unearth** it.
To discover something that has been under water is to **dredge it up**.
To discover something you have been pursuing is to **track it down**.
OPPOSITE hide

discovery *noun*
*Scientists have made an exciting new **discovery**.*
find, breakthrough

discrimination *noun*
1 *She shows **discrimination** in her choice of music.*
good taste, good judgement
2 *The school has a policy against racial **discrimination**.*
prejudice, bias, intolerance, unfairness
Discrimination against people because of their sex is **sexism**.
Discrimination against people because of their race is **racism**.

discuss *verb*
*I **discussed** the idea with my parents.*
talk about, confer about, debate

discussion *noun*
*We had a lively **discussion** about pocket money.*

a
b
c
d
e
f
g
h
i
t
u
v
w
x
y
z

conversation, argument, exchange of views
A formal discussion is a *conference* or *debate*.

disease *noun*
He was suffering from a serious disease.
illness, ailment, sickness, complaint, affliction
(*informal*) bug

disgrace *noun*
1 *He never got over the disgrace of being caught cheating.*
humiliation, shame, embarrassment, dishonour
2 *The way he treats them is a disgrace!*
outrage, scandal

disgraceful *adjective*
We were shocked by her disgraceful behaviour.
shameful, shocking, appalling, outrageous, scandalous
OPPOSITE honourable

disguise *verb*
I tried to disguise my feelings.
conceal, hide, cover up, camouflage, mask
to disguise yourself as
The spy disguised himself as a hotel porter.
dress up as, pretend to be

disguise *noun*
I didn't recognize him in that disguise.
costume, camouflage, make-up, mask

disgust *noun*
The sight of the carcass filled me with disgust.
repulsion, repugnance, distaste, dislike, horror, loathing, detestation
OPPOSITE liking

disgust *verb*
The smell of rotten eggs disgusts me.
repel, revolt, sicken, appal, offend, distress, shock, horrify
(*informal*) put you off, turn your stomach
OPPOSITE please

disgusting *adjective*
The brew in the cauldron looked disgusting.
repulsive, revolting, horrible, nasty, loathsome, repellent, repugnant, offensive, appalling, sickening, nauseating
(*informal*) yucky, icky, gross
OPPOSITE delightful, pleasing

dishonest *adjective*
1 *They were taken in by a dishonest salesman.*
deceitful, cheating, corrupt, disreputable, untrustworthy, immoral, lying, swindling, thieving
(*informal*) bent, crooked, dodgy, shady

2 *The author makes some dishonest claims.*
false, misleading, untruthful, fraudulent, devious

dishonesty *noun*
The MP was accused of dishonesty.
deceit, cheating, corruption, insincerity, lying, deviousness
(*informal*) crookedness
OPPOSITE honesty

disintegrate *verb*
The cloth is so old that it's starting to disintegrate.
break up, fall apart, break into pieces, crumble, decay, decompose

dislike *noun*
His colleagues regarded him with intense dislike.
hatred, loathing, detestation, disapproval, disgust, revulsion
OPPOSITE liking

dislike *verb*
I dislike people who hunt wild animals.
hate, loathe, detest, disapprove of
OPPOSITE like

disloyal *adjective*
The rebels were accused of being disloyal to the king.
unfaithful, treacherous, faithless, false, unreliable, untrustworthy
OPPOSITE loyal

dismal *adjective*
1 *How can we brighten up this dismal room?*
dull, drab, dreary, dingy, colourless, cheerless, gloomy, murky
OPPOSITE bright, cheerful
2 (*informal*) *It was a dismal performance by the home team.*
dreadful, awful, terrible, feeble, useless, hopeless
(*informal*) pathetic
OPPOSITE bright, cheerful

dismay *noun*
We listened with dismay to the bad news.
distress, alarm, shock, concern, anxiety, gloom

dismiss *verb*
1 *The teacher dismissed the class.*
send away, discharge, free, let go, release
2 *The firm dismissed ten workers.*
sack, give the sack, give notice to, make redundant
(*informal*) fire
3 *The weather was so bad that we dismissed the idea of having a picnic.*
discard, drop, reject

disobedient *adjective*
She said she had never known such a disobedient child.
naughty, badly behaved,

undisciplined, uncontrollable, unmanageable, unruly, ungovernable, troublesome, defiant, disruptive, mutinous, rebellious, contrary
OPPOSITE obedient

disobey *verb*
1 *You will be penalized if you disobey the rules.*
break, ignore, disregard, defy, violate
2 *Soldiers are trained never to disobey.*
be disobedient, rebel, revolt, mutiny
OPPOSITE obey

display *verb*
We planned the best way to display our work.
demonstrate, exhibit, present, put on show, set out, show, show off
To display something boastfully is to *flaunt* it.

display *noun*
We set out a display of our art work.
exhibition, show, presentation, demonstration

disrespectful *adjective*
She was very disrespectful towards her parents.
rude, bad-mannered, insulting, impolite, insolent, cheeky
OPPOSITE respectful

disrupt *verb*
Bad weather has disrupted the tennis tournament.
interrupt, upset, interfere with, throw into confusion or disorder

dissatisfied *adjective*
I was dissatisfied with my piano playing.
displeased, disappointed, discontented, frustrated, annoyed
OPPOSITE satisfied

distance *noun*
What is the distance from Earth to the Sun?
measurement, space, extent, reach, mileage
The distance across something is the *breadth* or *width*.
The distance along something is the *length*.
The distance between two points is a *gap* or *interval*.

distant *adjective*
1 *I'd love to travel to distant countries.*
faraway, remote, out-of-the-way, inaccessible, exotic
OPPOSITE close
2 *His distant manner puts me off.*
unfriendly, unapproachable, formal, reserved, withdrawn, cool, haughty, aloof
OPPOSITE friendly

distinct *adjective*
 1 *There is a **distinct** improvement in your handwriting.*
definite, evident, noticeable, obvious, perceptible
OPPOSITE **imperceptible**
 2 *It was a small photo, but the details were quite **distinct**.*
clear, distinguishable, plain, recognizable, sharp, unmistakable, visible, well defined
OPPOSITE **indistinct**
 3 *Organize your essay into **distinct** sections.*
individual, separate

distinguish *verb*
 1 *It was impossible to **distinguish** one twin from the other.*
tell apart, pick out, discriminate, differentiate, make a distinction, decide
 2 *In the dark we couldn't **distinguish** who was walking past.*
identify, tell, make out, determine, perceive, recognize, single out

distress *verb*
 *We could see that the bad news **distressed** her.*
upset, disturb, trouble, worry, alarm, dismay, torment
OPPOSITE **comfort**

distribute *verb*
 1 *The coach **distributed** water to the players at half-time.*
give out, hand round, circulate, dispense, issue, share out, take round
(*informal*) dish out, doll out
 2 *Distribute the seeds evenly.*
scatter, spread, disperse

distrust *verb*
 *I **distrusted** the professor from the moment I met him.*
doubt, mistrust, question, suspect, be suspicious or wary of, be sceptical about, feel uncertain or uneasy or unsure about
OPPOSITE **trust**

disturb *verb*
 1 *Don't **disturb** the baby when she's asleep.*
bother, interrupt, annoy, pester
 2 *They were **disturbed** by the bad news.*
distress, trouble, upset, worry, alarm, frighten
 3 *Please don't **disturb** the papers on my desk.*
muddle, mix up, move around, mess about with

ditch *noun*
 *We dug a **ditch** to drain away the water.*
trench, channel, drain, gully

dive *verb*
 1 *The mermaid **dived** into the water.*
plunge, jump, leap

*A dive in which you land flat on your front is a **bellyflop**.*
 2 *The eagle **dived** towards its prey.*
pounce, swoop

divide *verb*
 1 *We **divided** the class into two groups.*
separate, split, break up, move apart, part
OPPOSITE **combine**
 2 *I **divided** the cake between my friends.*
distribute, share out, give out, allot, deal out, dispense
 3 *Which way do we go? The path **divides** here.*
branch, fork
OPPOSITE **converge**

dizzy *adjective*
 *Going on a roundabout makes me feel **dizzy**.*
dazed, giddy, faint, reeling, unsteady

do *verb*
 1 *My friend always knows what to **do** in a crisis.*
act, behave, conduct yourself
 2 *The vet has a lot of work to **do** this morning.*
attend to, cope with, deal with, handle, look after, perform, undertake
 3 *It took me half an hour to **do** the washing-up.*
accomplish, achieve, carry out, complete, execute, finish
 4 *I need to **do** all of these sums.*
answer, puzzle out, solve, work out
 5 *Staring at the sun can **do** damage to your eyes.*
bring about, cause, produce, result in
 6 *If you don't have lemonade, water will **do**.*
be acceptable, be enough, be satisfactory, be sufficient, serve

dock *noun*
 *A boat was waiting for us at the end of the **dock**.*
harbour, quay, jetty, wharf, landing stage, dockyard, pier, port, marina

dodge *verb*
 *I just managed to **dodge** the snowball.*
avoid, evade, side-step

dive

dominate *verb*
 *The visiting team **dominated** the game.*
control, direct, monopolize, govern, take control of, take over

donation *noun*
 *The museum relies on **donations** from the public.*
contribution, gift, offering

done *adjective*
 1 *All my thank-you letters are **done** now.*
finished, complete, over
 2 *The cake will be brown on top when it's **done**.*
cooked, ready

doomed *adjective*
 *The expedition was **doomed** from the start.*
ill-fated, condemned, fated, cursed, jinxed, damned

door *noun*
 *A door in a floor or ceiling is a **hatch** or **trapdoor**.*
*The plank or stone underneath a door is the **threshold**.*
*The beam or stone above a door is the **lintel**.*
*The device on which most doors swing is the **hinge**.*

dot *noun*
 *She was furious when she saw **dots** of paint on the carpet.*
spot, speck, fleck, point, mark
*The dot you always put at the end of a sentence is a **full stop**.*
on the dot (*informal*) *We left the house at nine o'clock **on the dot**.*
exactly, precisely

double *adjective*
 *You enter the room through a **double** set of doors.*
dual, twofold, paired, twin, matching, duplicate

double *noun*
 *She's so like you—she's almost your **double**.*
twin
(*informal*) lookalike, spitting image, dead ringer
*A living organism created as an exact copy of another living organism is a **clone**.*

doubt *noun*
 1 *Have you any **doubt** about his honesty?*
distrust, suspicion, mistrust, hesitation, reservation, scepticism
OPPOSITE **confidence**
 2 *There is no **doubt** that you will pass your exam.*
question, uncertainty, ambiguity, confusion
OPPOSITE **certainty**

a
b
c
d
e
f
g
h
i
j
k
l
m
n
o
p
q
r
s
t
u
v
w
x
y
z

doubt verb

*There is no reason to **doubt** her story.*

distrust, feel uncertain or uneasy or unsure about, question, mistrust, suspect, be sceptical about, be suspicious or wary of

OPPOSITE **trust**

doubtful adjective

*He looked **doubtful**, but agreed to let us go.*

unsure, uncertain, unconvinced, hesitant, distrustful, sceptical, suspicious

OPPOSITE **certain**

doze verb

*Dad often **dozes** in the evening.*

rest, sleep, nod off
(*informal*) drop off

drab adjective

*That dress is too **drab** to wear to the party.*

dull, dingy, dreary, cheerless, colourless, dismal, gloomy, grey

OPPOSITE **bright, cheerful**

draft noun

*I jotted down a **draft** of my story.*

outline, plan, sketch, rough version

draft verb

*I began to **draft** my story.*

outline, plan, prepare, sketch, work out

drag verb

*The tractor **dragged** the car out of the ditch.*

pull, tow, tug, draw, haul, lug

OPPOSITE **push**

drain verb

1 *If they **drain** the marsh, lots of waterbirds will die.*

dry out, remove water from

2 *She **drained** the oil from the engine.*

draw off, empty

3 *The water slowly **drained** away.*

trickle, ooze, seep

4 *The tough climb **drained** my energy.*

use up, consume, exhaust

drastic adjective

*After being without food for three days, the explorers needed to take **drastic** action.*

desperate, extreme, radical, harsh, severe

OPPOSITE **moderate**

draw verb

1 *I **drew** some pictures of the flowers in our garden.*

sketch, trace, doodle

2 *I'm not very good at **drawing** faces.*

depict, portray, represent

3 *The horse was **drawing** a cart.*

pull, tow, drag, haul, tug, lug

4 *We expect tomorrow's match to **draw** a big crowd.*

attract, bring in, pull in

5 *The two teams **drew** 1–1.*

finish equal, tie

to draw near

*As the spaceship **drew** near, I began to get nervous.*

approach, advance, come near

drawback noun

*It's a **drawback** to be small if you play basketball.*

disadvantage, difficulty, handicap, obstacle, inconvenience, hindrance, downside, snag

dread noun

*Our teacher has a **dread** of spiders.*

fear, horror, terror, phobia (about), anxiety (about)

dreadful adjective

1 *There has been a **dreadful** accident at sea.*

horrible, terrible, appalling, horrendous, distressing, shocking, upsetting, tragic, grim

2 *The weather at the weekend was **dreadful**.*

bad, awful, terrible, abysmal, abominable, dire, foul, nasty

OPPOSITE **good, pleasant**

dream noun

A bad dream is a *nightmare*.
A dreamlike experience you have while awake is a *daydream*, *fantasy*, or *reverie*.
Something you see in a dream or daydream is a *vision*.
The dreamlike state when you are hypnotized is a *trance*.
Something you think you see that is not real is a *hallucination* or *illusion*.

dreary adjective

1 *The newsreader had a very **dreary** voice.*

dull, boring, flat, tedious, unexciting, uninteresting

OPPOSITE **lively**

2 *When will this **dreary** weather end?*

depressing, dismal, dull, gloomy, cheerless, murky, overcast

OPPOSITE **bright, sunny**

dress noun

1 *What kind of **dress** are you wearing to the party?*

frock, gown

2 *The invitation said to wear casual **dress**.*

clothes, clothing, outfit, costume, garments

dress verb

1 *I helped to **dress** my little brother.*

clothe, put clothes on

OPPOSITE **undress**

🕸 WORD WEB

dragon noun

*A fearsome **dragon** once lived in these hills.*

SOME WAYS TO DESCRIBE A DRAGON
ancient, fearsome, fiery, fire-breathing, mighty, monstrous, scaly

BODY PARTS A DRAGON MIGHT HAVE
claws, crest, forked tail or tongue, scales, spikes or spines, bat-like wings

A DRAGON'S SCALES MIGHT BE
dazzling, iridescent, patterned, shimmering

A DRAGON'S BREATH MIGHT BE
fiery, flaming, scorching, searing

THINGS A DRAGON MIGHT DO
breathe fire, puff smoke, roar, snort, change shape, fly, swoop

PLACES WHERE A DRAGON MIGHT LIVE
cave, den, lair

2 *A nurse dressed my wound.*
bandage, put a dressing on, bind up

dribble *verb*
1 *Careful, the baby's dribbling on your jumper.*
drool
2 *Water dribbled out of the hole in the tank.*
drip, trickle, leak, ooze, seep

drift *verb*
1 *The boat drifted downstream.*
float, be carried, move slowly
2 *The crowd lost interest and drifted away.*
stray, wander, meander, ramble, walk aimlessly
3 *The snow will drift in this wind.*
pile up, accumulate, make drifts

drift *noun*
1 *The car was stuck in a snow drift.*
bank, heap, mound, pile, ridge
2 *Did you understand the drift of the speech?*
gist, main idea, point

drill *verb*
It took a long time to drill through the wall.
bore, penetrate, pierce

drink *verb*
To drink greedily is to *gulp*, *guzzle*, or *swig*.
To drink noisily is to *slurp*.
To drink a small amount at a time is to *sip*.
To drink with the tongue as a cat does is to *lap*.

drip *noun*
Dad was worried by the drips of oil underneath the car.
spot, dribble, splash, trickle

drip *verb*
The oil dripped onto the garage floor.
drop, leak, dribble, splash, trickle

drive *verb*
1 *The dog drove the sheep through the gate.*
direct, guide, herd
2 *I couldn't drive the spade into the hard ground.*
push, thrust, hammer, plunge, ram
3 *When can I learn to drive a car?*
control, handle, manage
4 *Lack of money drove him to steal.*
force, compel, oblige
to drive someone out
The invading soldiers drove the people out.
eject, expel, throw out
To drive people out of their homes is to *evict* them.
To drive people out of their country is to *banish* or *exile* them.

drive *noun*
1 *We went for a drive in the country.*

ride, trip, journey, outing, excursion, jaunt
2 *Have you got the drive to succeed?*
ambition, determination, keenness, motivation, energy, zeal

droop *verb*
Plants tend to droop in dry weather.
sag, wilt, bend, flop, be limp

drop *noun*
1 *Large drops of rain began to fall.*
drip, droplet, spot, bead, blob
2 *Could I have another drop of milk in my tea?*
dash, small quantity
3 *We expect a drop in the price of fruit in the summer.*
decrease, reduction, cut
4 *There's a drop of two metres on the other side of the wall.*
fall, descent, plunge

drop *verb*
1 *The hawk dropped onto its prey.*
descend, dive, plunge, swoop
2 *I dropped to the ground exhausted.*
collapse, fall, sink, subside, slump, tumble
3 *Why did you drop me from the team?*
omit, eliminate, exclude, leave out
4 *They dropped the plan for a new bypass.*
abandon, discard, reject, give up, scrap

drown *verb*
The music from upstairs drowned our conversation.
overwhelm, overpower, drown out

drowsy *adjective*
If you feel drowsy, why not go to bed?
sleepy, tired, weary

drug *noun*
A new drug has been discovered for back pain.
medicine, remedy, treatment
A drug which relieves pain is an *analgesic* or *painkiller*.
A drug which calms you down is a *sedative* or *tranquillizer*.
Drugs which make you more active are *stimulants*.

dry *adjective*
1 *Nothing will grow in this dry soil.*
arid, parched, moistureless, waterless, dehydrated, desiccated, barren
A common simile is *as dry as a bone*.
OPPOSITE **wet**
2 *He gave rather a dry speech.*

dull, boring, dreary, tedious, uninteresting
OPPOSITE **interesting**
3 *I can't understand his dry sense of humour.*
ironic, wry, witty, subtle

duck *verb*
Oliver ducked to avoid the snowball.
bend down, bob down, crouch, stoop

dull *adjective*
1 *I don't like the dull colours in this room.*
dim, dingy, drab, dreary, dismal, faded, gloomy, sombre, subdued
OPPOSITE **bright, colourful**
2 *The sky was dull that day.*
cloudy, overcast, grey, sunless, murky
OPPOSITE **clear**
3 *I heard a dull thud from upstairs.*
indistinct, muffled, muted
OPPOSITE **distinct**
4 *He's rather a dull student.*
stupid, slow, unintelligent, dim, unimaginative, dense, obtuse
(*informal*) thick
OPPOSITE **clever**
5 *The play was so dull that I fell asleep.*
boring, dry, monotonous, tedious, uninteresting, unexciting, lacklustre
A common simile is *as dull as ditchwater*.
OPPOSITE **interesting**

dumb *adjective*
1 *The spectators were struck dumb with amazement.*
If you do not speak, you are *mute* or *silent*.
If you cannot speak because you are surprised, confused, or embarrassed, you are *speechless* or *tongue-tied*.
If you find it hard to express yourself, you are *inarticulate*.
2 (*informal*) *He's too dumb to understand.*
stupid, unintelligent, dim, slow, dense, obtuse
(*informal*) thick

dump *verb*
1 *I decided to dump some of my old toys.*
get rid of, throw away, throw out, discard, dispose of, scrap
2 *Just dump your things in the bedroom.*
put down, set down, deposit, place, drop, throw down, tip

dusk *noun*
Bats begin to emerge at dusk.
twilight, nightfall, sunset, sundown
OPPOSITE **dawn**

duty *noun*
1 *I have a duty to help my parents.*

responsibility, obligation
*2 I carried out my **duties** conscientiously.*
job, task, assignment, chore
*3 The government has increased the **duty** on petrol.*
charge, tax

dwindle *verb*
*Our enthusiasm **dwindled** as the day went on.*
become less, diminish, decline, decrease, lessen, subside, wane, weaken
OPPOSITE increase

dynamic *adjective*
*The team has a new, **dynamic** captain.*
energetic, lively, enthusiastic, vigorous, active, forceful, powerful
OPPOSITE apathetic

Ee

eager *adjective*
*He is always **eager** to help.*
keen, enthusiastic, desperate, anxious
OPPOSITE unenthusiastic

early *adjective*
*1 The bus was **early** today.*
ahead of time, ahead of schedule
OPPOSITE late
*2 The **early** computers were huge machines.*
first, old, primitive, ancient
OPPOSITE recent, new

earth *noun*
*The **earth** was so dry that many plants died.*
ground, land, soil
Rich, fertile earth is *loam*.
The top layer of fertile earth is *topsoil*.
Rich earth consisting of decayed plants is *humus*.
A heavy, sticky kind of earth is *clay*.

easy *adjective*
*1 Tonight's homework is really **easy**.*
undemanding, effortless, light
An informal word for an easy task is a *doddle*.
*2 The instructions were **easy** to understand.*
simple, straightforward, clear, plain, elementary
A common simile is *as easy as ABC*.
*3 Our cat has an **easy** life.*
carefree, comfortable, peaceful, relaxed, leisurely, restful, tranquil, untroubled
OPPOSITE difficult

eat *verb*
*Hannah was **eating** a cheese sandwich.*
consume, devour
(*informal*) scoff
When cattle eat grass they are *grazing*.
A person who eats a large amount is said to *eat like a horse*.
*I was so hungry, I **wolfed down** a whole pizza.*
bolt down, gobble, gulp, guzzle, gorge, polish off, wolf down
*Rabbits like to **chomp** raw carrots.*
chomp, crunch, gnash, gnaw, munch, slurp
*Do you have any biscuits we could **nibble**?*
nibble, peck, pick at or pick away at, taste
*Mr Hogg was **savouring** a sausage roll.*
relish, savour, tuck into
*The guests will be **dining** in the great hall.*
banquet, dine, feast

eccentric *adjective*
*What is the reason for his **eccentric** behaviour?*
odd, peculiar, strange, weird, abnormal, unusual, curious, unconventional, unorthodox, quirky, zany
(*informal*) way-out, dotty
OPPOSITE conventional, orthodox

echo *verb*
*1 The sound **echoed** across the valley.*
resound, reverberate
*2 'He's gone home.' 'Gone home?' she **echoed**.*
repeat, imitate, mimic

ecstatic *adjective*
*Samantha was feeling **ecstatic** about her party.*
elated, delighted, overjoyed, gleeful, joyful, blissful, rapturous, euphoric, exultant, delirious, fervent, frenzied

edge *noun*
The edge of a cliff or other steep place is the *brink*.

The edge of a cup or other container is the *brim* or *rim*.
The line round the edge of a circle is the *circumference*.
The line round the edge of any other shape is its *outline*.
The distance round the edge of an area is the *perimeter*.
The stones along the edge of a road are the *kerb*.
Grass along the edge of a road is the *verge*.
The space down the edge of a page is the *margin*.
The space round the edge of a picture is a *border*.
Something that fits round the edge of a picture is a *frame*.
The edge of a garment is the *hem*.
An edge with threads or hair hanging loosely down is a *fringe*.
The edge of a crowd also is the *fringe* of the crowd.
The area round the edge of a city is the *outskirts* or *suburbs*.
The edge of a cricket field is the *boundary*.
The edge of a football pitch is the *touchline*.

edge *verb*
*1 We **edged** away from the lion's den.*
creep, inch, move stealthily, steal, slink
*2 Her bonnet was **edged** with black lace.*
trim, hem

edgy *adjective*
*Horses become **edgy** during thunderstorms.*
nervous, restless, anxious, agitated, excitable, tense, jumpy, fidgety
(*informal*) uptight, jittery
OPPOSITE calm

educate *verb*
*The job of a school is to **educate** young people.*
teach, train, inform, instruct, tutor

eerie *adjective*
*I heard some **eerie** sounds in the night.*
strange, weird, uncanny, mysterious, frightening, creepy, ghostly, sinister, unearthly, unnatural
(*informal*) scary, spooky

effect *noun*
*1 The **effect** of eating too much was that I became fat!*
result, consequence, outcome, sequel, upshot
*2 Does this music have any **effect** on you?*
impact, influence
*3 The lighting gives an **effect** of warmth.*

feeling, impression, sense, illusion

efficient *adjective*
1 *An efficient worker can do the job in an hour.*
effective, competent, able, capable, proficient
2 *Dad tried to work out an efficient way of heating our house.*
economic, productive

effort *noun*
1 *A lot of effort went into making the film.*
work, trouble, exertion, industry, labour, toil
2 *She congratulated us on a good effort.*
attempt, try, endeavour, go, shot

elaborate *adjective*
The plot of the book is so elaborate that I got lost halfway through.
complicated, complex, detailed, intricate, involved, convoluted
OPPOSITE simple

elect *verb*
We elected a new captain.
vote for, appoint

elegant *adjective*
She always wears elegant clothes.
graceful, stylish, fashionable, chic, smart, tasteful, sophisticated
OPPOSITE inelegant

eliminate *verb*
The government wants to eliminate crime.
get rid of, put an end to
To be eliminated from a competition is to be *knocked out*.

embarrass *verb*
Will it embarrass you if I tell people our secret?
humiliate, distress, mortify, make you blush

embarrassed *adjective*
Don't feel embarrassed—it happens to everyone!
humiliated, ashamed, awkward, uncomfortable, bashful, distressed, flustered, mortified, self-conscious

embrace *verb*
1 *The mother gorilla embraced her baby.*
hug, clasp, cuddle, hold
2 *She's always ready to embrace new ideas.*
welcome, accept, adopt, take on

emerge *verb*
He didn't emerge from his bedroom until ten o'clock.
appear, come out

emergency *noun*
Try to keep calm in an emergency.
crisis, serious situation, danger, difficulty

emotional *adjective*
1 *He made an emotional farewell speech.*
moving, touching
2 *The music for the love scenes was very emotional.*
romantic, sentimental
3 *She's a very emotional woman.*
passionate, intense

emphasize *verb*
She emphasized the important points.
highlight, stress, focus on, dwell on, underline

empty *adjective*
1 *Please put the empty milk bottles outside the door.*
OPPOSITE full
2 *The house next to ours has been empty for weeks.*
unoccupied, uninhabited, vacant, deserted
OPPOSITE occupied
3 *After we put up our display, there was still some empty space on the wall.*
blank, bare, clear, unused

empty *verb*
1 *Empty the dirty water into the sink.*
drain, pour out
OPPOSITE fill
2 *The building emptied when the fire alarm went off.*
clear, evacuate, vacate
3 *Did you empty all the shopping out of the trolley?*
remove, unload

enchanting *adjective*
The ballet dancers were enchanting.
delightful, charming, appealing, attractive, bewitching, spellbinding

enchantment *noun*
1 *The forest had an air of enchantment.*
magic, wonder, delight, pleasure
2 *The witch recited an enchantment.*
spell, incantation

encourage *verb*
1 *We went to the match to encourage our team.*
inspire, support, motivate, cheer, spur on, egg on

embrace

2 *The poster encourages people to eat healthily.*
persuade, urge
3 *Is advertising likely to encourage sales?*
increase, boost, stimulate, further, promote, help, aid

encouraging *adjective*
The results of the tests were encouraging.
hopeful, positive, promising, reassuring, optimistic, cheering, favourable

end *noun*
1 *The fence marks the end of the garden.*
boundary, limit
2 *The end of the film was the most exciting part.*
ending, finish, close, conclusion, culmination
The last part of a show or piece of music is the *finale*.
A section added at the end of a letter is a *postscript*.
A section added at the end of a story is an *epilogue*.
3 *I was tired by the time we got to the end of the journey.*
termination, destination
4 *We arrived late and found ourselves at the end of the queue.*
back, rear, tail
5 *What end did you have in view when you started?*
aim, purpose, intention, objective, plan, outcome, result

end *verb*
1 *The meeting should end in time for lunch.*
finish, complete, conclude, break off, halt
(*informal*) round off
2 *When did they end public executions?*
abolish, do away with, get rid of, put an end to, discontinue, eliminate
3 *The festival ended with a show of fireworks.*
close, come to an end, stop, cease, terminate, culminate, wind up

ending *noun*
The ending of the film was the most exciting part.
end, finish, close, conclusion, culmination, last part
The ending of a show or piece of music is the *finale*.

endless *adjective*
1 *Teachers need endless patience.*
unending, limitless, infinite, inexhaustible, unlimited
2 *There's an endless procession of cars along the main road.*
continual, continuous, constant, incessant, interminable, perpetual, unbroken,

a b c d e f g h i j k l m n o p q r s t u v w x y z

uninterrupted, everlasting, ceaseless

endure verb
1 *She had to* **endure** *a lot of pain.*
bear, stand, suffer, cope with, experience, go through, put up with, tolerate, undergo
2 *These traditions have* **endured** *for centuries.*
survive, continue, last, persist, carry on, keep going

enemy noun
They used to be friends but now they are bitter **enemies***.*
opponent, adversary, foe, rival
OPPOSITE friend, ally

energetic adjective
1 *She's a very* **energetic** *person.*
dynamic, spirited, enthusiastic, animated, active, zestful
OPPOSITE inactive, lethargic
2 *It was a very* **energetic** *exercise routine.*
lively, vigorous, brisk, fast, quick moving, strenuous
OPPOSITE slow-paced, sluggish

energy noun
1 *The dancers had tremendous* **energy***.*
liveliness, spirit, vitality, vigour, life, drive, zest, verve, enthusiasm, dynamism
(*informal*) get-up-and-go, zip
OPPOSITE lethargy
2 *Wind power is a renewable source of* **energy***.*
power, fuel

enjoy verb
I really **enjoyed** *the film.*
like, love, get pleasure from, be pleased by, admire, appreciate

enjoyable adjective
It was an **enjoyable** *party.*
pleasant, agreeable, delightful, entertaining, amusing
OPPOSITE unpleasant

enlarge verb
The zoo is going to **enlarge** *the lion enclosure.*
expand, extend, develop, make bigger

energy

To make something wider is to **broaden** or **widen** it.
To make something longer is to **extend**, **lengthen**, or **stretch** it.
To make something seem larger is to **magnify** it.
OPPOSITE reduce

enormous adjective
Enormous *waves battered the ship.*
huge, gigantic, immense, colossal, massive, monstrous, monumental, mountainous, towering, tremendous, vast
(*informal*) ginormous, humungous
OPPOSITE small

enough adjective
Is there **enough** *food for ten people?*
sufficient, adequate, ample

enquire verb
to enquire about
I **enquired about** *train times to Bristol.*
ask for, get information about, request, investigate

enter verb
1 *Silence fell as I* **entered** *the room.*
come in, walk in
To enter a place without permission is to **invade** it.
OPPOSITE leave
2 *The arrow* **entered** *his shoulder.*
go into, penetrate, pierce
3 *Can I* **enter** *my name on the list?*
insert, record, register, put down, set down, sign, write, inscribe
OPPOSITE cancel
4 *Our class decided to* **enter** *the competition.*
take part in, enrol in, sign up for, go in for, join in, participate in, volunteer for
OPPOSITE withdraw from

entertain verb
1 *The storyteller* **entertained** *us with scary ghost stories.*
amuse, divert, keep amused,

make you laugh, please, cheer up
OPPOSITE bore
2 *You can* **entertain** *friends in the private dining room.*
receive, welcome, cater for, give hospitality to

entertainment noun
Our hosts had arranged some **entertainment** *for us.*
amusements, recreation, diversions, enjoyment, fun, pastimes

enthusiasm noun
1 *The young athletes showed plenty of* **enthusiasm***.*
keenness, keenness, ambition, commitment, drive, zeal, zest
OPPOSITE apathy
2 *Collecting fossils is one of my* **enthusiasms***.*
interest, passion, pastime, hobby, craze, diversion, fad

enthusiastic adjective
1 *He's an* **enthusiastic** *supporter of our local team.*
keen, passionate, avid, devoted, energetic, fervent, zealous
2 *The audience burst into* **enthusiastic** *applause.*
eager, excited, lively, vigorous, exuberant, hearty

entire adjective
Donald spent the **entire** *evening watching television.*
complete, whole, total, full

entirely adverb
I'm not **entirely** *sure that I agree with you.*
completely, absolutely, wholly, totally, utterly, fully, perfectly, quite

entrance noun
1 *Please pay at the* **entrance***.*
entry, way in, access, door, gate
When you go through the entrance to a building, you cross the **threshold***.*

2 *I'll meet you in the entrance.*
entrance hall, foyer, lobby, porch
3 *Her sudden entrance took everyone by surprise.*
entry, arrival, appearance

entrance *verb*
The crowd were entranced by the fireworks display.
charm, delight, please, enchant

envious *adjective*
He was envious of his brother's success.
jealous, resentful

environment *noun*
Animals should live in their natural environment, not in cages.
habitat, surroundings, setting, conditions, situation
the environment
We must do all we can to protect the environment.
the natural world, nature, the earth, the world

envy *noun*
I didn't feel any envy, even when I saw how rich she was.
jealousy, resentment, bitterness

envy *verb*
The evil queen envied Snow White's beauty.
be jealous of, begrudge, grudge, resent

episode *noun*
1 *I paid for the broken window, and I want to forget the whole episode.*
event, incident, experience
2 *I missed last night's episode of 'Dr Who'.*
instalment, part

equal *adjective*
1 *Give everyone an equal amount.*
equivalent, identical, matching, similar, corresponding, fair
2 *The scores were equal at half-time.*
even, level, the same, square
To make the scores equal is to *equalize*.

equipment *noun*
The shed is full of gardening equipment.
apparatus, gear, kit, tackle, tools, implements, instruments, materials, machinery, paraphernalia, things
Computing equipment is *hardware*.

erase *verb*
I erased the writing on the blackboard.
delete, remove, rub out, wipe out, get rid of

erode *verb*
The flood water eroded the river bank.
wear away, eat away, destroy

errand *noun*
I went on an errand to the corner shop.

job, task, assignment, trip, journey

error *noun*
1 *The accident was the result of an error by the driver.*
mistake, fault, lapse, blunder
2 *I think there is an error in your argument.*
flaw, inaccuracy, misunderstanding, inconsistency
The error of leaving something out is an *omission* or *oversight*.

escape *verb*
1 *Why did you let him escape?*
get away, get out, run away, break free, break out
(*informal*) give you the slip
A performer who escapes from chains, etc., is an *escape artist* or *escapologist*.
2 *She always escapes the nasty jobs.*
avoid, get out of, evade, dodge, shirk

escape *noun*
1 *The prisoner's escape was filmed by security cameras.*
getaway, breakout, flight
2 *The explosion was caused by an escape of gas.*
leak, leakage, seepage

essential *adjective*
Fruit and vegetables are an essential part of our diet.
important, necessary, basic, vital, principal, fundamental, chief, crucial, indispensable

establish *verb*
1 *He plans to establish a new business.*
set up, start, begin, create, found, initiate, institute, introduce, launch, originate
2 *The police have not managed to establish his guilt.*
prove, show to be true, confirm, verify

estimate *verb*
The builders estimate that the work will take four months.
calculate, assess, work out, compute, count up, evaluate, judge, reckon, think out

eternal *adjective*
1 *The magic fountain was said to give eternal youth.*
everlasting, infinite, lasting, unending, timeless
Beings with eternal life are said to be *immortal*.
2 *I'm sick of your eternal quarrelling!*
constant, continual, never-ending, non-stop, persistent, perpetual, endless, ceaseless, incessant, unceasing

even *adjective*
1 *You need an even*

surface for ice-skating.
level, flat, smooth, straight
OPPOSITE **uneven**
2 *The runners kept up an even pace.*
regular, steady, unvarying, rhythmical, monotonous
OPPOSITE **irregular**
3 *Mr Humphreys has an even temper.*
calm, cool, placid, unexcitable
OPPOSITE **excitable**
4 *The scores were even at half time.*
equal, level, matching, identical, the same, square
OPPOSITE **different**
5 *2, 4, and 6 are even numbers.*
OPPOSITE **odd**

evening *noun*
Towards evening it clouded over and began to rain.
dusk, nightfall, sundown, sunset, twilight

event *noun*
1 *Her autobiography describes the main events of her life.*
happening, incident, occurrence
2 *There was an event to mark the launch of the new film.*
function, occasion, ceremony, entertainment, party, reception
3 *The World Cup is an important event for football fans.*
competition, contest, fixture, engagement, meeting, game, match, tournament

eventually *adverb*
The journey took ages, but eventually we arrived safely.
finally, at last, in the end, ultimately

evidence *noun*
This piece of paper is evidence that he is lying.
proof, confirmation
Evidence that someone accused of a crime was not there when the crime was committed is an *alibi*.
Evidence given in a law court is a *testimony*.
To give evidence in court is to *testify*.

evil *adjective*
1 *The charm was used to keep away evil spirits.*
malevolent, fiendish, diabolical
2 *Who would do such an evil deed?*
wicked, immoral, cruel, sinful, villainous, malicious, foul, hateful, vile
OPPOSITE **good**

evil *noun*
1 *The good witch tried to fight against evil.*
wickedness, badness, wrongdoing, sin, immorality,

villainy, malevolence, malice
2 *They had to endure the **evils** of famine and drought.*
disaster, misfortune, suffering, pain, affliction, curse

exact *adjective*
1 *I gave the police an **exact** account of what happened.*
accurate, precise, correct, true, faithful, detailed, meticulous, strict
2 *Is this an **exact** copy of the original document?*
identical, perfect, indistinguishable
OPPOSITE inaccurate

exaggerate *verb*
*He tends to **exaggerate** his problems.*
magnify, inflate, overdo, make too much of
OPPOSITE minimize

examination *noun*
1 *The results of the **examinations** will be announced next month.*
test, assessment
(*informal*) exam
2 *The judge made a thorough **examination** of the facts.*
investigation, inspection, study, analysis, survey, review, appraisal
3 *He was sent to hospital for an **examination**.*
check-up
A medical examination of a dead person is a *post-mortem*.

examine *verb*
1 *The judge **examined** the evidence.*
inspect, study, investigate, analyse, look closely at, pore over, scrutinize, probe, survey, review, weigh up, sift
2 *They were **examined** on their knowledge of history.*
question, interrogate, quiz
To examine someone rigorously is to *grill* them.

example *noun*
1 *Give me an **example** of what you mean.*
instance, illustration, sample, specimen, case
2 *She's an **example** to us all.*
model, ideal

excellent *adjective*
*That's an **excellent** idea!*
first-class, first-rate, outstanding, exceptional, remarkable, tremendous, wonderful, superb, great, fine, marvellous, superior, superlative, top-notch
(*informal*) brilliant, fantastic, terrific, fabulous, sensational, super
OPPOSITE bad, awful, second-rate

exceptional *adjective*
*It is **exceptional** to have such cold weather in June.*
unusual, extraordinary, uncommon, unexpected, amazing, rare, odd, peculiar, strange, surprising, special, abnormal, phenomenal, unheard-of, bizarre
OPPOSITE normal, usual

exchange *verb*
*The shop will **exchange** faulty goods.*
change, replace
To exchange goods for other goods without using money is to *barter*. To exchange an old thing for part of the cost of a new one is to *trade it in*.
To exchange things with your friends is to *swap* or *swop* them.
To exchange players for other players in football, etc., is to *substitute* them.

excited *adjective*
*On Christmas Eve, my little brother was too **excited** to sleep.*
agitated, lively, enthusiastic, exuberant, thrilled, elated, eager, animated
OPPOSITE calm

excitement *noun*
*I could hardly bear the **excitement**!*
suspense, tension, drama, thrill

exciting *adjective*
*The last minutes of the match were the most **exciting** of all!*
dramatic, eventful, thrilling, gripping, sensational, stirring, rousing, stimulating, electrifying
OPPOSITE dull, boring

exclude *verb*
1 *Adults are **excluded** from joining our club.*
ban, bar, prohibit, keep out, banish, reject
2 *She had to **exclude** dairy products from her diet.*
leave out, omit

excuse *noun*
*What is your **excuse** for being so late?*
reason, explanation, defence, justification

excuse *verb*
*I can't **excuse** his bad behaviour.*
forgive, overlook, pardon
OPPOSITE punish

to be excused something
*May I **be excused** swimming?*
be exempt from, be let off, be released from

exercise *noun*
1 ***Exercise** helps to keep you fit.*
physical activity, working out, keep fit, training
2 *Doing **exercises** will improve your guitar playing.*
practice, training, drill

exercise *verb*
1 *If you **exercise** regularly, you will keep fit.*
keep fit, train, exert yourself
2 *I sometimes **exercise** our neighbour's dog.*
take for a walk, take out, walk
3 *We must **exercise** patience.*
show, use, apply, display, employ

exhausted *adjective*
*After a hard race, we lay **exhausted** on the grass.*
tired, weary, worn out, fatigued, breathless, gasping, panting
(*informal*) all in, done in, bushed, zonked

exhausting *adjective*
*Digging the garden is **exhausting** work.*
tiring, demanding, hard, laborious, strenuous, difficult, gruelling, wearisome
OPPOSITE easy

exhibition *noun*
*We went to see an **exhibition** of paintings by Picasso.*
display, show

expand *verb*
*Their computer business is **expanding** rapidly.*
increase, enlarge, extend, build up, develop, make bigger
To become larger is to *grow* or *swell*.
To become wider is to *broaden*, *thicken*, or *widen*.
To become longer is to *extend*, *lengthen*, or *stretch*.
OPPOSITE contract, reduce

expect *verb*
1 *I **expect** that it will rain today.*
anticipate, imagine, forecast, predict, foresee, prophesy
2 *She **expects** me to do everything for her!*
require, want, count on, insist on, demand
3 *I **expect** they missed the bus.*
believe, imagine, guess, suppose, presume, assume, think

expedition *noun*
An expedition into unknown territory is an *exploration*.
An expedition to carry out a special task is a *mission*.
An expedition to find something is a *quest*.
An expedition to worship at a holy place is a *pilgrimage*.
An expedition to see or hunt wild animals is a *safari*.

expel *verb*
1 *A fan **expels** the stale air and fumes.*
send out, force out
2 *He was **expelled** from school.*

dismiss, ban, remove, throw out, send away
To expel someone from their home is to *eject* or *evict* them.
To expel someone from their country is to *banish* or *exile* them.
To expel evil spirits is to *exorcise* them.

experience noun
1 *Have you had any experience of singing in a choir?*
practice, involvement, participation
2 *I had an unusual experience today.*
happening, event, occurrence, incident
An exciting experience is an *adventure*.
An unpleasant experience is an *ordeal*.

expert noun
He's an expert at chess.
specialist, authority, genius, wizard
(*informal*) dab hand, whizz

expert adjective
Only an expert sailor could cross the ocean.
brilliant, capable, clever, competent, experienced, knowledgeable, professional, proficient, qualified, skilful, skilled, specialized, trained
OPPOSITE amateur, unskilful

explain verb
1 *The doctor explained the procedure carefully.*
make clear, give an explanation of, clarify, describe
2 *Can you explain your strange behaviour?*
give reasons for, account for, excuse, make excuses for, justify

explode verb
1 *The firework exploded with a bang.*
blow up, make an explosion, go off, burst, shatter
2 *The slightest movement might explode the bomb.*
detonate, set off

explore verb
1 *The spacecraft will explore the solar system.*
search, survey, travel through, probe
2 *We must explore all the possibilities.*
examine, inspect, investigate, look into, research, analyse, scrutinize

⭐ **WORD WEB**

explorer noun
The explorers were looking for the legendary Lost City.
traveller, voyager, discoverer, wanderer

THINGS AN EXPLORER MIGHT FIND
catacombs, cave, cavern, chest, hieroglyphics, inscription, labyrinth, maze, mummy, parchment, pyramid, riddle, sarcophagus, seal, secret passage, skeleton, stone tablet, temple, tomb, treasure, tunnel, underground chamber

THINGS AN EXPLORER MIGHT USE OR CARRY
binoculars, chart, compass, machete, map, penknife, rope, rucksack, telescope, tent, torch, water bottle

explosion noun
The explosion rattled the windows.
blast, bang
An explosion from a volcano is an *eruption*.
An explosion of laughter is an *outburst*.
The sound of a gun going off is a *report*.

⭐ **WORD WEB**

expression noun
EXPRESSIONS YOU MIGHT SEE ON A FACE
beam, frown, glare, glower, grimace, grin, laugh, leer, long face, poker-face, pout, scowl, smile, smirk, sneer, wide-eyed look, wince, yawn

1 *'Tickled pink' is a colloquial expression.*
phrase, saying, term, wording
An expression that people use too much is a *cliché*.
2 *Did you see her expression when I told her the news?*
look, appearance, countenance, face

extra adjective
1 *There is an extra charge for taking your bike on the train.*
additional, further, added, supplementary, excess
2 *There is extra food in the kitchen if you need it.*
more, spare, surplus, reserve

extraordinary adjective
The astronauts saw many extraordinary sights.
amazing, astonishing, remarkable, outstanding, exceptional, incredible, fantastic, marvellous, miraculous, phenomenal, rare, special, strange, surprising, unheard of, unusual, weird, wonderful, abnormal, curious
OPPOSITE ordinary

extreme adjective
1 *Polar bears can withstand extreme cold.*
great, intense, severe, acute, excessive
2 *She lives on the extreme edge of the town.*
farthest, furthest

Ff

fabric *noun*
*This **fabric** will make a lovely dress for my doll.*
cloth, material, stuff
A plural word is *textiles*.

fabulous *adjective*
1 (*informal*) *We had a **fabulous** time at the party.*
excellent, first-class, marvellous, outstanding, superb, tremendous, wonderful (*informal*) brilliant, fantastic, smashing
2 *Dragons are **fabulous** creatures.*
fictitious, imaginary, legendary, mythical

face *noun*
1 *We saw the anger in the witch's face.*
expression, features, look, countenance
2 *The **face** of the clock had been smashed.*
front
3 *A cube has six **faces**.*
side, surface

face *verb*
1 *Stand and **face** your partner.*
be opposite to, look towards
2 *The astronauts had to **face** many dangers.*
cope with, deal with, face up to, stand up to, tackle, meet, encounter, confront
OPPOSITE avoid

fact *noun*
*It is a **fact** that dodos are now extinct.*
reality, truth, certainty
OPPOSITE fiction

the facts
*The detective considered **the facts** in the case.*
details, particulars, information, data
Facts which are useful in trying to prove something are *evidence*.
Facts expressed as numbers are *statistics*.

factual *adjective*
*Anne Frank wrote a **factual** account of her life during the war.*
real, true, truthful, accurate, authentic, faithful, genuine, objective, reliable

A film or story based on a person's life is *biographical*.
A film or story based on history is *historical*.
A film telling you about real events is a *documentary*.
OPPOSITE made-up, fictional

fade *verb*
1 *Sunlight has **faded** the curtains.*
make paler, bleach, blanch, whiten, dim
OPPOSITE brighten
2 *Those flowers will **fade** in a few days.*
wither, wilt, droop, flag, shrivel
OPPOSITE flourish
3 *Gradually, the light began to **fade**.*
weaken, decline, diminish, dwindle, fail, wane, disappear, melt away, vanish
OPPOSITE increase

fail *verb*
1 *Their plan to steal the crown jewels **failed** miserably.*
be unsuccessful, go wrong, fall through, founder, come to grief, miscarry (*informal*) flop, bomb
OPPOSITE succeed

2 *The rocket engine **failed** before take-off.*
break down, cut out, give up, stop working
3 *By late afternoon, the light had begun to **fail**.*
weaken, decline, diminish, dwindle, fade, get worse, deteriorate
OPPOSITE **improve**
4 *The professor **failed** to warn us of the danger.*
neglect, forget, omit
OPPOSITE **remember**
5 *I hope I don't **fail** my violin exam.*
OPPOSITE **pass**
failure *noun*
1 *The storm caused a power **failure**.*
breakdown, fault, malfuction, crash, loss, collapse, stoppage
2 *Their attempt to reach the North Pole was a **failure**.*
defeat, disappointment, disaster, fiasco
(*informal*) flop, wash-out
OPPOSITE **success**
faint *adjective*
1 *The details in the photograph are very **faint**.*
faded, dim, unclear, indistinct, vague, blurred, hazy, pale, shadowy, misty
OPPOSITE **clear, distinct**
2 *There was a **faint** smell of burning in the air.*
delicate, slight
OPPOSITE **strong**
3 *We heard a **faint** cry for help.*
weak, low, muffled, distant, hushed, muted, soft, thin
OPPOSITE **loud**
4 *Gordon was so hungry that he felt **faint**.*
dizzy, giddy, light-headed, unsteady, weak, exhausted, feeble
(*informal*) woozy
faint *verb*
*The explorers nearly **fainted** from exhaustion.*
become unconscious, collapse, pass out, black out
(*old use*) swoon
fair *adjective*
1 *I think the referee made a **fair** decision.*
just, proper, right, fair-minded, honest, honourable, impartial, unbiased, unprejudiced, disinterested
OPPOSITE **unfair**
2 *The twins both have **fair** hair.*
blond or blonde, light, golden, yellow
OPPOSITE **dark**
3 *Our team has a **fair** chance of winning the cup.*

reasonable, moderate, average, acceptable, adequate, satisfactory, passable, respectable, tolerable
4 *The weather should be **fair** today.*
dry, fine, sunny, bright, clear, cloudless, pleasant, favourable
fair *noun*
1 *My sister won a teddy bear at the **fair**.*
fairground, funfair, carnival, fête, gala
2 *Our school is holding a book **fair** next week.*
show, exhibition, display, market, bazaar
fairly *adverb*
1 *The competition will be judged **fairly**.*
honestly, properly, justly, impartially
2 *The ground is still **fairly** wet. I'm **fairly** certain that we are heading north.*
quite, rather, somewhat, slightly, moderately, up to a point, reasonably, tolerably
(*informal*) pretty

WORD WEB

fairy *noun*
THINGS A FAIRY MIGHT HAVE OR USE
fairy dust, lantern, wand, wings

A FAIRY'S WINGS OR CLOTHES MIGHT BE
diaphonous, feathery, glittering, glowing, gossamer, lustrous, sheer, sparkling, translucent, transparent

PLACES WHERE A FAIRY MIGHT LIVE
dell, glen, magic forest or tree, glade, mound, toadstool

SOME CREATURES LIKE FAIRIES
brownie, elf, imp, leprechaun, nymph, pixie, sprite

---

faithful *adjective*
*My dog, Scruffy, is my **faithful** friend.*
loyal, devoted, reliable, trustworthy, dependable, firm, constant, close
OPPOSITE **unfaithful**
fake *noun*
*That's not a real Roman coin—it's a **fake**.*
copy, imitation, reproduction, replica, forgery
(*informal*) phoney
An event which fakes a real event is a *hoax*, *sham*, or *simulation*.
A person who pretends to be another person is an *impostor*.
fake *verb*
*The spy tried to **fake** a foreign accent.*
imitate, copy, pretend, put on, reproduce, simulate

To fake someone's signature is to *forge* it.
fall *verb*
1 *The acrobat **fell** off a ladder and broke his leg.*
tumble, topple, crash down, pitch, plunge
2 *Snow was beginning to **fall** quite thickly.*
drop, come down, descend, rain down, plummet
3 *The level of the river had **fallen** since March.*
go down, subside, recede, sink, ebb
4 *The temperature in the cave **fell** to below freezing.*
go down, become lower, decrease, decline, lessen, diminish, dwindle
to fall in
*The roof of the cabin **fell in** during the storm.*
cave in, collapse, give way
to fall out
*The twins are always **falling out** with each other.*
argue, disagree, quarrel, squabble, bicker
fall *noun*
1 *Ellen had a **fall** and cut her knee.*
tumble
2 *We noticed a sharp **fall** in the temperature.*
drop, lowering
OPPOSITE **rise**
3 *There has been a **fall** in the price of coffee.*
decrease, reduction, decline
OPPOSITE **increase**
4 *This is a story about the **fall** of Troy.*
defeat, surrender
false *adjective*
1 *They gave us **false** information about the treasure.*
wrong, incorrect, untrue, inaccurate, mistaken, erroneous, faulty, invalid, misleading, deceptive
OPPOSITE **correct**
2 *The spy was travelling with a **false** passport.*
fake, bogus, sham, counterfeit, forged
OPPOSITE **genuine, authentic**
3 *Mrs Gummidge put in her **false** teeth.*
artificial, imitation
OPPOSITE **real, natural**
4 *The Black Knight turned out to be a **false** ally.*
unfaithful, disloyal, unreliable, untrustworthy, deceitful, dishonest, treacherous
OPPOSITE **faithful, loyal**
familiar *adjective*
1 *Seagulls are a **familiar** sight on the beach.*

common, everyday, normal, ordinary, usual, regular, customary, frequent, mundane, routine
OPPOSITE rare
2 *It seems a bit **familiar** to call her by her first name.*
informal, friendly, intimate, relaxed, close
OPPOSITE formal, unfriendly
to be familiar with something
*Are you **familiar with** the rules of chess?*
be acquainted with, be aware of, know

WORD WEB

family *noun*
*Some members of my **family** live in New Zealand.*
relations, relatives
An old-fashioned term for your family is your *kin*.
The official term for your closest relative is *next of kin*.
A group of related Scottish families is a *clan*.
A succession of people from the same powerful family is a *dynasty*.
In certain societies, a group of families living together is a *tribe*.
A single stage in a family is a *generation*.
The line of ancestors from which a family is descended is its *ancestry*.
A diagram showing how people in your family are related is a *family tree*.
The study of family history is *genealogy*.
A family of young birds is a *brood*.
A family of kittens or puppies is a *litter*.

MEMBERS OF A FAMILY MAY INCLUDE
adopted child, aunt, brother, child, cousin, daughter, father, foster-child, foster-parent, grandchild, grandparent, guardian, husband, mother, nephew, niece, parent, sister, son, spouse, step-child, step-parent, uncle, ward, wife

family

famous *adjective*
*Pele is a very **famous** football player.*
well-known, celebrated, renowned, acclaimed, notable, prominent, distinguished, eminent
To be famous for doing something bad is to be *notorious*.
OPPOSITE unknown, obscure
fan *noun*
*I used to be a **fan** of jazz music.*
enthusiast, admirer, devotee, follower, supporter
fanatic *noun*
*My brother is a rugby **fanatic**.*
enthusiast, addict, devotee (*informal*) freak, nut
fancy *adjective*
*Alice bought a **fancy** hat for her friend's wedding.*
elaborate, decorative, ornamental, ornate
OPPOSITE plain
fancy *verb*
1 *What do you **fancy** to eat?*
feel like, want, wish for, desire, prefer
2 *I **fancied** I heard a noise downstairs.*
imagine, think, believe, suppose
fantastic *adjective*
1 *The story is full of **fantastic** creatures.*
fanciful, extraordinary, strange, odd, weird, outlandish, far-fetched, incredible, imaginative
OPPOSITE realistic
2 (*informal*) *We had a **fantastic** time at camp.*
excellent, first-class, outstanding, superb, wonderful, tremendous, marvellous (*informal*) brilliant, fabulous, smashing
fantasy *noun*
*Rosie had a **fantasy** about being a mermaid.*
dream, daydream, delusion, fancy
far *adjective*
1 *The castle stood in the **far** north of the country.*
distant, faraway, remote
2 *The ferry took us to the **far** side of the river.*
opposite, other

WORD WEB

farm *noun*
The formal word for farming is *agriculture*.
A farm which uses no artificial fertilizers or chemicals is an *organic farm*.
A very small farm is a *smallholding*.
A small farm growing fruit and vegetables is a *market garden*.
A small farm in Scotland is a *croft*.
A large cattle farm in America is a *ranch*.

combine harvester

fascinate *verb*
*We were **fascinated** by the inventor's workshop.*
interest (in), engross, captivate, enthrall, absorb, beguile, entrance, attract, charm, enchant, delight
OPPOSITE bore
fashion *noun*
1 *The Martians behaved in a peculiar **fashion**.*
way, manner
2 *Zoe dresses according to the latest **fashion**.*
trend, vogue, craze, fad, style, look

FARM BUILDINGS
barn, byre or cowshed, dairy, farmhouse, granary, milking parlour, outhouse, pigsty, stable

OTHER PARTS OF A FARM
barnyard or farmyard, cattle pen, fields, haystack, meadow, paddock, pasture, rick, sheep fold, silo

ITEMS OF FARM EQUIPMENT
baler, combine harvester, cultivator, drill, harrow, harvester, mower, planter, plough, tractor, trailer

PEOPLE WHO WORK ON A FARM
agricultural worker, (old use) dairymaid, farmer, farm labourer, ploughman, shepherd, stockbreeder, tractor driver

SOME FARM ANIMALS
bull, bullock, chicken or hen, cow, duck, goat, goose, horse, pig, sheep, turkey

Birds kept on a farm are *poultry*. Animals kept for milk or beef are *cattle*. Farm animals in general are *livestock*.

Birds kept on a farm are *poultry*. Animals kept for milk or beef are *cattle*. Farm animals in general are *livestock*.

tractor

fashionable *adjective*
Megan has a fashionable new hairstyle.
stylish, chic, up-to-date, popular, elegant, smart
(*informal*) trendy, hip, in
OPPOSITE unfashionable, out-of-date

fast *adjective*
The robber made a fast exit when he heard us coming.
quick, rapid, speedy, swift, brisk, hurried, hasty, high-speed, headlong, breakneck
(*informal*) nippy
Something which goes faster than sound is *supersonic*.
A common simile is *as fast as lightning*.
OPPOSITE slow, unhurried

fast *adverb*
1 *Mr Toad was driving too fast in his motor car.*
quickly, speedily, swiftly, rapidly, briskly
2 *The boat was stuck fast on the rocks.*
firmly, securely, tightly
3 *Be quiet! The baby is fast asleep.*
deeply, sound, completely

fasten *verb*
1 *They fastened their ropes to the rock face.*
tie, fix, attach, connect, join, link, bind, hitch, clamp, pin, clip, tack, stick
To fasten a boat is to *anchor* or *moor* it.
To fasten an animal is to *tether* it.
2 *They fastened the gate with a heavy chain.*
secure, seal, lock, bolt, make fast

fat *adjective*
1 *You'll get fat if you eat too many crisps!*
overweight, obese, chubby, plump, podgy, dumpy, flabby, portly, stout, round, rotund
2 *The witch opened a big, fat book of spells.*
thick, bulky, chunky, weighty, substantial
OPPOSITE thin

fatal *adjective*
1 *The knight delivered a fatal wound to his enemy.*
deadly, lethal, mortal
A fatal illness is an *incurable* or *terminal* illness.
2 *Leaving the door unlocked was a fatal mistake.*
disastrous, catastrophic, dreadful, calamitous

fate *noun*
1 *The shipwrecked crew were in the hands of fate.*
fortune, destiny, providence, chance, luck
2 *The prisoner met with a terrible fate.*
death, end

fault *noun*
1 *This DVD has a fault in it.*
defect, flaw, malfunction, snag, problem, weakness
2 *It was my fault that we missed our bus.*
responsibility, liability

faulty *adjective*
The TV was faulty, so we took it back to the shop.
broken, not working, defective, out of order, unusable, damaged
OPPOSITE perfect

favour *noun*
1 *I asked my friend to do me a favour.*
good deed, good turn, kindness, service, courtesy
2 *The captain's plan found favour with most of the crew.*
approval, support, liking, goodwill

to be in favour of something
We're all in favour of longer holidays.
agree to, approve of, support, like the idea of

favourite *adjective*
What is your favourite book?
best-loved, preferred, treasured, dearest, special, top

fear *noun*
When Garth heard the monster, he trembled with fear.
fright, terror, horror, alarm, panic, dread, anxiety, apprehension, trepidation
A formal word for a special type of fear is *phobia*.
A fear of open spaces is *agoraphobia*.
A fear of spiders is *arachnophobia*.
A fear of enclosed spaces is *claustrophobia*.
A fear or dislike of foreigners is *xenophobia*.
OPPOSITE courage

fear *verb*
1 *My sister fears snakes and spiders.*
be frightened of, be afraid of, be scared of, dread
2 *I fear we may be too late.*
suspect, expect, anticipate

fearless *adjective*
The fearless explorers entered the dark cave.
brave, courageous, daring, heroic, valiant, intrepid, plucky
OPPOSITE cowardly

feast *noun*
The king held a great feast to celebrate his birthday.
banquet, dinner, (*informal*) spread

feat *noun*
The trapeze artists performed many daring feats.
act, action, deed, exploit, achievement, performance

feather *noun*
A large feather is a *plume*.
All the feathers on a bird are its *plumage*.
Soft, fluffy feathers are *down*.
A feather used as a pen is a *quill*.

feature *noun*
1 *The room has several unusual features.*
characteristic, detail, point, aspect, quality, peculiarity, trait, facet
A person's features are their *face*.

2 *There was a feature about our school in the newspaper.*
article, report, story, item, piece

feeble *adjective*
1 *The elderly knight looked tired and feeble.*
weak, frail, infirm, delicate, poorly, sickly, puny, weary, weedy
OPPOSITE strong, powerful
2 *I made a feeble attempt to stop the ball. Do you expect me to believe that feeble excuse?*
weak, poor, ineffective, inadequate, unconvincing, tame, flimsy, lame

feed *verb*
We have enough sandwiches to feed six people.
provide for, cater for, give food to, nourish
to feed on
The leopard was feeding on its prey.
eat, consume, devour

feel *verb*
1 *I felt the llama's soft, woolly fur.*
touch, caress, stroke, fondle
2 *It feels colder today.*
appear, seem, strike you as
3 *Older people tend to feel the cold.*
notice, be aware of, be conscious of, experience, suffer from
4 *I feel that it's time we made a start.*
think, believe, consider
to feel like
Do you feel like going for a walk?
fancy, want, wish for, desire

feel *noun*
I love the feel of warm sand between my toes.
feeling, sensation, touch

feeling *noun*
1 *The cat had lost all feeling in its paw.*
sense of touch, sensation, sensitivity
2 *I didn't mean to hurt your feelings.*
emotion, passion, sentiment
3 *I have a feeling that something is wrong.*
suspicion, notion, inkling, hunch, idea, impression, fancy, intuition

fence *noun*
The mansion was surrounded by a tall fence.
railing, barrier, wall, paling, stockade, hedge

ferocious *adjective*
The mansion was guarded by a ferocious dog.
fierce, fearsome, savage, wild, vicious, violent, bloodthirsty, brutal
OPPOSITE tame

fertile *adjective*
The surrounding countryside was green and fertile.
fruitful, productive, rich, fecund
OPPOSITE barren, sterile

festival *noun*
The town holds a festival every summer.
carnival, fiesta, fête, gala, fair, celebration, jamboree
A celebration of a special anniversary is a *jubilee*.

fetch *verb*
1 *I fetched the shopping from the car.*
get, bring, carry, collect, transfer, transport, convey, pick up, retrieve, obtain
2 *If we sell our car, how much will it fetch?*
make, raise, sell for, go for, bring in, earn

feud *noun*
There has been a feud between our families for years.
quarrel, dispute, conflict, hostility, enmity, rivalry, strife, antagonism
A feud that lasts a long time is a *vendetta*.

feverish *adjective*
1 *I felt feverish with the cold.*
When you are feverish you are *hot* and *shivery*.
With a bad fever you may become *delirious*.
2 *There was feverish activity in the kitchen.*

frenzied, frantic, frenetic, excited, agitated, hectic, busy, hurried, impatient, restless

fictional *adjective*
Harry Potter is a fictional character.
imaginary, made-up, invented, fanciful
OPPOSITE factual, real

fiddle *verb*
1 *Who's been fiddling with the DVD player?*
tinker, meddle, tamper, play about, mess about, twiddle
2 *(informal) Mr Filch had been fiddling the bank account for years.*
falsify, alter, rig
(informal) cook the books

fidget *verb*
I begin to fidget when I'm bored.
be restless, fiddle about, play about, mess about

field *noun*
1 *Cattle were grazing in the field.*
meadow, pasture
A small field for horses is a **paddock**.
An area of grass in a village is a **green**.
2 *The field is too wet to play football.*
ground, pitch, playing field
3 *Electronics is not my field.*
special interest, speciality, area of study

fierce *adjective*
1 *The travellers were killed in a fierce attack by armed bandits.*
vicious, ferocious, savage, brutal, violent, wild, cruel, merciless, ruthless, pitiless
2 *Our team will face fierce opposition in the final.*
strong, keen, eager, aggressive, competitive, passionate, relentless
3 *The explorers braved the fierce heat of the desert sun.*
blazing, intense, raging

fiery *adjective*
1 *It's best to avoid the fiery heat of the midday sun.*
blazing, burning, hot, intense, fierce, raging, flaming, red-hot, glowing
2 *My great aunt has always had a fiery temper.*
violent, passionate, excitable, angry, furious

fight *noun*
1 *The warriors faced each other for a fight to the death.*
Fighting is **combat** or **hostilities**.
A fight between armies is a **battle**.
A minor unplanned battle is a **skirmish**.
A series of battles is a **campaign**

or *war*.
A minor fight is a *brawl*, *scrap*, *scuffle*, or *tussle*.
A fight arranged between two people is a *duel*.
2 *We support the fight to save the rainforest.*
campaign, crusade, struggle

fight *verb*
1 *Two seagulls were fighting over a scrap of bread.*
have a fight, scrap, scuffle, exchange blows, come to blows
2 *The two countries fought each other in the war.*
do battle with, wage war with, attack
Fighting with swords is *fencing*.
Fighting with fists is *boxing*.
Fighting in which you try to throw your opponent to the ground is *wrestling*.
Fighting sports such as karate and judo are *martial arts*.
3 *We will fight the decision to close our local library.*
protest against, oppose, resist, make a stand against, campaign against

figure *noun*
1 *Please write the figure '8' on the board.*
number, numeral, digit, integer
2 *Ballet dancers need to have a good figure.*
body, build, form, shape
3 *Inside the temple were several clay figures.*
statue, carving, sculpture

figure *verb*
Donald Duck figures in many cartoons.
appear, feature, take part
to figure out
We couldn't figure out what the riddle meant.
work out, make out, understand, see

fill *verb*
1 *Dad filled the trolley with shopping.*
load, pack, stuff, cram, top up
To fill a tyre with air is to *inflate* it.
OPPOSITE empty

2 *What can I use to fill this hole?*
close up, plug, seal, block up, stop up
3 *Sightseers filled the streets.*
crowd, jam, block, obstruct
(informal) bung up

film *noun*
1 *There is a good film on TV tonight.*
movie, picture, video, DVD
A long film is a *feature film*.
A short excerpt from a film is a *clip*.
A script for a film is a *screenplay* and a writer of screenplays is a *screenwriter*.
A well-known film actor is a *film star*.
A theatre where films are shown is a *cinema*, *picture house*, or *(American) movie theatre*.
2 *There was a film of oil on the water.*
coat, coating, layer, covering, sheet, skin
A large patch of oil floating on water is a *slick*.

filthy *adjective*
Those trainers are filthy!
dirty, mucky, messy, grimy, grubby, muddy, soiled, stained
OPPOSITE clean

final *adjective*
1 *The final moments of the match were very tense.*
last, closing, concluding
OPPOSITE opening
2 *What was the final result?*
eventual, ultimate

finally *adverb*
I've finally managed to finish my book.
eventually, at last, in the end

find *verb*
1 *Did you find any fossils on the beach?*
come across, discover, see, spot, locate, encounter, stumble across, unearth
2 *The children never found the secret door again.*
trace, track down, recover, retrieve
OPPOSITE lose
3 *Did the doctor find what was wrong?*
detect, identify, diagnose, ascertain
4 *You will find that building a tree house is hard work.*
become aware, realize, learn, recognize, notice, observe

fine *adjective*
1 *The young musicians gave a fine performance.*
excellent, first-class, superb, splendid, admirable, commendable, good
OPPOSITE bad

2 *As the weather was **fine**, we took a picnic.*
sunny, fair, bright, clear, cloudless, pleasant
OPPOSITE dull
3 *Spiders spin very **fine** thread for their webs.*
delicate, fragile, thin, flimsy, slender, slim
OPPOSITE thick
4 *The desert dunes were made of **fine** sand.*
dusty, powdery
OPPOSITE coarse

finish *verb*
1 *When are you likely to **finish** your homework?*
complete, reach the end of, cease, round off
2 *The film should **finish** around nine o'clock.*
end, stop, conclude, terminate
(*informal*) wind up
3 *I've already **finished** my bag of crisps.*
consume, use up, get through, exhaust
(*informal*) polish off
OPPOSITE start

finish *noun*
*We stayed to watch the parade until the **finish**.*
end, close, conclusion, completion, result, termination
OPPOSITE start

fire *noun*
*The campers toasted marshmallows in the **fire**.*
blaze, flames, burning, combustion
*A very big hot fire is an **inferno**.*
*An open fire out of doors is a **bonfire**.*
*An enclosed fire which produces great heat is a **furnace**.*
*An enclosed fire for cooking food is an **oven**.*
*An enclosed fire for making pottery is a **kiln**.*
*A team of people whose job is to put out fires is a **fire brigade**.*
*A member of a fire brigade is a **firefighter**.*

fire *verb*
1 *The soldier aimed his rifle and **fired** two shots.*
shoot, discharge, let off, set off
*To fire a missile is to **launch** it.*
2 (*informal*) *Miss Stark **fired** her assistant for being late for work.*
dismiss, sack

firm *noun*
*Mr Perkins owns a **firm** that makes biscuits.*
company, business, organization, enterprise

firm *adjective*
1 *The surface of the planet was dry and **firm**.*

hard, solid, dense, compact, rigid, set
OPPOSITE soft
2 *Make sure the knots in the rope are **firm**.*
secure, tight, strong, stable, fixed, sturdy, steady
3 *Zelda had a **firm** belief in the power of magic.*
definite, certain, sure, decided, determined, resolute, unshakeable, unwavering
OPPOSITE unsure
4 *The two girls have become **firm** friends.*
close, devoted, faithful, loyal, constant, dependable, reliable

first *adjective*
1 *The **first** inhabitants of the area were Picts.*
earliest, original
2 *The **first** thing to do in an emergency is to keep calm.*
principal, key, main, fundamental, basic, chief

fit *adjective*
1 *Cinderella's gown was **fit** for a princess.*
suitable, appropriate, fitting, right, good enough, worthy (of)
OPPOSITE unsuitable
2 *I walk to school every day to keep **fit**.*
healthy, well, strong, robust
(*old use*) hale and hearty
*A common simile is **as fit as a fiddle**.*
OPPOSITE unhealthy
3 *After a long ride, the horses were **fit** to collapse.*
ready, liable, likely, about

fit *verb*
1 *We need to **fit** a new lock on the door.*
install, put in place, position
2 *This key doesn't **fit** the lock. He **fits** the description of the wanted criminal.*
match, correspond to, go together with, tally with
3 *Her speech perfectly **fitted** the occasion.*
be suitable for, be appropriate to, suit

fix *verb*
1 *The soldier **fixed** a bayonet to the end of his rifle.*
fasten, attach, connect, join, link
2 *We **fixed** the tent poles in the ground.*
set, secure, make firm, stabilize
3 *Let's **fix** a time for the party.*
decide on, agree on, set, arrange, settle, determine, specify, finalize
4 (*informal*) *Dad says he can **fix** my bike.*
repair, mend, sort, put right

fix *noun*
(*informal*) *Can you help me? I'm in a **fix**.*
difficulty, mess, predicament, plight
(*informal*) jam, hole

fizzy *adjective*
*Could I have a bottle of **fizzy** water, please?*
sparkling, bubbly, effervescent, gassy, foaming
OPPOSITE still

flag *noun*
*The street was decorated with **flags** for the carnival.*
banner, pennant, streamer
*The flag of a regiment is its **colours** or **standard**.*
*A flag flown on a ship is an **ensign**.*
*Decorative strips of small flags are **bunting**.*

flap *verb*
*The sail **flapped** in the wind.*
flutter, sway, swing, wave about, thrash about

flash *verb*
*We saw a light **flash** from an upstairs window.*
shine, beam, blaze, flare, glare, gleam, glint, flicker, glimmer, sparkle

flash *noun*
*There were **flashes** of lightning in the sky.*
blaze, flare, beam, ray, shaft, burst, gleam, glint, flicker, glimmer, sparkle

flat *adjective*
1 *You need a **flat** surface to write on.*
even, level, smooth, plane
*A common simile is **as flat as a pancake**.*
OPPOSITE uneven
2 *I lay **flat** on the ground.*
horizontal, outstretched, spread out
*To be lying face downwards is to be **prone**.*
*To be lying face upwards is to be **supine**.*
OPPOSITE upright
3 *The robot spoke in a **flat**, electronic voice.*
dull, boring, lifeless, uninteresting, monotonous, tedious
OPPOSITE lively
4 *The front tyre of my bike was **flat**.*
deflated, punctured
OPPOSITE inflated
5 *Our request met with a **flat** refusal.*
outright, straight, positive, absolute, total, utter, point-blank

flatten *verb*
1 *We flattened the crumpled map on the desk.*
smooth, press, roll out, iron out
2 *The earthquake flattened several buildings.*
demolish, destroy, knock down, pull down, level
3 *The young plants were flattened by the rain.*
squash, crush, trample

flavour *noun*
1 *I don't like the flavour of raw onions.*
taste, tang
2 *Which flavour of ice cream do you like best?*
kind, sort, variety

flexible *adjective*
1 *I need a pair of trainers with flexible soles.*
bendable, supple, pliable, bendy, elastic, springy
OPPOSITE rigid, inflexible
2 *My working hours are very flexible.*
adjustable, adaptable, variable, open
OPPOSITE fixed

flicker *verb*
The candlelight flickered in the draught.
twinkle, glimmer, waver, flutter, blink, shimmer

flimsy *adjective*
1 *The kite was so flimsy that it broke apart.*
fragile, delicate, frail, brittle, weak, wobbly, shaky, rickety
OPPOSITE sturdy, robust
2 *The fairy wore a dress of the flimsiest silk.*
thin, fine, light, lightweight, floaty

flinch *verb*
He flinched as an arrow flew past his head.
back off, draw back, falter, recoil, shrink back, start, wince

fling *verb*
I flung a stone into the pond.
throw, cast, sling, toss, hurl, pitch
(*informal*) chuck, bung

float *verb*
We watched the twigs float gently down the river.
sail, drift, glide, slip, slide, waft

flood *noun*
1 *The flood of water swept away the bridge.*
deluge, inundation, rush, torrent, spate
2 *The restaurant has received a flood of complaints.*
succession, barrage, storm, volley

flood *verb*
1 *The river burst its banks and flooded the valley.*

flood

drown, swamp, inundate, submerge, immerse, engulf
2 *We have been flooded with entries for our competition.*
overwhelm, swamp, besiege

flop *verb*
1 *I was so tired that I just flopped onto my bed.*
collapse, drop, fall, slump
2 *The plants will flop if you don't water them.*
dangle, droop, hang down, sag, wilt
3 (*informal*) *The first film flopped, but the sequel was a big hit.*
be unsuccessful, fail, founder, fall flat

floppy *adjective*
The dog had long, floppy ears.
droopy, limp, saggy, soft
OPPOSITE stiff, rigid

flow *verb*
The rain water flowed along the gutter.
run, stream, pour, glide
To flow slowly is to *dribble*, *drip*, *ooze*, *seep*, or *trickle*.
To flow fast is to *cascade*, *gush*, or *sweep*.
To flow with sudden force is to *spurt* or *squirt*.
To flow over the edge of something is to *overflow* or *spill*.
When blood flows from a wound, it *bleeds*.
When the tide flows out, it *ebbs*.

flow *noun*
1 *It's hard work rowing against the flow.*
current, tide, drift
2 *There was a steady flow of water into the pond.*
stream, flood, cascade, gush, rush, spate

fluffy *adjective*
Four fluffy ducklings were swimming in the pond.
feathery, downy, furry, fuzzy, hairy, woolly, shaggy, soft

flush *verb*
Rory flushed with embarrassment.
blush, go red, colour, redden, burn

flustered *adjective*
I get flustered when I have to read in assembly.

confused, upset, bothered, agitated, unsettled, ruffled
(*informal*) rattled
OPPOSITE calm

flutter *verb*
A moth fluttered about the light bulb.
flap, beat, flicker, quiver, tremble, vibrate

foam *noun*
The bath water was covered with pinkish foam.
bubbles, froth, suds, lather
Foam made by sea water is *surf* or *spume*.

foam *verb*
The mixture in the cauldron foamed and gurgled.
froth, bubble, fizz, boil, seethe, ferment, lather

fog *noun*
The top of the mountain was covered with fog.
Thin fog is *haze* or *mist*.
A thick mixture of fog and smoke is *smog*.

fold *verb*
Fold the paper along the dotted line.
bend, double over, crease, pleat

fold *noun*
She smoothed the soft folds of her dress.
crease, furrow, layer
A fold which is pressed into a garment is a *pleat*.

follow *verb*
1 *Why does thunder always follow lightning?*
come after, succeed, replace
OPPOSITE precede
2 *I think that car is following us!*
go after, chase, pursue, track, trail, tail, stalk, hunt, shadow
3 *Follow this path until you reach the river.*
go along, keep to
4 *I followed the instructions on the packet.*
carry out, comply with, heed, obey, observe
5 *Which football team do you follow?*
be a fan of, support
6 *We found it hard to follow what the creature was saying.*

understand, comprehend, grasp, take in, catch

fond *adjective*
1 *Mrs Walker gave her pet poodle a* **fond** *kiss.*
loving, tender, affectionate
2 *Anna had a* **fond** *hope that she would become a film star.*
foolish, silly, unrealistic, fanciful

to be fond of
I'm very **fond of** *chocolate cake.*
be keen on, be partial to, like, love

fool *noun*
Only a **fool** *would believe that ridiculous story.*
idiot, dope, ass, clown, halfwit, dimwit, dunce, simpleton, blockhead, buffoon, clot, dunderhead, imbecile, moron (*informal*) twit, chump, nitwit, nincompoop

fool *verb*
The spy **fooled** *everyone with his disguises.*
deceive, trick, mislead, hoax, dupe, hoodwink
(*informal*) con, kid, have you on, take you in, pull the wool over your eyes

to fool about or **around**
We were told not to **fool about** *in the swimming pool.*
play about, mess about, misbehave

foolish *adjective*
It would be **foolish** *to stand too close to the lions.*
stupid, silly, idiotic, senseless, ridiculous, nonsensical, unwise, ill-advised, half-witted, unintelligent, absurd, crazy, mad, hare-brained
(*informal*) daft
OPPOSITE sensible

foot *noun*
1 *Rhona walked on the sand in her bare* **feet**.
The foot of an animal that has claws is a *paw*.
The foot of a cow, deer, or horse is a *hoof*.
A pig's foot is a *trotter*.
A bird's feet are its *claws*.
The feet of a bird of prey are its *talons*.
2 *We set up camp at the* **foot** *of the mountain.*
base, bottom

WORD WEB

food *noun*
The banquet table was laid out with all kinds of **food**.
foodstuffs, rations, provisions, refreshments, eatables, nourishment, nutrition (*informal*) grub, nosh
The food that you normally eat or choose to eat is your *diet*.
A diet which includes no meat is a *vegetarian* diet.
A diet which includes no animal products is a *vegan* diet.
Food which includes fish or shellfish is *seafood*.
Foods made from milk, butter, cheese, or eggs are *dairy foods*.
Food for farm animals is *fodder*.

FOODS MADE FROM FLOUR OR CEREALS
batter, biscuits, bread, bun, cornflakes, cracker, crispbread, muesli, noodles, oatcake, pancake, pastry, popcorn, porridge, ricecake, roll, scone, toast

SOME PREPARED DISHES OF FOOD
balti, bhaji, broth, casserole, chilli, chips, chop suey, chow mein, curry, dhal, fritters, goulash, houmous, hotpot, omelette, pakora, panini, pasta, pie, pizza, quiche, samosa, sandwich, soufflé, soup, stew, stir-fry, sushi

SOME PUDDINGS AND OTHER SWEET FOODS
brownie, cake, chocolate, flan, gateau, honey, jam, jelly, marmalade, marzipan, meringue, mousse, muffin, sponge, steamed pudding, sugar, tart, treacle, trifle

SOME FLAVOURINGS AND SAUCES FOR FOOD
chilli, chutney, French dressing, garlic, gravy, herbs, ketchup, mayonnaise, mustard, pepper, pickle, salsa, salt, spice, vinegar

Things like salt and pepper which you add to food are *condiments* or *seasoning*.

SOME TYPES OF SEAFOOD
bloater, bream, caviare, cod, crab, eel, haddock, halibut, herring, kipper, lobster, mackerel, monkfish, mussels, oysters, pilchard, plaice, prawn, salmon, sardine, scampi, sea bass, shrimp, sole, sprat, trout, tuna, whelks, whitebait, whiting

SOME DAIRY FOODS
butter, cheese, cream, curds, custard, eggs, ice cream, milk, yoghurt

---

WORD WEB

football *noun*
Football is also known as *soccer*.
Someone who plays football is a *footballer*.
Football is played on a *field* or *pitch* in a *ground*, *park*, or *stadium*.

MEMBERS OF A FOOTBALL TEAM
captain, defender, fullback, forward, goalkeeper or (*informal*) goalie, midfielder, striker, substitute, sweeper, winger

referee

forbidden *adjective*
*Skateboarding is **forbidden** in the playground.*
banned, barred, prohibited, disallowed, outlawed
OPPOSITE **allowed**

force *noun*
1 *The firefighters had to use **force** to open the door.*
strength, power, might, muscle, vigour, effort, energy
2 *The **force** of the explosion broke all the windows.*
impact, effect, shock, intensity
3 *The soldiers are part of a peace-keeping **force**.*
group, unit, team, corps, army, troops

force *verb*
1 *The slaves were **forced** to work in the mines.*
compel, make, order, require, oblige, pressurize, coerce
2 *The king **forced** a new law upon the country.*
impose, inflict
3 *The firefighters had to **force** the door.*
break open, burst open, prise open, smash, wrench
(*informal*) yank

foreign *adjective*
1 *Lots of **foreign** tourists visit Edinburgh in the summer.*
overseas, international
OPPOSITE **native, domestic**
2 *I like travelling to **foreign** countries.*
overseas, distant, faraway, exotic, remote, far-flung

forever *adverb*
*Timmy is **forever** complaining about something.*
constantly, continually, always, perpetually

forgery *noun*
*One of these paintings is a **forgery**.*
fake, copy, imitation, reproduction, replica
(*informal*) phoney

forget *verb*
1 *I **forgot** my toothbrush when I packed my suitcase.*
leave out, leave behind, overlook
2 *I **forgot** to switch off the computer.*
omit, neglect, fail

forgive *verb*
*Please **forgive** me for being so rude.*
excuse, pardon, let off, overlook, spare

form *noun*
1 *I made out the **form** of a man through the mist.*
shape, figure, outline, silhouette
2 *Ice is a **form** of water.*
kind, sort, type, variety
3 *My brother moves up into a higher **form** next term.*
class, year, grade, set

form *verb*
1 *The sculptor **formed** the clay into the shape of a bird.*
shape, mould, model, fashion, work, cast
2 *My friends and I have **formed** a chess club.*
set up, establish, found, create, start
3 *Icicles had **formed** on the roof of the cave.*
appear, develop, grow, emerge, take shape

formal *adjective*
1 *I was invited to the **formal** opening of the museum.*
official, ceremonial
2 *The letter was written in a very **formal** style.*
correct, proper, conventional, dignified, solemn
OPPOSITE **informal, casual**

fortune *noun*
1 *By good **fortune**, I stumbled across a secret doorway.*
chance, luck, accident, fate
2 *The millionairess left her **fortune** to charity.*
wealth, riches, possessions, property, assets, estate
(*informal*) millions

foul *adjective*
1 *The knight fainted at the **foul** smell of the dragon's breath.*
disgusting, revolting, repulsive, rotten, stinking, offensive, unpleasant, loathsome, nasty, horrible, vile
OPPOSITE **pleasant**
2 *The walls and floor of the dungeon were **foul**.*
dirty, unclean, filthy, mucky, messy
OPPOSITE **clean, pure**
3 *The player was sent off for using **foul** language.*
rude, offensive, insulting, abusive, improper, indecent, obscene

fragile *adjective*
*Fossil dinosaur bones are very **fragile**.*
breakable, delicate, frail, brittle, easily damaged, weak
OPPOSITE **strong**

footballer

SOME MOVES A FOOTBALLER MIGHT MAKE
chip, dribble, dummy, header, kick, mazy run, miss, pass, score, shot, tackle, volley

SOME OTHER TERMS USED IN FOOTBALL
corner, crossbar, deflection, dugout, equalizer, extra time, final whistle, foul, free kick, goal, goalposts, half-time, kick-off, net, offside, penalty, penalty shootout, red or yellow card, sending off, throw-in

OTHER PEOPLE INVOLVED IN FOOTBALL
ballboy or ballgirl, coach, linesman, manager, referee

boots

corner flag

football

frail *adjective*
1 *My grandad felt frail after his illness.*
weak, infirm, feeble
2 *That step-ladder looks a bit frail.*
flimsy, fragile, delicate, rickety, unsound
OPPOSITE strong, robust

frantic *adjective*
1 *I was frantic with worry when our kitten got lost.*
beside yourself, fraught, desperate, distraught, hysterical, worked up, berserk
2 *There was frantic activity on the day of the wedding.*
excited, hectic, frenzied, feverish, wild, mad

fraud *noun*
1 *The bank manager was found guilty of fraud.*
deceit, deception, dishonesty, swindling, cheating
2 *The prize draw was just a fraud—no-one won anything.*
swindle, trick, hoax, pretence, sham
(*informal*) con, scam
(*informal*) con man, phoney

free *adjective*
1 *You are free to wander anywhere in the building.*
able, allowed, permitted, at liberty
OPPOSITE restricted
2 *After ten years in jail, the prisoners were free at last.*
freed, liberated, emancipated, at large, on the loose
A common simile is *as free as a bird*.
OPPOSITE imprisoned, enslaved
3 *I got a free drink with my sandwich.*
complimentary, free of charge, gratis, on the house
4 *Are you free this weekend?*
available, unoccupied
OPPOSITE busy, occupied
5 *The bathroom is free now.*
available, unoccupied, vacant, empty
OPPOSITE engaged

free *verb*
1 *The soldiers freed the prisoners of war.*
release, liberate, set free, deliver
To free slaves is to *emancipate* them.
To free prisoners by paying money to the captors is to *ransom* them.
OPPOSITE imprison
2 *We freed the dogs and let them run about.*
loose, turn loose, let go, untie, unchain
OPPOSITE confine

freedom *noun*
The animals have a lot of freedom in the safari park.
liberty, independence

freeze *verb*
1 *Water begins to freeze at 0°C.*
become ice, ice over, harden, solidify
2 *If you freeze food, you can store it for a long time.*
deep-freeze, chill, refrigerate

freezing *adjective*
It's freezing cold outside in winter.
chilly, frosty, icy, wintry, raw, bitter

frequent *adjective*
1 *I send frequent email messages to my friends.*
numerous, constant, continual, recurring, recurrent, repeated, countless
OPPOSITE infrequent
2 *Badgers are frequent visitors to the garden.*
regular, habitual, common, familiar, persistent
OPPOSITE rare

fresh *adjective*
1 *This pudding is made with fresh fruit.*
natural, raw, unprocessed
2 *The shop bakes fresh bread every day.*
new
OPPOSITE old, stale
3 *Sally went outside to get some fresh air.*
clean, cool, crisp, refreshing
OPPOSITE stuffy
4 *Have you put fresh sheets on the bed?*
new, clean, laundered, washed
OPPOSITE dirty
5 *Having a shower makes me feel nice and fresh.*
refreshed, revived, restored, invigorated
6 *We need some fresh ideas for our magazine.*
new, original, different, novel, innovative
OPPOSITE old

friend *noun*
I am inviting four friends to my birthday party.
companion, comrade
(*informal*) mate, pal, buddy, chum
A friend you play games with is a *playmate*.
A friend you work with or live with is your *partner*.
A friend you write to but don't normally meet is a *penfriend*.
A friend you know only slightly is an *acquaintance*.

OPPOSITE enemy

friendly *adjective*
1 *Our neighbour's pet dog is very friendly.*
affectionate, loving, good-natured, likeable, amiable, approachable, kind-hearted, kindly, amicable, genial, sociable, outgoing, sympathetic
2 *Those two are very friendly with each other.*
close, familiar, intimate
(*informal*) pally, chummy
3 *I like this cafe—it has a very friendly atmosphere.*
warm, welcoming, hospitable, cordial, neighbourly

fright *noun*
1 *The girl jumped up in fright and began to scream.*
fear, terror, alarm, horror, panic, dread
2 *The explosion gave us an awful fright!*
scare, shock, surprise, start, turn, jolt

frighten *verb*
Sorry—I didn't mean to frighten you.
scare, terrify, startle, alarm, shock, panic, petrify

frightened *adjective*
Mia always felt frightened in the dark.
afraid, scared, terrified, alarmed, fearful, panicky, petrified

frightening *adjective*
The ghost story she told was quite frightening.
terrifying, horrifying, scary, alarming, nightmarish, chilling, spine-chilling, hair-raising, bloodcurdling, chilling, eerie, sinister, fearsome
(*informal*) creepy, spooky

frisky *adjective*
The new lion cubs in the zoo are very frisky.
playful, lively, high-spirited, sprightly

frivolous *adjective*
Don't waste my time asking frivolous questions.
foolish, silly, ridiculous, shallow, superficial, pointless, unimportant, trivial, petty

front *noun*
1 *We stood at the front of the queue.*
head, start, beginning, lead, top
2 *The front of the house was painted white.*
face, facing, frontage, facade
The front of a ship is the *bow* or *prow*.
The front of a picture is the *foreground*.

front *adjective*
1 *The front runners came into sight round the corner.*

WORD WEB

fruit *noun*
SOME COMMON VARIETIES OF FRUIT
apple, apricot, avocado, banana, bilberry, blackberry or bramble, blackcurrant, blueberry, cherry, coconut, cranberry, damson, date, fig, gooseberry, grape, guava, kiwi fruit, loganberry, lychee, mango, melon, nectarine, pawpaw or papaya, peach, pear, pineapple, plum, pomegranate, quince, raspberry, redcurrant, rosehip, sloe, strawberry, tomato

CITRUS FRUITS
clementine, grapefruit, kumquat, lemon, lime, mandarin, orange, satsuma, tangerine

DRIED FRUITS
currant, prune, raisin, sultana

Rhubarb is not a fruit, although it is often eaten like one. A person who sells fruit and vegetables is a *greengrocer*.

first, leading, most advanced
OPPOSITE back
2 *The horse had injured one of its* ***front*** *legs.*
fore
OPPOSITE back, rear, hind
frosty *adjective*
1 *It was a clear,* ***frosty*** *night.*
cold, crisp, icy, freezing, wintry
2 *The shopkeeper gave us a* ***frosty*** *stare.*
unfriendly, unwelcoming, cold, cool, stony
frown *noun*
On Christmas Eve, Scrooge had a ***frown*** *on his face.*
scowl, glare, grimace, glower, black look
frown *verb*
The witch ***frowned*** *when her spell didn't work.*
scowl, glare, grimace, glower, knit your brow, look sullen
fruit *noun see panel above*
frustrate *verb*
1 *It was* ***frustrating*** *to have to wait in the long queue.*
exasperate, discourage, dispirit, irritate
2 *Our plan for the day was* ***frustrated*** *by the weather.*
block, foil, thwart, defeat, check, hinder, prevent
full *adjective*
1 *My suitcase is* ***full*** *to the brim.*
filled, loaded, topped up
OPPOSITE empty
2 *The shopping centre was* ***full*** *on Saturday.*

busy, crowded, jammed, packed, crammed, congested
OPPOSITE empty
3 *The detective gave a* ***full*** *account of his findings.*
complete, detailed, exhaustive comprehensive, thorough,
OPPOSITE incomplete
4 *The horses were galloping at* ***full*** *speed.*
top, maximum, greatest, highest
OPPOSITE minimum
fun *noun*
We had great ***fun*** *at the beach on our holiday.*
amusement, diversion, enjoyment, entertainment, games, jokes, laughter, merriment, play, pleasure, recreation, sport
to make fun of someone
It was cruel to ***make fun of*** *her when she fell over.*
jeer at, laugh at, mock, ridicule, taunt, tease
funny *adjective*
1 *There are some very* ***funny*** *jokes in the film.*
amusing, humorous, comic, comical, hilarious, witty, entertaining, diverting
(*informal*) hysterical, priceless
OPPOSITE serious
2 *There's a* ***funny*** *smell in here.*
strange, odd, peculiar, curious, puzzling, weird, queer, bizarre
furious *adjective*
The manager was ***furious*** *when his team lost.*

angry, mad, enraged, infuriated, incensed, livid, fuming, raging, seething
furry *adjective*
A small, ***furry*** *creature was curled inside the box.*
hairy, fleecy, woolly, fuzzy, downy, feathery
fuss *noun*
There was a lot of ***fuss*** *when the queen arrived.*
bother, commotion, excitement, trouble, hullabaloo
fuss *verb*
Please don't ***fuss***!
worry, fret, bother, get worked up
fussy *adjective*
1 *Our cat is* ***fussy*** *about her food.*
finicky, hard to please, particular
(*informal*) choosy, picky
An informal name for a fussy person is a ***fusspot***.
2 *I don't like clothes with* ***fussy*** *designs.*
fancy, elaborate, ornate, florid
future *noun*
She has a bright ***future*** *as a tennis player.*
outlook, prospects
OPPOSITE past
fuzzy *adjective*
1 *The TV picture has gone* ***fuzzy***.
blurred, bleary, unfocused, unclear, indistinct, hazy, cloudy
OPPOSITE clear
2 *Mia was wearing a* ***fuzzy*** *cardigan.*
fluffy, frizzy, furry, woolly, fleecy

Gg

gadget *noun*
This torch is a handy little gadget.
tool, instrument, implement, device, contraption, gizmo

game *noun*
1 *My favourite game is hide-and-seek.*
amusement, pastime, sport, activity, recreation
2 *The big game is on this Saturday.*
match, contest, competition, tournament

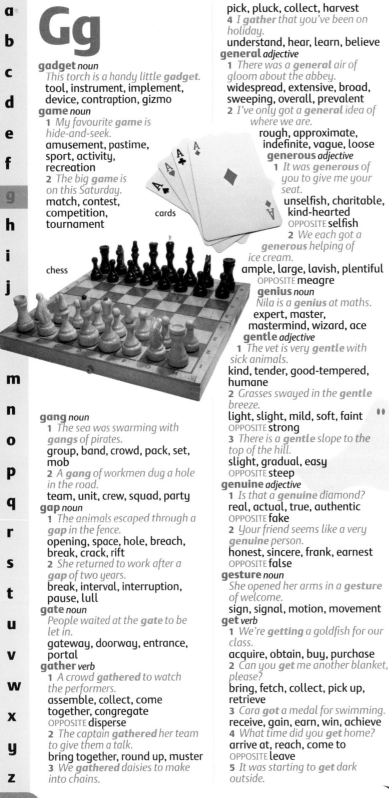

cards

chess

gang *noun*
1 *The sea was swarming with gangs of pirates.*
group, band, crowd, pack, set, mob
2 *A gang of workmen dug a hole in the road.*
team, unit, crew, squad, party

gap *noun*
1 *The animals escaped through a gap in the fence.*
opening, space, hole, breach, break, crack, rift
2 *She returned to work after a gap of two years.*
break, interval, interruption, pause, lull

gate *noun*
People waited at the gate to be let in.
gateway, doorway, entrance, portal

gather *verb*
1 *A crowd gathered to watch the performers.*
assemble, collect, come together, congregate
OPPOSITE disperse
2 *The captain gathered her team to give them a talk.*
bring together, round up, muster
3 *We gathered daisies to make into chains.*

pick, pluck, collect, harvest
4 *I gather that you've been on holiday.*
understand, hear, learn, believe

general *adjective*
1 *There was a general air of gloom about the abbey.*
widespread, extensive, broad, sweeping, overall, prevalent
2 *I've only got a general idea of where we are.*
rough, approximate, indefinite, vague, loose

generous *adjective*
1 *It was generous of you to give me your seat.*
unselfish, charitable, kind-hearted
OPPOSITE selfish
2 *We each got a generous helping of ice cream.*
ample, large, lavish, plentiful
OPPOSITE meagre

genius *noun*
Nila is a genius at maths.
expert, master, mastermind, wizard, ace

gentle *adjective*
1 *The vet is very gentle with sick animals.*
kind, tender, good-tempered, humane
2 *Grasses swayed in the gentle breeze.*
light, slight, mild, soft, faint
OPPOSITE strong
3 *There is a gentle slope to the top of the hill.*
slight, gradual, easy
OPPOSITE steep

genuine *adjective*
1 *Is that a genuine diamond?*
real, actual, true, authentic
OPPOSITE fake
2 *Your friend seems like a very genuine person.*
honest, sincere, frank, earnest
OPPOSITE false

gesture *noun*
She opened her arms in a gesture of welcome.
sign, signal, motion, movement

get *verb*
1 *We're getting a goldfish for our class.*
acquire, obtain, buy, purchase
2 *Can you get me another blanket, please?*
bring, fetch, collect, pick up, retrieve
3 *Cara got a medal for swimming.*
receive, gain, earn, win, achieve
4 *What time did you get home?*
arrive at, reach, come to
OPPOSITE leave
5 *It was starting to get dark outside.*

become, grow, turn
6 *I got a stomach bug on holiday last year.*
catch, develop, pick up, come down with
7 *You'll never get Oscar to eat celery.*
persuade, urge, influence, coax
8 *I don't get the point of that film.*
understand, follow, comprehend, grasp

to get out of
My brother got out of doing the washing up.
avoid, evade, shirk

to get over
He hasn't got over the accident yet.
get better from, recover from, shake off, survive

ghastly *adjective*
The boy's face turned a ghastly shade of green.
appalling, awful, dreadful, frightful, grim, grisly, horrible, horrifying, shocking, monstrous, terrible

WORD WEB

ghost *noun*
Meldrop House was haunted by several ghosts.
spirit, spectre, phantom, ghoul, apparition, shade, wraith
(*informal*) spook
A ghost that makes a lot of noise is a **poltergeist**

A GHOST OR GHOSTLY EXPERIENCE MIGHT BE
bloodcurdling, chilling, grisly, gruesome, hair-raising, macabre, nightmarish, spine-chilling, spine-tingling

THINGS A GHOST MIGHT DO
flit, float, glide, glow, haunt a person or place, hover, lurk, materialize, pass through walls, rattle chains, shimmer, vanish, waft

NOISES A GHOST MIGHT MAKE
cackle, clang, clank, creak, groan, hoot, howl, moan, screech, sigh, sob, wail

PLACES A GHOST MIGHT BE FOUND
catacombs, crypt, haunted house or mansion, graveyard, sepulchre, tomb, vault

OTHER THINGS THAT MIGHT BE IN A HAUNTED HOUSE
bats, candles, cellar, cobwebs, dungeon, gargoyle, mummy, owl, secret door or passage, skeleton, skull, trap door, turret

ghostly *adjective*
The candlelight cast ghostly shadows on the wall.
spectral, phantom, ghoulish, unearthly, eerie, sinister, uncanny
(*informal*) spooky, creepy

giant *adjective*
A giant tree towered above us.
gigantic, huge, enormous, massive, immense, mammoth, colossal, monstrous
OPPOSITE **tiny**

giddy *adjective*
I felt giddy when I stood at the edge of the cliff.
dizzy, faint, unsteady

gift *noun*
1 *I received some nice gifts on my birthday.*
present
2 *Elsa has a gift for music.*
talent, ability, flair, knack, genius

gigantic *adjective*
The dragon reared its gigantic head.
huge, giant, enormous, massive, colossal, immense, mammoth, monstrous
(*informal*) whopping, humungous
OPPOSITE **tiny**

giggle *verb*
Ailsa and I couldn't stop giggling.
snigger, titter, chuckle, laugh

girl *noun*
A synonym used in some parts of Britain is *lass*.
Old-fashioned words are *damsel*, *maid*, and *maiden*.

give *verb*
1 *Santa Claus gave each child a present.*
deal out, distribute, issue, supply, offer, present, hand over, pass, award
2 *Will you give something to our collection for charity?*
contribute, donate
3 *The giant gave a loud sneeze.*
utter, emit, let out
4 *We are giving a concert at the end of term.*
present, put on, lay on, organize, arrange

5 *Will this branch give if I sit on it?*
collapse, give way, bend, break, buckle
to give in
The boxer gave in after a long fight.
surrender, yield, submit, quit
to give up
He gave up trying to start the car.
abandon, stop, cease, quit

glad *adjective*
I'm glad to hear that you're feeling better.
pleased, happy, delighted, thrilled
OPPOSITE **sad**

glance *verb*
The bus driver glanced quickly at his watch.
look quickly, peek, peep, glimpse

glare *verb*
The troll glared at us from under his bushy eyebrows.
stare, frown, scowl, glower

glare *noun*
1 *The glare of the lights dazzled me.*
dazzle, blaze, brightness, brilliance
2 *Miss Frump silenced the children with an angry glare.*
stare, scowl, glower, frown, nasty look

gleam *noun*
I saw a gleam of moonlight between the clouds.
glimmer, glint, flash, ray, shaft

gleam *verb*
The lights gleamed on the water.
glimmer, glint, glisten, shimmer, shine

glide *verb*
The boat glided gently across the lake.
move smoothly, slide, slip, drift, float, coast

glimmer *verb*
The city lights glimmered in the distance.
gleam, glint, glow, glisten, shimmer, flicker, blink

glimpse *verb*
I glimpsed a deer running through the forest.
catch sight of, spot, spy, sight

glimpse *verb*
We caught a glimpse of a whale in the sea.
peek, peep, glance, sighting, view

glint *verb*
Sunlight glinted on the windows.
flash, glitter, sparkle, twinkle

glisten *verb*
The pavement glistened with frost.
gleam, shine, glint, shimmer, glimmer

glitter *verb*
The jewels glittered under the bright lights.
sparkle, twinkle, shimmer, glimmer, glint, glisten, flash, shine

gloat *verb*
He was gloating about winning the poetry prize.
boast, brag, crow, show off

global *adjective*
The Internet is a global network of computers.
worldwide, international, universal

gloom *noun*
1 *We could hardly see in the gloom of the cave.*
darkness, dimness, shade, shadow, murk
The gloomy light late in the evening is *dusk* or *twilight*.
2 *There was an air of gloom in the abandoned tower.*
depression, sadness, unhappiness, melancholy, misery, despair

gloomy *adjective*
1 *It was cold and gloomy in the cellar.*
dark, dingy, dim, dismal, dreary, sombre, cheerless, murky, shadowy
OPPOSITE **bright**
2 *Eeyore was feeling gloomy again.*
depressed, sad, unhappy, glum, miserable, melancholy, low, downcast, dejected
(*informal*) down in the dumps
OPPOSITE **cheerful**

glimmer

glorious *adjective*
Look at that glorious sunset!
magnificent, splendid, stunning, spectacular, superb, magnificent, wonderful, marvellous

glossy *adjective*
The bear had a thick, glossy coat of black fur.
shiny, sleek, silky, shining, gleaming, lustrous
OPPOSITE **dull**

glow *noun*
The soft glow of burning candles lit the room.
brightness, shine, gleam, radiance

glow *verb*
The embers of the bonfire were still glowing.
shine, gleam, burn
Something that glows in the dark is *luminous* or *phosphorescent*.

glum *adjective*
Why are you looking so glum?
depressed, sad, unhappy, gloomy, miserable, melancholy, low, downcast, dejected
OPPOSITE **cheerful**

gnarled *adjective*
The branches of the tree were gnarled with age.
bent, twisted, crooked, distorted, knobbly, knotty

gnaw *verb*
The wolves gnawed at a pile of bones.
chew, bite, nibble, munch

go *verb*
1 *A carriage was going slowly along the road.*
move, progress, proceed
2 *My granny has always wanted to go to China.*
travel, journey
3 *Some of the guests had already gone.*
leave, depart, get away, withdraw
4 *By morning, the ice had all gone.*
disappear, vanish
5 *The canal goes all the way from Inverness to Fort William.*
extend, lead, reach, stretch, run
6 *The mountaineer's face went blue with cold.*
become, turn, grow
7 *Is that old grandfather clock still going?*
function, operate, work, run
8 *Cups and saucers go on the bottom shelf.*
belong, be kept, be placed
9 *Time goes slowly when you're stuck indoors.*
pass, go by, elapse
to go back
Sarah has gone back to the house.
return, retreat, retrace your steps
to go off
1 *A bomb went off nearby.*

explode, blow up, detonate
2 *The milk will go off if it's not in the fridge.*
turn sour, go bad, rot
to go on
1 *What's going on over there?*
happen, occur, take place
2 *Please go on with your story.*
carry on, continue, keep going, proceed

go *noun*
Would you like to have a go on my computer?
try, turn, chance, opportunity
(*informal*) shot, bash, stab

goal *noun*
The goal of the society is to protect wildlife.
aim, ambition, intention, object, objective, purpose, target

gobble *verb*
Ladybirds love to gobble greenfly.
guzzle, gulp, bolt, devour

good *adjective see panel opposite*
That is a really good idea!
excellent, fine, lovely, nice, wonderful
(*informal*) fantastic, great, super, cool
OPPOSITE **bad**

gorgeous *adjective*
The gardens look gorgeous in the summer.
beautiful, glorious, dazzling, stunning, splendid, superb, glamorous, handsome

gossip *verb*
Two neighbours were gossiping over the fence.
chatter, tell tales
(*informal*) natter

gossip *noun*
1 *Don't believe all the gossip you hear.*
chatter, rumour, hearsay, scandal
(*informal*) tittle-tattle
2 *Our next-door*

neighbour is a dreadful *gossip*.
busybody, chatterer, telltale, scandalmonger

govern *verb*
The ancient Romans governed a vast empire.
rule, run, administer, direct, command, manage, be in charge of

grab *verb*
The cowboy grabbed the reins of the runaway horse.
seize, grasp, catch, clutch, grip, get hold of, snatch

graceful *adjective*
The gymnast made a graceful landing.
elegant, beautiful, stylish, smooth, flowing, agile, nimble
OPPOSITE **clumsy, graceless**

grade *noun*
My sister has reached the top grade in judo.
class, standard, level, stage, rank, degree

gradual *adjective*
There's been a gradual change in the weather.
steady, slow, gentle, moderate, regular, even
OPPOSITE **sudden**

grand *adjective*
1 *The wedding was a grand occasion.*
magnificent, splendid, stately, impressive, big, great, important, imposing

gnarled

2 (*informal*) *Keep going—you're doing a grand job!*
excellent, fine, good, first-class

grapple *verb*
The guard grappled with the thief, but he got away.
struggle, wrestle, fight, tussle

grasp *verb*
1 *The climber grasped the end of the rope.*
clutch, grab, grip, seize, catch, snatch, take hold of, hang on to
2 *The ideas were quite difficult to grasp.*
understand, comprehend, follow, take in

grateful *adjective*
I'm grateful for your help.
thankful, appreciative, obliged, indebted
OPPOSITE ungrateful

grave *adjective*
1 *They looked grave when they heard the news.*
grim, sad, serious, thoughtful
OPPOSITE cheerful
2 *She made a grave mistake.*
crucial, important, serious, vital
OPPOSITE trivial

graze *verb*
I grazed my knee when I fell off my bike.
scrape, cut, scratch, scuff

great *adjective*
1 *The inventor had made a great discovery.*
important, significant, major, leading, noteworthy
OPPOSITE insignificant, minor
2 *Mozart was a great composer.*
famous, notable, celebrated, eminent, distinguished, outstanding, brilliant
3 *Their voices echoed round the great hall.*
big, huge, large, enormous, vast, immense, gigantic, extensive, cavernous
OPPOSITE small
4 *Beth took great care over her knitting.*
considerable, extreme, exact
OPPOSITE little
5 (*informal*) *That is a great idea!*
very good, excellent, marvellous, outstanding, superb, tremendous, wonderful
(*informal*) brilliant, fantastic,
super, smashing, terrific
OPPOSITE bad, awful

greed *noun*
The king wanted more gold to satisfy his greed.
avarice, selfishness, hunger, craving, gluttony

greedy *adjective*
1 *The boys were so greedy that they ate all the cakes.*
gluttonous
(*informal*) piggish
A common simile is **as greedy as a pig**.
2 *Mr Skimp is very greedy with his money.*
selfish, miserly, tight-fisted, grasping

greet *verb*
My aunt greeted us with a friendly wave.
welcome, hail, receive, salute

grey *adjective*
1 *The old wizard had a bushy grey beard.*
silver, silvery, grizzly, hoary, whitish
2 *The mother's face was grey with worry.*
ashen, pale, leaden, wan
3 *The day began cold and grey.*
dull, cloudy, overcast

grief *noun*
He couldn't hide his grief at his friend's death.
sorrow, sadness, mourning, unhappiness, distress, anguish, heartache
OPPOSITE joy

grieve *verb*
The family is still grieving over her death.
mourn, lament, sorrow, weep
OPPOSITE rejoice

grim *adjective*
1 *The judge wore a grim expression on his face.*
stern, severe, harsh, bad-tempered, sullen
OPPOSITE cheerful
2 *The detective made the grim discovery of the body.*
unpleasant, horrible, dreadful, terrible, hideous, shocking, gruesome, grisly
OPPOSITE pleasant

grimy *adjective*
Don't wipe those grimy feet on the carpet!
dirty, filthy, grubby, mucky, soiled
OPPOSITE clean

grin *noun, verb*
Mark arrived with a silly grin on his face.
smile, beam, smirk
A large grin is a **broad**, **wide**, or **cheesy** grin.

! OVERUSED WORD

good *adjective*
Try to vary the words you use for **good**. Here are some other words you could use.

FOR A good person
honest, worthy, honourable, moral, decent, virtuous, noble, kind, humane, charitable, merciful *The virtuous knight defeated the evil queen.*
OPPOSITE evil, wicked
A good character in a story or film is a **hero** or **heroine** or (*informal*) **goody**.

FOR good behaviour
well-behaved, obedient, angelic, exemplary *The twins are surprisingly well-behaved.*
A common simile is **as good as gold**.
OPPOSITE naughty, disobedient

FOR A good friend
true, loyal, loving, reliable, trusty, trustworthy *My dog, Rusty, is a loyal companion.*

FOR A good feeling OR good mood
happy, cheerful, light-hearted, positive, contented *Mr Fox was in a cheerful mood after his tea.*

FOR A good experience OR good news
pleasant, enjoyable, delightful, agreeable, pleasing

OPPOSITE unpleasant, disagreeable *The girls had an enjoyable time at the party. The letter contained some pleasing news.*

FOR A good performer OR good work
capable, skilful, clever, able, talented, competent, commendable, sound *My friend, Chris, is a talented dancer.*
OPPOSITE poor, awful

FOR good food OR A good meal
delicious, healthy, nourishing, nutritious, tasty, well-cooked, wholesome, substantial, hearty *The crew ate a hearty breakfast together.*

FOR A good excuse OR good reason
acceptable, valid, proper, satisfactory, legitimate *I hope you have a valid excuse for being late.*
OPPOSITE poor, unacceptable

FOR good timing
convenient, suitable, fortunate, appropriate, opportune *Is this a convenient time for a chat?*
OPPOSITE inconvenient, unsuitable

FOR good weather
fine, favourable *We are hoping for fine weather tomorrow.*
OPPOSITE harsh, adverse

a
b
c
d
e
f
g
h
i
j
k
l
m
n
o
p
q
r
s
t
u
v
w
x
y
z

grind *verb*
1 *Grind the spices into a fine powder.*
crush, pound, powder, pulverize, mill
2 *This tool is used for grinding knives.*
sharpen, file, hone, whet

grip *verb*
1 *Grip the handle tightly.*
grasp, seize, clutch, clasp, hold
2 *The audience was gripped by the film.*
fascinate, engross, absorb, enthrall

grisly *adjective*
We found the grisly remains of a dead sheep.
gruesome, gory, ghastly, hideous, nasty, revolting, sickening

groan *verb*
The wounded soldier groaned with pain.
cry out, moan, sigh, wail

gross *adjective*
1 *That is a gross exaggeration!*
extreme, glaring, obvious, sheer, blatant, outright
2 *Most ogres have gross table manners.*
offensive, rude, coarse, vulgar

ground *noun*
1 *I planted some seeds in the ground.*
earth, soil, land
2 *The ground was too wet to play on.*
field, pitch, park, stadium, arena

group *noun*
1 *Japan consists of a group of islands.*
collection, set, batch, cluster, clump
2 *A group of children was waiting at the bus stop.*
crowd, bunch, gathering, band, body, gang
3 *The book group meets once a month.*
club, society, association, circle
4 *We sorted the fossils into different groups.*
category, class, type, kind, sort

grow *verb*
1 *I've grown an inch taller since last summer.*
get bigger, put on growth, spring up, sprout
2 *The number of children in the school has grown.*
increase, develop, enlarge, expand, build up
OPPOSITE decrease
3 *Our neighbour grows orchids in her greenhouse.*
cultivate, produce, raise, farm
4 *It is growing dark outside.*
become, get, turn

growth *noun*
There's been a growth of interest in golf for kids.
increase, rise, spread, expansion, development, enlargement

grubby *adjective*
My hands were grubby from working in the garden.
dirty, filthy, grimy, messy, mucky, soiled
OPPOSITE clean

gruesome *adjective*
The battlefield was a gruesome sight.
grisly, gory, ghastly, hideous, monstrous, revolting, sickening, appalling, dreadful, frightful, shocking, abominable

gruff *adjective*
The ogre spoke in a gruff voice.
harsh, rough, hoarse, husky, throaty

grumble *verb*
You're always grumbling about the weather!
complain, moan, groan, protest, whine, gripe

grumpy *adjective*
Marge was grumpy because she had a headache.
bad-tempered, cross, irritable, testy, tetchy, cantankerous

grow

(informal) grouchy
OPPOSITE good-humoured

guard *verb*
The cave was guarded by a one-eyed giant.
protect, defend, stand guard over, patrol, safeguard, shield, watch over

guard *noun*
A guard was on duty at the gate.
sentry, sentinel, warder, lookout, watchman

guess *verb*
1 *There was a prize for guessing the weight of the cake.*
estimate, judge, work out, guage, predict, reckon
2 *I guess you must be tired after your journey.*
suppose, imagine, expect, assume, think

guest *noun*
We are having guests for tea on Sunday.
visitor, caller, company

guide *noun*
1 *Our guide showed us around the zoo.*
courier, escort, leader, chaperon
2 *We bought a useful guide to the city.*
guidebook, handbook, manual

guide *verb*
The explorers used the stars to guide them at night.
direct, lead, steer, conduct, escort, show the way

guilty *adjective*
1 *The prisoner was found guilty of the crime.*
responsible, to blame, at fault, in the wrong, liable
OPPOSITE innocent
2 *You have a guilty look on your face!*
ashamed, guilt-ridden, remorseful, sorry, conscience-stricken, repentant, shamefaced, sheepish
OPPOSITE unrepentant

gulp *verb*
Peter gulped down the cake in one go.
swallow, bolt, gobble, guzzle, devour

gush *noun*
There was a gush of water from the pipe.
rush, stream, torrent, rush, cascade, flood, jet, spout, spurt

gush *verb*
Water gushed from the broken pipe.
rush, stream, flow, pour, flood, spout, spurt, squirt

guzzle *verb*
The seagulls guzzled all the bread.
gobble, gulp, bolt, devour

Hh

habit *noun*
1 *It's her habit to go for a walk each morning.*
custom, practice, routine, rule
2 *My dog has a habit of scratching his ear.*
mannerism, way, tendency, inclination, quirk

haggard *adjective*
The warriors looked haggard after the battle.
drawn, gaunt, thin, pinched, wasted, shrunken, wan
OPPOSITE healthy

haggle *verb*
The men haggled over the price of the gems.
bargain, negotiate, argue, wrangle

 WRITING TIPS

hair *noun*
You can use these words to describe **hair**.
TO DESCRIBE ITS *colour*
auburn, blond (male) or blonde (female), brunette, carroty, dark, fair, flaxen, ginger, grey, grizzled, hoary, mousy, platinum blonde, raven, red, silver
TO DESCRIBE HOW IT *looks* OR *feels*
bushy, coarse, curly, dishevelled, fine, frizzy, glossy, greasy, lank, limp, ringletted, shaggy, shiny, silky, spiky, straggly, straight, stringy, tangled, thick, tousled, tuggy, unkempt, wavy, windswept, wispy *The elderly knight had a grizzled, straggly beard.*

---

hairy *adjective*
Mammoths were like elephants with thick hairy coats.
shaggy, bushy, bristly, woolly, fleecy, furry, fuzzy, long-haired, hirsute

hall *noun*
1 *The hall was full for the concert.*
assembly hall, auditorium, concert hall, theatre
2 *You can use the coat stand in the hall.*
entrance hall, hallway, lobby, foyer

halt *verb*
1 *The car halted at the red light.*
stop, come to a halt, draw up, pull up, wait
2 *A traffic jam halted the traffic.*
stop, check, obstruct

3 *Work halted when the whistle went.*
end, cease, terminate, break off
OPPOSITE start, go

hand *verb*
The postman handed me several letters.
give, pass, present, offer, deliver

handle *verb*
1 *Please don't handle the exhibits.*
touch, feel, hold, stroke, fondle, finger, grasp
2 *The referee handled the game well.*
manage, control, conduct, deal with, cope with, tackle

handsome *adjective*
1 *Prince Charming was very handsome.*
attractive, good-looking, nice-looking, gorgeous
(*informal*) dishy
OPPOSITE ugly, unattractive
2 *They sold their house for a handsome profit.*
big, large, substantial, sizeable
OPPOSITE slight

handy *adjective*
1 *This handy gadget is for peeling potatoes.*
useful, helpful, convenient, practical
OPPOSITE awkward
2 *I always keep my umbrella handy.*
accessible, available, close at hand, nearby, ready
OPPOSITE inaccessible

hang *verb*
1 *A monkey was hanging from the tree branch.*
dangle, be suspended, swing, sway
2 *The dog had hair hanging down over his eyes.*
droop, drape, flop, trail, cascade
3 *I hung the picture on the wall.*
fix, attach, fasten, stick, peg
4 *Smoke hung in the air.*
float, hover, drift, linger, cling
to hang about or **around**
Don't hang about, we'll miss the bus.
delay, dawdle, linger, loiter
to hang on
(*informal*) *Try to hang on a bit longer.*
carry on, continue, stay, remain, persist, keep going, persevere
to hang on to something
1 *Hang on to the rope.*
hold, grip, grasp
2 *Hang on to your bus ticket.*
keep, retain, save

happiness *noun*
The bride's face glowed with happiness.
joy, joyfulness, delight, jubilation, pleasure,

contentment, gladness, cheerfulness, merriment, ecstasy, bliss
OPPOSITE sorrow

happy *adjective*
1 *The girls look really happy in the photograph.*
cheerful, joyful, jolly, merry, light-hearted, contented, gleeful, delighted OPPOSITE unhappy, sad
2 *Sandy was happy when she won first prize.*
thrilled, ecstatic, elated, overjoyed
(*informal*) over the moon, thrilled to bits, tickled pink
3 *They spent a happy summer on the island.*
enjoyable, joyous, glorious, blissful, heavenly, idyllic

harbour *noun*
Several yachts were tied up in the harbour.
port, dock, mooring, quay, pier, wharf

hard *adjective*
1 *The ground was hard and covered with frost.*
solid, firm, dense, compact, rigid, stiff
OPPOSITE soft
2 *The climber gave the rope a hard pull.*
strong, forceful, heavy, powerful, violent
OPPOSITE light
3 *Digging the tunnel was hard work.*
tough, gruelling, strenuous, tiring, exhausting, laborious, backbreaking
OPPOSITE easy
4 *None of us could solve the hard riddle.*
difficult, complicated, complex, intricate, perplexing, puzzling, baffling, knotty, thorny
OPPOSITE simple

hard *adverb*
1 *Ros is working hard at learning French.*
strenuously, energetically, diligently, keenly, intently
2 *It has been raining hard all afternoon.*
heavily, steadily
(*informal*) cats and dogs

hardly *adverb*
I could hardly see in the fog.
barely, scarcely, only just, with difficulty

harm *verb*
1 *His captors didn't harm him.*
hurt, injure, ill-treat, wound
2 *Too much direct sunlight may harm this plant.*
damage, spoil, ruin

a b c d e f g **h** i j k l m n o p q r s t u v w x y z

harm noun

I didn't mean to cause him any harm.

damage, hurt, injury, pain
OPPOSITE benefit

harmful adjective

Junk food can be harmful to your health.

damaging, dangerous, destructive, injurious, unhealthy
OPPOSITE harmless, beneficial

harmless adjective

1 *You can drink the potion—it is quite harmless.*

safe, non-toxic, innocuous
OPPOSITE harmful, dangerous

2 *It was just a bit of harmless fun.*

innocent, inoffensive

harsh adjective

1 *The trumpet sounded loud and harsh.*

rough, rasping, grating, jarring, shrill, raucous
OPPOSITE soft, gentle

2 *We blinked in the harsh light.*

bright, brilliant, dazzling, glaring
OPPOSITE soft, subdued

3 *The rescue team braved the harsh weather.*

severe, strict, cruel, hard, tough, bleak
OPPOSITE mild

4 *The coach had some harsh words to say.*

strong, sharp, unkind, unfriendly

hasty adjective

1 *The robbers made a hasty exit.*

fast, hurried, quick, sudden, swift, rapid, speedy
OPPOSITE slow

2 *The king regretted his hasty decision.*

rash, reckless, impatient, foolhardy, thoughtless
OPPOSITE careful

hate verb

1 *Eddie hates broccoli and peas.*

dislike, detest, despise, loathe

2 *I hate to bother you.*

be sorry, be reluctant, regret

have verb

1 *I have my own CD player.*

own, possess

2 *Our house has three bedrooms.*

consist of, comprise, include, incorporate

3 *We are having a barbecue at the weekend.*

hold, organize, provide, host, throw

4 *Dad had trouble finding a place to park.*

experience, go through, meet with, run into, face, suffer

5 *The girls had a great time at the party.*

experience, enjoy

6 *The BBC has had lots of email messages.*

receive, get, be given, be sent

7 *Sharon had the last toffee.*

take, consume, eat

8 *One of the giraffes has had a baby.*

give birth to, bear, produce

9 *I have to be home by six o'clock.*

must, need to, ought to, should

hazy adjective

1 *The things in the distance were rather hazy.*

blurred, misty, unclear, dim, faint

2 *He's only got a hazy knowledge of history.*

uncertain, vague

head noun

1 *My dad hit his head on the attic ceiling.*

skull, crown
(*informal*) nut

2 *Can you add up these figures in your head?*

brain, mind, intellect, intelligence

3 *There is a new head of the music department.*

chief, leader, manager, director, controller
(*informal*) boss

4 *The girls waited at the head of the queue.*

front, lead, top
OPPOSITE back, rear

head verb

The professor was chosen to head the expedition.

lead, be in charge of, direct, command, manage, oversee, supervise

to head for

At the end of the day we headed for home.

go towards, make for, aim for

heal verb

1 *It took two months for my leg to heal properly.*

get better, mend, recover

2 *Part of a vet's job is to heal sick animals.*

cure, make better, treat, restore

health noun

The puppies are in excellent health.

condition, fitness, shape, strength, vigour, wellbeing

healthy adjective

1 *Neil has always been a healthy child.*

well, fit, strong, sturdy, vigorous, robust
(*informal*) in good shape
OPPOSITE ill

2 *Porridge makes a very healthy breakfast.*

health-giving, wholesome, invigorating
OPPOSITE unhealthy

heap noun

There was an untidy heap of clothes on the floor.

mound, pile, stack, mountain, collection, mass

heap verb

We heaped up all the rubbish in the corner.

pile, stack, collect, bank, mass

hear verb

1 *Did you hear what she said?*

catch, listen to, make out, pick up, overhear, pay attention to
A sound that you can hear is audible.
A sound that you cannot hear is inaudible.

2 *Have you heard the news?*

be told, discover, find out, learn, gather

heart noun

1 *Have you no heart?*

compassion, feeling, sympathy, tenderness, affection, humanity, kindness, love

2 *The hotel is located right in the heart of the city.*

centre, middle, hub

3 *They tried to get to the heart of the problem.*

core, essence

heat noun

1 *The cat basked in the heat of the fire.*

warmth, hotness, glow

2 *Last summer, the heat made me feel ill.*

hot weather, high temperatures, closeness
A long period of hot weather is a heatwave.

heave verb

The men heaved the sacks onto a lorry.

haul, drag, pull, draw, tow, tug, hoist, lug, lift, raise, throw

heavy adjective

1 *The box was too heavy for me to lift.*

weighty, massive, dense, bulky

2 *Digging the garden is heavy work.*

hard, tough, gruelling, back-breaking, strenuous

3 *This book makes heavy reading.*

serious, intense, demanding

4 *The rain has caused heavy flooding.*

severe, extreme, torrential

5 *Both sides suffered heavy losses in the battle.*

large, substantial, considerable

6 *A heavy mist hung over the landscape.*

dense, thick

hectic *adjective*
The days before the wedding were **hectic**.
busy, frantic, feverish, frenzied, chaotic, (*informal*) manic
OPPOSITE quiet, leisurely

help *noun*
1 *Thank you for your* **help**.
aid, assistance, support, guidance, cooperation, advice
OPPOSITE hindrance
2 *Would a torch be of any* **help** *to you?*
use, benefit

help *verb*
1 *Could you please* **help** *me with my luggage?*
aid, assist, cooperate with (*informal*) give a hand to
2 *The Red Cross is an organization that* **helps** *people in need.*
be helpful to, support, serve, stand by
3 *This medicine will* **help** *your cough.*
make better, cure, ease, relieve, improve
OPPOSITE aggravate, worsen
4 *I can't* **help** *coughing.*
stop, avoid, prevent, refrain from

helpful *adjective*
1 *The staff were friendly and* **helpful**.
obliging, cooperative, kind, considerate, thoughtful, sympathetic
OPPOSITE unhelpful
2 *The shop assistant gave us some* **helpful** *advice.*
useful, valuable, worthwhile, beneficial, profitable
OPPOSITE worthless

helpless *adjective*
Kittens are born blind and **helpless**.
powerless, weak, feeble, dependent, defenceless, vulnerable
OPPOSITE independent, strong

heroic *adjective*
The firefighters made a **heroic** *effort to put out the blaze.*
bold, brave, courageous, daring, fearless, noble, selfless, valiant
OPPOSITE cowardly

hesitate *verb*
I **hesitated** *for a moment before ringing the doorbell.*
pause, delay, wait, hold back, dither, falter, waver
(*informal*) think twice

hidden *adjective*
1 *The giant kept his gold* **hidden** *in a wooden chest.*
concealed, out of sight, unseen, invisible, covered, disguised
OPPOSITE visible
2 *There's a* **hidden** *message in the riddle.*
secret, mysterious, obscure,
coded, cryptic
OPPOSITE obvious

hide *verb*
1 *Quick!—someone's coming— we'd better* **hide**.
go into hiding, take cover, take refuge, keep out of sight, lie low, go to ground
2 *They* **hid** *the jewels in a secret drawer.*
conceal, secrete, bury (*informal*) stash
OPPOSITE expose
3 *The clouds* **hid** *the sun.*
blot out, cover, screen, shroud, veil, mask
OPPOSITE uncover
4 *I tried to* **hide** *my feelings.*
disguise, keep secret, suppress, camouflage, cloak
OPPOSITE show

hideous *adjective*   hide

hideous *adjective*
The troll had a **hideous** *grin on his face.*
repulsive, revolting, ugly, grotesque, monstrous, ghastly, gruesome, horrible, appalling, dreadful, frightful
OPPOSITE beautiful

high *adjective*
1 *The castle was surrounded by a* **high** *wall.*
tall, towering, elevated, lofty
OPPOSITE low
2 *Sir Grinalot was a knight of* **high** *rank and status.*
senior, top, leading, important, prominent, powerful
OPPOSITE low, junior
3 *House prices are very* **high** *at the moment.*
expensive, dear, costly, excessive
OPPOSITE low
4 *A* **high** *wind was blowing.*
strong, powerful, forceful, extreme
OPPOSITE gentle
5 *The pixie spoke in a* **high** *squeaky voice.*
high-pitched, sharp, shrill, piercing
A high singing voice is **soprano** *or* **treble**.
OPPOSITE deep

hilarious *adjective*
The boys thought the cartoon was **hilarious**.
funny, amusing, comical (*informal*) hysterical

hill *noun*
1 *From the top of this* **hill** *you can see for miles.*
mount, peak, ridge
A small hill is a **hillock** *or* **mound**.
The top of a hill is the **summit**.
2 *Jenny pushed her bike up the steep* **hill**.
slope, rise, incline, ascent, gradient

hinder *verb*
The snowstorm **hindered** *the rescue attempt.*
hamper, hold up, obstruct, impede, slow down, stand in the way of, restrict, handicap
OPPOSITE help

hint *noun*
1 *I don't know the answer—can you give me a* **hint**?
clue, indication, sign, suggestion, inkling
2 *The magazine offers handy* **hints** *for decorating.*
tip, pointer

hint *verb*
Mum **hinted** *that we might be getting a puppy.*
give a hint, suggest, imply, indicate

hit *noun*
1 *Matt got a nasty* **hit** *on the head.*
bump, blow, bang, knock, whack
A hit with your fist is a **punch**.
A hit with your open hand is a **slap** *or* **smack**.
A hit with a bat or club is a **drive**, **stroke**, *or* **swipe**.
2 *Their new CD was an instant* **hit**.
success, triumph (*informal*) winner

hit *verb*
1 *Auntie Flo* **hit** *the burglar on the head with her umbrella.*
strike, knock, bang, bash, thump, bump, crack, rap, slam, swipe, slog, cuff
(*informal*) whack, wham, wallop, sock, clout, clobber, belt, biff
(*old use*) smite
To hit with your fist is to **punch**.
To hit with the palm of your hand is to **slap** *or* **smack**.
To punish someone by hitting them is to **beat** *them.*
To hit someone with a stick is to **club** *them.*

a
b
c
d
e
f
g
h
i
j
k
l
m
n
o
p
q
r
s
t
u
v
w
x
y
z

To hit your toe on something is to **stub** it.

To kill an insect by hitting it is to **swat** it.

To hit something repeatedly is to **batter**, **buffet**, or **pound** it.

To hit something gently is to **tap** it.

2 *The drought has **hit** many farms in the area.*
affect, damage, harm, hurt

hoard *noun*
*Hamish keeps a **hoard** of sweets in his desk.*
cache, store, stock, supply, pile, stockpile
A hoard of treasure is a **treasure trove**.

hoard *verb*
*Squirrels **hoard** nuts for the winter.*
store, collect, gather, save, put by, pile up, stockpile
(*informal*) stash away

hoard

hoarse *adjective*
*Mr Barker's voice was **hoarse** from shouting.*
rough, harsh, husky, croaky, throaty, gruff, rasping, gravelly

hobby *noun*
*My favourite **hobby** is snorkelling.*
pastime, pursuit, interest, activity, recreation

hold *verb*
1 *Please **hold** the dog's lead.*
clasp, grasp, grip, cling to, hang on to, clutch, seize
2 *Can I **hold** the baby?*
embrace, hug, cradle
3 *They **held** the suspect until the police arrived.*
confine, detain, keep
4 *Will the ladder **hold** my weight?*
bear, support, carry, take
5 *If our luck **holds**, we could reach the final.*
continue, last, carry on, persist, stay
6 *She **holds** strong opinions.*
believe in, maintain, stick to
to hold out
1 *The robot **held out** one of his arms.*
extend, reach out, stick out, stretch out
2 *Our supplies won't **hold out** much longer.*
keep going, last, carry on,

continue, endure
to hold something up
1 *Please **hold up** your hand.*
lift, put up, raise
2 *The accident **held up** the traffic.*
delay, hinder, slow down

hole *noun*
1 *The meteor created a massive **hole** in the ground.*
pit, hollow, crater, dent, depression, cavity, chasm, abyss
2 *The rabbits escaped through a **hole** in the fence.*
gap, opening, breach, break, cut, slit, gash, split, tear, vent

hollow *adjective*
*Tennis balls are **hollow**.*
empty, unfilled
OPPOSITE solid

hollow *noun*
*The ball rolled into a **hollow** in the ground.*
dip, dent, depression, hole, pit, crater
A hollow between two hills is a **valley**.

holy *adjective*
1 *The pilgrims knelt to pray in the **holy** shrine.*
sacred, blessed, revered
2 *The pilgrims were **holy** people.*
religious, spiritual, devout, pious, godly, saintly

home *noun*
*The hurricane forced people to flee their **homes**.*
house, residence, dwelling, abode, lodging
A home for the sick is a **convalescent home** or **nursing home**.
A place where a bird or animal lives is its **habitat**.

honest *adjective*
1 *He's an **honest** boy, so he gave the money back.*
good, honourable, law-abiding, moral, trustworthy, upright, virtuous
OPPOSITE dishonest
2 *Please give me your **honest** opinion.*
sincere, genuine, truthful, direct, frank, candid, plain, straightforward, unbiased
OPPOSITE insincere

honour *noun*
1 *Her success brought **honour** to the school.*
credit, good reputation, good name, respect, praise, acclaim
2 *It's an **honour** to meet you.*
privilege, distinction

honour *verb*
*The winners were **honoured** at a special ceremony.*
praise, celebrate, salute, give credit to, pay tribute to, glorify

honourable *adjective*
1 *The knight was an **honourable** man.*
good, honest, sincere, noble, principled, moral, righteous, trustworthy, upright, virtuous, worthy, decent, fair, trusty
2 *It was an **honourable** thing to do.*
noble, admirable, praiseworthy, decent

hop *verb*
*The goblins **hopped** about in excitement.*
jump, leap, skip, spring, prance, caper, bound, dance

hope *verb*
*I **hope** to see you again soon.*
wish, trust, expect, look forward

hope *noun*
1 *Her dearest **hope** was to see her family again.*
ambition, dream, desire, wish
2 *There's **hope** of better weather tomorrow.*
prospect, expectation, likelihood

hopeful *adjective*
1 *I am feeling **hopeful** about tomorrow's match.*
optimistic, confident, positive, expectant
OPPOSITE pessimistic
2 *The future is beginning to look more **hopeful**.*
promising, encouraging, favourable, reassuring
OPPOSITE discouraging

hopeless *adjective*
1 *The shipwrecked crew were in a **hopeless** situation.*
desperate, wretched, beyond hope
OPPOSITE hopeful
2 *I'm **hopeless** at ice-skating.*
bad, poor, incompetent
(*informal*) useless, rubbish
OPPOSITE good, competent

horrible *adjective*
*What a **horrible** smell!*
awful, terrible, dreadful, appalling, unpleasant, disagreeable, offensive, objectionable, disgusting, repulsive, revolting, horrendous, horrid, nasty, hateful, odious, loathsome, beastly, ghastly
OPPOSITE pleasant

horrific *adjective*
*The film has some **horrific** scenes of battle.*
horrifying, terrifying, shocking, gruesome, dreadful, appalling, ghastly, hideous, atrocious, grisly, sickening

horrify *verb*
*We were **horrified** by the sight of the monster.*

appal, shock, terrify, frighten, alarm, scare, sicken, disgust

horror noun
1 *Ingrid screamed in* **horror** *when she saw the snake.*
terror, fear, fright, alarm, dread
2 *The film depicts the full* **horror** *of war.*
awfulness, hideousness, gruesomeness, ghastliness, frightfulness

hostile adjective
The warriors shook their weapons in a **hostile** *manner.*
aggressive, antagonistic, unfriendly, unwelcoming, warlike, malevolent
OPPOSITE friendly

hot adjective
1 *The weather has been* **hot** *this summer.*
warm, balmy, blazing, roasting, scorching, blistering, sweltering, stifling
OPPOSITE cold, cool
2 *Careful—the soup's really* **hot**.
burning, boiling, baking hot, piping hot, scalding, searing, sizzling, steaming
OPPOSITE cold, cool
3 *I like curry, but only if it's not too* **hot**.
spicy, peppery, fiery
OPPOSITE mild
4 *My sister, Diana, has a* **hot** *temper.*
fierce, fiery, violent, passionate, raging, angry, intense
OPPOSITE calm, mild

hover

✻ WORD WEB

house noun
WORDS FOR THE PLACE YOU LIVE IN
abode, dwelling, home, lodging, quarters, residence

BUILDINGS WHERE PEOPLE LIVE
apartment, bungalow, chalet, cottage, council house, croft, detached house, farmhouse, flat, hovel, hut, igloo, lodge, manor, manse, mansion, rectory, semi-detached house, shack, shanty, tenement, terraced house, thatched house, vicarage, villa

---

hover verb
1 *A flock of seagulls* **hovered** *overhead.*
fly, flutter, float, hang, drift
2 *He* **hovered** *outside the room, afraid to knock.*
linger, pause, wait about, hesitate, dally, loiter, dither
(*informal*) hang about

howl verb
1 *The injured boy* **howled** *in pain.*
cry, yell, scream, yelp, shriek, wail
2 *They heard wolves* **howling** *in the night.*
bay, yowl

huddle verb
The penguins **huddled** *together to get warm.*
crowd, gather, flock, cluster, squeeze, pack, nestle, cuddle, snuggle
OPPOSITE scatter

hug verb
Ellie was **hugging** *her favourite teddy bear.*
cuddle, clasp, embrace, cling to, hold close, squeeze

huge adjective
Elephants are **huge** *animals.*
enormous, gigantic, massive, colossal, giant, immense, vast, mighty, mammoth, monumental, hulking, great, big, large
(*informal*) whopping, ginormous, humungous
OPPOSITE small, little, tiny

hum verb
We heard insects **humming** *in the air.*
buzz, drone, murmur, purr, whirr

humble adjective
1 *The gentle giant was both* **humble** *and kind.*
modest, meek, unassuming, polite, respectful, submissive
OPPOSITE proud
2 *Hansel and Gretel lived a* **humble** *cottage.*
simple, modest, plain, ordinary, commonplace, lowly
OPPOSITE grand

humid adjective
I don't like this **humid** *weather.*
muggy, clammy, close, sticky, steamy, sweaty
OPPOSITE fresh

humiliate verb
He **humiliated** *her in front of her friends.*
embarrass, disgrace, shame, make ashamed, humble, crush, degrade
(*informal*) put you in your place, take you down a peg

humour noun
1 *I liked the* **humour** *in the film.*
comedy, wit, amusement, jokes
2 *The ogre was in a very bad* **humour**.

mood, temper, disposition, frame of mind, spirits

hunger noun
After a week without food, the crew were faint with **hunger**.
lack of food, starvation, famine
Bad health caused by not having enough food is *malnutrition*.

hungry adjective
Our dog always seems to be **hungry**.
starving, famished, ravenous
(*informal*) peckish

hunt noun
Police have begun the **hunt** *for clues.*
search, quest, chase, pursuit (of)

hunt verb
1 *Some Native Americans tribes used to* **hunt** *buffalo.*
chase, pursue, track, trail, hound, stalk
An animal which hunts other animals for food is a *predator*.
2 *I* **hunted** *in the attic for our old photos.*
search, seek, look, rummage, ferret, root around

hurry verb
1 *If you want to catch the bus, you'd better* **hurry**.
be quick, hasten, make speed
(*informal*) get a move on, step on it
OPPOSITE dawdle
2 *Alice saw the White Rabbit* **hurrying** *past.*
rush, dash, fly, speed, hurtle, scurry
OPPOSITE amble, stroll

hurt verb
1 *Be careful not to* **hurt** *yourself with the scissors.*
harm, injure, damage, wound, maim
To hurt someone deliberately is to *torment* or *torture* them.
2 *My feet* **hurt**.
be sore, be painful, ache, throb, sting, smart
3 *Your letter* **hurt** *me deeply.*
upset, distress, offend, grieve

hurtful adjective
That was a very **hurtful** *remark.*
upsetting, unkind, cruel, mean, painful, spiteful, nasty

hut noun
The walkers came across a **hut** *in the forest.*
shed, shack, cabin, den, shelter, shanty, hovel

hysterical adjective
1 *The fans became* **hysterical** *when the band appeared.*
crazy, frenzied, mad, delirious, raving, wild, uncontrollable
2 (*informal*) *We laughed at the* **hysterical** *jokes in the film.*
hilarious, funny, amusing, comical

a
b
c
d
e
f
g
h
i
j
k
l
m
n
o
p
q
r
s
t
u
v
w
x
y
z

Ii

ice hockey

ice noun
WAYS TO DESCRIBE ICE
brittle, cracked,
frozen solid, glacial,
glassy, gleaming,
glinting, hard, packed,
slippery or (informal)
slippy, smooth, treacherous

THINGS YOU MIGHT DO ON ICE
glide, skate, skid, slide, slip,
slither

SPORTS THAT ARE PLAYED ON ICE
curling, figure skating, ice skating,
ice hockey, speed skating
Ice sports are played on an *ice
rink*.

icy adjective
1 *You need to dress warmly in* **icy**
weather.
cold, freezing, frosty, wintry,
arctic, bitter, biting
2 **Icy** *roads are dangerous.*
frozen, slippery, glacial, glassy
(informal) slippy
idea noun
1 *I've got a great* **idea**!
plan, scheme, proposal,
suggestion, inspiration
2 *She has some funny* **ideas** *about
life.*
belief, notion, opinion, view,
theory, concept, conception,
hypothesis
3 *What's the main* **idea** *of this poem?*
point, meaning, intention,
thought
4 *Give me an* **idea** *of what you are
planning.*
clue, hint, inkling, impression
ideal adjective
It's **ideal** *weather for a picnic.*
perfect, excellent, the best,
faultless, suitable
identical adjective
The twins were wearing **identical**
clothes.
matching, similar, alike,
indistinguishable
OPPOSITE different
identify verb
1 *The police asked if I could*
identify *the thief.*
recognize, name, distinguish,
pick out, single out
2 *The doctor couldn't* **identify**
what was wrong.
diagnose, discover, spot
(informal) put a name to
idiotic adjective
That was an **idiotic** *thing to do.*

stupid, silly, foolish, unwise,
senseless, ridiculous, half-
witted, unintelligent, crazy,
mad, hare-brained
(informal) daft
OPPOSITE sensible
idle adjective
1 *The ogre was an* **idle**,
foul-smelling creature.
lazy, indolent,
slothful, work-shy
OPPOSITE hard-
working
2 *The computers
lay* **idle** *all week.*
inactive, unused,
inoperative
OPPOSITE busy, active
idol noun
1 *The floor of the
temple was littered
with broken* **idols**.
god, deity, image,
statue
2 *He was a pop* **idol**
of the fifties.
star, celebrity,
icon, pin-up,
favourite
ignorant adjective
Trolls are often described as
ignorant *creatures.*
uneducated, simple, stupid
ignore verb
Ignoring *the weather, Lynn went
for a walk.*
disregard, take no notice of,
overlook, neglect, spurn, snub
(informal) turn a blind eye to
ill adjective
1 *I missed school for a week when
I was* **ill**.
sick, unwell, poorly, sickly,
ailing, infirm, unfit, indisposed,
diseased, infected, nauseous,
queasy, off colour, peaky
(informal) under the weather
OPPOSITE healthy, well
2 *Did the plants suffer* **ill** *effects in
the frost?*
bad, harmful, adverse, damaging
OPPOSITE good
illegal adjective
Stealing is **illegal**.
unlawful, against the law,
banned, prohibited, criminal,
forbidden, wrong
OPPOSITE legal
illustrate verb
1 *I used some photos to* **illustrate**
my story.
depict, picture, portray
2 *The accident* **illustrates** *the
importance of road safety.*
show, demonstrate, make clear
illustration noun
1 *I like cookery books with lots of*
illustrations.
picture, photograph, drawing,

sketch, diagram
2 *I'll give you an* **illustration** *of
what I mean.*
example, instance,
demonstration, specimen
image noun
1 *The film contained frightening*
images *of war.*
picture, portrayal, depiction,
representation
2 *The temple contained* **images** *of
the gods.*
figure, idol, statue, carving
3 *You can see your* **image** *in the
mirror.*
reflection, likeness
imaginary adjective
The story takes place in an
imaginary *universe.*
imagined, non-existent, unreal,
made up, invented, fanciful,
fictitious, fictional
OPPOSITE real
imagination noun
Use your **imagination** *to draw an
alien spaceship.*
creativity, inventiveness,
ingenuity, inspiration, originality,
vision, artistry, fancy
imaginative adjective
Roald Dahl wrote highly
imaginative *stories.*
creative, inventive, inspired,
original, artistic, fanciful,
ingenious, clever
OPPOSITE unimaginative, dull
imagine verb
1 **Imagine** *what it would be like to
visit Mars.*
picture, visualize, pretend, think
up, dream up, fancy, conjure up
2 *I* **imagine** *you'd like something
to eat.*
suppose, assume, presume,
believe, guess
imitate verb
Parrots can **imitate** *the human
voice.*
copy, reproduce, mimic, mirror,
echo, simulate, impersonate,
follow, match
(informal) send up, take off
imitation noun
This is an **imitation** *of a Viking
helmet.*
copy, replica, reproduction,
duplicate
*An imitation made to deceive
someone is a* **fake** *or a* **forgery**.
immediate adjective
1 *Please can I have an* **immediate**
reply.
instant, instantaneous, prompt,
speedy, swift, urgent, quick,
direct
(informal) snappy
OPPOSITE slow
2 *Are you friends with your*
immediate *neighbours?*

closest, nearest, adjacent, next
OPPOSITE **distant**

immediately *adverb*
You must fetch a doctor
immediately!
at once, now, straight away,
right away, instantly, promptly,
directly

immense *adjective*
The giant wiggled one of his
immense toes.
huge, great, massive, enormous,
colossal, vast, giant, gigantic,
mighty, mammoth, monumental
(*informal*) whopping, ginormous,
humungous
OPPOSITE **tiny**

immoral *adjective*
It would be immoral to steal the
money.
wrong, wicked, bad, sinful,
dishonest, corrupt
OPPOSITE **moral, right**

immortal *adjective*
The ancient Greeks believed their
gods were immortal.
undying, ageless, eternal,
everlasting
OPPOSITE **mortal**

impact *noun*
1 *The crater was caused by the*
impact of a meteor.
crash, collision, smash, blow,
bump, bang, knock, jolt
2 *Computers have a big impact*
on our lives.
effect, influence

impatient *adjective*
1 *As time went on, Henry grew*
more and more impatient.
restless, agitated, anxious, edgy,
fidgety, irritable, snappy, testy,
jumpy
OPPOSITE **patient**
2 *The crowd were impatient for*
the show to begin.
anxious, eager, in a hurry, keen
(*informal*) itching

important *adjective*
1 *The World Cup is an important*
sporting event.
major, significant, big, central,
momentous, outstanding,
historic
2 *I have some important business*
to attend to.
serious, urgent, pressing,
weighty, vital, essential, crucial
3 *The prime minister is an*
important person.
prominent, powerful, influential,
notable, eminent, distinguished

impossible *adjective*
We used to think that space travel
was impossible.
impractical, unthinkable,
unrealistic, unachievable,
unworkable, out of the question
OPPOSITE **possible**

impact

impress *verb*
Frank impressed the coach with
his football skills.
make an impression on,
influence, leave its mark on, stick
in your mind

impression *noun*
1 *I had the impression that*
something was wrong.
feeling, idea, sense, notion,
suspicion, hunch
2 *The film made a big impression*
on them.
effect, impact, influence, mark
3 *My sister does a good*
impression of the Queen.
imitation, impersonation
(*informal*) send-up

impressive *adjective*
The film includes some impressive
special effects.
striking, effective, powerful,
remarkable, spectacular,
exciting, inspiring
OPPOSITE **unimpressive,**
uninspiring

imprison *verb*
The thief was imprisoned for
two years.
send to prison, jail, lock up,
incarcerate, confine, detain
(*informal*) put away, send down,
put under lock and key
OPPOSITE **liberate**

improve *verb*
1 *Her work improved this term.*
get better, advance, progress,
develop, move on
OPPOSITE **deteriorate**
2 *Has he improved since his*
illness?
get better, recover, recuperate,
pick up, rally, revive
OPPOSITE **get worse**
3 *How can I improve this story?*
make better, enhance, refine,
amend, revise, correct, upgrade

improvement *noun*
1 *Your handwriting shows signs of*
improvement.
getting better, advance, progress,
development, recovery, upturn
2 *The author made some*
improvements to the book.
amendment, correction, revision,
modification, enhancement

impulsive *adjective*
She regretted her impulsive
decision to dye her hair.
hasty, rash, reckless, sudden,
spontaneous, thoughtless,
unthinking, impetuous
OPPOSITE **deliberate**

inaccurate *adjective*
That spelling of my surname is
inaccurate.
wrong, incorrect, mistaken, false,
inexact, untrue
OPPOSITE **accurate**

inadequate *adjective*
They had brought an inadequate
supply of matches.
insufficient, not enough, limited,
scarce, scanty, meagre
OPPOSITE **adequate**

incident *noun*
There was an amusing incident
at school this morning.
event, happening, occurrence,
episode, affair

include *verb*
Does the cost include postage
and packing?
contain, incorporate, comprise,
involve, take in, allow for, take
into account, cover
OPPOSITE **exclude**

inconsiderate *adjective*
It's inconsiderate to play the radio
so loudly.
selfish, unthinking, thoughtless,
insensitive, rude, tactless,
unkind, uncaring
OPPOSITE **considerate**

inconvenient *adjective*
The guests arrived at an
inconvenient moment.
awkward, difficult, unsuitable,
unfortunate, untimely,
inopportune
OPPOSITE **convenient**

increase *verb*
1 *They've increased the size of the*
tennis courts.
make bigger, enlarge, expand,
develop, add to, widen,
broaden
2 *She increased the cooking time*
in the recipe.
extend, lengthen, prolong
3 *The police increased their efforts*
to find the murderer.
intensify, step up
4 *Will you be increasing the bus*
fares?
put up, raise
5 *Can you increase the volume of*
the TV?
turn up, amplify, boost
6 *The number of cars on the roads*
continues to increase.
grow, mount, go up, rise,
soar, build up, escalate,
multiply

incredible *adjective*
1 *Do you expect us to believe that*
incredible story?
unbelievable, unlikely,
improbable, far-fetched, absurd,
implausible
OPPOSITE **credible**
2 *The Forth Bridge is an incredible*
feat of engineering.
extraordinary, amazing,
astounding, magnificent,
marvellous, spectacular

independent *adjective*
1 *My granny is a very*
independent person.
free, liberated, self-sufficient,
self-reliant
OPPOSITE **dependent**
2 *Luxembourg is an independent*
country.
autonomous, self-governing
3 *We need an independent*
opinion on the matter.
impartial, neutral, objective,
unbiased
OPPOSITE **biased**

indifferent *adjective*
1 *I felt indifferent as I watched*
the game.
uninterested, detached,
uncaring, unenthusiastic,
unmoved, uninvolved,
unconcerned
OPPOSITE **enthusiastic**
2 *The food in the restaurant was*
indifferent.
mediocre, ordinary, unexciting,
average
OPPOSITE **excellent**

indignant *adjective*
The player was indignant when he
was sent off.
annoyed, angry, cross, affronted,
offended, outraged, piqued

indirect *adjective*
The bus took an indirect route into
town.
roundabout, winding,
meandering, rambling, zigzag
OPPOSITE **direct**

individual *adjective*
Her singing has an individual
style.
characteristic, distinct,
distinctive, special, unique,
personal, singular

inevitable *adjective*
If it rains, it is inevitable that the
pitch will get wet.
certain, sure, definite,
unavoidable, inescapable

infect *verb*
A virus may have infected the
water supply.
contaminate, pollute, poison

infection *noun*
The infection spread rapidly.
disease, virus, contagion,
contamination

infectious *adjective*
Chickenpox is highly infectious.
contagious, catching

inferior *adjective*
1 *The clothes were of inferior*
quality.
poor, bad, second-rate,
mediocre, cheap, shoddy
2 *Officers can give orders to those*
of inferior rank.
lesser, lower, junior, subordinate

infinite *adjective*
You need infinite patience to train
a puppy.
endless, limitless, unlimited,
boundless, never-ending,
unending, inexhaustible
OPPOSITE **finite**

influence *noun*
Rock music had a big influence on
her life.
effect, impact, power,
dominance, guidance, authority,
control

influence *verb*
The money he was offered
influenced his decision.
affect, have an effect on, direct,
guide, control, motivate

inform *verb*
Please inform us if you move
house.
tell, let you know, notify, advise

informal *adjective*
1 *The party will be a very*
informal event.
casual, relaxed, easygoing,
friendly, homely, natural
2 *Emails are usually*

written in an informal
style.
colloquial, familiar,
chatty, personal

information *noun*
There is more
information on our website.
details, particulars, facts, data,
advice, guidance, knowledge
(*informal*) info

inhabit *verb*
People inhabited the caves
thousands of years ago.
live in, occupy, dwell in, reside
in, populate, settle in

initiative *noun*
You must use your initiative on
the treasure hunt.
resourcefulness, inventiveness,
originality, enterprise

injure *verb*
Was anyone injured in the
accident?
hurt, harm, wound
To injure someone causing
permament damage is to
maim them.

innocent *adjective*
1 *The jury found the man innocent.*
guiltless, blameless, free from
blame
OPPOSITE **guilty**
2 *Baby tigers look so innocent.*
angelic, harmless, faultless,
virtuous, pure, simple,
inexperienced, naïve
OPPOSITE **wicked**

inquire *verb*
to inquire into
Detectives are inquiring into the
robbery.
look into, investigate, examine,
explore

insane *adjective*
1 *It was rumoured that the king*
had gone insane.
mentally ill, mad, crazy,
deranged, demented, disturbed,
unhinged
(*informal*) off your head, out of
your mind
OPPOSITE **sane**
2 *It would be insane to swim in the*
sea in January!
crazy, mad, daft, senseless,
stupid, foolish, idiotic
OPPOSITE **sensible, wise**

insect *noun see panel opposite*

insensitive *adjective*
I'm sorry if my comments were
insensitive.
thoughtless,
tactless, unfeeling,
uncaring,

WORD WEB

insect *noun*
SOME TYPES OF INSECT
ant, aphid, bee, beetle, bluebottle, bumble-bee, butterfly, cicada, cockroach, crane fly or daddy-long-legs, cricket, dragonfly, earwig, firefly, flea, fly, glow-worm, gnat, grasshopper, greenfly, hornet, horsefly, ladybird, locust, louse, mantis, mayfly, midge, mosquito, moth, stick insect, termite, tsetse fly, wasp, weevil

LIFE STAGES OF SOME INSECTS
caterpillar, chrysalis, grub, larva, maggot, pupa

PARTS OF INSECTS' BODIES
head, thorax, abdomen, antennae, legs, wings

SOME CREATURES SIMILAR TO INSECTS
centipede, earthworm, mite, slug, spider, woodlouse, worm

unsympathetic, callous
OPPOSITE **sensitive**

inside *noun*
*The **inside** of the nest was lined with feathers.*
interior, inner surface, centre, core, heart, middle
OPPOSITE **outside**

insignificant *adjective*
*The author made a few **insignificant** changes.*
unimportant, minor, trivial, negligible, slight, meaningless
OPPOSITE **significant**

insincere *adjective*
*The butler welcomed us with an **insincere** smile.*
false, pretended, hypocritical, dishonest, deceitful, deceptive, lying
(*informal*) two-faced
OPPOSITE **sincere**

insist *verb*
*Griselda **insisted** that she was not a witch.*
declare, state, assert, maintain, stress, emphasize, swear, vow, claim
to insist on
*The magician **insisted on** silence before he began.*
demand, require

inspect *verb*
*They **inspected** the damage done by the storm.*
check, examine, investigate, look over, study, survey, scrutinize

inspire *verb*
*The crowd **inspired** the team to play well.*
motivate, prompt, stimulate, encourage, stir, arouse, spur on

instant *adjective*
*Gardeners don't expect **instant** results.*
immediate, quick, rapid, fast, prompt, snappy, speedy, swift, direct

instant *noun*
*The shooting star was gone in an **instant**.*
moment, second, split second, flash
(*informal*) tick, jiffy

instinct *noun*
*The detective always followed his own **instincts**.*
impulse, inclination, intuition, hunch, feeling, urge

instruct *verb*
1 *All the staff are **instructed** in first aid.*
teach, train, coach, tutor
2 *The police officer **instructed** the cars to wait.*
tell, order, direct, command

instructions *plural noun*
*Please follow the **instructions** carefully.*
directions, guidelines, orders, commands

instrument *noun*
*Dentists use special **instruments** to check your teeth.*
tool, implement, utensil, appliance, device, gadget, contraption

insult *verb*
*He was **insulted** not to be invited to the wedding.*
offend, outrage, be rude to, hurt, injure, slight, snub

insult *noun*
*It is considered an **insult** to refuse a gift.*
rudeness, offence, affront, slight, slur, snub

insulting *adjective*
*She made an **insulting** comment about my clothes.*
offensive, rude, impolite, derogatory, scornful
OPPOSITE **complimentary**

intelligent *adjective*
The aliens from Planet Zog are highly intelligent.
clever, bright, smart, quick, sharp, perceptive, shrewd, able, brilliant, rational, thinking
(*informal*) brainy
OPPOSITE **unintelligent, stupid**

intense *adjective*
1 *I felt a sudden, **intense** pain in my chest.*
extreme, acute, severe, sharp, great, strong, violent
OPPOSITE **slight, mild**
2 *The contest aroused **intense** feelings.*
deep, passionate, powerful, strong, profound
OPPOSITE **mild**

interest *verb*
*Politics doesn't **interest** me at all.*
appeal to, attract, capture your imagination, excite, fascinate, stimulate, absorb
OPPOSITE **bore**

interest *noun*
1 *The dog showed no **interest** in the bone.*
curiosity, attention, concern, involvement
2 *The information was of no **interest** to anyone.*
importance, significance, consequence, value
3 *My **interests** include judo and playing the trombone.*
hobby, pastime, pursuit, activity, diversion

interesting *adjective*
Everyone wanted to hear about our interesting adventures.
fascinating, absorbing, enthralling, intriguing, engrossing, stimulating, riveting, gripping, entertaining diverting
OPPOSITE **boring, dull**

interfere *verb*
to interfere in
*Don't **interfere in** other people's affairs.*
intervene in, intrude in, meddle in, pry into, encroach on, butt in on
to interfere with
*The bad weather **interfered with** our plans.*
hamper, hinder, get in the way of, obstruct

international *adjective*
*Interpol is an **international** police organization.*
global, worldwide, intercontinental

a
b
c
d
e
f
g
h
i
j
k
l
m
q
r
u
v
w
x
y
z

interrupt *verb*
1 *Please don't interrupt while I am speaking.*
intervene, interject, break in, butt in, cut in
2 *Heavy rain interrupted the tennis match.*
stop, suspend, disrupt, break off, cut short

interruption *noun*
He wrote for an hour without any interruption.
break, pause, stop, gap, halt, disruption, suspension

interval *noun*
1 *There will be a short interval after the first act.*
break, pause, wait, delay, lapse, lull
Another word for an interval in a play or film is *interlude* or *intermission*.
An interval in a meeting is a *recess*.
An interval when you take a rest is a *breather* or *breathing space*.
2 *There were signs at regular intervals along the road.*
space, gap, distance

interview *verb*
He interviewed the author about her new book.
question, talk to, interrogate, examine

intimate *adjective*
1 *They have been intimate friends for years.*
close, cherished, dear, friendly, informal
OPPOSITE distant
2 *The newspaper printed intimate details about her life.*
personal, private, confidential, secret

intriguing *adjective*
The results of the experiment are intriguing.
interesting, attractive, fascinating, captivating, beguiling

introduce *verb*
1 *Let me introduce you to my friend.*
present, make known
2 *The director stood up to introduce the film.*
give an introduction to, announce, lead into
3 *They are introducing a new bus service next year.*
set up, start, begin, create, establish, initiate, bring in

introduction *noun*
Something which happens as an introduction to a bigger event is a *prelude*.
An introduction to a book is a *preface*.

An introduction to a play is a *prologue*.
A piece played as an introduction to a concert or opera is an *overture*.

invade *verb*
The Vikings invaded many parts of Europe.
attack, enter, occupy, overrun, march into, raid

invent *verb*
James Dewar invented the thermos flask.
create, devise, think up, conceive, design, originate

inventor *noun*
James Dewar was the inventor of the thermos flask.
creator, designer, originator, discoverer

investigate *verb*
Police are investigating the cause of the accident.
examine, explore, inquire into, look into, study, consider, follow up, probe, research, scrutinize
(*informal*) go into

investigation *noun*
An investigation showed how the accident happened.
examination, inquiry, inspection, study, review, survey

invisible *adjective*
The wizard was invisible when he wore his magic cloak.
out of sight, unseen, unnoticed, hidden, concealed, covered, obscured, camouflaged, disguised, undetectable, unnoticeable, inconspicuous
OPPOSITE visible

invite *verb*
Our neighbours invited us round for tea.
ask, request your company, welcome, summon

involve *verb*
1 *My job involves a lot of travel.*
include, comprise, require, demand, necessitate, mean
2 *Protecting the environment involves us all.*
affect, concern, interest, touch

involved *adjective*
1 *The film has a long and involved plot.*
complex, complicated, elaborate, intricate, confusing, difficult, convoluted
OPPOSITE simple
2 *Are you involved in the theatre?*
concerned, participating, engaged, caught up, mixed up

irregular *adjective*
1 *The bricks were arranged in an irregular pattern.*
varying, erratic, haphazard, random, unpredictable, fitful
OPPOSITE regular

2 *It is highly irregular to eat pizza with a spoon!*
abnormal, unusual, exceptional, unconventional, improper
OPPOSITE normal

irresponsible *adjective*
It's irresponsible to drive too fast.
reckless, rash, thoughtless, inconsiderate, uncaring, unthinking, negligent
OPPOSITE responsible

irritable *adjective*
After a bad night, he woke in an irritable mood.
bad-tempered, grumpy, short-tempered, cross, impatient, snappy, touchy, testy, prickly, peevish
(*informal*) stroppy, shirty
OPPOSITE good-humoured, cheerful

irritate *verb*
The noise from next door began to irritate me.
annoy, bother, exasperate, anger, provoke, madden, vex
(*informal*) get on your nerves, bug

isolated *adjective*
They sheltered in an isolated cave in the mountains.
remote, out-of-the-way, secluded, outlying, inaccessible, cut off, deserted
OPPOSITE accessible

issue *verb*
1 *They issued blankets to the refugees.*
give out, distribute, supply
2 *They have issued a new set of stamps.*
bring out, put out, produce, publish, release, circulate, print
3 *Green smoke issued from the dragon's nostrils.*
come out, emerge, appear, flow out, gush, erupt

issue *noun*
1 *The new issue of the magazine comes out this week.*
edition, number, instalment, copy
2 *They print stories about local issues in the magazine.*
matter, subject, topic, affair, concern, question, problem

itch *noun*
1 *I had an annoying itch on my foot.*
tickle, tingling, prickle
2 *Olga had a great itch to travel.*
desire, longing, urge, wish, yearning, ache, impulse

item *noun*
1 *I bought a few items in the jumble sale.*
thing, object, article
2 *There was an item about our school in the paper.*
article, piece, report, feature

Jj

jab *verb*
A passer-by jabbed me in the ribs.
poke, prod, elbow, nudge, stab, thrust

jagged *adjective*
This dinosaur had jagged teeth.
rough, uneven, ragged, spiky, toothed, serrated
OPPOSITE smooth

jam *noun*
1 *We got stuck in a jam on the motorway.*
traffic jam, hold-up, tailback, blockage
2 (*informal*) *I'm in a bit of a jam.*
difficulty, mess, predicament, plight
(*informal*) fix, tight corner

jam *verb*
1 *Someone had jammed the door open.*
prop, wedge, stick
2 *The roads are jammed at rush hour.*
block, clog, obstruct, congest
(*informal*) bung up
3 *I jammed my things into a backpack.*
cram, pack, stuff, squeeze, squash, crush, ram, crowd

jangle *verb*
Silver bracelets jangled on her wrists.
jingle, chink, clink, tinkle

jealous *adjective*
Cinderella's sisters were jealous of her beauty.
envious, resentful, grudging

jeer *verb*
Some of the audience whistled and jeered.
boo, hiss, sneer, taunt, mock, scoff, ridicule
OPPOSITE cheer

jerk *verb*
The rider jerked on the horse's reins.
pull, tug, yank, pluck, wrench, tweak

jerky *adjective*
The stagecoach drew to a jerky halt.
jolting, jumpy, shaky, bouncy, bumpy, uneven
OPPOSITE steady

jet *noun*
A jet of water shot high in the air.
spout, spurt, squirt, gush, stream, fountain

jingle *verb*
Some coins jingled in his back pocket.
jangle, chink, clink, tinkle

job *noun*
1 *My sister wants a job as a TV reporter.*
post, position, profession, occupation, employment, trade, work, career
The job you particularly want to do is your mission or vocation.
2 *Whose job is it to do the washing-up?*
duty, task, assignment, chore, errand

jog *verb*
1 *He jogs round the park every morning.*
go jogging, run, trot
2 *A boy sitting next to me jogged my elbow.*
nudge, prod, jolt, knock, bump, jar, jostle
3 *The photograph may jog her memory.*
prompt, stir, arouse, set off, stimulate

join *verb*
1 *Our families joined together to buy the present.*
combine, come together, merge, unite, amalgamate
OPPOSITE separate
2 *Join one piece of rope to the other.*
connect, fasten, attach, fix, link, put together, tack on
OPPOSITE detach
3 *The two roads join here.*
meet, merge, converge
OPPOSITE divide
4 *I joined the crowd going into the cinema.*
follow, go with, tag along with
OPPOSITE leave
5 *We have joined a local sports club.*
become a member of, enrol in, sign up for
To join the army is to enlist.
OPPOSITE leave, resign from

join *noun*
If you look hard, you can still see the join.
joint, connection, link, mend, seam

joint *adjective*
The preparation of the meal was a joint effort.
combined, shared, common, communal, cooperative, united, collective, mutual
OPPOSITE individual

joke *noun*
Do you know any good jokes?
jest, quip, crack, witticism, wisecrack
(*informal*) gag

joke *verb*
Those two are always laughing and joking.
jest, clown, have a laugh, make jokes

jolly *adjective*
We had a jolly time on holiday.
cheerful, merry, happy, joyful, pleasant, enjoyable
OPPOSITE gloomy

jolt *verb*
The car jolted over the bumps in the road.
jerk, jog, bump, bounce, shake, shudder

journey *noun*
On their journey, the astronauts will pass the Moon.
voyage, trip, expedition, travels, tour, route

joy *noun*
I remember the sheer joy of scoring a goal!
happiness, joyfulness, delight, cheerfulness, gladness, mirth, glee, jubilation, gaiety, rejoicing, bliss, ecstasy, elation
OPPOSITE sorrow

joyful *adjective*
The wedding was a joyful occasion.
happy, cheerful, merry, joyous, jolly, jovial, good-humoured
OPPOSITE sad

judge *verb*
1 *The umpire judged that the ball was out.*
rule, decide, decree, adjudicate
2 *Who's judging the flower show this year?*
decide on, assess, evaluate, appraise
3 *He judged the coin to be about 1000 years old.*
reckon, suppose, consider, gauge, guess, estimate

judgement *noun*
1 *What is the judgement of the court?*
decision, finding, ruling, verdict, decree
2 *His comments show a lack of judgement.*
wisdom, common sense, understanding, discrimination
3 *In my judgement, you're making a big mistake.*
opinion, view, belief, assessment, estimate

jumble *noun*
There was a jumble of clothes on the floor.
mess, muddle, clutter, chaos, confusion, disorder

jumble *verb*
Please don't jumble the pages.
muddle, mix up, mess up, disorganize, shuffle
OPPOSITE arrange

jump *verb*
1 *Suddenly a rabbit jumped in front of us.*
leap, spring, bound, bounce, hop
When a cat jumps it pounces.

2 *All the horses jumped the first hurdle.*
leap over, vault, clear
3 *The loud bang made them all jump.*
start, flinch, jolt
jump *noun*
With a jump, the grasshopper landed on the leaf.
leap, spring, bound, vault, hop
junk *noun*
The garage is full of old junk.
rubbish, clutter, garbage, jumble, trash, waste, scrap, odds and ends
just *adjective*
It was a just punishment, considering the crime.
fair, fitting, appropriate, deserved, proper, reasonable, justified
OPPOSITE unjust, unfair

Kk

keen *adjective*
1 *Rhona is a keen hockey player.*
enthusiastic, eager, fervent, avid, devoted, committed, motivated
A common simile is **as keen as mustard**.
OPPOSITE unenthusiastic
2 *A carving knife should have a keen edge.*
sharp, razor-sharp, cutting
OPPOSITE blunt
3 *Owls must have keen eyesight.*
sharp, acute, piercing
OPPOSITE poor
4 *A keen wind was blowing from the east.*
bitter, cold, icy, penetrating
OPPOSITE mild
keep *verb*
1 *Let's keep the rest of the cake for later.*
save, conserve, preserve, retain, hang on to, hold on to, guard, store
2 *Please keep still.*
stay, remain
3 *A man in the audience kept coughing.*
persist in, go on, carry on, continue
4 *You're late. What kept you?*
delay, detain, hold up, keep waiting
5 *Where do you keep the knives and forks?*
store, house, put, stow
6 *Will the milk keep until tomorrow?*
last, be usable, stay good
7 *It costs money to keep a pet.*
support, maintain, provide for, pay for

to keep something up
Keep up the good work!
carry on, continue, maintain
key *noun*
Have you found the key to the riddle?
answer, solution, explanation, clue
kick *noun*
1 *He gave the television a kick.*
hit, boot, blow
2 *(informal) Some people might get a kick out of crossing the Atlantic in an old bath.*
thrill, excitement, (informal) buzz
kick *verb*
1 *Merv kicked the ball out.*
boot, hit, drive, send, punt, heel
2 *(informal) It's a habit I have to kick.*
give up, quit, break, abandon, cease, desist from
kidnap *verb*
In the story, a boy is kidnapped by bandits.
abduct, capture, seize, carry off, snatch
kill *verb*
Several people were killed in the explosion.
(informal) bump off, do away with (old use) slay
To kill someone deliberately is to **murder** them.

To kill someone brutally is to **butcher** them.
To kill large numbers of people is to **massacre** or **slaughter** them.
To kill someone as a punishment is to **execute** them or **put them to death**.
To kill someone for political reasons is to **assassinate** them.
kind *noun*
What kind of music do you like to play?
sort, type, variety, style, category, class, set
kind *adjective*
It was very kind of you to help me.
kind-hearted, caring, good-natured, kindly, affectionate, warm, genial, loving, sweet, gentle, lenient, amiable, friendly, generous, sympathetic, thoughtful, obliging, considerate, understanding, compassionate, unselfish, giving, gracious, merciful, benevolent, charitable, humane, neighbourly
OPPOSITE unkind
kit *noun*
I've forgotten my games kit.
gear, outfit, equipment, paraphernalia, tools, tackle
knack *noun*
George has a knack for taking photographs.
skill, talent, gift, flair

⭐ **WORD WEB**

knight *noun*
THINGS A MEDIEVAL KNIGHT MIGHT WEAR OR CARRY
armour, baldric (leather belt), coat of arms, falcon or hawk, lance, mace (metal club), pennant, shield, surcoat, sword, tabard, tunic

A fight between knights on horseback was a *joust*.
A series of sporting contests between knights was a *tournament*.
A boy training to be a knight was first a *page* and then a *squire*.
An expedition made by a knight was a *quest*.

knock *verb*
I knocked my head as I came out of the car.
bump, bang, hit, strike, thump (*informal*) bash

knot *verb*
The sailors knotted the two ropes together.
tie, bind, fasten, join, entwine, lash
OPPOSITE untie

know *verb*
1 *Do you know how to mend a puncture?*
understand, have knowledge of, comprehend
2 *As soon as she saw the unicorn, she knew what it was.*
recognize, realize, appreciate, be aware of
3 *Do you know Stewart well?*
be acquainted with, be familiar with, be a friend of

knowledge *noun*
1 *She has a good knowledge of Italian.*
understanding, grasp, command, familiarity (with)
2 *An encyclopedia contains a lot of knowledge.*
information, data, facts, learning, know-how, wisdom, scholarship

Ll

label *noun*
The washing instructions are on the label.
tag, ticket, sticker

lack *noun*
The judge dismissed the case because of a lack of evidence.
absence, shortage, scarcity, want
A general lack of food is a famine.
A general lack of water is a drought.
OPPOSITE abundance

lack *verb*
The game lacked excitement.
be short of, be without, want, need, require, miss

lag *verb*
One runner was lagging behind the others.
straggle, trail, fall behind, drop behind, dawdle, linger, loiter

lake *noun*
We rowed across the lake.
pond, pool

(*Scottish*) loch
A salt-water lake is a *lagoon*.
A lake used to supply water is a *reservoir*.

land *noun*
1 *The castle is surrounded by several acres of land.*
grounds, estate, property
2 *The land here is good for growing strawberries.*
ground, soil, earth
3 *China is a land with an ancient history.*
country, nation, state, region, territory

land *verb*
1 *The plane landed exactly on time.*
touch down, arrive
OPPOSITE take off
2 *The ship will land at Dover.*
dock, berth, come ashore
3 *How did these papers land on my desk?*
arrive, turn up, end up, wind up, settle

landscape *noun*
We sat on the hill and admired the landscape.
countryside, scenery, view, scene, outlook, prospect

lap *noun*
1 *My cat, Snowy, likes to sit on my lap.*
knees, thighs
2 *The cars were on the last lap of the race.*
circuit, round, loop

large *adjective*
1 *Elephants are large animals.*
big, huge, enormous, colossal, giant, gigantic, immense, great, massive, bulky, heavy, hefty, weighty, mighty, towering
(*informal*) whopping, ginormous
2 *The cook gave me a large helping of pudding.*
ample, generous, plentiful, abundant, lavish
3 *Is this room large enough for dancing in?*
spacious, roomy, sizeable
4 *The gales caused damage over a large area.*
wide, broad, extensive, widespread, vast
5 *The meeting was attended by a large number of people.*
considerable, substantial

last *adjective*
1 *Z is the last letter of the alphabet.*
final, closing, concluding, terminating, ultimate
OPPOSITE first
2 *Did you see the last Harry Potter film?*

latest, most recent
OPPOSITE next

last *noun*
at last
The holidays are here at last!
finally, eventually, in the end

late *adjective*
1 *The bus is late.*
delayed, overdue
OPPOSITE early, punctual, on time
2 *Mr Pettigrew showed us a portrait of his late wife.*
dead, deceased, departed, former

lately *adverb*
There has been a lot of snow lately.
recently, latterly, of late

later *adverb*
I'm busy now, but I'll phone you later.
afterwards, in a while, subsequently, next

laugh *verb*
1 *The childen laughed when the clown fell over.*
chuckle, chortle, giggle, titter, burst out laughing, roar or scream with laughter, roll or fall about laughing, guffaw
(*informal*) have hysterics, be in stitches
2 *It's rude to laugh at his way of singing.*
make fun of, mock, ridicule, scoff at, tease, deride

laughter *noun*
We heard bursts of laughter coming from the kitchen.
laughing, amusement, hilarity, mirth, merriment

lavish *adjective*
The king put on a lavish feast for his birthday.
generous, extravagant, sumptuous, luxurious, opulent, grand, abundant, copious, plentiful, bountiful
OPPOSITE meagre, paltry

law *noun*
A law passed by parliament is an *act*.
A proposed law to be discussed by parliament is a *bill*.
The laws of a game are *regulations* or *rules*.
A regulation which must be obeyed is a *commandment*, *decree*, *edict*, or *order*.

lay *verb*
1 *He laid the parchment carefully on his desk.*
put down, set down, place, position, spread, deposit, leave
2 *Please lay the table for dinner.*
set out, arrange

layer *noun*
1 *The walls needed two layers of paint.*

coat, coating, covering, thickness, film, sheet, skin
2 *You can see various **layers** of rock in the cliff.*
seam, stratum

laze *verb*
*We spent the day **lazing** in the garden.*
be lazy, idle, loaf, lounge, lie about, relax, loll

lazy *adjective*
*My **lazy** little brother stayed in bed all day!*
idle, inactive, lethargic, slack, slothful, indolent
*An informal name for a lazy person is **lazybones**.*

lead *verb*
1 *The rescuers **led** the climbers to safety.*
guide, conduct, escort, usher, steer, pilot, shepherd
OPPOSITE follow
2 *Dr Martez will **lead** the expedition to Peru.*
be in charge of, direct, command, head, manage, supervise
3 *The British cyclist **led** from the start of the race.*
be in front, be in the lead, head the field
4 *The animals in the zoo **lead** a peaceful life.*
have, pass, spend, experience

lead *noun*
1 *The team followed the captain's **lead**.*
example, guidance, leadership, direction
2 *The Australian swimmer is in the **lead**.*
first place, front position
3 *Don't trip over the electrical **lead**.*
cable, flex, wire

leader *noun*
*The **leader** of the pirates was Captain Cutlass.*
head, chief, commander, captain, director, principal, ruler
(*informal*) boss
*The leader of a group of wrongdoers is the **ringleader**.*

leak *noun* **leak** *verb*
1 *The juice had **leaked** all over my schoolbag.*
escape, drip, seep, ooze, trickle
2 *Details of a secret plan were **leaked** to the newspaper.*
reveal, disclose, make known, pass on, give away, let out

lean *verb*
1 *I **leaned** against the wall.*
recline, rest, prop

yourself, support yourself
2 *The yacht **leaned** to one side in the wind.*
slope, tilt, tip, incline, slant, list, bank

leap *verb*
*The dog **leaped** in the air to catch the ball.*
jump, spring, bound, vault

learn *verb*
1 *We are **learning** about the Vikings this term.*
discover, find out, gather, grasp, pick up
2 *I've got to **learn** the words of this song.*
learn by heart, memorize, master

learner *noun*
*This swimming class is for **learners** only.*
beginner, starter, novice
*Someone learning things at school or college is a **pupil** or **student**.*
*Someone learning a trade is an **apprentice** or **trainee**.*

leave *verb*
1 *Do you have to **leave** now?*
go, go away, depart, withdraw, take your leave, go out, set off, say goodbye
(*informal*) take off, disappear
OPPOSITE arrive
2 *The doctor **left** the room in a hurry.*
exit, go out of, depart from, quit, vacate
OPPOSITE enter
3 *Don't **leave** me here on my own!*
abandon, desert, forsake
4 *The crew **left** the sinking ship.*
evacuate, get out of
5 *My sister has **left** her job at the bank.*
give up, quit, resign from
(*informal*) walk out of
6 *Leave the milk bottles by the front door.*
place, position, put down, set down, deposit
7 *Lady Bigwig **left** all her money to charity.*
bequeath, hand down, will, endow

lecture *noun*
1 *There is a **lecture** about dinosaurs at the museum today.*
talk, lesson, speech, address
2 *The teacher gave us a **lecture** on how to behave.*
reprimand, warning
(*informal*)
telling off

ledge *noun*
*The climbers rested on a **ledge** of rock.*
shelf, projection
*A ledge under a window is a **windowsill**.*

leg *noun*
1 *Boris fell and bruised his **leg**.*
FOR PARTS OF YOUR BODY, SEE body.
2 *The rowers completed the first **leg** of the race.*
part, stage, section, phase, stretch

legal *adjective*
*Is it **legal** to park here on Sundays?*
lawful, legitimate, permissible, permitted, allowed
OPPOSITE illegal

legend *noun*
*I like reading **legends** about ancient heroes.*
myth, story, folk tale, fairy tale, fable, tradition

leisure *noun*
*Grandad has plenty of **leisure** since he retired.*
free time, spare time, relaxation, recreation, rest

lend *verb*
*Can you **lend** me some money until the weekend?*
loan, advance, let you have
OPPOSITE borrow

length *noun*
1 *My heart sank when I saw the **length** of the queue.*
extent, size
2 *We only had to wait a short **length** of time.*
space, period, stretch

lengthen *verb*
1 *Is it possible to **lengthen** these curtains?*
extend, make longer, increase, stretch
2 *The days **lengthen** in spring.*
draw out, get longer, stretch out

lenient *adjective*
*The teacher was **lenient** and let us off.*
easygoing, soft-hearted, tolerant, forgiving, indulgent, kind, merciful
OPPOSITE strict

lesson *noun*
*My piano **lesson** is on Friday afternoon.*
class, period, tutorial, instruction

let *verb*
1 *Abby's parents **let** her go to the party.*
allow, give permission to, permit, consent to, agree to
OPPOSITE **forbid**
2 *Our friends are **letting** their house for the summer.*
lease, rent out, hire out

lethal *adjective*
*This bottle contains a **lethal** potion.*
deadly, fatal, mortal, poisonous

level *adjective*
1 *You need a **level** field for playing rounders.*
even, flat, horizontal, smooth
OPPOSITE **uneven**
2 *At half-time the scores were **level**.*
equal, even, the same, matching
(*informal*) neck-and-neck

level *noun*
1 *The water had reached a high **level**.*
height
2 *The lift takes you up to the sixth **level**.*
floor, storey, tier
3 *What **level** have you reached in judo?*
grade, standard, stage, rank, degree

lid *noun*
*Can you help me get the **lid** off this jar?*
cap, cover, covering, top

lie *noun*
*He accused the newspaper of printing **lies**.*
deceit, falsehood, dishonesty
(*informal*) fib
OPPOSITE **truth**

lie *verb*
1 *It's twelve o'clock and he's still **lying** in bed!*
recline, stretch out, lounge, sprawl, rest
To lie face down is to be **prone**.
To lie face upwards is to be **supine**.
2 *The castle **lies** in a valley.*
be sited, be situated, be located, be found
3 *I don't trust her—I think she's **lying**.*
deceive someone, bluff
(*informal*) fib

life *noun*
1 *My hamster, Fluffy, leads a very easy **life**.*
existence, being, way of life
2 *Our **lives** depended on finding water.*
survival
3 *You seem to be full of **life** today!*
energy, liveliness, vigour, vitality, spirit, sprightliness, animation

4 *I'm reading a **life** of Elvis Presley.*
life story, autobiography, biography

lift *verb*
1 *The removal men **lifted** the piano carefully.*
pick up, raise, elevate, pull up, hoist
2 *The plane **lifted** off the ground.*
rise, ascend, soar

> ✎ **WRITING TIPS**
>
> light
>
> **light** *noun*
> You can use these words to describe **light**.
> TO DESCRIBE *how light appears*
> bright, brilliant, harsh, luminous, lustrous, strong; diffused, dim, muted, soft, warm
> **light** MAY:
> beam, blaze, dazzle, flash, flicker, glare, gleam, glimmer, glint, glisten, glitter, glow, shimmer, shine, sparkle, twinkle

light *adjective*
1 *The artist worked in a **light** and airy studio.*
bright, well-lit, illuminated
OPPOSITE **dim, gloomy**
2 *She was wearing **light** blue jeans.*
pale
OPPOSITE **dark**
3 *The parcel looks big, but it is quite **light**.*
lightweight, portable, weightless, slight
A common simile is *as light as a feather*.
OPPOSITE **heavy**
4 *A **light** wind rippled the surface of the water.*
gentle, faint, slight
OPPOSITE **strong**
5 *We had a **light** meal before we went out.*
small, modest, simple, insubstantial
OPPOSITE **heavy, substantial**

light *verb*
1 *We **lit** the candles on my*

birthday cake.
ignite, kindle, set alight, set fire to, switch on
OPPOSITE **extinguish**
2 *The fireworks **lit** the sky.*
light up, brighten, illuminate, shed light on, shine on
OPPOSITE **darken**

like *verb*
1 *Lauren **likes** her new puppy more than anything.*
admire, adore, be attached to, be fond of, care for, cherish, esteem, hold dear, love
(*informal*) have a soft spot for
2 *Alex **likes** chocolate cake very much. What sort of films do you **like**?*
appreciate, be interested in, be keen on, be partial to, delight in, enjoy, prefer, relish
OPPOSITE **dislike**

likely *adjective*
*It's **likely** that the shop will be closed tomorrow.*
probable, expected, anticipated, predictable, foreseeable
OPPOSITE **unlikely**

limit *noun*
1 *There is a **limit** of twenty pupils for this class.*
maximum, restriction, threshold, ceiling, cut-off point
A limit on time is a **deadline** or **time limit**.
2 *The fence marks the **limit** of the school grounds.*
border, boundary, edge, perimeter, frontier

limit *verb*
*I had to **limit** the invitations to my party.*
put a limit on, restrict, control, ration

limp *adjective*
*The leaves on the plant are looking **limp**.*
drooping, floppy, sagging, wilting, soft, flabby, slack
OPPOSITE **rigid**

line *noun*
1 *I drew a pencil **line** across the page.*
stroke, rule, underline, stripe, streak, band, bar, dash
A line that is cut into a surface is a **groove**, **score**, or **scratch**.
A line on a person's skin is a **wrinkle**.
A deep groove or wrinkle is a **furrow**.
A line on fabric is a **crease**
2 *There was a long **line** of people waiting at the bus stop.*
queue, row, file, column, rank, procession, chain
A line of police officers forming a barrier is a **cordon**.
A line of schoolchildren walking

in pairs is a *crocodile*.
3 *The clothes were drying on the washing* **line**.
cord, rope, string, thread, wire, cable, flex, lead

linger *verb*
1 *The smell of burning wood* **lingered** *in the air.*
continue, remain, stay, last, persist
OPPOSITE disappear
2 *Don't* **linger** *outside in this cold weather.*
hang about, wait about, loiter, dawdle, dally, delay
OPPOSITE hurry

link *noun*
The two schools have close **links** *with each other.*
relationship, association, connection, bond, tie

link *verb*
They **linked** *the trailer to the tractor.*
attach, connect, fasten, join, couple
OPPOSITE separate

list *noun*
A list of people's names is a *roll* or *register*.
A list of people who have tasks to do is a *rota*.
A list of books in the library or of goods for sale is a *catalogue*.
A list of topics mentioned in a book is an *index*.
A list of things to choose from is a *menu*.
A list of things to do or remember is a *checklist*.

list *verb*
I helped to **list** *the books in the library.*
record, write down, catalogue, index, register

little

listen *verb*
to listen to something
The spy **listened** *carefully to the instructions.*
pay attention to, take notice of, attend to, heed
To listen secretly to a private conversation is to *eavesdrop*.

litter *noun*
The street was covered with **litter**.
rubbish, waste, refuse, garbage, junk, clutter, mess, odds and ends

little *adjective*
1 *The camera is so* **little** *it will fit in your pocket.*
compact, mini, miniature, minute, petite, small, tiny (*informal*) teeny (*Scottish*) wee
OPPOSITE big, large
2 *My granny lived in India when she was* **little**.
small, young
OPPOSITE big, old

live *adjective*
The fishermen caught a **live** *octopus in their nets.*
alive, living, breathing
OPPOSITE dead

live *verb*
Will these plants **live** *through the winter?*
stay alive, survive, exist, flourish, last, continue, remain
OPPOSITE die

lively *adjective*
1 *The toddlers were in a* **lively** *mood.*
active, energetic, animated, spirited, boisterous, excited, vivacious, sprightly, frisky, chirpy, perky
OPPOSITE inactive
2 *The city centre is always* **lively** *at night.*
busy, bustling, crowded, exciting, buzzing
OPPOSITE quiet, dead

living *adjective*
1 *Miss Millicent had no* **living** *relatives.*
alive
OPPOSITE dead
2 *There are no dinosaurs still* **living**.
existing, surviving
OPPOSITE extinct

living *noun*
1 *He makes a* **living** *from painting.*
income, livelihood
2 *What does she do for a* **living**?
job, occupation, profession, trade, career

load *noun*
1 *Camels can carry heavy* **loads**.
burden, weight
2 *The lorry delivered its* **load** *to the supermarket.*

cargo, consignment, goods, freight

load *verb*
1 *We* **loaded** *the suitcases into the car.*
pack, pile, heap, stow
2 *He arrived* **loaded** *with shopping bags.*
weigh down, burden, saddle

loathe *verb*
My brother **loathes** *the colour pink.*
hate, detest, dislike, despise
OPPOSITE love, adore

local *adjective*
Our **local** *shop delivers newspapers.*
neighbourhood, nearby, neighbouring

lock *noun*
1 *There was a heavy* **lock** *on the lid of the chest.*
fastening, clasp, padlock, bolt, latch
2 *The princess cut a* **lock** *from her hair.*
tress, curl, tuft

lock *verb*
Make sure you **lock** *the door when you go out.*
fasten, secure, bolt, close, shut, seal

logical *adjective*
The robot always gave a **logical** *answer.*
rational, reasonable, sensible, sound, valid, intelligent, clear, lucid, methodical, systematic
OPPOSITE illogical

lone *adjective*
A **lone** *rider galloped past.*
single, solitary, unaccompanied, isolated

lonely *adjective*
1 *Cara felt* **lonely** *while her friends were away.*
alone, friendless, lonesome, solitary, abandoned, neglected, forlorn, forsaken
2 *The climbers sheltered in a* **lonely** *hut.*
deserted, isolated, remote, secluded, out-of-the-way

long *adjective*
It seemed a **long** *time before the bus came.*
lengthy, prolonged, extended, extensive, long-lasting
OPPOSITE short

long *verb*
to long for something
I'm **longing for** *a drink.*
yearn for, crave, want, wish for, desire, fancy, hunger for, pine for, hanker after, itch for (*informal*) be dying for

look *verb*
1 *If you look carefully, you'll see an owl in the tree.*
watch, observe, view, regard, keep your eyes open
2 *My pet snake looks a bit hungry.*
appear, seem
3 *The secret agent looked at her watch.*
glance, glimpse, peek, peep
4 *The fossil hunters looked at the rocks.*
stare, peer, study, scrutinize, examine, inspect, take a good look at
5 *The grumpy knight looked at his servant.*
glare, glower, grimace, frown, scowl
To look steadily is to *gaze*.
To look quickly is to *glance, glimpse, peek* or *peep*.
To look in amazement is to *gape*.
To look over a wide area is to *scan* or *survey* it.

look *noun*
1 *Did you have a look at what she was wearing?*
glance, glimpse, peep, sight, view
2 *The guard had an unfriendly look.*
appearance, bearing, manner, air, expression, face

loop *noun*
Make a loop in the string and then tie a knot.
coil, hoop, circle, ring, noose, bend, curl, kink, twist

loop *verb*
The cowboy looped the reins round a fence post.
coil, wind, curl, bend, turn, twist

loose *adjective*
1 *Some of the cobbles on the road are loose.*
insecure, unfixed, movable, unsteady, shaky, wobbly
OPPOSITE firm, secure
2 *The fire was started by a loose wire.*
disconnected, unattached, detached
3 *These jeans are loose around the waist.*
slack, baggy, roomy, loose-fitting
OPPOSITE tight
4 *The chickens wander loose about the farm.*
free, at large, at liberty, on the loose, unconfined, unrestricted
OPPOSITE confined

loot *noun*
The thieves buried their loot in a safe place.
haul, plunder, takings

loot *verb*
Rioters looted the shops.
raid, ransack, rob, steal from, pillage, plunder

lose *verb*
1 *Debbie has lost one of her gloves.*
be unable to find, mislay, misplace
OPPOSITE find
2 *Unfortunately, we lost the game on Saturday.*
be defeated, get beaten, suffer a defeat
OPPOSITE win

lot *noun*
We are having another lot of visitors this weekend.
group, batch, set, crowd, collection

a lot of
My brother needs a lot of help with his spelling.
a large amount of, a good or great deal of, plenty of

lots of
There are lots of toys to choose from in the shop.
a great number of, many, numerous, plenty (of)
(*informal*) loads of, tons of, masses of, oodles of, hundreds of

loud *adjective*
The whole house was kept awake by the loud music.
noisy, blaring, booming, deafening, rowdy, resounding, thunderous, penetrating, piercing
A noise which is loud enough to hear is *audible*.
OPPOSITE quiet, soft

love *noun*
She often mentions her love of the outdoors.
liking, passion, fondness, affection, devotion, admiration, adoration
(*informal*) soft spot (for)

love *verb*
1 *They love each other and want to get married.*
be in love with, care for, adore, cherish, hold dear, treasure, worship, idolize
A relationship between two people who love each other is a *romance*.
2 *My friend, Dot, loves knitting.*
like, have a passion for, be fond of, be partial to, enjoy

lovely *adjective*
1 *Jemma is a*

lovely girl. charming, delightful, lovable, likeable, dear, sweet, enchanting, endearing
2 *It's a lovely day for a bicycle trip.*
fine, glorious
3 *The girls had an lovely time camping*
pleasant, pleasing, enjoyable
OPPOSITE nasty
4 *The roses look lovely in that vase.*
appealing, attractive, beautiful, pretty

low *adjective*
1 *The garden is surrounded by a low wall.*
short, shallow, sunken
2 *They were soldiers of low rank in the army.*
junior, inferior, lowly, modest, humble
3 *We spoke in low whispers.*
quiet, soft, muted, subdued, muffled
4 *The tuba plays low notes.*
bass, deep
OPPOSITE high

lower *verb*
1 *The supermarket lowered its prices.*
reduce, cut, bring down, decrease, lessen
(*informal*) slash
2 *Please lower the volume of your radio.*
quieten, turn down
3 *At the end of the Olympic Games, they lower the flag.*
take down, let down, dip

loyal *adjective*
Sir Valiant had always been a loyal knight.
true, trusty, faithful, steadfast, reliable, dependable, devoted, constant, sincere
OPPOSITE disloyal

luck *noun*
1 *He found the secret entrance by luck.*
accident, chance, coincidence, fluke, fate, destiny
2 *She had a bit of luck today.*
good fortune, success

a
b
c
d
e
f
g
h
i
j
k
l
m
n
o
p
q
r
s
t
u
v
w
x
y
z

lucky *adjective*
1 *I got the right answer by a* **lucky** *guess.*
accidental, chance, unintentional, unplanned
2 *Some* **lucky** *person won a million pounds.*
fortunate, favoured, successful

luggage *noun*
The **luggage** *can go in the boot of the car.*
baggage, cases, suitcases, bags

lump *noun*
1 **Lumps** *of sticky clay stuck to his boots.*
chunk, piece, cluster, clump, wad, mass, hunk, wedge, block
A round lump of something is a **ball**.
A lump of gold is a **nugget**.
A lump of earth is a **clod**.
A lump of blood is a **clot**.
2 *I could feel a* **lump** *where I'd bumped my head.*
bump, swelling, bulge, protrusion

lunge *verb*
Robin **lunged** *at the sheriff with his sword.*
thrust, charge, rush, dive, pounce, throw yourself

lurch *verb*
1 *The bus passengers* **lurched** *from side to side.*
reel, sway, rock, stagger, stumble, totter
2 *The ship* **lurched** *as the waves pounded it.*
pitch, roll, heave, lean, list

lure *verb*
Spiders **lure** *insects into their webs.*
attract, entice, tempt, coax, draw, invite, persuade
Something used to lure an animal into a trap is **bait**.

lurk *verb*
The jaguar **lurked** *in wait for its prey.*
skulk, loiter, prowl, crouch, hide, lie in wait, lie low

lush *adjective*
Rainforests have **lush** *vegetation.*
rich, dense, thick, rampant, abundant

luxurious *adjective*
The dress was trimmed with **luxurious** *lace.*
grand, lavish, lush, rich, expensive, costly, deluxe, plush, magnificent, splendid, sumptuous
OPPOSITE simple, austere

luxury *noun*
The millionaire lived a life of **luxury**.
affluence, wealth, richness, splendour, comfort, ease
OPPOSITE poverty

Mm

machine *noun*
Do you know how this **machine** *works?*
apparatus, appliance, device, engine, contraption

mad *adjective*
1 *You must be* **mad** *to go out on a day like this.*
crazy, daft, insane, senseless, stupid, foolish, idiotic
(*informal*) out of your mind, potty, nuts
OPPOSITE sensible, wise
2 *The emperor was* **mad** *with rage.*
angry, furious, beside yourself, frenzied, hysterical
3 (*informal*) *Sandra is* **mad** *about horses.*
enthusiastic, fanatical, passionate

magazine *noun*
I bought a **magazine** *to read on the train.*
journal, periodical, paper, comic

magic *adjective*
1 *My uncle taught me some* **magic** *tricks.*
conjuring
2 *The castle was surrounded by a* **magic** *spell.*
magical, supernatural

✸ WORD WEB

magic *noun*
Do you believe in magic?
sorcery, witchcraft, wizardry, spells, charms, enchantments

PEOPLE WHO USE MAGIC
enchanter or enchantress, magician, sorceror or sorceress, warlock, witch, wizard

THINGS WHICH A SORCEROR MIGHT DO
bewitch, enchant, cast or undo a spell, become invisible or vanish, brew a potion, put a curse on you

THINGS WHICH A SORCEROR MIGHT HAVE OR USE
apprentice, cauldron, charm, elixir, magic potion, magic spell or incantation, talisman, wand

magician *noun*
1 *The* **magician** *pulled a scarf out of his hat.*
conjuror
2 *King Arthur was helped by the* **magician**, *Merlin.*
sorcerer, witch, wizard

magnificent *adjective*
1 *The mountain scenery was* **magnificent**.
beautiful, glorious, splendid, spectacular, impressive, majestic
2 *The film star lived in a* **magnificent** *house.*
grand, imposing, stately
(*informal*) posh
3 *That was a* **magnificent** *meal!*
excellent, first-class, marvellous, superb
(*informal*) fabulous, fantastic

magnify *verb*
Objects are **magnified** *through binoculars.*
enlarge, make larger
(*informal*) blow up
OPPOSITE reduce, minimize

main *adjective*
1 *What was the* **main** *point of the story?*
central, chief, most important, basic, essential, fundamental, primary, predominant
2 *This is the* **main** *shopping area in the town.*
major, principal, biggest, foremost, largest, leading, prime
OPPOSITE minor, unimportant

mainly *adverb*
Chimpanzees eat **mainly** *fruit and vegetables.*
largely, mostly, chiefly, principally, predominantly, primarily

maintain *verb*
1 *The referee tried to* **maintain** *order.*
keep, preserve
2 *A team of gardeners* **maintain** *the grounds.*
look after, take care of, keep in order
3 *He still* **maintains** *that he's innocent.*
claim, declare, assert, insist, state, contend

major adjective
1 *There are delays on all the* **major** *roads into the city.*
chief, principal, primary, leading
2 *Writing her first novel was a* **major** *achievement.*
big, great, considerable, significant, important
OPPOSITE minor
make verb
1 *We* **made** *a shelter out of leaves and branches.*
build, construct, assemble, put together, produce, manufacture
2 *Those two are always* **making** *trouble.*
cause, bring about, give rise to, provoke
3 *They* **made** *me captain.*
appoint, elect, nominate
4 *They've* **made** *the attic into a games room.*
change, turn, convert, modify, transform, alter
5 *She'll* **make** *a good actress when she's older.*
become, grow into, turn into, change into
6 *We can't* **make** *her go if she doesn't want to.*
force, compel, order
7 *He* **made** *a lot of money last year.*
gain, get, obtain, acquire, receive, earn, win
8 *The ship finally* **made** *land.*
reach, arrive at, get to, get as far as
9 *What time do you* **make** *it?*
calculate, estimate, reckon
10 *2 and 2* **make** *4.*
add up to, come to, total
11 *I'll* **make** *you an offer for your old bike.*
propose, suggest
12 *Have you* **made** *your bed this morning?*
arrange, tidy
to make someone or **something out**
I can't **make out** *why everything went wrong.*
understand, work out, comprehend, fathom, make sense of
to make up
I **made up** *a new flavour of ice cream.*
create, invent, think up, concoct
make noun
What **make** *of computer do you have?*
brand, model, label
man noun
A polite word for a man is *gentleman.*
Informal words are *bloke, chap, fellow,* and *guy.*
A married man is a *husband.*
A man who has children is

a *father.*
An unmarried man is a *bachelor.*
A man whose wife has died is a *widower.*
A man on his wedding day is a *bridegroom.*
A man who is engaged to be married is a *fiancé.*
Words for a young man are *boy, lad,* and *youth.*
manage verb
1 *His eldest son* **manages** *the business now.*
be in charge of, run, direct, lead, control, govern, rule, supervise, oversee, preside over
2 *I can't* **manage** *any more work this week.*
cope with, deal with, take on, carry out
3 *We'll have to* **manage** *without the car.*
cope, make do, get along, get by
manner noun
1 *They did the work in an efficient* **manner.**
way, style, fashion, method
2 *I was put off by her frosty* **manner.**
behaviour, conduct, attitude, disposition, air, look, bearing
manners
Trolls have no **manners** *at all!*
politeness, courtesy, graces
manufacture verb
The factory **manufactures** *pine furniture.*
make, build, assemble, fabricate
many adjective
I've been on an aeroplane **many** *times.*
a lot of, plenty of, numerous, frequent, countless, innumerable, untold
(*informal*) umpteen, lots of
OPPOSITE few
map noun
The travel agent gave us a free **map** *of Paris.*
chart, diagram, plan
A book of maps is an *atlas.*
A person who draws maps is a *cartographer.*
march verb
The brass band **marched** *down the High Street.*
parade, file, troop, stride, pace
mark noun
1 *There were muddy paw* **marks** *all over the kitchen floor.*
spot, stain, blemish, blotch, blot, smear, smudge, streak
A mark left by a pen or pencil is a *scribble.*
A mark left by fingers is a *fingermark.*
A mark on your skin that you are born with is a *birthmark.*
2 *They stood in silence as a* **mark** *of respect.*

sign, token, indication, symbol, emblem
3 *What* **mark** *did you get in the spelling test?*
score, grade
mark verb
1 *Please be careful not to* **mark** *the photographs.*
stain, smudge, dirty, blot
2 *The teacher had a pile of essays to* **mark.**
correct, grade, assess
marry verb
In what year did your grandparents **marry?**
get married, wed
(*informal*) tie the knot, get hitched
A couple who have promised to marry are **engaged** to each other.
A man who is engaged to be married is a *fiancé* and the woman he is engaged to is his *fiancée.*
marsh noun
Wading birds are found in coastal **marshes.**
swamp, bog, wetland, marshland, fen
marvel verb
to marvel at
The crowd **marvelled at** *the juggler's skill.*
admire, wonder at, be amazed by, be astonished by
marvellous adjective
1 *The professor showed us his* **marvellous** *inventions.*
amazing, remarkable, extraordinary, incredible, miraculous, astonishing, phenomenal
OPPOSITE ordinary
2 *We had a* **marvellous** *day at the zoo.*
excellent, superb, tremendous, wonderful, splendid
(*informal*) brilliant, fantastic, terrific, super, smashing
OPPOSITE bad, awful
mash verb
Mash *the potatoes until they're smooth.*
crush, pound, pulp, smash, squash
To make something into powder is to *grind* or *pulverize* it.
mask verb
The entrance was **masked** *by an overhanging tree.*
conceal, hide, cover, obscure, screen, veil, shroud, camouflage
mass noun
She sifted through the **mass** *of papers on her desk.*
heap, pile, mound, stack, collection, quantity, accumulation
(*informal*) load

master noun
1 *We played a game in which I was master of the castle.*
lord, ruler, governor, chief
2 *Sherlock Holmes was a master of disguises.*
expert (at), genius, ace, wizard
master verb
1 *Have you mastered chess yet?*
grasp, learn, understand
(*informal*) get the hang of, get to grips with
2 *I've managed to master my fear of heights.*
overcome, conquer, defeat, triumph over, get the better of, control, curb, subdue, tame
match noun
The semi-final was a really exciting match.
game, contest, competition, fixture, tournament, tie
match verb
Does this tie match my shirt?
go with, suit, fit with, blend with, tone in with
OPPOSITE contrast with
material noun
1 *I'm collecting material for the school magazine.*
information, facts, data, ideas, notes
2 *The cleaning materials are in the cupboard.*
stuff, substances, things
3 *The kite is made of lightweight material.*
cloth, fabric
matter noun
1 *The manager will deal with this matter.*
affair, concern, issue, business, situation, incident, subject, topic, thing
2 *Peat consists mainly of plant matter.*
material, stuff, substance
3 *What's the matter with the car?*
problem, difficulty, trouble, worry
matter verb
Will it matter if I'm late?
be important, count, make a difference
mature adjective
1 *The zoo has two mature gorillas.*
adult, fully grown, well developed
OPPOSITE young
2 *He acts very mature for his age.*
grown-up, responsible, sensible
OPPOSITE immature, childish
mean adjective
1 *Scrooge was too mean to buy any presents.*
selfish, miserly, uncharitable
(*informal*) stingy, tight-fisted, penny-pinching
OPPOSITE generous

2 *That was a mean trick to play.*
unkind, unpleasant, nasty, spiteful, vicious, cruel, malicious
OPPOSITE kind
mean verb
1 *A red traffic light means that cars have to stop.*
indicate, signify, denote, express, imply, convey, communicate, stand for, symbolize
2 *I mean to get better at swimming this year.*
intend, plan, aim, propose, want
meaning noun
What is the meaning of this riddle?
sense, significance, explanation, interpretation, definition
measure verb
Measure the height of the wall.
calculate, gauge, assess, survey
To measure the weight of something is to **weigh** it.
measure noun
They are taking measures to improve the park.
step, action, course, procedure, means
medium adjective
The man was of medium height.
average, middle, middling, standard, moderate, normal
meek adjective
Koalas look meek, but they have fierce claws.
gentle, mild, tame, submissive, modest, docile, quiet, humble
OPPOSITE aggressive
meet verb
1 *I met an old friend at the party.*
come across, encounter, run into, see
(*informal*) bump into
2 *My parents met me at the station.*
greet, pick up, welcome
3 *We're meeting outside the cinema at eight.*
gather, assemble, collect, muster, rally
4 *The two roads meet here.*
come together, merge, connect, join, cross, intersect
meeting noun
The bandits held a meeting to discuss their plan.
gathering, assembly, council, forum, congress, conference
A large outdoor public meeting is a **rally**.
A formal meeting with a king or queen is an **audience**.
melt verb
The ice began to melt in the sun.
thaw, soften, unfreeze
To melt frozen food is to **defrost** it.
To melt ore to get metal

from it is to **smelt** it.
Rock or metal that has melted through great heat is **molten**.
OPPOSITE freeze
mend verb
Workmen were mending the pavement.
fix, repair, put right, restore, renovate, patch
mention verb
1 *Please don't mention the idea to anyone.*
refer to, speak about, touch on, hint at
2 *You mentioned that you spoke Japanese.*
say, remark, reveal, disclose
(*informal*) let out
3 *The director mentioned all the cast.*
name, acknowledge, list
mercy noun
The evil queen showed no mercy.
compassion, humanity, sympathy, pity, leniency, kindness, charity
OPPOSITE cruelty
merge verb
1 *They plan to merge the two schools.*
join together, combine, integrate, put together, unite, amalgamate
2 *Two streams merge here to form a river.*
come together, converge, join, meet
OPPOSITE separate
merry adjective
The postman was whistling a merry tune.
cheerful, happy, jolly, bright, joyful, light-hearted, lively, spirited
OPPOSITE gloomy
mess noun
1 *Please clear up this mess.*
muddle, untidiness, chaos, disorder, confusion, clutter, jumble, litter, dirt
(*informal*) shambles
2 *Zoe made a mess of her audition.*
disaster, botch
(*informal*) hash

mess verb
to mess about
We spent the day messing about on the beach.
play about, fool around, lounge about
(*informal*) muck about
to mess things up
I hope you haven't messed up my CDs.
confuse, mix up, muddle, jumble, make a mess of, tangle
to mess something up
I think I messed up my interview.
bungle, botch
(*informal*) make a hash of
message noun
Did you get my message?
note, letter, communication
messy adjective
My bedroom is really messy!
muddled, untidy, disorderly, chaotic, dirty, filthy, grubby, mucky
(*informal*) higgledy-piggledy
OPPOSITE neat
method noun
My granny has a secret method for making jam.
technique, way, procedure, process
A specially skilful method for doing something is a *knack*.
middle adjective
The middle lane is reserved for buses.
central, inner, inside, midway
middle noun
A scarecrow stood in the middle of the field.
centre, core, heart, midpoint
The middle of a wheel is the *hub*.
The middle part of an atom or cell is the *nucleus*.
mighty adjective
The dragon let out a mighty roar.
powerful, forceful, vigorous, ferocious, violent, great, enormous, hefty
OPPOSITE weak
mild adjective
1 *He's a mild person who never complains.*
amiable, docile, easygoing, gentle, good-tempered, harmless, kind, lenient, merciful, placid, soft-hearted
2 *The weather has been mild for this time of year.*
pleasant, warm, temperate
OPPOSITE severe
mind noun
1 *Her mind was as sharp as ever.*
brain, intelligence, intellect, head, sense, understanding, wits, judgement, mental powers, reasoning

2 *Are you sure you won't change your mind?*
wishes, intention, fancy, inclination, opinion, outlook, point of view
mind verb
1 *Will you mind my bag for a minute?*
guard, look after, watch, care for
(*informal*) keep an eye on
2 *Mind the step.*
look out for, watch out for, beware of, pay attention to, heed, note
3 *They won't mind if I'm late.*
bother, care, worry, be upset, take offence, object, disapprove
mingle verb
The secret agent mingled with the crowd.
mix in, circulate, blend, combine, merge, fuse
miniature adjective
A piccolo looks like a miniature flute.
tiny, minute, diminutive, small-scale, baby, mini
minor adjective
I only had a minor part in the play.
small, unimportant, insignificant, inferior, subordinate, trivial, petty
OPPOSITE major
minute adjective
You can hardly see the minute crack.
tiny, minuscule, microscopic, negligible
OPPOSITE large
miraculous adjective
The patient made a miraculous recovery.
amazing, astonishing, astounding, extraordinary, incredible, marvellous, unbelievable, wonderful, mysterious, inexplicable
misbehave verb
My puppy has been misbehaving again!
behave badly, be naughty, be disobedient, get up to mischief
OPPOSITE behave
miserable adjective
1 *You look miserable—what's the matter?*
sad, unhappy, sorrowful, gloomy, glum, downhearted, despondent, dejected, depressed, melancholy, mournful, tearful
OPPOSITE cheerful, happy
2 *The poor animals lived in miserable conditions.*
distressing, uncomfortable, wretched, pitiful, pathetic, squalid
OPPOSITE comfortable
misery noun
The slaves must have led a

life of **misery**.
sadness, sorrow, unhappiness, grief, distress, despair, anguish, wretchedness, suffering, torment, heartache, depression
OPPOSITE happiness
misfortune noun
I heard about my family's misfortune.
bad luck, trouble, hardship, adversity, affliction, setback, mishap
OPPOSITE good luck
misleading adjective
The directions he gave were quite misleading.
confusing, unreliable, deceptive, ambiguous, unclear
miss verb
1 *I missed the bus.*
be too late for
2 *The arrow missed the target.*
fall short of, go wide of
3 *If we leave now, we should miss the traffic.*
avoid
4 *I missed dad when he was in hospital.*
long for, yearn for, pine for
to miss something out
I missed out the boring bits of the story.
leave out, omit, ignore, overlook, skip
mission noun
1 *Her mission in life was to help those in need.*
aim, purpose, objective, task, job, campaign
2 *The astronauts are on a mission to Mars.*
expedition, journey, voyage, exploration
mist noun
We drove slowly through the mist.
fog, haze, cloud, drizzle
mistake noun
This piece of writing is full of mistakes.
error, inaccuracy, blunder, slip, slip-up, lapse
A spelling mistake is a *misspelling*.
A mistake where something is left out is an *omission*.
A mistake in a printed book is a *misprint*.
misty adjective
1 *If it's misty outside, take a torch.*
foggy, hazy
2 *I can't see through the misty window.*
steamy, cloudy, smoky, opaque
mix verb
Mix the ingredients in a bowl.
combine, blend, mingle
to mix something up
Please don't mix up my CDs.

muddle, jumble, confuse
To mix up playing cards is to **shuffle** them.

mixed *adjective*
Add a teaspoon of **mixed** herbs.
assorted, various, different, miscellaneous
OPPOSITE separate

mixture *noun*
1 Put the cake **mixture** in a baking tin.
mix, blend, combination
A mixture of metals is an **alloy**.
A mixture of two different species of plant or animal is a **hybrid**.
2 There's an odd **mixture** of things in the drawer.
assortment, collection, variety, jumble
A confused mixture is a **mishmash**.

moan *verb*
1 The wounded warrior **moaned** in pain.
cry, groan, sigh, wail, howl, whimper
2 Ned's always **moaning** about the food.
complain, grumble, grouse, whine
(*informal*) whinge

monster

mob *noun*
An angry **mob** stormed the gates of the castle.
crowd, horde, throng, mass, rabble, gang, pack, herd, bunch

mock *verb*
It was mean of them to **mock** his singing.
jeer at, laugh at, make fun of, scoff at, sneer at, ridicule, scorn, deride
(*informal*) take the mickey out of

model *noun*
1 I'm building a **model** of a space rocket.
copy, replica, toy
2 This is the latest **model** of skateboard.
design, type, version
3 She's a **model** of good behaviour.
example, ideal

moderate *adjective*
Her first book was a **moderate** success.
average, fair, modest, medium, reasonable, passable, tolerable
OPPOSITE exceptional

modern *adjective*
1 All the equipment in their kitchen was **modern**.
up to date, contemporary, advanced, the latest

OPPOSITE out of date
2 She always dresses in **modern** clothes.
fashionable, stylish, modish
(*informal*) trendy, hip
OPPOSITE old-fashioned

modest *adjective*
1 He's very **modest** about his success.
humble, quiet, reserved, shy, bashful, coy
OPPOSITE conceited
2 There has been a **modest** increase in sales.
moderate, reasonable, average, medium

moist *adjective*
1 The walls of the dungeon were **moist**.
damp, wet, watery, clammy, dank
2 Tropical plants grow well in a **moist** atmosphere.
humid, muggy, steamy, rainy

moisture *noun*
There is still a lot of **moisture** on the ground.
wetness, dampness, damp, dew, condensation, humidity

moment *noun*
1 I'll be ready in a **moment**.
minute, second, instant, flash
(*informal*) jiffy, tick
2 It was a great **moment** in the history of space travel.
time, occasion, period

money *noun*
How much **money** do you have with you?
cash, currency, funds, finance
(*informal*) dough, dosh
A large amount of money is a **fortune**, **riches**, or **wealth**.

monster *noun*
A sea **monster** reared its head above the waves.
beast, giant, ogre, brute

monstrous *adjective*
1 The town was engulfed by a **monstrous** wave.
huge, gigantic, enormous, immense, massive, colossal, great, hulking, mighty, towering, vast
2 The nation was shocked by the **monstrous** crime.
horrifying, shocking, wicked, evil, hideous, horrible, terrible, atrocious, dreadful, gruesome, outrageous, scandalous

mood *noun*
What sort of **mood** is he in today?
temper, humour, state of mind, disposition

moody *adjective*
She's been **moody** and withdrawn

for weeks.
sulky, sullen, grumpy, bad-tempered, temperamental, touchy, miserable, gloomy, glum
OPPOSITE cheerful

moral *noun*
The **moral** of this story is that crime doesn't pay.
lesson, message, meaning

more *adjective*
The soup needs **more** pepper.
extra, further, added, additional
OPPOSITE less

mostly *adverb*
I spend my money **mostly** on books and CDs.
mainly, largely, chiefly, primarily, generally, usually, normally, typically, principally, predominantly

motive *noun*
The police can find no **motive** for the crime.
cause, motivation, reason, purpose, grounds

mould *verb*
The sculptor **moulded** the figures from clay.
shape, form, fashion, model, cast

mouldy *adjective*
All I found in the fridge was some **mouldy** cheese.
rotten, rotting, decaying, musty, damp

mound *noun*
1 Her desk was covered with **mounds** of paper.
heap, pile, stack, mass
2 There used to be a castle on top of that **mound**.
hill, hillock, rise, hump
An ancient mound of earth over a grave is a **barrow**.

mountain *noun* see panel opposite

mourn *verb*
He was still **mourning** the loss of his friend.
grieve for, lament for

move *noun*
1 Don't make a **move**!
movement

2 *The spy was watching their every move.*
action, step, deed, manoeuvre
3 *Is it my move next?*
turn, go, chance, opportunity
move *verb*
to move from one place to another
carry, remove, transfer, transport, shift *They shifted the piano into the front room.*
to move from a position
go, leave, depart, quit, budge *The camel stared and refused to budge.*
to move restlessly
toss, turn, stir, twist, shake, fidget, twitch, flap *Please stop twitching in your seat.*
to move from side to side
sway, swing, wave, wag, wiggle *The knight swung a sword above his helmet.*
to move along
travel, walk, proceed *Few people travel on these roads after dark.*
to move along quickly
hurry, dash, race, run, rush, hasten, hurtle, career, fly, speed, sweep, shoot, zoom *A boy went careering past on a scooter.*
to move along slowly
amble, stroll, saunter, dawdle, crawl, drift *Gerald the tortoise sauntered down the path.*
to move towards something

WORD WEB

mountain *noun*
The top of a mountain is the **peak** or **summit**.
A line of mountains is a **range**.
A long, narrow mountain is a **ridge**.
A mountain with a hole at the top caused by an eruption is a **volcano**.
An area of land with many mountains is said to be **mountainous**.

THINGS YOU MIGHT SEE ON OR NEAR A MOUNTAIN
avalanche, boulder, cave, cliff, crag, crevice, glacier, gorge, ledge, mountain pass, mountain stream, precipice, rocks, slope, valley or (*Scottish*) glen

SOME WORDS TO DESCRIBE A MOUNTAIN
barren, craggy, forbidding, jagged, lofty, massive, misty, rocky, rugged, snow-capped, soaring, towering, treacherous

---

advance, approach, come, proceed, progress *The lookout saw a pirate ship approaching.*
to move back or move away
back, retreat, reverse, withdraw *The serpent retreated, hissing, into its lair.*
to move downwards
drop, descend, fall, sink, swoop *A pair of vultures swooped down from the sky.*
to move upwards
rise, ascend, climb, mount, soar, arise *A hot-air balloon mounted into the air.*
movement *noun*
1 *The robot made a sudden, jerky movement.*
motion, move, action, gesture
2 *She was involved in the peace movement.*
organization, group, party, campaign
moving *adjective*
The story was so moving that I started to cry.
emotional, inspiring, stirring, touching
(*informal*) tear-jerking
muck *noun*
They cleared the muck out of the stable.
dirt, filth, grime, mud, sludge, dung, manure
mud *noun*
The tractor left a trail of mud on the road.
dirt, muck, mire, sludge, clay, soil
muddle *noun*
1 *There was a muddle over the date of the party.*
confusion, misunderstanding
(*informal*) mix-up
2 *There was a muddle of clothes on the floor.*
jumble, mess, tangle
muddle *verb*
1 *Who muddled the papers on my desk?*
mix up, mess up, disorder, jumble up, shuffle, tangle
OPPOSITE tidy
2 *They got muddled and took the wrong turning.*
confuse, bewilder, puzzle, perplex

---

muffled *adjective*
They heard muffled voices from the next room.
faint, indistinct, unclear, muted, deadened
OPPOSITE clear
muggy *adjective*
The weather is often muggy before a storm.
humid, close, clammy, sticky, moist, damp, oppressive
OPPOSITE fresh
mumble *verb*
We couldn't hear the actor as he was mumbling.
mutter, talk indistinctly
munch *verb*
Kim sat munching popcorn all through the film.
chew, crunch
murky *adjective*
A creature loomed out of the murky waters of the loch.
dark, clouded, cloudy, dim, dull, dingy, gloomy, grey, foggy, misty
OPPOSITE clear
murmur *verb*
We heard voices murmuring in the room above.
mutter, mumble, whisper
music *noun*
see panel on following page
musical *adjective*
Helena has a very musical voice.
tuneful, melodic, melodious, harmonious, sweet-sounding
musty *adjective*
There was a musty smell in the cellar.
damp, dank, mouldy, stale, stuffy, airless
OPPOSITE fresh
mutter *verb*
The goblin sat muttering to himself in the corner.
mumble, murmur, whisper
mysterious *adjective*
They uncovered a mysterious sign on the wall.
strange, puzzling, baffling, mystifying, perplexing, obscure, unexplained, incomprehensible, inexplicable, curious, weird
mystery *noun*
What really happened was a mystery.
puzzle, riddle, secret

a b c d e f g h i j k l m n o p q r s t u v w x y z

WORD WEB

music noun

VARIOUS KINDS OF MUSIC
blues, classical music, country and western, dance music, disco music, folk music, gospel, hip hop, jazz, orchestral music, pop music, punk, ragtime, rap, reggae, rock, soul, swing

TYPES OF MUSICAL COMPOSITION
anthem, ballad, carol, concerto, folk song, fugue, hymn, lullaby, march, melody, musical, opera, operetta, sonata, song, symphony, tune

FAMILIES OF MUSICAL INSTRUMENTS
brass, keyboard, percussion, strings, woodwind

STRINGED INSTRUMENTS THAT CAN BE PLAYED WITH A BOW
cello, double bass, viola, violin or fiddle

STRINGED INSTRUMENTS PLAYED BY PLUCKING OR STRUMMING
banjo, cittern, guitar, harp, lute, lyre, mandolin, sitar, ukulele, zither

BRASS INSTRUMENTS
bugle, cornet, euphonium, flugelhorn, French horn, trombone, trumpet, tuba

OTHER INSTRUMENTS PLAYED BY BLOWING
bagpipes, bassoon, clarinet, cor anglais, flute, harmonica or mouth organ, oboe, piccolo, recorder, saxophone

KEYBOARD INSTRUMENTS
accordion, harmonium, harpsichord, keyboard, organ, piano, synthesizer

PERCUSSION INSTRUMENTS
bass drum, bongo drum, castanets, cymbals, drum, glockenspiel, gong, kettledrum, maracas, marimba, rattle, snare drum, tabor, tambour, tambourine, timpani, tom-tom, triangle, tubular bells, vibraphone, xylophone

PEOPLE WHO PLAY VARIOUS INSTRUMENTS
bugler, cellist, clarinettist, drummer, fiddler, flautist, guitarist, harpist, lutenist, oboist, organist, percussionist, pianist, piper, timpanist, trombonist, trumpeter, violinist

SOME OTHER MUSICIANS
accompanist, composer, conductor, instrumentalist, singer, vocalist

GROUPS OF MUSICIANS
band, choir or chorus, duet or duo, ensemble, group, orchestra, quartet, quintet, trio

TERMS USED IN MUSIC
chord, counterpoint, discord, harmony, melody, note, octave, pitch, rhythm, scale, semitone, tempo, theme, tone, tune

NAMES OF NOTES AND SIGNS IN WRITTEN MUSIC
clef, crotchet, flat, key signature, minim, natural, quaver, semibreve, semiquaver, sharp, stave, time signature

violin

accordion

saxophone

guitar

drums

Nn

nag *verb*
*He was always **nagging** her to work harder.*
badger, pester, scold

naked *adjective*
*He walked **naked** into the bathroom.*
bare, nude, unclothed, undressed
OPPOSITE **clothed**

name *noun*
The official names you have are your *first names* or *forenames*, and *surname*.
Names a Christian is given at baptism are *Christian names*.
A false name is an *alias*.
A name people use instead of your real name is a *nickname*.
A false name an author uses is a *pen name* or *pseudonym*.
The name of a book or film is its *title*.

name *verb*
*The zoo **named** the new lion cubs, Kiara and Kovu.*
call
To name someone at the ceremony of baptism is to *baptize* or *christen* them.

nap *noun*
*Granny always takes a **nap** on Sunday afternoons.*
rest, sleep, doze, lie-down, siesta
(*informal*) snooze, forty winks

narrow *adjective*
*The rabbit squeezed through a **narrow** opening in the fence.*
thin, slender, slim
OPPOSITE **wide**

nasty *adjective*
1 *Ogres have a thoroughly **nasty** temper.*
unkind, unpleasant, unfriendly, disagreeable, objectionable, odious, mean, malicious, cruel, spiteful, vicious
2 *A **nasty** smell wafted from the laboratory.*
unpleasant, offensive, disgusting, repulsive, revolting, horrible, foul, rotten, sickening
OPPOSITE **agreeable, pleasant**
3 *The weather suddenly turned **nasty**.*
unpleasant, rough, stormy, squally

national *adjective*
*The programme will be broadcast on **national** television.*
nationwide
OPPOSITE **local**

natural *adjective*
1 *Karen has a **natural** gift for music.*
born, inborn, instinctive, intuitive, native
2 *It's only **natural** to be nervous before an exam.*
normal, common, understandable, reasonable, predictable
OPPOSITE **unnatural**

nature *noun*
1 *I like TV programmes about **nature**.*
natural history, wildlife
2 *The old sheepdog has a very kind **nature**.*
character, disposition, personality, manner
3 *I collect coins, medals, and things of that **nature**.*
kind, sort, type, description, variety

naughty *adjective*
*The puppies were quite **naughty** when they were young.*
bad, badly behaved, disobedient, mischievous, uncontrollable, unmanageable, troublesome, unruly
OPPOSITE **well behaved**

near *adjective*
1 *We get on well with our **near** neighbours.*
next-door, nearby, close, adjacent, surrounding
2 *My birthday is **near**.*
approaching, coming
(*informal*) round the corner
3 *We sent cards to all our **near** relatives.*
close, dear, familiar, intimate
OPPOSITE **distant**

nearly *adverb*
*Thank goodness, it's **nearly** dinner time!*
almost, practically, virtually, just about, approaching

neat *adjective*
1 *Please leave the room as **neat** as possible.*
clean, orderly, tidy, uncluttered, immaculate
(*informal*) spick and span
2 *Craig always looks **neat** in his school uniform.*
smart, elegant, spruce, trim
3 *Her handwriting is very **neat**.*
precise, skilful, well-formed
OPPOSITE **untidy**

necessary *adjective*
*The recipe lists all the **necessary** ingredients.*
essential, required, needed, needful, compulsory, obligatory, unavoidable
OPPOSITE **unnecessary**

need *noun*
*There's a **need** for more shops in our area.*
call, demand, requirement

need *verb*
1 *I **need** a pound coin for the locker.*
require, want, be short of, lack
2 *The charity **needs** our support.*
depend on, rely on

neglect *verb*
*She's been **neglecting** her work.*
forget, ignore, overlook, abandon, disregard, pay no attention to, shirk

nervous *adjective*
*She always feels **nervous** before an exam.*
anxious, worried, apprehensive, concerned, uneasy, fearful, edgy, fraught, tense, troubled
(*informal*) uptight, jittery
OPPOSITE **calm**

neutral *adjective*
*A referee has to be **neutral**.*
impartial, unbiased, unprejudiced, even-handed
OPPOSITE **biased, prejudiced**

new *adjective*
1 *Start on a **new** sheet of paper.*
clean, fresh, unused, brand-new
Something new and unused is *in mint condition*.
2 *They went to the motor show to see the **new** models.*
latest, current, modern, recent, up-to-date
3 *They've found a **new** bug in the computer program.*
additional, extra, unexpected, unfamiliar
4 *Haven't you got any **new** ideas?*
fresh, original, novel, innovative, creative, different
OPPOSITE **old**

news *noun*
*What's the latest **news**?*
information, word, report, bulletin
(*old use*) tidings

next *adjective*
1 *He lives in the house **next** to the chip shop.*
adjacent, closest, nearest
OPPOSITE **distant**
2 *If you miss this bus, you can catch the **next** one.*
following, subsequent
OPPOSITE **previous**

nice *adjective* see panel on following page
1 *That's not a very **nice** thing to say!*
pleasant, agreeable
OPPOSITE **nasty**
2 *There is a **nice** distinction between borrowing and stealing.*
delicate, fine, precise, subtle

night *noun*
*Badgers usually come out at **night**.*
night-time, dark
Animals which are active at night are *nocturnal* animals.

OVERUSED WORD

nice *adjective*
Try to vary the words you use for **nice**. Here are some other words you could use.

FOR A *nice person*
good, kind, friendly, helpful, generous, likeable, amiable, charming, polite, genial *Our singing teacher is very **likeable**.*
FOR A *nice experience*
delightful, enjoyable, wonderful, marvellous, splendid *Did you have an **enjoyable** time in France?*
FOR SOMETHING THAT *looks nice*
beautiful, attractive, pleasing, lovely *There is an **attractive** view from the upstairs window.*
FOR A *nice smell*
agreeable, fragrant, sweet-smelling *The **fragrant** scent of lavender filled the garden.*
FOR *nice food*
delicious, tasty, appetizing, satisfying *They serve **tasty** sandwiches in the cafe.*
FOR *nice weather*
fine, sunny, warm *The weather has been **fine** all week.*

noble *adjective*
1 *The knight belonged to an ancient **noble** family.*
aristocratic, high-born, upper-class
2 *The rescuers were congratulated for their **noble** efforts.*
brave, heroic, courageous, honourable, worthy, virtuous, gallant
OPPOSITE cowardly, unworthy
nod *verb*
*Simon **nodded** his head in agreement.*
bob, bow, dip, lower
noise *noun*
*Where is that dreadful **noise** coming from?*
din, racket, row, uproar, commotion, tumult, hullabaloo, pandemonium
noisy *adjective*
1 *The people next door were playing **noisy** music.*
loud, blaring, booming, deafening, ear-splitting, thunderous
2 *The children are very **noisy** this morning.*
rowdy, raucous, chattering, talkative
nonsense *noun*
*Stop talking **nonsense**!*
rubbish, drivel, balderdash, piffle, gibberish, claptrap, gobbledegook
(*informal*) rot, tripe, twaddle

normal *adjective*
1 *He had a **normal** kind of day at work.*
average, common, customary, familiar, habitual, ordinary, predictable, regular, routine, standard, typical, unsurprising, usual
2 *No **normal** person would sleep on a bed of nails.*
healthy, rational, reasonable, sane
OPPOSITE abnormal
nosy *adjective (informal)*
*Stop being so **nosy** and asking all these questions!*
inquisitive, curious, prying, snooping, intrusive
An informal name for a nosy person is a *nosy parker*.

note *noun*
1 *I sent a **note** thanking him for the present.*
message, letter, communication
2 *There was a **note** of anger in her voice.*
sound, tone, feeling, quality
note *verb*
1 *The detective **noted** the address on a scrap of paper.*
jot down, make a note of, write down, record, scribble
2 *Did you **note** what she was wearing?*
notice, see, take note of, pay attention to, heed, mark, observe

nothing *noun*
*Four minus four equals **nothing**.*
nought, zero
In cricket a score of nothing is a *duck*; in tennis it is *love*, and in football it is *nil*.
notice *noun*
*Someone put up a **notice** about the meeting.*
sign, advertisement, placard, poster, warning
to take notice of something
*They **took** no **notice of** the warning.*
heed, pay attention to
notice *verb*
1 *Did you **notice** what he was wearing?*
note, see, take note of, pay attention to, heed, mark, observe
2 *I **noticed** a funny smell in the room.*
become aware of, detect
now *adverb*
1 *My cousins are **now** living in Melbourne.*
at present, at the moment, currently, nowadays
2 *I'll give them a ring **now**.*

immediately, at once, straight away, without delay, instantly
nudge *verb*
*She **nudged** me with her elbow.*
poke, prod, shove, bump, jog, jolt
nuisance *noun*
*The traffic noise is a real **nuisance**.*
annoyance, irritation, inconvenience, bother, menace, pest, drawback
numb *adjective*
*My toes are **numb** with cold.*
unfeeling, deadened, frozen, insensitive, paralysed
OPPOSITE sensitive
number *noun*
1 *Add the **numbers** together to get the answer.*
figure, numeral
Any of the numbers from 0 to 9 is a *digit*.
A negative or positive whole number is an *integer*.
An amount used in measuring or counting is a *unit*.
2 *A large **number** of people applied for the job.*
amount, quantity, collection, crowd
3 *The band played some well-known **numbers**.*
song, piece, tune

Oo

obedient *adjective*
*The dog seems very **obedient**.*
well-behaved, disciplined, manageable, dutiful, docile
OPPOSITE disobedient
obey *verb*
1 *The dog **obeyed** his owner's commands.*
follow, carry out, execute, implement, observe, adhere to, heed
2 *The soldiers **obeyed** without question.*
do what you are told, take orders, be obedient, conform
OPPOSITE disobey
object *noun*
1 *We saw some strange **objects** in the museum.*
article, item, thing
2 *What is the **object** of this exercise?*
point, purpose, aim, goal, intention, objective
object *verb*
to object to something
*Several residents have **objected to** the plan.*
complain about, be opposed to, disapprove of, take exception to,

protest against
OPPOSITE accept, agree to

observant *adjective*
If you're **observant**, you might see a fox tonight.
alert, attentive, sharp-eyed, vigilant, watchful
OPPOSITE inattentive

observation *noun*
1 They took him to hospital for **observation**.
study, watching, scrutiny
2 The detective made an interesting **observation**.
comment, remark, statement

observe *verb*
1 Astronomers **observed** the eclipse last night.
watch, look at, view, study
2 I have **observed** a change in his behaviour.
notice, note, see, detect, spot, discern, perceive, witness
3 It's important to **observe** the rules.
follow, abide by, adhere to, heed, keep to, obey
4 My friend **observed** that I had grown taller.
mention, say, comment, remark, declare

obsession *noun*
Football is Frank's **obsession**.
passion, fixation, addiction, mania

obstacle *noun*
1 They drove around the **obstacles** in the road.
obstruction, barrier, barricade
2 His age proved to be an **obstacle**.
problem, difficulty, hindrance, hurdle, snag, catch

obvious *adjective*
1 It was silly to make so many **obvious** mistakes.
glaring, noticeable, pronounced
2 The castle is an **obvious** landmark.
conspicuous, notable, prominent, visible
OPPOSITE inconspicuous
3 It was **obvious** that the woman was a spy.
clear, evident, apparent, plain, undeniable, unmistakable
OPPOSITE hidden

occasion *noun*
1 I've been to Italy on several **occasions**.
time, moment, instance, opportunity, chance
2 The wedding was a happy **occasion**.
affair, event, happening, incident, occurrence

occasional *adjective*
The weather forecast said there would be **occasional** showers.
intermittent, odd, scattered,

irregular, infrequent
OPPOSITE frequent, regular

occasionally *adverb*
The dragon **occasionally** lifted its head and roared.
sometimes, now and again, once in a while, every so often
OPPOSITE frequently, often

occupation *noun*
1 He's not happy with his present **occupation**.
job, post, employment, profession, trade, work
2 Vita's favourite **occupation** is reading.
activity, hobby, pastime, pursuit

occupy *verb*
1 They **occupy** the house next door.
live in, reside in, dwell in, inhabit
2 The rebel army **occupied** the town.
capture, seize, take over, conquer, invade

occur *verb*
1 She told us what had **occurred**.
happen, take place, come about, arise
2 The disease only **occurs** in certain plants.
develop, crop up, turn up

odd *adjective*
1 Her behaviour seemed very **odd**.
strange, unusual, abnormal, peculiar, curious, puzzling, queer, unconventional, eccentric, funny, weird
OPPOSITE normal
2 He could only find a couple of **odd** socks.
left over, single, spare
3 He does **odd** jobs to earn money.
occasional, casual, irregular, various

offend *verb*
I hope my letter didn't **offend** you.
give or cause offence to, insult, upset, hurt your feelings, anger, displease, annoy, affront, disgust, vex

offensive *adjective*
1 The gas produces an **offensive** smell.
unpleasant, repellent, disgusting, revolting, nasty
OPPOSITE pleasant
2 He apologized for his **offensive** remarks.
insulting, impolite, rude, abusive

offer *verb*
1 A reward was **offered** for the capture of the outlaws.
propose, put forward, suggest, make available
2 He **offered** to help with the washing-up.
volunteer

offer *noun*
Their **offer** of help was gratefully received.
proposal, suggestion

often *adverb*
It **often** rains in April.
frequently, regularly, repeatedly, time after time, many times, again and again, constantly

old *adjective*
1 The **old** Norman church is to be restored.
ancient, historic, original
2 I put on **old** jeans to do some gardening.
worn, scruffy, shabby, threadbare
OPPOSITE new
3 The museum has a display of **old** computers.
old-fashioned, out of date, antiquated, early, obsolete
Things which are valuable because they are old are **antique**.
OPPOSITE up to date, current, modern

old-fashioned *adjective*
That hairstyle is quite **old-fashioned** now.
out of date, outdated, outmoded, antiquated
OPPOSITE modern, up to date

omit *verb*
1 His article was **omitted** from the magazine.
exclude, leave out, miss out, cut, eliminate, overlook, skip
2 Don't **omit** to turn off the lights.
forget, fail, neglect

ooze *verb*
The filling started to **ooze** out my sandwich.
leak, seep, escape, dribble, drip

open *adjective*
1 The puppy escaped through the **open** door.
unlocked, unfastened, ajar, gaping
OPPOSITE closed
2 The jam jar had been left **open**.
uncovered, unsealed
3 There is a view of **open** country from the back window.
clear, unrestricted, unenclosed, extensive
OPPOSITE enclosed 4 He was **open** about what he had done wrong.
frank, honest, sincere, straightforward, candid
OPPOSITE deceitful 5 The captain faced **open** rebellion from the crew.
unconcealed, undisguised, obvious, plain
OPPOSITE concealed

open *verb*
1 Please **open** the door.

unfasten, unlock, unbolt2 *I can't wait to open my birthday presents!*
undo, unwrap, untie, unseal

To open an umbrella is to **unfurl** it.
To open a wine bottle is to **uncork** it.
To open a map is to **unfold** or **unroll** it.
3 *The jumble sale opens at 10 a.m.*
begin, start, commence (*informal*) get going

opening *noun*
1 *The sheep got out through an opening in the fence.*
gap, hole, breach, break, split
2 *The film has a very dramatic opening.*
beginning, start, commencement
3 *We are invited to the opening of the new sports centre.*
launch, initiation

opinion *noun*
What was your honest opinion of the film?
view, judgement, impression, belief, attitude, point of view, thought, conclusion, assessment, notion, feeling, idea

opportunity *noun*
1 *There were few opportunities to relax.*
chance, occasion, moment, time
2 *The job offers a good opportunity for a keen young person.*
opening
(*informal*) break

oppose *verb*
Many people opposed the building of the new road.
object to, disapprove of, be against, be hostile towards, argue against, fight against, attack, resist
OPPOSITE support, defend

opposite *adjective*
1 *They have opposite views about politics.*
contrasting, conflicting, contradictory, opposed, opposing, different, contrary
OPPOSITE similar
2 *My friend lives on the opposite side of the road.*
facing

opposite *noun*
She says one thing and does the opposite.
contrary, reverse, converse

optimistic *adjective*
She's optimistic about her chances of success.
hopeful, positive, confident, expectant, cheerful, buoyant
OPPOSITE pessimistic

ordeal *noun*
The shipwrecked sailor told us about his ordeal.

suffering, troubles, trial, anguish, torture, nightmare

order *noun*
1 *The captain gave the order to abandon ship.*
command, instruction, direction
2 *I've put in an order for the new book.*
request, demand, reservation, booking
3 *The police restored order after the riot.*
peace, calm, control, quiet, harmony, law and order
4 *The CDs are arranged in alphabetical order.*
arrangement, sequence, series, succession
5 *She keeps her bike in good order.*
condition, state

order *verb*
1 *She ordered them to be quiet.*
command, instruct, require, tell
2 *He ordered the new magazine.*
request, reserve, apply for, book

ordinary *adjective*
1 *It was just an ordinary sort of day.*
normal, typical, usual, customary, habitual, everyday
2 *This is more than just an ordinary robot.*
standard, average, common, conventional, regular
3 *It was a very ordinary game.*
mediocre, unexceptional, run-of-the-mill, routine

organize *verb*
1 *It took her ages to organize the party.*
coordinate, plan, make arrangements for, see to, set up, run
2 *The librarian has to organize the books in the library.*
arrange, put in order, classify, sort out, tidy up

original *adjective*
1 *The settlers drove out the original inhabitants.*
earliest, first, initial, native, aboriginal
2 *The story was very original.*
inventive, new, novel, creative, fresh, imaginative, unusual, unconventional
3 *Is that an original work of art or a copy?*
genuine, real, authentic, unique

ornament *noun*
A few ornaments will make the room more attractive.
decoration, adornment, trinket, bauble

outrageous *adjective*
1 *The behaviour of the trolls was outrageous.*
disgraceful, scandalous, shocking, atrocious, appalling, monstrous, shameful
2 *They charge outrageous prices at that shop.*
excessive, unreasonable

outside *adjective*
Lookouts were stationed on the outside wall of the castle.
exterior, external, outer

outside *noun*
Insects have their skeletons on the outside of their bodies.
exterior, shell, surface
OPPOSITE inside

outstanding *adjective*
1 *She will be an outstanding tennis player in a few years.*
excellent, exceptional, superb, extraordinary, superlative, brilliant, great, fine, distinguished, celebrated, remarkable, superior, striking, notable
OPPOSITE ordinary
2 *There are still some outstanding bills to pay.*
overdue, unpaid, owing

overcome *verb*
He managed to overcome his fear of flying.
conquer, defeat, master, get the better of

overpowering *adjective*
I felt an overpowering urge to giggle.
overwhelming, powerful, strong, compelling, irresistible, uncontrollable

overtake *verb*
We overtook the car in front.
pass, leave behind, pull ahead of, outstrip

own *verb*
It was the first bike she had owned.
be the owner of, have, possess
to own up to
No one owned up to breaking the window.
confess to, admit to, tell the truth about
(*informal*) come clean about

order

Pp

pace noun
  1 *Move forward two **paces**.*
  step, stride
  2 *The front runner set a fast **pace**.*
  rate, speed
  A formal word is *velocity*.
pack noun
  *There were four candles in each **pack**.*
  package, packet, bundle, bale
pack verb
  1 *She **packed** her suitcase and called a taxi.*
  fill, load up
  2 *I forgot to **pack** my hairdryer.*
  stow away, wrap up
  3 *They tried to **pack** too many passengers onto the train.*
  cram, crowd, squeeze, stuff, jam, wedge
page noun
  1 *Several **pages** have been torn out of this book.*
  sheet, leaf
  2 *He wrote two **pages** of notes.*
  side
pain noun
  *Dirk felt a sudden jabbing **pain** in his foot.*
  anguish, suffering
  A dull pain is an *ache* or *soreness*.
  Severe pain is *agony*, *torment*, or *torture*.
  A slight pain is *discomfort*.
  A slight pain which doesn't last long is a *twinge*.
  A sudden pain is a *pang* or *stab*.
  Pain in your head is a *headache*.
  Pain in your teeth is *toothache*.
painful adjective
  1 *My shoulder is still really **painful**.*
  sore, aching, tender, hurting, smarting, stinging, throbbing
  2 *The conversation brought back many **painful** memories.*
  unpleasant, upsetting, distressing, disagreeable, traumatic
paint verb
  1 *The bedroom walls were **painted** green.*
  colour, decorate
  2 *Samantha **painted** the flowers in bright colours.*
  depict, portray, represent
painting noun
  A picture painted on a wall is a *fresco* or a *mural*.
  A picture painted by a famous artist of the past is an *old master*.

pair noun
  A pair of people who go out together are a *couple*.
  Two people who sing or play music together are a *duet*.
  Two people who work together are *partners* or a *partnership*.
  Two babies born together are *twins*.
pale adjective
  1 *Are you all right? You're looking a little **pale**.*
  white, pallid, pasty, wan, ashen, sallow, anaemic
  To go pale with fear is to *blanch*.
  OPPOSITE ruddy, flushed
  2 *That shade of pink is too **pale**.*
  light, pastel, faded, faint, dim, bleached, colourless
  OPPOSITE bright
panic noun
  *People fled the streets in **panic**.*
  alarm, fright, terror, frenzy, hysteria
panic verb
  *If a fire starts, don't **panic**!*
  be alarmed, take fright, become hysterical
  (*informal*) lose your head, get in a flap
  To panic is also to be *panic-stricken*.
pant verb
  *Some of the runners were **panting** by the last lap.*
  breathe quickly, gasp, wheeze, puff
paper noun
  1 *She started her diary on a fresh sheet of **paper**.*
  A piece of paper is a *leaf* or a *sheet*.
  2 *The doctor had some important **papers** to sign.*
  document, deed, certificate
  3 *The story made the front page of the local **paper**.*
  newspaper, journal
  (*informal*) rag

parade noun
  *A circus **parade** passed along the street.*
  procession, march, spectacle, show, display
  A parade of vehicles or people or horseback is a *cavalcade*.
  A parade of people in costume is a *pageant*.
parcel noun
  *The postman delivered a bulky **parcel**.*
  package, packet
pardon verb
  *The king decided to **pardon** the prisoners.*
  release, free, set free, let off, spare, excuse, forgive
  To pardon someone who is condemned to death is to *reprieve* them.
part noun
  1 *All the **parts** of the engine are now working properly.*
  bit, component, constituent
  2 *I only saw the first **part** of the programme.*
  section, piece, portion, element
  3 *Which **part** of the business do they own?*
  branch, department, division
  4 *Granny lives in another **part** of the town.*
  area, district, region, neighbourhood, sector
  5 *He's just right to act the **part** of Peter Pan.*
  character, role
part verb
  1 *It was the first time she'd been **parted** from her parents.*
  separate, divide, remove
  OPPOSITE join
  2 *They exchanged a final kiss before **parting**.*
  go away, leave, depart, say goodbye
  OPPOSITE meet   mural

a
b
c
d
e
f
g
h
i
j
k
l
m
n
o
p
q
r
s
t
u
v
w
x
y
z

particular *adjective*
1 *The tickets must be used on a particular day.*
specific, certain, distinct, definite, exact
2 *She took particular care not to damage the parcel.*
special, exceptional, unusual, extreme, marked, notable
3 *The cat's very particular about his food.*
fussy, finicky, hard to please (*informal*) choosy, picky
partner *noun*
The two women have been business partners for years.
colleague, associate, ally
In marriage, your partner is your **spouse** or your **husband** or **wife**.
An animal's partner is its **mate**.
party *noun*
1 *We had a class party at the end of term.*
celebration, festivity, function, gathering, reception (*informal*) get-together, do
2 *A party of tourists was going round the museum.*
group, band, crowd, gang
pass *verb*
1 *We watched the parade as it passed.*
go by, move past
2 *She tried to pass the car in front.*
overtake, go ahead of
3 *We passed over the bridge.*
go, advance, proceed, progress
4 *Could you pass me the sugar, please?*
hand, give, deliver, offer, present
5 *Do you think you will pass your music exam?*
be successful in, get through, succeed in
6 *How did you pass the time on holiday?*
spend, use, occupy, fill, while away
7 *Three years passed before we met again.*
go by, elapse
8 *The pain will soon pass.*
go away, come to an end, disappear, fade
pass *noun*
We had a pass to get into the concert for free.
permit, licence, ticket
passage *noun*
1 *A secret passage led from the chamber to the outside.*
passageway, corridor, tunnel
2 *The guards forced a passage through the crowd.*
path, route, way
3 *Our homework is to choose a favourite passage from a book.*
episode, excerpt, extract, piece, quotation, section

4 *He hadn't changed, despite the passage of time.*
passing, progress, advance
passion *noun*
1 *'Romeo and Juliet' is a story of youthful passion.*
love, emotion
2 *She has a passion for sports.*
enthusiasm, eagerness, appetite, desire, craving, urge, zest, thirst, mania
passionate *adjective*
1 *The captain gave a passionate speech before the battle.*
emotional, intense, moving, heartfelt
OPPOSITE unemotional
2 *He is a passionate follower of football.*
eager, keen, avid, enthusiastic, fanatical, fervent
OPPOSITE apathetic
past *noun*
In the past, things were different.
past times, old days, olden days, days gone by
The study of what happened in the past is **history**.
The things and ideas that have come down to us from the past are our **heritage** or **traditions**.
OPPOSITE future
past *adjective*
Things were very different in past centuries.
earlier, former, previous, old
OPPOSITE future
pat *verb*
Andy patted the Shetland pony on the head.
tap, touch, stroke, pet
To touch something quickly and lightly is to **dab** it.
To stroke someone with an open hand is to **caress** them.
patch *verb*
I need some material to patch my jeans.
mend, repair
Another way to mend holes in clothes is to **darn** them or **stitch** them up.
path *noun*
Please keep to the path as you walk through the gardens.
pathway, track, trail, footpath, walk, walkway, lane
A path for horse-riding is a **bridleway**.
A path by the side of a road is a **pavement**.
A path above a beach is an **esplanade** or **promenade**.
A path along a canal is a **towpath**.
A path between buildings is an **alley**.
pathetic *adjective*
1 *The abandoned kittens were a*

pathetic sight.
moving, touching, pitiful, distressing, heartbreaking, sad, sorry
2 *The goalie made a pathetic attempt to stop the ball.*
hopeless, useless, weak, feeble, inadequate, incompetent
patience *noun*
She waited with great patience for an hour.
calmness, tolerance, self-control, endurance, restraint, perseverance, persistence, resignation
OPPOSITE impatience
patient *adjective*
1 *The nurse was very patient with the children.*
calm, composed, even-tempered, easygoing, tolerant, lenient, mild, quiet, uncomplaining, resigned, long-suffering
2 *It took hours of patient work to restore the painting.*
persevering, persistent, unhurried, untiring, steady, determined
OPPOSITE impatient
pause *noun*
There was a pause while the singers got their breath back.
break, gap, halt, rest, lull, stop, wait, interruption, stoppage
A pause in the middle of a performance is an **interlude** or **interval**.
A pause in the middle of a cinema film is an **intermission**.
pause *verb*
1 *The stranger paused at the door before knocking.*
hesitate, wait, delay, hang back
2 *The cyclists paused to let the others catch up.*
halt, stop, rest, take a break, break off
pay *verb*
1 *How much did you pay for your new bike?*
spend, give out, hand over (*informal*) fork out
2 *Who's going to pay the bill?*
pay off, repay, settle, clear, refund
3 *They had to pay for all the damage they caused.*
compensate, pay back
4 *I'll make you pay for this!*
suffer
pay *noun*
We should get an increase in pay next year.
wages, salary, income, earnings
A payment you get for doing a single job is a **fee**.
peace *noun*
1 *After the war there was a period of peace.*

agreement, harmony, friendliness
2 She enjoys the **peace** of the countryside.
calmness, peacefulness, quiet, tranquillity, stillness, serenity, silence
peaceful *adjective*
They enjoyed a **peaceful** day fishing.
calm, quiet, relaxing, tranquil, restful, serene, undisturbed, untroubled, gentle, placid, soothing, still
OPPOSITE noisy, troubled
peak *noun*
1 The **peak** of the mountain was covered in snow.
summit, cap, crest, crown, pinnacle, top, tip, point
2 She is at the **peak** of her career as an athlete.
top, height, highest point, climax
peculiar *adjective*
1 What's that **peculiar** smell?
strange, unusual, odd, curious, extraordinary, abnormal, funny, weird, bizarre
OPPOSITE ordinary
2 He recognized her **peculiar** way of writing.
characteristic, distinctive, individual, particular, personal, special, unique, identifiable
people *plural noun*
1 How many **people** are you inviting?
persons, individuals
People as opposed to animals are **humans** or **human beings** or **mankind**.
2 The government is elected by the **people** of the country.
population, citizens, the public, society, nation, race
perceptive *adjective*
It was very **perceptive** of you to spot my mistake.
observant, clever, sharp, shrewd, quick, alert
OPPOSITE unobservant
perfect *adjective*
1 Each petal on the flower was **perfect**.
faultless, flawless, ideal, intact, undamaged, complete, whole
2 The dress is a **perfect** fit.
exact, faithful, precise, accurate, correct
OPPOSITE imperfect
3 I received a letter from a **perfect** stranger.
complete, total, absolute, utter
perform *verb*
1 Is this your first time **performing** on stage?
act, appear, play, dance, sing
2 The children **performed** a play about Cinderella.

present, stage, produce, put on
3 Soldiers are expected to **perform** their duty.
do, carry out, execute, fulfil
To perform a crime is to **commit** a crime.
performance *noun*
1 Tonight's **performance** is already sold out.
show, production, presentation
2 He congratulated the players on their outstanding **performance**.
effort, work, endeavour, exertion, behaviour, conduct
permanent *adjective*
1 Sugar can do **permanent** damage to your teeth.
lasting, long-lasting, long-term, everlasting, enduring
2 Traffic noise is a **permanent** problem in the city centre.
never-ending, perpetual, persistent, chronic, perennial
3 She has been offered a **permanent** job in the firm.
stable, steady, fixed, lifelong
permission *noun*
They had the teacher's **permission** to leave.
consent, agreement, approval
(*informal*) go-ahead
permit *verb*
The council doesn't **permit** fishing in the lake.
allow, consent to, give permission for, authorize, license, grant, tolerate, admit
permit *noun*
You need a **permit** to fish in the river.
licence, pass, ticket
persecute *verb*
People were **persecuted** for their religious beliefs.
oppress, discriminate against, harass, intimidate, bully, terrorize, torment
persevere *verb*
The rescuers **persevered** despite the bad weather.
continue, carry on, keep going, persist
(*informal*) keep at it, stick at it
OPPOSITE give up
person *noun*
Not a single **person** has replied to my email.
individual, human being, character, soul
personal *adjective*
1 The book is based on the writer's **personal** experience.
own, individual, particular
2 The contents of the letter are **personal**.
confidential, private, secret, intimate
personality *noun*
Like all ogres, he has an ugly

personality.
character, nature, disposition, temperament, make-up
persuade *verb*
I **persuaded** my friend to join the choir.
convince, coax, induce
To persuade someone to do something is also to **talk them into** doing it.
OPPOSITE dissuade
persuasive *adjective*
She used some very **persuasive** arguments.
convincing, effective, sound, strong, forceful, compelling, valid
OPPOSITE unconvincing
pessimistic *adjective*
The players are **pessimistic** about their chances of winning.
negative, unhopeful, gloomy, despairing, resigned, cynical
OPPOSITE optimistic
pester *verb*
Please don't **pester** me while I'm busy!
annoy, bother, trouble, harass, badger, hound, nag
(*informal*) bug
petrified *adjective*
Jack stood **petrified** as the monster lumbered towards him.
terrified, horrified, terror-struck, paralysed, frozen
phase *noun*
Going to school is the start of a new **phase** in your life.
period, time, stage, step
phone *verb*
I'll **phone** you later this evening.
telephone, call, ring, dial
photograph *noun*
I put my holiday **photographs** in an album.
photo, snap or snapshot, shot
The photographs you get when a film is processed are **prints**.
A photograph on the original film from which a print is made is a **negative**.
A photograph for projecting onto a screen is a **slide** or **transparency**.
pick *verb*
1 They've **picked** the players for the hockey team.
choose, select, decide on, settle on, opt for, single out
2 Irene **picked** some flowers from the garden.
gather, collect, cut
3 I **picked** an apple off the tree.
pluck, pull off, take
to pick up
1 He was too weak to **pick up** the box.
lift, raise, hoist

a
b
c
d
e
f
g
h
i
j
k
l
m
n
o
p
q
r
s
t
u
v
w
x
y
z

2 *I'll* **pick up** *some milk on the way home.*
get, collect, fetch

picture *noun*
1 *There's a* **picture** *of a pyramid in this book.*
illustration, image, print
A picture which represents a particular person is a *portrait*.
A picture which represents the artist himself or herself is a *self-portrait*. A picture which represents

a group of objects is a *still life*.
A picture which represents a country scene is a *landscape*.
Pictures on a computer are *graphics*.
2 *Mum took some* **pictures** *of us building a sandcastle.*
photograph, snapsot, snap

picture *verb*
1 *The girl is* **pictured** *against a background of flowers.* depict, illustrate, represent, show, portray

2 *Can you* **picture** *what the world will be like in 100 years?*
imagine, visualize

piece *noun*
1 *They collected* **pieces** *of wood to build a raft.*
bar, block, length, stick, chunk, lump, hunk, bit, chip, fragment, particle, scrap, shred
2 *I've only got two* **pieces** *of chocolate left.* bit, portion, part, section, segment, share, slice
3 *I've lost one of the* **pieces** *of the jigsaw.*

✦ WORD WEB

pirate *noun*
The ship was overrun by bloodthirsty pirates.
buccaneer, marauder

THINGS YOU MIGHT FIND ON A PIRATE SHIP
barrels, cabin, crow's nest, deck, hammock, lantern, mast, plank, pirate flag, rigging, sail, treasure chest, wheel

telescope

A pirate flag is a *Jolly Roger* or *skull-and-crossbones*.
A pirate ship might sail on the *high seas* or the *Spanish Main*.

PEOPLE YOU MIGHT FIND ON A PIRATE SHIP
cabin boy or girl, captain, captives, cook, crew, first mate, lookout, stowaway

PIRATE TREASURE MIGHT CONTAIN
doubloons or ducats, gold bullion, pieces of eight
Goods or treasure seized by pirates is *booty*.

WEAPONS A PIRATE MIGHT USE
cannon, cutlass, dagger, gunpowder, musket, pistol

OTHER THINGS A PIRATE MIGHT WEAR OR CARRY
bandanna or kerchief, bottle of rum, breeches, cocked hat, earrings, eye patch, hook, parrot or cockatoo, pigtail, sea chart, spyglass or telescope, treasure map, wooden leg or peg leg

SOME WORDS TO DESCRIBE A PIRATE
barbaric, black-hearted, bloodthirsty, cut-throat, daring, dastardly, fearless, heartless, lawless, merciless, murderous, pitiless, ruthless, savage, swashbuckling, vengeful, vicious, villainous

hat

parrot

dagger

musket

jolly roger

treasure map

treasure

part, element, unit, component, constituent

4 *There's a piece about our school in the local paper.*
article, item, report, feature

pierce *verb*
The arrow had pierced the knight's armour.
enter, go through, make a hole in, penetrate, bore through
To pierce a hole through paper is to **punch** a hole or **perforate** it.
To pierce a hole in a tyre is to **puncture** it.
To pierce someone with a spike is to **impale** or **spear** them.

pile *noun*
1 *Where did this pile of rubbish come from?*
heap, mound, mountain, stack, hoard, mass, quantity, collection, assortment
2 *I've still got piles of homework to do.*
plenty, a lot, a great deal
(*informal*) lots, masses

pile *verb*
Pile everything in the corner and we'll sort it out later.
heap, stack, collect, gather, assemble, hoard

to pile up
The bills are beginning to pile up.
build up, mount up, accumulate

pillar *noun*
The roof was supported by tall pillars.
column, pier, post, prop, support

pinch *verb*
1 *The baby pinched my arm and wouldn't let go.*
nip, squeeze, press, tweak, grip
2 (*informal*) *Who pinched my calculator?*
steal, take, snatch, pilfer
(*informal*) nick, swipe, make off with

pipe *noun*
The water flows away along this pipe.
tube
A pipe used for watering the garden is a *hose*.
A pipe in the street which supplies water for fighting fires is a *hydrant*.
A pipe which carries oil, etc., over long distances is a *pipeline*.
The system of water pipes in a house is the *plumbing*.

pirate *noun*
see panel on previous page

pity *noun*
The pirates showed no pity towards the captives.
mercy, compassion, sympathy, humanity, kindness, concern, feeling
OPPOSITE cruelty

a pity
It's a pity that you have to leave so early.
a shame, unfortunate, bad luck

pity *verb*
We pitied anyone who was caught up in the storm.
feel sorry for, feel for, sympathize with, take pity on

place *noun*
1 *This is a good place to park.*
site, venue, spot, location, position, situation
2 *They are looking for a quiet place to live.*
area, district, locality, neighbourhood, region, vicinity
3 *Save me a place on the bus.*
seat, space

place *verb*
1 *The hotel is placed next to the beach.*
locate, situate, position, station
2 *You can place your coats on the bed.*
put down, set down, leave, deposit, lay
(*informal*) dump, plonk

plain *adjective*
1 *The furniture in the room was very plain.*
simple, modest, basic, unelaborate
OPPOSITE elaborate
2 *Some people say she looks plain compared with her sister.*
unattractive, ordinary
OPPOSITE attractive
3 *It is plain to me that you are not interested.*
clear, evident, obvious, apparent, unmistakable
OPPOSITE unclear
4 *She told us what she thought in very plain terms.*
direct, frank, blunt, outspoken, honest, sincere, straightforward
5 *We need to wear a plain t-shirt for sports.*
unpatterned, self-coloured

plan *noun*
1 *The captain explained her plan to the rest of the team.*
idea, proposal, scheme, strategy, project, suggestion, proposition
A plan to do something bad is a *plot*.
2 *They looked at the plans for the new sports centre.*
design, diagram, chart, map, drawing, blueprint

plan *verb*
1 *The outlaws planned an attack upon the sheriff.*
scheme, design, devise, work out, formulate, prepare, organize
To plan to do something bad is to *plot*.
2 *What do you plan to do next?*
aim, intend, propose, mean

WORD WEB

planet *noun*
The new space probe will travel to far-off *planets*.
world

THE PLANETS OF THE SOLAR SYSTEM (IN ORDER FROM THE SUN) ARE Mercury, Venus, Earth, Mars, Jupiter, Saturn, Uranus, Neptune.

The path followed by a planet is its *orbit*. Minor planets orbiting the sun are *asteroids*.

Something which orbits a planet is a *satellite*.

The earth's large satellite is the *Moon*.

WRITING TIPS

You can use these words to describe an **alien planet**
Earth-like, gaseous, inhospitable, uninhabitable

TO DESCRIBE ITS *surface*
barren, desolate, dusty, frozen, icy, molten, rocky, volcanic

TO DESCRIBE ITS *atmosphere* OR *air*
airless, noxious, poisonous, thin, unbreathable

play noun
1 *There was a good **play** on TV last night.*
drama, performance, production
2 *It is important to balance work and **play**.*
playing, recreation, amusement, fun, games, sport
play verb
1 *The children went out to **play**.*
amuse yourself, have fun, romp about
2 *Do you like **playing** basketball?*
take part in, participate in, compete in
3 *We are **playing** the home team next week.*
compete against, oppose, challenge, take on
4 *Mira **played** the piano at the school concert.*
perform in
5 *My sister **played** Goldilocks in the school **play**.*
act, take the part of, portray, represent
playful adjective
*The kittens were in a **playful** mood.*
lively, spirited, frisky, mischievous, roguish, impish, joking, teasing
OPPOSITE serious
plead verb
to plead with
*The children **pleaded with** the witch to let them go.*
beg, entreat, implore, appeal to, ask, request, petition
pleasant adjective
1 *The owner of the shop is always **pleasant** to us.*
kind, friendly, likeable, charming, amiable, amicable, cheerful, genial, good-natured, good-humoured, approachable, hospitable, welcoming
2 *We spent a very **pleasant** evening playing cards.*
pleasing, enjoyable, agreeable, delightful, lovely, entertaining
pleased adjective
*Why do you look so **pleased** today?*
contented, delighted, elated, glad, grateful, happy, satisfied, thankful, thrilled
OPPOSITE annoyed
pleasure noun
1 *Mrs Ramsay gets a lot of **pleasure** from her garden.*
delight, enjoyment, happiness, joy, satisfaction, comfort, contentment, gladness
Very great pleasure is *bliss* or *ecstasy*.
2 *He talked about the **pleasures** of living in the country.*
joy, comfort, delight

plenty noun
*Don't buy any milk—there's **plenty** in the fridge.*
a lot, a large amount, an abundance, a profusion
A lot more than you need is a *glut* or *surplus*.
OPPOSITE scarcity
plenty of
*We've still got **plenty of** time.*
a lot of, lots of, ample, abundant
(*informal*) loads of, masses of, tons of
plot noun
1 *Guy Fawkes was part of a **plot** against the government.*
conspiracy, scheme, secret plan
2 *It was hard to follow the **plot** of the film.*
story, storyline, narrative, thread
3 *They bought a **plot** of ground to build a new house.*
area, piece, lot, patch
A plot of ground for growing flowers or vegetables is an *allotment*.
A large plot of land is a *tract* of land.
plot verb
1 *The gang were **plotting** a daring bank raid.*
plan, devise, concoct, hatch
(*informal*) cook up
2 *They were accused of **plotting** against the queen.*
conspire, intrigue, scheme
plump adjective
*The goblin was short and **plump**, with pointy ears.*
chubby, dumpy, fat, tubby, podgy, round, stout, portly
OPPOSITE skinny
plunge verb
1 *One by one, the girls **plunged** into the pool.*
dive, jump, leap, throw yourself
2 *As the wind died down, the kite **plunged** to the ground.*
drop, fall, pitch, tumble, plummet, swoop
3 *I **plunged** my hand in the cold water.*
dip, lower, sink, immerse, submerge
4 *Finn **plunged** his spear into the dragon's throat.*
thrust, stab, push, stick, shove, force
point noun
1 *Be careful—that knife has a very sharp **point**.*
tip, end, spike, prong
2 *The stars looked like **points** of light in the sky.*
dot, spot, speck, fleck
3 *He marked on the map the exact **point** where the

treasure lay.*
location, place, position, site
4 *At that **point** the rain started to come down.*
moment, instant, time
5 *I agree with your last **point**.*
idea, argument, thought
6 *His sense of humour is one of his good **points**.*
characteristic, feature, attribute
7 *There is no **point** in phoning at this hour.*
purpose, reason, aim, object, use, usefulness
8 *I think I missed the **point** of that film.*
meaning, essence, core, gist
point verb
1 *She **pointed** the way.*
draw attention to, indicate, point out, show, signal
2 *Can you **point** me in the right direction for the station?*
aim, direct, guide, lead, steer
pointless adjective
*It's **pointless** to argue with him—he's so stubborn.*
useless, futile, vain
OPPOSITE worthwhile
poisonous adjective
*Some of those mushrooms may be **poisonous**.*
toxic, venomous, deadly, lethal
poke verb
*Someone **poked** me in the back with an umbrella.*
prod, dig, jab, stab, thrust
to poke out
*The kitten's head was **poking out** of the basket.*
stick out, project, protrude
pole noun
*Four **poles** marked the corners of the field.*
post, bar, rod, stick, shaft
A pole that you use when walking or as a weapon is a *staff*.
A pole for a flag to fly from is a *flagpole*.
A pole to support sails on a boat or ship is a *mast* or *spar*.
A pole with a pointed end to stick in the ground is a *stake*.
Poles which a circus entertainer walks on are *stilts*.
polish verb
*Beeswax is used to **polish** furniture.*
rub down, shine, buff, burnish, wax
polish noun
*The silverware had been cleaned to give it a good **polish**.*
shine, sheen, gloss, lustre, sparkle, brightness, glaze, finish
polite adjective
*My aunt is always **polite** to visitors.*
courteous, well-

point

mannered, respectful, civil, well-behaved, gracious, gentlemanly or ladylike, chivalrous, gallant
OPPOSITE rude, impolite

pollute *verb*
The river has been **polluted** by chemicals.
contaminate, infect, poison

poor *adjective*
1 You can't afford luxuries if you're **poor**.
impoverished, poverty-stricken, penniless, needy, badly off, hard-up
OPPOSITE rich
2 His handwriting is very **poor**.
bad, inferior, inadequate, incompetent, unsatisfactory, shoddy, weak, worthless
OPPOSITE good, superior
3 They pitied the **poor** animals standing in the rain.
unlucky, unfortunate, pitiful, wretched
OPPOSITE lucky

popular *adjective*
1 Disney has made a lot of **popular** children's films.
well-liked, well-loved, celebrated, favourite
OPPOSITE unpopular
2 Rollerblades are very **popular** just now.
fashionable, widespread, current, in demand
(*informal*) trendy
OPPOSITE unpopular

port *noun*
A large cruise ship sailed into the **port**.
harbour, dock, anchorage
A harbour for yachts and pleasure boats is a *marina*.

portrait *noun*
There's a **portrait** of the Queen on every stamp.
picture, image, likeness, representation
A portrait which shows a side view of someone is a *profile*.
A portrait which shows just the outline of someone is a *silhouette*.
A portrait which exaggerates some aspect of a person is a *caricature*.

posh *adjective*
(*informal*)
We went to a **posh** restaurant for a treat.
smart, stylish, high-class, elegant, fashionable, up-market, luxurious, luxury, deluxe, plush
(*informal*) classy, swanky, swish, snazzy

position *noun*
1 Mark the **position** on the map.
location, place, point, spot, site, whereabouts
2 He shifted his **position** to avoid getting cramp.
pose, posture, stance
3 Losing all her money put her in a difficult **position**.
situation, state, condition, circumstances
4 A referee should adopt a neutral **position**.
opinion, attitude, outlook, view
5 Being a head teacher is an important **position**.
job, post, appointment, function

positive *adjective*
1 The detective was **positive** that the cook was lying.
certain, sure, convinced, assured, confident
OPPOSITE uncertain
2 Miss Andrews made some **positive** comments on my singing.
helpful, useful, worthwhile, beneficial, constructive
OPPOSITE negative

possible *adjective*
1 Is it **possible** that life exists on other planets?
likely, probable, conceivable, credible
2 It wasn't **possible** to shift the piano.
feasible, practicable, practical

post *noun*
1 The farmer put up some **posts** for a new fence.
pole, pillar, shaft, stake, support, prop
2 The **post** was delivered late.
mail, letters, delivery
3 Are you thinking of applying for the **post**?
job, position, situation, appointment, vacancy

post *verb*
1 Did you **post** those letters?
mail, send, dispatch
2 The names of the winners will be **posted** on the noticeboard.
display, put up, announce, advertise

postpone *verb*
They **postponed** the match because of bad weather.

portrait

put off, defer, delay
To stop a game or meeting that you intend to start again later is to *adjourn* or *suspend* it.

potion *noun*
A magic **potion** was brewing in the wizard's cauldron.
drug, medicine, mixture

pounce *verb*
to pounce on
The cat **pounced on** the mouse.
jump on, leap on, spring on, swoop down on, lunge at, ambush, attack

pour *verb*
1 Water **poured** through the hole.
flow, run, gush, stream, spill, spout
2 I **poured** some milk into my cup.
tip, serve

power *noun*
1 They were amazed by the **power** of the robot.
strength, force, might, energy
2 The storyteller has the **power** to enthrall an audience.
skill, talent, ability, competence
3 A policeman has the **power** to arrest someone.
authority, right
4 The empress had **power** over all the people.
authority, command, control, dominance, domination

powerful *adjective*
1 Sir Joustalot was the most **powerful** knight in the kingdom.
influential, leading, commanding, dominant, high-powered
2 The wrestler had a **powerful** punch.
strong, forceful, hard, mighty, vigorous, formidable, potent
3 He used some **powerful** arguments.
strong, convincing, effective, persuasive, impressive

practical *adjective*
1 I'll ask Katie what to do—she is always very **practical**.
down-to-earth, matter-of-fact, sensible, level-headed
OPPOSITE impractical
2 The robbers' plan was not very **practical**.
workable, realistic, sensible, feasible, viable, achievable
OPPOSITE impractical
3 Do you have any **practical** experience of childminding?
real, actual, hands-on
OPPOSITE theoretical

practice *noun*
1 We have extra football **practice** this week.

a b c d e f g h i j k l m n o p q r s t u v w x y z

training, exercises, preparation, rehearsal, drill

2 *Is it the* **practice** *amongst ogres to eat grubs for breakfast?*
custom, habit, convention, routine

in practice
What will the plan involve **in practice***?*
in effect, in reality, actually, really

practise verb
1 *My piano teacher asked me to* **practise** *for longer.*
do exercises, rehearse, train, drill
To practise just before the start of a performance is to **warm up**.
2 *My sister wants to* **practise** *veterinary medicine.*
do, perform, carry out, put into practice, follow, pursue

praise verb
The critics **praised** *the actress for her outstanding performance.*
commend, applaud, admire, compliment, congratulate, pay tribute to
(*informal*) rave about
OPPOSITE criticize

praise noun
She received a lot of **praise** *for her painting.*
approval, admiration, compliments, congratulations, applause

prance verb
Milly started **prancing** *about in a silly way.*
dance, skip, hop, leap, romp, cavort, caper, frolic, gambol

precious adjective
1 *Her most* **precious** *possession was an old photograph.*
treasured, cherished, valued, prized, dearest, beloved
2 *The throne glittered with* **precious** *gems and gold.*
valuable, costly, expensive, priceless
OPPOSITE worthless

precise adjective
1 *Can you tell me the* **precise** *time, please?*
exact, accurate, correct, true, right
OPPOSITE rough
2 *The map gave* **precise** *directions for finding the treasure.*
careful, detailed, specific, particular, definite
OPPOSITE vague

predict verb
You can't **predict** *what may happen in the future.*
forecast, foresee, foretell, prophesy

prefer verb
Would you **prefer** *juice or lemonade?*
rather have, go for, opt for, plump for, choose, fancy

prejudice noun
The school has a policy against racial **prejudice***.*
bias, discrimination, intolerance, narrow-mindedness, bigotry
Prejudice against other races is *racism*.
Prejudice against other nations is *xenophobia*.
Prejudice against the other sex is *sexism*.
OPPOSITE fairness, tolerance

prepare verb
The museum staff are **preparing** *for the new exhibition.*
get ready, make arrangements for, organize, plan, set up
To prepare for a play is to *rehearse*.
To prepare to take part in a sport is to *train*.

present adjective
1 *Is everyone* **present***?*
here, in attendance, at hand
2 *Who is the* **present** *world chess champion?*
current, existing

present noun
What would you like for your birthday **present***?*
gift
(*informal*) prezzie

present verb
1 *The head* **presents** *the prizes on sports day.*
award, hand over
2 *Our class is* **presenting** *a play about the Vikings.*
put on, perform, stage, mount
3 *Dr Smart* **presented** *her amazing invention to the world.*
put forward, show, display, exhibit, make known

press verb
1 **Press** *the fruit through a sieve to get rid of the seeds.*
push, force, squeeze, squash, crush, shove, cram, compress
2 *She* **pressed** *her blouse for the party.*
iron, flatten, smooth
3 *Our friends* **pressed** *us to stay a bit longer.*
beg, urge, entreat, implore

press noun
1 *We read about the competition in the* **press***.*
newspapers, magazines
2 *The* **press** *came to the opening of the new arts centre.*
journalists, reporters, the media

pressure noun
1 *The nurse applied* **pressure** *to the wound.*
force, compression, squeezing, weight, load
2 *In the final, the home team were*

under a lot of **pressure***.*
stress, strain, tension

presume verb
I **presume** *you'd like something to eat.*
assume, take it, imagine, suppose, think, believe, guess

pretend verb
She's not really crying—she's only **pretending***.*
put on an act, bluff, fake, sham, pose
(*informal*) kid, put it on

pretend adjective
That's not a real spider—it's just a **pretend** *one!*
fake, false, artificial, made-up
OPPOSITE real

pretty
adjective
The doll was dressed in a **pretty** *blue outfit.*
attractive, beautiful, lovely, nice, pleasing, charming, dainty, picturesque, quaint
(*informal*) cute
A common simile is *as pretty as a picture*.
OPPOSITE ugly

prevent verb
1 *The driver could do nothing to* **prevent** *the accident.*
stop, avert, avoid, head off
2 *The police* **prevented** *an attempted bank raid.*
block, foil, frustrate, thwart
3 *There's not much you can do to* **prevent** *colds.*
stave off, ward off

price noun
What is the **price** *of a return ticket to Sydney?*
cost, amount, figure, expense, payment, sum, charge, rate
The price you pay for a journey on public transport is a *fare*.
The price you pay to send a letter is the *postage*.
The price you pay to use a private road, bridge, or tunnel is a *toll*.

priceless adjective
The museum contained many **priceless** *antiques.*
precious, rare, valuable, costly, expensive, dear

prick verb
Jamie burst the balloon by **pricking** *it with a pin.*
pierce, puncture, stab, jab, perforate

prickly adjective
Holly leaves are very **prickly***.*
spiky, spiny, thorny, bristly,

sharp, scratchy
pride noun
1 *Mr Dodds takes great pride in his garden.*
satisfaction, pleasure, delight
2 *The medal winner was a source of great pride to his family.*
self-esteem, self-respect, dignity, honour
3 *Pride comes before a fall.*
arrogance, conceit, bigheadedness, vanity, snobbery
OPPOSITE humility

prim adjective
Aunt Jemima is always very prim and proper.
prudish, strait-laced, formal, demure

prisoner noun
The prisoner tried to escape from jail.
convict, captive, inmate
A person who is held prisoner until some demand is met is a *hostage*.

private adjective
1 *Everything I write in my diary is private.*
secret, confidential, personal, intimate
Secret official documents are *classified* documents.
2 *Can we go somewhere a little more private?*
quiet, secluded, hidden, concealed

prize noun
Our team won first prize in the relay race.
award, reward, trophy
Money that you win as a prize is your *winnings*.
Prize money that keeps increasing until someone wins it is a *jackpot*.

prize verb
Chrissie prized her grandmother's ring above all else.
treasure, value, cherish, hold dear, esteem, revere
OPPOSITE dislike

probable adjective
A burst pipe was the most probable cause of the flood.
likely, feasible, possible, predictable, expected
OPPOSITE improbable

problem noun
1 *Our maths teacher set us a difficult problem.*
puzzle, question
(*informal*) brainteaser, poser
2 *I'm having a problem with my computer.*
difficulty, trouble, snag, worry
(*informal*) headache

procession noun
The procession made its way
slowly down the hill.
parade, march, column, line

prod verb
Someone prodded me in the back with an umbrella.
poke, dig, jab, nudge, push

production noun
1 *Production at the factory has increased this year.*
output
2 *We went to see a production of 'The Sound of Music'.*
performance, show

programme noun
1 *We worked out a programme for sports day.*
plan, schedule, timetable
A list of things to be done at a meeting is an *agenda*.
2 *There was a really good programme on TV last night.*
broadcast, show, production, transmission

progress noun
1 *I traced their progress on the map.*
journey, route, movement, travels
2 *I'm not making much progress learning Dutch.*
advance, development, growth, improvement, headway
An important piece of progress is a *breakthrough*.

progress verb
Work on the new building is progressing well.
proceed, advance, move forward, make progress, make headway, continue, develop, improve
(*informal*) come along

prohibit verb
Skateboarding is prohibited in the school grounds.
ban, forbid, outlaw, rule out, veto
OPPOSITE permit, allow

project noun
1 *We did a history project on the Victorians.*
activity, task, assignment, piece of research
2 *There is a project to create a bird sanctuary in the area.*
plan, proposal, scheme

project verb
1 *A narrow ledge projects from the cliff.*
extend, protrude, stick out, jut out, overhang
2 *The lighthouse projects a beam of light.*
cast, shine, throw out

promise noun
1 *We had promises of help from many people.*
assurance, pledge, guarantee,
commitment, vow, oath, word of honour
2 *That young pianist shows promise.*
potential, talent

promise verb
Dad promised that we'd go camping this summer.
assure someone, give your word, guarantee, swear, take an oath, vow

promote verb
1 *Gareth has been promoted to captain.*
move up, advance, upgrade, elevate
2 *The singer is here to promote her new CD.*
advertise, publicize, market, push, sell (*informal*) plug
3 *The school is trying to promote healthy eating.*
encourage, foster, advocate, back, support

prompt adjective
I received a prompt reply to my email.
punctual, quick, rapid, swift, immediate, instant
OPPOSITE delayed

prompt verb
Having a dog prompted her to take more exercise.
cause, lead, induce, motivate, stimulate, encourage, provoke

proof noun
There is no proof that he is a secret agent.
evidence, confirmation

proper adjective
1 *The nurse showed them the proper way to tie a bandage.*
correct, right, accurate, precise, true, genuine
OPPOSITE wrong, incorrect
2 *It's only proper that he should pay for the broken window.*
fair, just, fitting, appropriate, deserved, suitable
OPPOSITE inappropriate
3 *It's not proper to speak with your mouth full.*
decent, respectable, tasteful
OPPOSITE rude

property noun
1 *This office deals with lost property.*
belongings, possessions, goods
2 *The website lists property that is for sale in the city.*
buildings, houses, land, premises
3 *Many herbs have healing properties.*
quality, characteristic, feature, attribute, trait

protect verb
1 *A sentry was posted outside*

a
b
c
d
e
f
g
h
i
j
k
l
m
n
o
p
q
r
s
t
u
v
w
x
y
z

to **protect** the palace.
defend, guard, safeguard,
keep safe, secure
2 I wore a hat to **protect**
myself from the sun.
shield, shade, screen,
insulate

protest noun
1 There were **protests** at the
plan to close the cinema.
complaint, objection
A general protest is an
outcry.
2 Some streets will be closed
for a **protest** in the city centre.
demonstration, march, rally
(informal) demo

protest verb
We wrote a letter **protesting**
about the closure of the
cinema.
complain, make a protest,
object
(to), take exception (to), express
disapproval (of)

proud adjective
1 Jennie's father was very **proud**
when she passed her music exam.
delighted (with), pleased (with)
A common simile is **as proud as
a peacock**.
2 He's too **proud** to mix with the
likes of us!
conceited, big-headed, arrogant,
vain, haughty, self-important,
snobbish, superior
(informal) stuck-up
OPPOSITE humble

prove verb
The evidence will **prove** that he is
innocent.
confirm, demonstrate, establish,
verify
OPPOSITE disprove

provide verb
1 We'll **provide** the juice if you
bring the sandwiches.
bring, contribute, arrange for,
lay on
To provide food and drink for
people is to **cater** for them.
2 The ski centre can **provide** you
with boots and skis.
supply, equip, furnish

provoke verb
1 Don't do anything to **provoke**
the lions!
annoy, irritate, anger, incense,
infuriate, exasperate, tease,
taunt, goad
(informal) wind up
OPPOSITE pacify
2 The referee's decision **provoked**
anger from the crowd.
arouse, produce, prompt, cause,
generate, induce, stimulate,
spark off, stir up, whip up

prowl verb
Guard dogs **prowled** about the

prowl

grounds of the palace.
roam, slink, sneak, creep, steal

public adjective
1 The **public** entrance is at the
front of the gallery.
common, communal, general,
open, shared
OPPOSITE private
2 The name of the author is now
public knowledge.
well-known, acknowledged,
published, open, general,
universal
OPPOSITE secret

publish verb
1 The magazine is **published** every
week.
issue, print, produce, bring out,
release, circulate
2 When will they **publish** the
results?
announce, declare, disclose,
make known, make public,
report, reveal
To publish information on radio
or TV is to **broadcast** it.

pudding noun
Do you want any **pudding**?
dessert, sweet
(informal) afters

puff noun
1 A **puff** of wind caught his hat.
gust, breath, flurry
2 A **puff** of smoke rose from the
chimney.
cloud, whiff

puff verb
1 The dragon **puffed** green smoke
from its nostrils.
blow out, send out, emit, belch
2 By the end of the race I was
puffing.
breathe heavily, pant, gasp,
wheeze
3 The sails **puffed** out as the wind
rose.
become inflated, billow, swell

pull verb
1 She **pulled** her chair nearer
to the desk.
drag, draw, haul, lug, trail,
tow
OPPOSITE push
2 Be careful—you nearly
pulled my arm off!
tug, rip, wrench, jerk, pluck

to pull out
1 The dentist **pulled out** one of
his teeth.
extract, take out, remove
2 He had to **pull out** of the race.
back out, withdraw, retire

to pull up
The bus **pulled up** at the traffic
lights.
draw up, stop, halt

pump verb
The fire brigade **pumped** water out
of the cellar.
drain, draw off, empty
To move liquid from a higher
container to a lower one through
a tube is to **siphon** it.

punch verb
1 Mrs Rafferty **punched** the robber
on the nose.
jab, poke, prod, thump
2 I need to **punch** a hole through
the card.
bore, pierce

punish verb
Those responsible for the crime
will be **punished**.
penalize, discipline, chastise

pupil noun
There are 33 **pupils** in our class.
schoolchild, student, learner,
scholar
Someone who follows a great
teacher is a **disciple**.

pure adjective
1 The bracelet is made of **pure**
gold.
authentic, genuine, real
2 He was talking **pure** nonsense.
complete, absolute, utter, sheer,
total
3 All our dishes are made from
pure ingredients.
natural, wholesome
4 They swam in the **pure**, clear
water of the lake.
clean, fresh, unpolluted
OPPOSITE impure

purpose noun
1 Have you got a particular
purpose in mind?
intention, aim, end, goal,
target, objective, outcome,
result
2 What's the **purpose** of your
invention?
point, use, usefulness, value

push verb
1 We **pushed** our way through the
crowd.

shove, thrust, force, propel,
barge, elbow, jostle
OPPOSITE pull
2 *Pete **pushed** his things into a bag.*
pack, press, cram, crush,
compress, ram, squash, squeeze
3 *They **pushed** him to work even
harder.*
pressurize, press, drive, urge,
compel, bully
(*informal*) lean on
put *verb*
1 *You can **put** your schoolbags in
the corner.*
place, set down, leave, deposit,
dump, stand
2 *The dog **put** its head on my lap.*
lay, lean, rest
3 *I'll **put** some pictures on the
wall.*
attach, fasten, fix, hang
4 *Where are they planning to **put**
the car park?*
locate, situate
5 *I'm not sure of the best way to
put this.*
express, word, phrase, say, state
to put someone off
*The colour of the food **put** me **off**
eating.*
deter, discourage, distract
to put something off
*They **put** off their journey because
of the fog.*
delay, postpone, defer
to put something out
*The firefighters quickly **put out** the
blaze.*
extinguish, quench, smother
to put something up
1 *It doesn't take long to **put up**
the tent.*
set up, construct, erect
2 *I'm going to buy a new bike
before they **put up** the price.*
increase, raise
to put up with something
*I don't know how you **put up with**
that noise.*
bear, stand, tolerate, endure
puzzle *noun*
*Has anyone managed to solve
the **puzzle**?*
question, mystery, riddle,
conundrum, problem
(*informal*) brainteaser, poser
puzzle *verb*
1 *Phil was **puzzled** by the
mysterious message.*
confuse, baffle, bewilder,
bemuse, mystify, perplex, fox

2 *We **puzzled** over the problem
for hours.*
ponder, think, meditate, worry,
brood
puzzled *adjective*
*Why are you looking so **puzzled**?*
confused, baffled, bewildered,
mystified, perplexed

Qq

quaint *adjective*
*They stayed in a **quaint** thatched
cottage.*
charming, picturesque, sweet,
old-fashioned, old-world
quake *verb*
*The ground **quaked** with the thud
of the giant's footsteps.*
shake, shudder, tremble, quiver,
shiver, vibrate, rock, sway,
wobble
quality *noun*
1 *We only use ingredients of the
highest **quality**.*
grade, class, standard
2 *The most obvious **quality** of
rubber is that it stretches.*
characteristic, feature, property,
attribute, trait
quantity *noun*
1 *She receives a huge **quantity** of
fan mail every week.*
amount, mass, volume, bulk,
weight
(*informal*) load
2 *We recycled a large **quantity** of
empty bottles.*
number
When you add up numbers, you
get a *sum* or *total*.
quarrel *noun*
*We have **quarrels**, but really we
are good friends.*
argument, disagreement,
dispute, difference of opinion,
row, squabble, clash, tiff
Continuous quarrelling is *strife*.
A long-lasting quarrel is a *feud*
or *vendetta*.
A quarrel in which people
become violent is a *brawl* or
fight.
quarrel *verb*
*The twins **quarrelled** over who
should sit in the front.*
disagree, argue, row, squabble,

quay

bicker, clash, fight, fall out
to quarrel with something
*I can't **quarrel with** your decision.*
disagree with, object to, take
exception to, oppose
quay *noun*
*The ship unloaded its cargo onto
the **quay**.*
dock, harbour, pier, wharf, jetty,
landing stage
quest *noun*
*The knights set out on a **quest** to
find the enchanted tower.*
search, hunt, expedition, mission
question *noun*
1 *Does anyone have any
questions?*
enquiry, query, problem
A question which someone sets
as a puzzle is a *brain-teaser* or
conundrum or *riddle*.
A series of questions asked as a
game is a *quiz*.
A set of questions which
someone asks to get
information is a *questionnaire*
or *survey*.
2 *There's some **question** over the
player's fitness.*
uncertainty, doubt, argument,
debate, dispute
question *verb*
1 *The detective decided to
question the suspect.*
ask, examine, interview, quiz,
interrogate
To question someone intensively
is to *grill* them.
2 *He **questioned** the referee's
decision.*
challenge, dispute, argue
over, quarrel with, object to,
query
queue *noun*
*There was a **queue** of people
outside the cinema.*
line, file, column, string
A long queue of traffic on a
road is a *tailback*.

a
b
c
d
e
f
g
h
i
j
k
l
m
n
o
p
q
r
s
t
u
v
w

queue

queue *verb*
Please queue at the door.
line up, form a queue

quick *adjective*
1 *You'd better be quick—the bus leaves in 10 minutes.*
fast, swift, rapid, speedy, hasty
(*informal*) nippy
A common simile is *as quick as a flash*.
OPPOSITE slow
2 *Do you mind if I make a quick phone call?*
short, brief, momentary, immediate, instant, prompt, snappy
OPPOSITE long, lengthy
3 *She's very quick at mental arithmetic.*
bright, clever, sharp, acute, alert
(*informal*) on the ball
OPPOSITE slow

quiet *adjective*
1 *The deserted house was still and quiet.*
silent, noiseless, soundless
A common simile is *as quiet as a mouse*.
OPPOSITE noisy
2 *The children spoke in quiet whispers.*
hushed, low, soft
Something that is so quiet that you can't hear it is *inaudible*.
OPPOSITE loud
3 *Amy has always been a quiet child.*
shy, reserved, subdued, placid, uncommunicative, retiring, withdrawn
OPPOSITE talkative
4 *We found a quiet place for a picnic.*
peaceful, secluded, isolated, restful, tranquil, calm, serene
OPPOSITE busy

quite *adverb*
Take care how you use **quite**, as the two senses are almost opposites.
1 *The two puppies have quite different personalities.*
completely, totally, utterly, entirely, absolutely, wholly
2 *They played quite well, but far from their best.*
fairly, reasonably, moderately, rather

quiz *noun*
Our class took part in a general knowledge quiz.
test, competition, questionnaire, exam, examination

Rr

race *noun*
1 *We had a race to see who was the fastest runner.*
competition, contest, chase
A race to decide who will take part in the final is a *heat*.
2 *We belong to different races but we're all humans.*
nation, people, ethnic group

race *verb*
1 *We raced each other to the end of the road.*
have a race with, run against, compete with
2 *She had to race home because she was late.*
run, rush, dash, hurry, sprint, fly, tear, whizz, zoom

racket *noun*
Please stop making that awful racket!
noise, row, din, commotion, disturbance, uproar, rumpus

ragged *adjective*
They met a traveller wearing ragged clothes.
tattered, tatty, threadbare, torn, frayed, patched, ripped, shabby, worn out

raid *noun*
The enemy raid caught them by surprise.
attack, assault, strike, onslaught, invasion, blitz

raid *verb*
1 *Long ago, Vikings raided the towns on the coast.*
attack, invade, ransack, plunder, loot, pillage
Someone who raids ships at sea is a *pirate*.
Someone who raids and steals cattle is a *rustler*.
2 *Police raided the house at dawn.*
descend on, rush, storm, swoop on

rain *noun*
A formal word for rain is *precipitation*.
The rainy season in south and southeast Asia is the *monsoon*.
When there is no rain for a long time you have a *drought*.

raise *verb*
1 *Raise your hand if you need help.*
hold up, put up, lift
2 *The box was too heavy for him to raise.*
lift, pick up, elevate, hoist, jack up
3 *The Post Office is raising the price of stamps.*
increase, put up
4 *The runners hope to raise £1000*

for charity.
collect, gather, take in, make
5 *He raised some objections to the plan.*
bring up, mention, put forward, present, introduce
6 *The doctor didn't want to raise their hopes.*
encourage, build up, arouse
7 *It's hard work trying to raise a family.*
bring up, care for, look after, nurture, rear

ram *verb*
The car skidded and rammed into a lamp-post.
bump, hit, strike, crash into, collide with, smash into

random *adjective*
They picked a random selection of pupils.
arbitrary, chance, haphazard, casual, unplanned
OPPOSITE deliberate

range *noun*
1 *There is a range of mountains to the south.*
chain, line, row, series, string
2 *Supermarkets sell a wide range of goods.*
variety, assortment, selection, choice, spectrum
3 *The shop caters for all age ranges from toddlers to teenagers.*
span, scope

range *verb*
1 *Prices range from five to twenty euros.*
vary, differ, extend, fluctuate
2 *Rows of jam jars were ranged on the shelf.*
arrange, order, lay out, set out, line up
3 *Wild deer range over the hills.*
wander, ramble, roam, rove, stray

rapid *adjective*
The cyclists set off at a rapid pace.
fast, quick, speedy, swift, brisk
OPPOSITE slow

rare *adjective*
1 *These flowers are now very rare in the wild.*
uncommon, unusual, infrequent, scarce, sparse
OPPOSITE common

rain

2 *He has a **rare** ability to make people laugh.*
exceptional, remarkable, special
rarely *adverb*
*Our next-door neighbour **rarely** goes out.*
seldom, infrequently, hardly ever
OPPOSITE **often**
rash *adjective*
*Don't make any **rash** promises.*
reckless, foolhardy, hasty, hurried, impulsive, unthinking
OPPOSITE **careful**
rate *noun*
1 *The cyclists were pedalling at a furious **rate**.*
pace, speed
2 *What's the usual **rate** for washing a car?*
charge, cost, fee, payment, price, figure, amount
rate *verb*
*How do you **rate** their chance of winning?*
judge, regard, consider, estimate, evaluate
rather *adverb*
1 *It's **rather** chilly today.*
quite, fairly, moderately, slightly, somewhat, a bit, a little
2 *I'd **rather** not go out tonight.*
preferably, sooner
rave *verb*
1 *Connie **raved** about the film she saw last week.*
be enthusiastic, talk wildly
2 *The head **raved** on about their bad behaviour.*
shout, rage, storm, yell, roar
raw *adjective*
1 *Raw vegetables are supposed to be good for you.*
uncooked
OPPOSITE **cooked**
2 *The factory imports a lot of **raw** materials from abroad.*
crude, natural, unprocessed, untreated
OPPOSITE **manufactured**, processed
3 *Her knee felt **raw** after she fell off her bike.*
red, rough, sore, tender, inflamed
4 *There was a **raw** wind blowing from the east.*
bitter, cold, chilly, biting, freezing, piercing
ray *noun*
*A **ray** of light shone into the dark cave.*
beam, shaft, stream
reach *verb*
1 *They hoped to **reach** Oxford by lunch time.*

arrive at, go as far as, get to, make
2 *The appeal fund has **reached** its target.*
achieve, attain
3 *I'm not tall enough to **reach** the top shelf.*
get hold of, grasp, touch
to reach out
Reach out your hands.
extend, hold out, put out, stick out, stretch out
reach *noun*
1 *The shelf was just within his **reach**.*
grasp
2 *The shops are within easy **reach**.*
distance, range
react *verb*
*How did he **react** when he read the letter?*
respond, behave, answer, reply
reaction *noun*
*What was her **reaction** when you said you were sorry?*
response, answer, reply
read *verb*
*They couldn't **read** the doctor's handwriting.*
make out, understand, decipher
To read through something very quickly is to *skim through* it.
To read here and there in a book is to *dip into* it.
To read something intently is to *pore over* it.
ready *adjective*
1 *When will tea be **ready**?*
prepared, set, done, available, in place
OPPOSITE **not ready**
2 *He's always **ready** to help.*
willing, glad, pleased, happy, keen, eager
OPPOSITE **reluctant**
real *adjective*
1 *History is about **real** events.*
actual, true, factual, verifiable
OPPOSITE **fictitious, imaginary**
2 *The necklace was made from **real** rubies.*
authentic, genuine, bona fide, natural
OPPOSITE **artificial, fake**
3 *She doesn't often show her **real** feelings.*
true, honest, sincere, genuine, heartfelt
OPPOSITE **insincere**
realistic *adjective*
1 *The portrait of the artist is very **realistic**.*
lifelike, true to life, faithful, convincing, recognizable
2 *It's not **realistic** to expect a puppy to be quiet.*
feasible, practical, sensible, possible, workable

realize *verb*
*It took him a long time to **realize** what she meant.*
understand, appreciate, grasp, comprehend, recognize, see
(*informal*) catch on to, tumble to, twig
really *adverb*
1 *Are you **really** going to Peru?*
actually, definitely, truly, in fact, certainly, genuinely, honestly
2 *I saw a **really** good film last night.*
very, extremely, exceptionally
reasonable *adjective*
1 *That seems like a **reasonable** plan.*
sensible, intelligent, rational, logical, sane, sound
OPPOSITE **irrational**
2 *They bought the house for a **reasonable** price.*
fair, acceptable, average, moderate, respectable, normal, proper
OPPOSITE **excessive**
reassure *verb*
*The doctor **reassured** her that the wound was not serious.*
calm, comfort, encourage, hearten, give confidence to
OPPOSITE **threaten**
rebel *verb*
*The king feared that the people would **rebel**.*
revolt, rise up
To rebel against the captain of a ship is to *mutiny* and someone who does this is a *mutineer*.
OPPOSITE **obey**
rebellion *noun*
*The protest soon became a widespread **rebellion**.*
revolt, revolution, uprising, resistance
A rebellion on a ship is a *mutiny*.
recent *adjective*
*We watch the news to keep up with **recent** events.*
current, up-to-date, contemporary, new, the latest, fresh
recite *verb*
*Zoe **recited** a poem she had written.*
say aloud, read out, narrate
reckless *adjective*
*A man has been charged with **reckless** driving.*
careless, irresponsible, mindless, thoughtless, negligent, foolhardy, rash, wild
OPPOSITE **careful**
reckon *verb*
1 *I tried to **reckon** how much she owed me.*
calculate, work out, add up, figure out, assess, estimate

a
b
c
d
e
f
g
h
i
j
k
l
m
n
o
p
q
r
s
t
u
v
w
x
y
z

2 *Do you reckon it's going to rain?*
think, believe, guess, imagine, feel

recognize *verb*
1 *I didn't recognize her with her new haircut.*
identify, know, distinguish, make out, recall, recollect, remember
2 *He refused to recognize that he was to blame.*
acknowledge, admit, accept, grant, concede, confess, realize

recommend *verb*
1 *The doctor recommended a complete rest.*
advise, counsel, propose, suggest, advocate, prescribe, urge
2 *The restaurant was recommended by a friend of mine.*
approve of, endorse, praise, commend

record *noun*
The zookeepers keep a record of the animals' diet.
account, report
A record of daily events is a *diary* or *journal*.
The record of a voyage at sea or in space is the *log*.
The record of what happened at a meeting is the *minutes*.
A record of people's names is a *register*.
Records consisting of historical documents are *archives*.

record *verb*
1 *The concert is being recorded by the BBC.*
tape, video
2 *She recorded our interview in a notebook.*
write down, note, set down, put down, enter

recover *verb*
1 *It took a long time to recover after my illness.*
get better, heal, improve, recuperate, pick up, mend, come round, pull through, revive, rally
2 *The police have recovered the stolen vehicles.*
get back, retrieve, reclaim, repossess, find, trace

recycle *verb*
You can recycle glass by putting it in the bottle bank.
reuse, reprocess, salvage, use again

red *adjective*
1 *I chose a red ribbon for my doll.*
Something which is rather red is *reddish*.
A common simile is *as red as a beetroot*.
2 *My nose and cheeks were red*

with cold.
flushed, glowing, rosy, ruddy, blushing
3 *Her eyes were red from lack of sleep.*
bloodshot, inflamed, red-rimmed
4 *The fairy queen had flaming red hair.*
ginger, auburn, coppery
(*informal*) carroty

reduce *verb*
She's reduced the amount of sugar in her diet.
decrease, lessen, lower, cut, cut back, slash
To reduce something by half is to *halve* it.
To reduce the width of something is to *narrow* it.
To reduce the length of something is to *shorten* or *trim* it.
To reduce speed is to *decelerate*.
To reduce the strength of a liquid is to *dilute* it.
OPPOSITE **increase**

refer *verb*
The shop assistant referred me to another department.
hand over, pass on, direct, send
to refer to
1 *Please don't refer to this matter again.*
mention, speak of, make reference to, allude to, bring up
2 *If you can't spell a word, refer to a dictionary.*
look up, consult, go to, turn to

reflect *verb*
1 *Cat's-eyes reflect the light from car headlights.*
send back, throw back, shine back
2 *Their success reflects their hard work.*
show, indicate, demonstrate, exhibit, reveal
to reflect on
We need time to reflect on what to do next.
think about, contemplate, consider, ponder, mull over

refuse *verb*
1 *Why did you refuse my offer of help?*
decline, reject,
turn down, say no to

OPPOSITE **accept**
2 *They were refused permission to enter the building.*
deny, deprive of
OPPOSITE **allow**

region *noun*
1 *The Arctic and Antarctic are polar regions.*
area, place, land, territory, part of the world
2 *There are two local radio stations serving this region.*
area, district, neighbourhood, locality, vicinity, zone

regret *verb*
She regretted her decision to leave Ireland.
be sorry for, repent, feel sad about

regular *adjective*
1 *Signs are placed at regular intervals along the cycle path.*
evenly spaced, fixed
OPPOSITE **irregular, uneven**
2 *The drummer kept up a regular rhythm.*
constant, consistent, steady, uniform, unvarying
A common simile is *as regular as clockwork*.
OPPOSITE **erratic**
3 *Is this your regular route to school?*
normal, usual, customary, habitual, ordinary, routine
OPPOSITE **unusual**
4 *Craig is a regular customer at the sweet shop.*
frequent, familiar, persistent
OPPOSITE **rare, unusual**

rehearse *verb*
We had to rehearse the scene all over again.
go over, practise, try out

reign *verb*
Which British monarch reigned the longest?
be king or queen, be on the throne, govern, rule

reject *verb*
1 *At first, she rejected their offer of help.*
decline, refuse, turn down, say no to
2 *As we picked the berries, we rejected any bad ones.*
discard, get rid of, throw out, scrap

rejoice *verb*
The people rejoiced when the wicked queen died.
celebrate, delight, be happy, exult
OPPOSITE **grieve**

relate *verb*
1 *Do you think the two crimes are related?*
connect, link, associate
2 *The travellers related the story of their adventures.*

recycle

tell, narrate, report, describe
relate to
The letter relates to your great grandfather.
be about, refer to, have to do with, concern
relationship *noun*
1 *There is a relationship between your diet and health.*
connection, link, association, bond
The relationship between two numbers is a ratio.
2 *The twins have a close relationship.*
friendship, attachment, understanding
relax *verb*
1 *I like to relax by listening to music.*
unwind, rest, take it easy
2 *This exercise will relax your shoulder muscles.*
loosen, ease
OPPOSITE **tighten**
3 *He relaxed his hold on the dog's leash.*
slacken, loosen, ease, lessen, reduce
OPPOSITE **tighten**
relaxed *adjective*
They liked the relaxed atmosphere of village life.
informal, casual, carefree, leisurely, easygoing, peaceful, restful, unhurried, calm
(*informal*) laid-back
OPPOSITE **tense, stressful**
release *verb*
1 *The prisoners were released early.*
free, let go, discharge, liberate, set free
To release slaves is to *emancipate* them.
OPPOSITE **imprison**
2 *The dog was tied up—who released him?*
let loose, set loose, unfasten, unleash, untie
3 *The band will release their new CD in April.*
issue, publish, put out
relevant *adjective*
1 *The detective noted everything that was relevant to the case.*
applicable, pertinent, appropriate, suitable, significant, related, connected
2 *Don't interrupt unless your comments are relevant.*
to the point
reliable *adjective*
1 *The king summoned his most reliable knights.*
faithful, dependable, trustworthy, loyal, constant, devoted, staunch, true
2 *The secret agent always sent*

reliable information.
dependable, valid, trustworthy, safe, sound, steady, sure
relieve *verb*
The doctor said the pills would relieve the pain.
ease, help, lessen, diminish, relax, soothe, comfort
religious *adjective*
1 *The choir sang a selection of religious music.*
sacred, holy, divine
OPPOSITE **secular**
2 *My grandparents were very religious.*
devout, pious, reverent, spiritual, godly
OPPOSITE **ungodly**
reluctant *adjective*
The old woman was reluctant to open the door.
unwilling, hesitant, slow, grudging, half-hearted, resistant
OPPOSITE **eager**
rely *verb*
Are you sure that we can rely on their help?
depend on, count on, have confidence in, trust
(*informal*) bank on
remain *verb*
1 *The boys were told to remain behind after school.*
stay, wait, linger
(*informal*) hang about
2 *It will remain warm and sunny all weekend.*
continue, persist, keep on, carry on
3 *Little remained of the house after the fire.*
be left, survive
remains *plural noun*
They cleared away the remains of the picnic.
remnants, leftovers, leavings, fragments, traces, scraps, debris
The remains at the bottom of a cup are *dregs*.
Remains still standing after a building has collapsed are *ruins*.
Historic remains are *relics*.
remarkable *adjective*
1 *He described his remarkable escape from the island.*
amazing, extraordinary, astonishing, memorable, wonderful, incredible, unforgettable, breathtaking
2 *The young violinist shows remarkable skill for her age.*
exceptional, notable, noteworthy, striking, outstanding, impressive, phenomenal
remember *verb*
1 *Can you remember what she looked like?*

recall, recollect, recognize, place
2 *He was trying to remember his lines for the play.*
learn, memorize, keep in mind
OPPOSITE **forget**
3 *My granny likes to remember the old days.*
reminisce about, think back to
remind *verb*
Remind me to buy a newspaper.
prompt, jog your memory
to remind you of something
What does this tune remind you of?
make you think of, take you back to
remote *adjective*
1 *The tour will explore a remote part of Brazil.*
distant, faraway, isolated, cut-off, inaccessible, out-of-the-way, unfrequented
OPPOSITE **accessible**
2 *The chances of us winning are remote.*
poor, slender, slight, small, faint, doubtful
OPPOSITE **likely**
remove *verb*
1 *Please remove your rubbish.*
clear away, take away
2 *The rowdy passengers were removed from the bus.*
throw out, turn out, eject, expel
(*informal*) kick out
To remove people from a house where they are living is to *evict* them.
To remove a monarch from the throne is to *depose* him or her.
3 *The author decided to remove the last paragraph.*
cut out, delete, erase, get rid of, do away with, eliminate
4 *The dentist removed my bad tooth.*
extract, pull out, take out, withdraw
5 *The divers slowly removed their wetsuits.*
take off, peel off, strip off, shed, cast off
renew *verb*
1 *The church roof has been completely renewed.*
repair, renovate, restore, replace, rebuild, reconstruct, revamp, refurbish, overhaul
(*informal*) do up
2 *You must renew your passport before you go abroad.*
bring up to date, update
repeat *verb*
1 *The parrot repeated everything he said.*
say again, copy, duplicate, reproduce, echo
2 *The actors had to repeat the opening scene.*

a
b
c
d
e
f
g
h
i
j
k
l
m
n
o
p
q
r
s
t
u
v
w
x
y
z

do again, redo

replace *verb*
1 *The spy carefully* **replaced** *the missing document.*
put back, return, restore, reinstate
2 *Who will* **replace** *the head teacher when she retires?*
follow, succeed, take over from, take the place of
3 *I need to* **replace** *one of the tyres on my bike.*
change, renew

reply *noun*
He has received no **replies** *to his email.*
response, answer, reaction, acknowledgement
An angry reply is a **retort**.

reply *verb*
to reply to
She took a long time to **reply to** *my letter.*
answer, respond to, give a reply to, react to, acknowledge

report *verb*
1 *The newspapers* **reported** *what happened.*
give an account of, record, state, describe, announce, publish
2 *We were told to* **report** *to reception when we arrived.*
present yourself, make yourself known, check in
3 *If you cause any damage, I'll* **report** *you to the police.*
complain about, inform on, denounce

report *noun*
There was a **report** *in the paper about the crash.*
account, record, story, article, description

reporter *noun*
The film star was being interviewed by a TV **reporter**.
journalist, correspondent

represent *verb*
1 *The picture* **represents** *an ancient legend.*
depict, illustrate, portray, picture, show, describe
2 *A dove is often said to* **represent** *peace.*
stand for, symbolize
3 *He appointed a lawyer to* **represent** *him.*
speak for

🕸 **WORD WEB**

reptile *noun*
SOME ANIMALS WHICH ARE REPTILES
alligator, chameleon, crocodile, gecko, iguana, lizard, slow-worm, snake, terrapin, tortoise, turtle
A reptile found in myths and legends is the **basilisk**.

repulsive *adjective*
We were put off eating by the **repulsive** *smell.*
disgusting, revolting, offensive, repellent, disagreeable, foul, repugnant, obnoxious, sickening, hateful, hideous, horrible, loathsome, objectionable, vile
OPPOSITE **attractive**

reputation *noun*
The singer's **reputation** *spread throughout the world.*
fame, celebrity, name, renown, eminence, standing, stature

request *verb*
She has **requested** *a transfer to a different job.*
ask for, appeal for, apply for, beg for, call for, entreat, implore, invite, pray for, seek

request *noun*
They have ignored our **request** *for help.*
appeal, plea, entreaty, call, cry
A request for a job or membership is an **application**.
A request signed by a lot of people is a **petition**.

require *verb*
1 *They* **require** *a draw to win the championship.*
need, must have
2 *Visitors are* **required** *to sign the register.*
instruct, oblige, request, direct, order, command

rescue *verb*
1 *A helicopter was sent to* **rescue** *the trapped climbers.*
free, liberate, release, save, set free
To rescue someone by paying money is to **ransom** them.
2 *The divers* **rescued** *some items from the sunken ship.*
retrieve, recover, salvage

reserve *verb*
1 *The astronauts had to* **reserve** *fuel for the return voyage.*
keep, put aside, set aside, save, preserve, retain, hold back
2 *Have you* **reserved** *your seats on the train?*
book, order, secure

reserve *noun*
1 *The climbers kept a* **reserve** *of food in their base camp.*
stock, store, supply, hoard, stockpile
A reserve of money is a **fund** or **savings**.
2 *They put him down as a* **reserve** *for Saturday's game.*
substitute, standby, stand-in,

crocodile

replacement
Someone who can take the place of an actor is an **understudy**.
3 *The wildlife* **reserve** *has a new baby rhino.*
reservation, park, preserve, sanctuary

resign *verb*
The manager of the football team was forced to **resign**.
leave, quit, stand down, step down, give in your notice
When a monarch resigns from the throne, he or she **abdicates**.

resist *verb*
1 *They were too weak to* **resist** *the sorcerer's magic.*
stand up to, defend yourself against, withstand, defy, oppose, fend off
OPPOSITE **yield to, surrender to**
2 *I couldn't* **resist** *having another piece of chocolate.*
avoid, hold back from, refuse
OPPOSITE **give in, accept**

resources *plural noun*
1 *The country is rich in natural* **resources**.
materials, raw materials, reserves
2 *The library has limited* **resources** *for buying CDs.*
funds, money, capital, assets, means, wealth

respect *noun*
1 *Her colleagues have the deepest* **respect** *for her.*
admiration, esteem, regard, reverence, honour
2 *Have some* **respect** *for other people's feelings.*
consideration, sympathy, thought, concern
3 *In some* **respects**, *he's a better player than I am.*
way, point, aspect, feature, characteristic, detail, particular

respect *verb*
1 *Everyone* **respects** *her for her courage.*
admire, esteem, revere, honour, look up to, value
OPPOSITE **scorn, despise**

lizard

2 *She tried to respect the wishes of her dead husband.*
obey, follow, observe, adhere to, comply with
OPPOSITE **ignore**

respectable *adjective*
1 *He came from a very respectable family.*
decent, honest, upright, honourable, worthy
2 *I finished the race in a respectable time.*
reasonable, satisfactory, acceptable, passable, adequate, fair, tolerable

respond *verb*
to respond to
He didn't respond to my question.
reply to, answer, react to, acknowledge

response *noun*
Did you get a response to your letter?
reply, answer, reaction, acknowledgement
An angry response is a retort.

responsible *adjective*
1 *Parents are legally responsible for their children.*
in charge
OPPOSITE **not responsible**
2 *He's a very responsible sort of person.*
reliable, sensible, trustworthy, dependable, conscientious, dutiful, honest
OPPOSITE **irresponsible**
3 *Looking after people's money is a responsible job.*
important, serious
4 *Who is responsible for all this mess?*
to blame, guilty (of), at fault

rest *noun*
1 *The actors had a short rest in the middle of the rehearsal.*
break, breather, breathing-space, pause, respite, lie-down, nap
2 *The doctor said the patient needed complete rest.*
relaxation, leisure, inactivity, ease, quiet, time off
the rest
Take a few sweets now, but leave the rest for later.
the remainder, the surplus, the others, the remains

rest *verb*
1 *I think we should stop and rest for a while.*
have a rest, lie down, relax, lounge, have a nap
2 *Rest the ladder against the wall.*
lean, prop, stand, place, support

restless *adjective*
The animals became restless during the storm.
agitated, nervous, anxious, edgy, fidgety, excitable,

jumpy, jittery
OPPOSITE **relaxed**

result *noun*
1 *The water shortage is a result of a long drought.*
consequence, effect, outcome, sequel (to), upshot
The result of a game is the score.
The result of a trial is the verdict.
2 *If you multiply 9 by 12, what is the result?*
answer, product

result *verb*
The bruising on his leg resulted from a bad fall.
come about, develop, emerge, happen, occur, follow, ensue, take place, turn out
to result in
Severe flooding resulted in chaos on the roads.
cause, bring about, give rise to, lead to, develop into

retreat *verb*
1 *The army retreated to a safe position.*
move back, draw back, fall back, withdraw, retire
To retreat in a shameful way is to run away or (informal) turn tail.
2 *The snail retreated into its shell.*
shrink back, recoil

retrieve *verb*
I had to climb the fence to retrieve our ball.
get back, bring back, fetch, recover, rescue, salvage

return *verb*
1 *We hope to return to Paris next summer.*
go back, revisit
2 *My husband returns on Friday.*
get back, come back, come home
3 *I returned the book to its rightful owner.*
give back, restore
4 *Faulty goods may be returned to the shop.*
send back, take back
5 *Please return the money I lent you.*
give back, repay, refund
6 *We hoped that the fever would not return.*
happen again, recur

reveal *verb*
1 *The spy refused to reveal his real identity.*
declare, disclose, make known, confess, admit, announce, proclaim, publish, tell

2 *She swept aside the curtain to reveal a secret door.*
uncover, unveil, expose

revenge *noun*
He sought revenge for the killing of his brother.
reprisal, vengeance
to take revenge on someone
He declared that he would take revenge on them all.
get even with, repay
(*informal*) get your own back on

review *noun*
1 *They are carrying out a review of after-school clubs.*
study, survey, examination, inspection
2 *We had to write reviews of our favourite books.*
report, criticism, appraisal, critique

review *verb*
The judge began to review the evidence.
examine, go over, study, survey, consider, assess, appraise, evaluate, weigh up

tortoise

revise *verb*
1 *We revised the work we did last term.*
go over, review, study
2 *The new evidence forced me to revise my opinion.*
change, modify, alter, reconsider, re-examine
3 *The last chapter has been revised by the author.*
correct, amend, edit, rewrite, update

revive *verb*
1 *The patient revived slowly after the operation.*
come round, come to, recover, rally, wake up
2 *A cold drink will revive you.*
refresh, restore, invigorate, bring back to life, revitalize

revolt *verb*
1 *The people revolted against the cruel king.*
rebel, riot, rise up
To revolt on a ship is to mutiny.
2 *They were revolted by the stench in the dungeon.*
disgust, repel, sicken, nauseate, offend, appal

snake

revolting *adjective*
*What is that **revolting** smell?*
disgusting, foul, horrible, nasty, loathsome, offensive, obnoxious, repulsive, repugnant, sickening, nauseating, vile, unpleasant
OPPOSITE pleasant, attractive

revolution *noun*
1 *The **revolution** brought in a new government.*
rebellion, revolt, uprising
2 *Computers brought about a **revolution** in the way people work.*
change, transformation, shift
3 *One **revolution** of the earth takes 24 hours.*
rotation, turn, circuit, cycle

revolve *verb*
*The earth **revolves** once every 24 hours.*
rotate, turn
To revolve quickly is to *spin* or *whirl*.
To move round something is to *circle* or *orbit* it.

reward *noun*
*There is a **reward** for finding the missing cat.*
prize, bonus, payment, award, decoration
OPPOSITE punishment

reward *verb*
1 *The firefighters were **rewarded** for their bravery.*
honour, decorate
2 *She was generously **rewarded** for her work.*
compensate, repay

rhythm *noun*
*We tapped our feet to the **rhythm** of the music.*
beat, pulse
The speed or type of rhythm of a piece of music is the *tempo*.
The type of rhythm of a piece of poetry is its *metre*.

rich *adjective*
1 *They must be **rich** to live in a castle.*
wealthy, affluent, prosperous, well-off, well-to-do
OPPOSITE poor
2 *The palace was full of **rich** furnishings.*
expensive, costly, luxurious, sumptuous, opulent, lavish, splendid, ornate
3 *The dancer wore a dress of a **rich** red colour.*
deep, strong, vivid, intense

rickety *adjective*
*Take care—that ladder looks **rickety**.*
shaky, unsteady, unstable, wobbly, flimsy
OPPOSITE solid

riddle *noun*
*They had to solve the **riddle** to find the treasure.*
puzzle, mystery, question, conundrum, problem

ride *verb*
*My little brother is learning to **ride** a bike.*
control, handle, manage, steer

ride *noun*
*They took us for a **ride** in their new car.*
drive, run, journey, trip
(*informal*) spin

ridiculous *adjective*
1 *My little sister looked **ridiculous** in high-heeled shoes.*
silly, stupid, foolish, daft, absurd, funny, laughable
2 *That is a **ridiculous** price for a pair of trainers?*
ludicrous, senseless, nonsensical, preposterous, outrageous, absurd, unreasonable, crazy

right *adjective*
1 *Put up your hand if you got the **right** answer.*
correct, accurate, true, exact
OPPOSITE wrong
2 *She was waiting for the **right** moment to tell him.*
proper, appropriate, fitting, suitable, ideal
OPPOSITE wrong
3 *It's not **right** to steal.*
fair, honest, decent, just, honourable, lawful, moral, upright, virtuous, ethical
OPPOSITE wrong

right *noun*
1 *The post office is on the **right** along the High Street.*
OPPOSITE left
2 *People have the **right** to walk across the common.*
freedom, liberty
3 *You don't have the **right** to tell me what to do.*
authority, power

ring *noun*
1 *The children danced around in a **ring**.*
circle, round, loop, circuit
2 *The wooden barrel had metal **rings** round it.*
band, hoop

ring *verb*
1 *The whole area was **ringed** by a high fence.*
surround, encircle, enclose, circle
2 *The doorbell **rang**.*
chime, peal, toll, jangle, tinkle, sound, buzz
3 ***Ring** me tomorrow evening.*
phone, call, telephone, ring up
(*informal*) give a buzz

riot *noun*
*The police moved in to stop the **riot**.*
commotion, disorder, disturbance, turmoil, uproar, uprising

riot *verb*
*The crowds were **rioting** in the streets.*
run riot, run wild, run amok, rampage, revolt, rise up, rebel

ripe *adjective*
*Some of the plums on the tree are **ripe** now.*
mature, ready to eat
To become ripe is to *ripen*.

rise *verb*
1 *The kite **rose** high into the air.*
climb, mount, fly up, ascend, soar
When a plane rises into the air, it *takes off*.
When a rocket rises into the air, it *lifts off*.
OPPOSITE descend
2 *The outer wall of the castle **rose** before us.*
tower, loom, reach up, stick up
3 *House prices **rose** again last year.*
go up, increase
OPPOSITE fall
4 *The audience **rose** and applauded wildly.*
stand up, get up
OPPOSITE sit

rise *noun*
*There will be a **rise** in temperature over the next few days.*
increase, jump
OPPOSITE fall

risk *verb*
1 *If you place a bet, you **risk** losing the money.*
chance, dare, gamble, venture
2 *The firefighter **risked** his life to save them.*
endanger, put at risk, jeopardize, hazard

risk *noun*
1 *All outdoor activities carry an element of **risk**.*
danger, hazard, peril
2 *The forecast says there's a **risk** of snow.*
chance, likelihood, possibility

risky *adjective*
*Cycling on icy roads is **risky**.*
dangerous, hazardous, perilous, unsafe
OPPOSITE safe

rival *noun*
*He has no serious **rival** for the championship.*
competitor, adversary, challenger, opponent, contender, contestant

river *noun*
A small river is a *stream* or *rivulet* or (*Scottish*) *burn*.
A small river which flows into a larger river is a *tributary*.
The place where a river begins is its *source*.
The place where a river goes into

the sea is its *mouth*.
A wide river mouth is an *estuary* or (*Scottish*) *firth*.
The place where the mouth of a river splits before going into the sea is a *delta*.
A river of ice is a *glacier*.

river

roar *noun, verb*
The dragon lifted its might head and roared.
bellow, cry, yell, bawl, howl, thunder

rob *verb*
The thieves planned to rob several banks in the city.
steal from, break into, burgle, hold up, raid, loot, ransack, rifle

rock *verb*
1 *I rocked the baby's cradle to and fro.*
sway, swing
2 *The ship rocked in the storm.*
roll, toss, lurch, pitch, tilt, reel

rod *noun*
The framework is held together by steel rods.
bar, rail, pole, strut, shaft, stick, spoke, staff

role *noun*
1 *Who is playing the lead role in the play?*
character, part
2 *Each player has an important role in the team.*
job, task, function, position

roll *verb*
1 *The wheels of the carriage began to roll.*
move round, turn, revolve, rotate, spin, twirl, whirl
2 *Roll the paper around your finger.*
curl, wind, wrap, twist, coil
To roll up a sail on a yacht is to *furl* it.

roar

3 *Roll the pastry into a large circle.*
flatten, level out, smooth
4 *The ship rolled about in the storm.*
pitch, rock, sway, toss, wallow, lurch

romantic *adjective*
1 *The film had a very romantic ending.*
sentimental, emotional, tender
(*informal*) soppy, mushy
2 *The life of an explorer sounds very romantic.*
exotic, glamorous, exciting

room *noun*
1 *How many rooms are there in your house?*
An old word for room is *chamber*.
2 *Is there room in the car for another suitcase?*
space, capacity

root *noun*
We need to get to the root of the problem.
origin, source, cause, basis, starting point

rope *noun*
The sailors threw a rope to the men in the water.
cable, cord, line
The ropes that support a ship's mast and sails are the *rigging*.
A rope with a loop at one end used for catching cattle is a *lasso*.

rot *verb*
The wooden fence had begun to rot.
decay, decompose, become rotten, crumble, disintegrate
If metal rots it is said to *corrode*.
If rubber rots it is said to *perish*.
If food rots it is said to *go bad* or *putrefy*.

rotten *adjective*
1 *The window frame is rotten.*
decayed, decaying, decomposed, crumbling, disintegrating
Rotten metal is *corroded* or *rusty* metal.
OPPOSITE sound
2 *The fridge smelled of rotten eggs.*
bad, mouldy, mouldering, foul, putrid, smelly
OPPOSITE fresh
3 (*informal*) *The weather has been rotten all week.*
bad, unpleasant, disagreeable, awful, abysmal, dreadful, nasty

(*informal*) lousy
OPPOSITE good

rough *adjective*
1 *A rough track led to the farm.*
bumpy, uneven, irregular, rocky, stony, rugged, craggy, jagged
OPPOSITE even, smooth
2 *The sea was rough and the boat lurched from side to side.*
stormy, turbulent, heaving
If the sea is rough with small waves it is said to be *choppy*.
OPPOSITE calm
3 *The woman wore a rough woollen cloak.*
coarse, harsh, scratchy, bristly
OPPOSITE soft
4 *The prisoners had suffered rough treatment.*
harsh, severe, cruel, hard, tough, violent
OPPOSITE gentle, mild
5 *I had only a rough idea of where we were.*
approximate, vague, inexact, imprecise, hazy
OPPOSITE exact
6 *Our guide made a rough sketch of the route.*
quick, hasty, crude, basic
OPPOSITE detailed, careful

round *adjective*
Holly bushes have small round berries.
rounded, spherical
A flat round shape is *circular*.

round *noun*
Our team got through to the second round of the competition.
stage, heat, bout, contest, game

round *verb*
The motorbike rounded the corner at top speed.
go round, travel round, turn
to round something off
They rounded the evening off with some songs.
bring to an end, conclude, end, finish, complete
to round up people or **things**
The captain rounded up his players.
assemble, gather, bring together, collect, muster, rally

routine *noun*
1 *Brushing my teeth is part of my morning routine.*
pattern, procedure, way, custom, habit, practice, order
2 *The ice-skaters practised their new routine.*
act, programme, performance, number

row *noun*
1 *The gardener planted the vegetables in rows.* (rhymes with *go*)
column, line, string, series, sequence

A row of people waiting for something is a *queue*.

A row of people walking behind each other is a *file*.

A row of soldiers standing side by side on parade is a *rank*.

2 *The class next door was making a terrible* **row**. *(rhymes with* cow*)*

noise, racket, din, commotion, disturbance, uproar, rumpus

3 *One of the pirates had a* **row** *with the captain. (rhymes with* cow*)*

argument, fight, quarrel, squabble, disagreement, dispute

rowdy *adjective*

Later in the evening, the party became **rowdy**.

noisy, unruly, wild, disorderly, boisterous, riotous

OPPOSITE quiet

rub *verb*

1 *Kathy* **rubbed** *her sore elbow.*

stroke, knead, massage

2 *I* **rubbed** *some suncream on my arms.*

spead, smooth, smear, apply (to)

3 *These boots are* **rubbing** *against my ankles.*

graze, scrape, chafe

4 *She* **rubbed** *the mirror until it gleamed.*

polish, wipe, shine, buff

to rub something out

Can you **rub out** *those pencil marks?*

erase, wipe out, delete, remove

rubbish *noun*

1 *Mike took the* **rubbish** *out to the bin.*

refuse, waste, trash, garbage, junk, litter, scrap

2 *Don't talk* **rubbish**!

nonsense, drivel, balderdash, piffle, gibberish, claptrap, gobbledegook

(informal) rot, tripe, twaddle

rude *adjective*

1 *It's very* **rude** *to talk with your mouth full.*

impolite, discourteous, disrespectful, impertinent, impudent, insolent, offensive, insulting, bad-mannered, ill-bred

To be rude to someone is to *insult* or *snub* them.

To be rude about sacred things is to be

rubbish

blasphemous or *irreverent*.

OPPOSITE polite

2 *Some of the jokes in the film are rather* **rude**.

indecent, improper, offensive, coarse, crude

OPPOSITE decent, clean

ruin *verb*

The storm had **ruined** *the farmer's crops.*

damage, destroy, spoil, wreck, devastate, demolish, lay waste, shatter

ruin *noun*

When they lost the match, it was the **ruin** *of their dream.*

collapse, failure, breakdown

Financial ruin is *bankruptcy*.

ruins

Archaeologists have discovered the **ruins** *of a Roman fort.*

remains, remnants, fragments

rule *noun*

1 *Players must stick to the* **rules** *of the game.*

law, regulation, principle

A set of rules is a *code*.

2 *The country was formerly under French* **rule**.

control, authority, command, power, government, reign

rule *verb*

1 *The Romans* **ruled** *a vast empire.*

command, govern, control, direct, lead, manage, run, administer

2 *Queen Victoria continued to* **rule** *for many years.*

reign, be ruler

3 *The umpire* **ruled** *that the batsman was out.*

judge, decree, pronounce, decide, determine, find

rumour *noun*

There was a **rumour** *that the queen was a witch in disguise.*

gossip, hearsay, talk

(informal) tittle-tattle

run *verb*

1 *We* **ran** *as fast as our legs could carry us.*

race, sprint, dash, tear, bolt, career, speed, hurry, rush, streak, fly, whiz, zoom, scurry, scamper, scoot

To run at a gentle pace is to *jog*. When a horse runs, it *gallops*, *canters*, or *trots*.

2 *Tears* **ran** *down the mermaid's cheeks.*

stream, flow, pour, gush, flood, cascade, spill, trickle, dribble, leak

3 *That old sewing machine still* **runs** *well.*

function, operate, work, go, perform

4 *My uncle* **runs** *a restaurant in Leeds.*

manage, be in charge of, direct, control, supervise, govern, rule

5 *The High Street* **runs** *through the city centre.*

pass, go, extend, stretch, reach

to run away or **off**

The thieves **ran off** *when they heard footsteps.*

bolt, fly, flee, escape, take off, hurry off

(informal) make off, clear off, scarper

to run into

1 *Guess who I* **ran into** *the other day?*

meet, come across, encounter

(informal) bump into

2 *A cyclist skidded and* **ran into** *a tree.*

hit, collide with

run *noun*

1 *She goes for a* **run** *in the park every morning.*

A fast run is a *dash*, *gallop*, *race*, or *sprint*.

A gentle run is a *jog*.

2 *We went for a* **run** *in the car.*

drive, journey, ride

3 *They've had a* **run** *of good luck recently.*

sequence, stretch, series

runny *adjective*

This custard is too **runny**.

watery, thin, liquid, fluid

OPPOSITE thick

rush *verb*

I **rushed** *home with the good news.*

hurry, hasten, race, run, dash, fly, bolt, charge, shoot, speed, sprint, tear, zoom

When cattle or other animals rush along together they *stampede*.

rush *noun*

1 *We've got plenty of time, so what's the* **rush**?

hurry, haste, urgency

2 *There was a sudden* **rush** *of water.*

flood, gush, spurt, stream, spate

ruthless *adjective*

The pirates launched a **ruthless** *attack.*

cruel, brutal, bloodthirsty, barbaric, heartless, pitiless, merciless, callous, ferocious, fierce, savage, vicious, violent

OPPOSITE merciful

runny

a b c d e f g h i j k l m n o p q r s t u v w x y z

Ss

sack *verb*
The manager threatened to sack the whole team.
dismiss, discharge
(*informal*) fire, give you the sack

sad *adjective*
Mia felt sad when her best friend moved away.
unhappy, sorrowful, miserable, depressed, downcast, downhearted, despondent, crestfallen, dismal, gloomy, glum, blue, low, dejected, forlorn, desolate, doleful, wretched, woeful, woebegone, tearful, heartbroken, broken-hearted
If you are sad because you are away from home, you are *homesick*.
OPPOSITE **happy**

sadden *verb*
The news of her friend's illness saddened her.
distress, upset, depress, grieve, disappoint
(*informal*) break your heart
OPPOSITE **cheer up**

safe *adjective*
1 *The kitten was found safe and well in a neighbour's garden.*
unharmed, unhurt, uninjured, undamaged, sound, intact
(*informal*) in one piece
OPPOSITE **hurt, damaged**
2 *They felt safe indoors as the storm raged outside.*
protected, guarded, defended, secure
OPPOSITE **vulnerable**
3 *The secret code is in safe hands.*
reliable, trustworthy, dependable
4 *Is the tap water safe to drink?*
harmless, uncontaminated, innocuous
OPPOSITE **dangerous**

safety *noun*
You must wear a seat belt for your own safety.
protection, security, well-being
OPPOSITE **danger**

sail *verb*
We sailed to Norway rather than going by air.
travel by ship
To have a holiday sailing on a ship is to *cruise*.
To begin a sea voyage is to *put to sea* or *set sail*.

same *adjective*
the same
1 *Each pirate was given the same ration of rum.*
equal, identical, equivalent
2 *Everyone in the choir wore the same outfit.*
matching, similar, alike, uniform
3 *Her feelings have remained the same.*
unaltered, unchanged, constant
OPPOSITE **different**

sarcastic *adjective*
He made a sarcastic remark about my hat.
mocking, satirical, ironical, sneering, taunting

satisfaction *noun*
He gets a lot of satisfaction from growing vegetables.
happiness, pleasure, enjoyment, contentment, fulfilment, sense of achievement, pride
OPPOSITE **dissatisfaction**

satisfactory *adjective*
I'm afraid this work is not satisfactory.
acceptable, adequate, passable, good enough, tolerable, competent
(*informal*) all right, up to scratch
OPPOSITE **unsatisfactory**

satisfy *verb*
Nothing satisfies him—he's always complaining.
please, content, make you happy
To satisfy your thirst is to *quench* or *slake* it.
OPPOSITE **dissatisfy**

savage *adjective*
1 *The invaders launched a savage attack on the town.*
vicious, cruel, barbaric, brutal, bloodthirsty, pitiless, ruthless, merciless, inhuman
OPPOSITE **humane**
2 *A savage beast is said to live in the cave.*
untamed, wild, ferocious, fierce
OPPOSITE **domesticated**

save *verb*
1 *They managed to save most of the books from the fire.*
rescue, recover, retrieve, salvage
2 *The knight pledged to save the princess from the witch's curse.*
protect, defend, guard, shield, preserve
3 *She saved him from making a fool of himself.*
stop, prevent, deter
4 *I saved you a piece of my birthday cake.*
keep, reserve, set aside, hold on to
5 *If you share a car, then you can save petrol.*
be sparing with, conserve, use wisely

say *verb*
1 *He found it hard to say what he meant.*
express, communicate, put into words, convey
2 *I would like to say a few words before we start.*
utter, speak, recite, read

⚠ OVERUSED WORD

Try to vary the words you use for **say**, especially in direct speech. Here are some other words you could use.

TO SAY *loudly*
call, cry, exclaim, bellow, bawl, shout, yell, roar *'Land ahoy!' bellowed the cabin boy.*

TO SAY *quietly*
whisper, mumble, mutter *'That woman,' I whispered, 'is a secret agent.'*

TO SAY *strongly*
state, announce, assert, declare, pronounce, insist, maintain, profess *'I never cut my toenails,' the ogre declared.*

TO SAY *casually*
remark, comment, observe, note, mention *'It's very warm for this time of year,' Mr Lewis remarked.*

TO SAY *angrily*
snap, snarl, growl, thunder, bark, rasp, rant, rave *'Give me that piece of paper!' snapped Miss Crabbit.*

TO SAY *suddenly*
blurt out *'That's just a pretend dinosaur!' Ben blurted out.*

TO SAY *unclearly*
babble, burble, gabble, stammer *The stranger kept babbling about hidden treasure.*

TO SAY *in surprise* OR *alarm*
gasp, cry, squeal *'The tunnel is sealed! There's no way out!' gasped Alex.*

TO SAY *something funny*
joke, quip, tease *'Were you singing? I thought it was a cat,' teased my big sister.*

TO GIVE *an order*
command, demand, order *A voice outside demanded, 'Open the door at once!'*

TO ASK *a question*
enquire, demand, query *'How do you spell your name?' the judge enquired.*

TO GIVE *a reply*
answer, reply, respond, retort *'Certainly not!' retorted Lady Dimsley.*

TO MAKE *a request*
beg, entreat, implore, plead, urge *The mouse pleaded, 'Please let go off my tail!'*

TO MAKE *a suggestion*
suggest, propose *'Let's make them walk the plank,' suggested Captain Hook.*

TO SAY *again*
repeat, reiterate, echo *The Martians repeated, 'Take us to your leader!'*

saying *noun*
*'Many hands make light work' is a common **saying**.*
expression, phrase, motto, proverb, catchphrase
An overused saying is a *cliché*.

scan *verb*
1 *The lookout **scanned** the horizon, hoping to see land.*
search, study, survey, examine, scrutinize, stare at, eye
2 *I **scanned** through some magazines in the waiting room.*
skim, glance at, flick through

scandal *noun*
1 *The waste of food after the party was a **scandal**.*
disgrace, embarrassment, shame, outrage
2 *Some newspapers like to publish the latest **scandal**.*
gossip, rumours, dirt

scar *noun*
*The warrior had a **scar** across his forehead.*
mark, blemish, wound

scar *verb*
*The injuries he received **scarred** him for life.*
mark, disfigure, deface

scarce *adjective*
*Water is very **scarce** in the desert.*
hard to find, in short supply, lacking, sparse, scanty, rare, uncommon
(*informal*) thin on the ground
OPPOSITE **plentiful**

scarcely *adverb*
*She was so tired that she could **scarcely** walk.*
barely, hardly, only just

scare *noun*
*The explosion gave them a nasty **scare**.*
fright, shock, alarm

scare *verb*
*My brother tried to **scare** us by making ghost noises.*
frighten, terrify, petrify, alarm, startle, panic
OPPOSITE **reassure**

scared *adjective*
*When she heard the footsteps, Lily was too **scared** to move.*
frightened, terrified, petrified, horrified, alarmed, fearful, panicky

scary *adjective* (*informal*)
*I had to close my eyes at the **scary** bits in the film.*
frightening, terrifying, horrifying, alarming, nightmarish, fearsome, chilling, spine-chilling, hair-raising, bloodcurdling, chilling, eerie, sinister

scatter *verb*
1 *She **scattered** the seeds on the ground.*
spread, sprinkle, sow, strew, throw about, shower
OPPOSITE **collect**
2 *The animals **scattered** when the children ran towards them.*
break up, separate, disperse, disband
OPPOSITE **gather**

scene *noun*
1 *The police arrived quickly at the **scene** of the crime.*
location, position, site, place, situation, spot
2 *They were rehearsing a **scene** from the play.*
episode, part, section, act
3 *I gazed out of the window at the moonlit **scene**.*
landscape, scenery, view, sight, outlook, prospect, spectacle, setting, backdrop
4 *He didn't want to create a **scene** in the restaurant.*
fuss, commotion, disturbance, quarrel, row

scenery *noun*
*We admired the **scenery** from the top of the hill.*
landscape, outlook, prospect, scene, view, panorama

scent *noun*
*Rowena loves the **scent** of roses.*
smell, fragrance, perfume, aroma

schedule *noun*
*The athletes had a rigorous training **schedule**.*
programme, timetable, plan, calendar, diary
A schedule of topics to be discussed at a meeting is an *agenda*.
A schedule of places to be visited on a journey is an *itinerary*.

scheme *noun*
*They worked out a **scheme** to raise some money.*
plan, proposal, project, procedure, method, system

scheme *verb*
*The smugglers were **scheming** against each other.*
plot, conspire, intrigue

scold *verb*
*He **scolded** the paper boy for being late.*
reprimand, reproach, tell off
(*informal*) tick off

scorch *verb*
*The dragon's breath **scorched** the wizard's beard.*
burn, singe, sear, blacken, char

scorch

score *noun*
We added up each other's scores.
marks, points, total
The final score is the *result*.

score *verb*
1 *How many goals did you **score**?*
win, get, make, gain, earn
2 *Some lines were **scored** into the bark of the tree.*
cut, gouge, mark, scrape, scratch

scorn *noun*
*She dismissed my suggestion with **scorn**.*
contempt, derision, disrespect, mockery, ridicule
OPPOSITE **admiration**

scowl *verb*
*The witch **scowled** under her floppy black hat.*
frown, glower

scramble *verb*
1 *The smugglers escaped by **scrambling** over the rocks.*
clamber, climb, crawl, scrabble
2 *The children **scrambled** to get the best seats.*
push, jostle, struggle, fight, scuffle

scrap *noun*
1 *They fed the **scraps** of food to the birds.*
bit, piece, fragment, morsel, crumb, speck, particle
2 *He took a pile of **scrap** to the tip.*
rubbish, waste, junk, refuse, litter
Scraps of cloth are *rags* or *shreds*.
3 (*informal*) *There was a **scrap** between the two gangs.*
fight, brawl, scuffle, tussle, squabble

scrap *verb*
*The author **scrapped** the last paragraph.*
discard, throw away, abandon, cancel, drop, give up
(*informal*) dump

scrape *verb*
1 *She **scraped** her knee when she fell over.*
graze, scratch, scuff
2 *I tried to **scrape** the mud off my trainers.*
rub, scour, scrub, clean

scratch *verb*
1 *Someone **scratched** the side of the car.*
mark, score, scrape, gouge, graze
2 *The cat tried to **scratch** her.*
claw

scratch *noun*
*Who made this **scratch** on the side of the car?*
gash, groove, line, mark, scrape

scream *noun, verb*
*A woman ran out of the house **screaming**. We heard a woman's **scream** in the distance.*
shriek, screech, shout, yell, cry, bawl, howl, wail, squeal, yelp

scribble *verb*
*He **scribbled** his phone number on a scrap of paper.*

scrawl, jot down, dash off, write
To scribble a rough drawing, especially when you are bored, is to *doodle*.

scrub *verb*
She scrubbed the floor clean.
rub, brush, clean, wash, scour

scruffy *adjective*
Magnus wore an old jumper and scruffy jeans.
untidy, messy, ragged, tatty, tattered, worn-out, shabby
OPPOSITE smart

sculpture *noun*
The temple was full of marble sculptures.
carving, figure, statue

WORD WEB

sea *noun*
The very large seas of the world are called *oceans*.
An area of sea partly enclosed by land is a *bay* or *gulf*.
A wide inlet of the sea is a *sound*.
A wide inlet where a river joins the sea is an *estuary*, or in Scotland a *firth*.
A narrow stretch of water linking two seas is a *strait*.
The bottom of the sea is the *seabed*.
The land near the sea is the *coast* or the *seashore*.
Creatures that live in the sea are *marine* creatures.

THINGS YOU MIGHT SEE ON THE SEA
breaker, iceberg, sea spray, surf, swell, waves; boat, cruise ship, ocean liner, yacht

SOME CREATURES THAT LIVE IN THE SEA
dolphin, eel, fish, killer whale, octopus, porpoise, seahorse, seal, sea lion, shark, squid, stingray, turtle, whale

starfish

WORD WEB

*We explored the **seashore**, looking for shells and fossils.*
seaside, beach, shore, coast

THINGS YOU MIGHT SEE ON THE SEASHORE
cave, cliff, coral reef, driftwood, dunes, lighthouse, mudflats, pebbles, rock pool, rocks, sand, seashell, seaweed, shingle

CREATURES THAT LIVE ON THE SEASHORE
barnacle, clam, cockle, coral, crab, cuttlefish, jellyfish, limpet, mussel, oyster, prawn, razor shell, sea anemone, sea bird, seagull, sea urchin, shrimp, sponge, starfish, whelk

*If it's sunny tomorrow, we might go to the **seaside**.*
beach, sands, seashore

THINGS YOU MIGHT SEE AT THE SEASIDE
beach huts, funfair, harbour, ice-cream van, jetty, pier, promenade

A town where you go to have fun by the sea is a *seaside resort*.

THINGS YOU MIGHT TAKE TO THE SEASIDE
beach ball, bucket and spade, deckchair, fishing net, snorkel, sunglasses, sunhat, sunshade, suncream, surfboard, surfsuit, swimming costume, towel, windbreak

THINGS YOU MIGHT DO AT THE SEASIDE
ball games, beachcombing, building sandcastles, collecting shells, fishing, paddling, scuba diving, snorkelling, sunbathing, surfing, swimming, water-skiing, windsurfing

---

WRITING TIPS

You can use these words to describe **the sea**.
TO DESCRIBE *a calm sea*
calm, crystal clear, glassy, sparkling, tranquil, unruffled
TO DESCRIBE *a rough sea*
choppy, raging, rough, stormy, tempestuous, turbulent, wild
waves on the sea MIGHT
billow, break, crash, heave, pound, roll, surge, swell, tumble, wash

crab

lighthouse

seaweed

shell

fish

a
e
f
g
h
i
j
k
m
n

a b c d e f g h i j k l m n o p q r s t u v w x y z

seal *verb*
The entrance to the burial chamber had been sealed.
close, fasten, shut, lock, secure
To seal a leak is to *plug* it or *stop* it.

search *verb*
1 *He was searching for the book he had lost.*
hunt, look, seek
To search for gold or some other mineral is to *prospect*.
2 *The police searched the house but didn't find anything.*
explore, scour, ransack, rummage through, comb
3 *Security staff searched all the passengers.*
check, inspect, examine, scrutinize
(*informal*) frisk

search *noun*
After a long search, she found her keys.
hunt, look, check
A long journey in search of something is a *quest*.

season *noun*
The hotels are full during the holiday season.
period, time

seat *noun*
We found two empty seats at the back of the cinema.
chair, place
A long seat for more than one person is a *bench*.
A long wooden seat in a church is a *pew*.
A seat on a bicycle or horse is a *saddle*.
A special seat for a king or queen is a *throne*.

second *adjective*
Would anyone like a second helping of pudding?
another, additional, extra, further

seat

second *noun*
1 *The magic potion only takes a second to work.*
instant, moment, flash
(*informal*) jiffy, tick
2 *Inga was second in the cross-country race.*
runner-up

second *verb*
We need someone to second the proposal.
back, support

secret *adjective*
1 *The spy managed to get hold of a*

secret *document.*
confidential, classified, restricted
(*informal*) hush-hush
2 *The detectives are part of a secret operation.*
undercover, covert
3 *The things I write in my diary are secret.*
private, confidential, personal, intimate
4 *The cook showed us a secret passageway into the castle.*
hidden, concealed, disguised

secretive *adjective*
Why is she being so secretive about her past?
uncommunicative, tight-lipped, reticent, reserved, mysterious, quiet
(*informal*) cagey
OPPOSITE communicative, open

section *noun*
The website has a special section aimed at children.
part, division, sector, portion, segment, bit, fragment
A section of a book is a *chapter*.
A section from a piece of classical music is a *movement*.
A section taken from a book or a long piece of music is a *passage*.
A section of a journey is a *stage*.

secure *adjective*
1 *The ladder was not very secure.*
steady, firm, solid, fixed, fast, immovable
2 *She is still trying to find a secure job.*
permanent, regular, steady
3 *They bolted the doors to make the castle secure.*
safe, guarded, protected, defended

see *verb*
1 *If you look closely, you might see a dragonfly.*
catch sight of, spot, notice, observe, make out, distinguish, note, perceive, recognize, sight, spy
To see something briefly is to *glimpse* it.
To see an accident or some unusual event is to *witness* it.
2 *Did you see the news yesterday?*
watch, look at, view
3 *You may see me in my office after work.*
go to, report to

4 *I didn't expect to see you here!*
meet, run into, encounter
(*informal*) bump into
5 *Will we have time to see them on the way home?*
visit, call on, drop in on
6 *I see what you mean.*
understand, appreciate, comprehend, follow, grasp, realize, take in
7 *I find it hard to see him in the role of Peter Pan.*
imagine, picture, visualize
8 *Please see that the windows are shut.*
make sure, make certain, ensure
9 *I'll see what I can do.*
think about, consider, ponder, reflect on, weigh up
10 *I'll see you to the door.*
conduct, escort, accompany, guide, lead, take

seem *verb*
Everything seems to be all right. She is far more friendly than she seems.
appear, look, give the impression of being

seize *verb*
1 *The climber stretched out to seize the rope.*
grab, catch, snatch, take hold of, grasp, grip, clutch
2 *The police seized the robbers as they left the bank.*
arrest, capture
(*informal*) collar, nab
To seize someone's property as a punishment is to *confiscate* it.
To seize someone's power or position is to *usurp* it.
To seize an aircraft or vehicle during a journey is to *hijack* it.

seldom *adverb*
It seldom rains in the desert.
rarely, infrequently
OPPOSITE often

select *verb*
They had to select a new captain.
choose, pick, decide on, opt for, settle on, appoint, elect

selection *noun*
The shop has a wide selection of rollerskates.
choice, range, variety, assortment

selfish *adjective*
He's so selfish that he kept all the chocolate to himself.
greedy, mean, miserly, grasping, self-centred, thoughtless
OPPOSITE unselfish, generous

sell *verb*
The corner shop sells newspapers and sweets.
deal in, trade in, stock, retail
Uncomplimentary synonyms are *peddle* and *hawk*.
OPPOSITE buy

send verb
1 *I sent each of my friends a postcard.*
post, mail, dispatch
2 *They plan to send a rocket to Mars.*
launch, propel, direct, fire, shoot
to send for someone
I think we should send for a doctor.
call, summon, fetch
to send something out
The device was sending out weird noises.
emit, issue, give off, discharge

sensational adjective
1 *The newspaper printed a sensational account of the murder.*
shocking, horrifying, startling, lurid
2 (informal) *Did you hear the sensational result of yesterday's match?*
amazing, extraordinary, remarkable, fantastic, spectacular, stupendous

sense noun
1 *A baby learns about the world through its senses.*
Your five senses are *hearing, sight, smell, taste,* and *touch*.
2 *A drummer needs to have a good sense of rhythm.*
awareness, consciousness, perception, feeling (for)
3 *If you had any sense you'd stay at home.*
common sense, intelligence, wisdom, wit, brains
4 *The sense of the word is not clear.*
meaning, significance, import
to make sense of something
They couldn't make sense of the garbled message.
understand, make out, interpret, follow

sense verb
1 *He sensed that she didn't like him.*
be aware, realize, perceive, feel, guess, notice, suspect
2 *The device senses any change of temperature.*
detect, respond to

sensible adjective
1 *It would be sensible to wait until the weather improves.*
wise, intelligent, shrewd, rational, reasonable, careful, prudent, logical, sane, sound
OPPOSITE stupid
2 *You will need sensible shoes for the hiking trip.*
comfortable, practical
OPPOSITE impractical

sensitive adjective
1 *She has sensitive skin which gets sunburnt.*

delicate, tender, fine, soft
2 *Take care what you say—he's very sensitive.*
easily offended, easily upset, touchy
3 *She's very sensitive towards other people.*
tactful, considerate, thoughtful, sympathetic, understanding

sentimental adjective
1 *He gets sentimental looking at old photographs.*
emotional, nostalgic, tearful
2 *I hate sentimental messages on birthday cards.*
romantic, tender
(informal) soppy, mushy

separate adjective
1 *The zoo kept the male lions separate from the cubs.*
apart, separated, distinct, independent
OPPOSITE together
2 *They slept in separate rooms.*
different, detached, unattached
OPPOSITE attached, joined

separate verb
1 *The sheepdog separated the sheep from the lambs.*
cut off, divide, fence off, isolate, keep apart, remove, segregate, set apart, take away
To separate something which is connected to something else is to *detach* or *disconnect* it.
To separate things which are tangled together is to *disentangle* them.
OPPOSITE combine, mix
2 *They walked along together until their paths separated.*
split, branch, fork
OPPOSITE merge
3 *Her friend's parents have separated.*
split up, break up, part company
To end a marriage legally is to *divorce*.

series noun
1 *We had to answer a series of questions in our exam.*
succession, sequence, string, set, chain, train
2 *Are you watching the new series on TV?*
serial

serious adjective
1 *His serious expression told them something was wrong.*
solemn, sombre, unsmiling, grave, grim
OPPOSITE cheerful
2 *She is writing a serious book about global warming.*
learned, intellectual, scholarly
(informal) heavy
OPPOSITE light
3 *Are you serious about wanting to learn to ski?*

sincere, genuine, in earnest
4 *This hospital ward is for people with serious injuries.*
severe, acute, critical, bad, terrible, appalling, dreadful, major, grave
OPPOSITE minor, trivial

servant noun
This part of the house was where the servants lived.
attendant, retainer, helper, domestic, manservant, maid
The chief manservant in a private house is a *butler*.
The servant of a medieval knight was a *page* or *squire*.

serve verb
1 *The shopkeeper was busy serving customers.*
help, assist, aid
2 *When everyone had sat down they served the first course.*
give out, dish up, pass round, distribute

service noun
1 *The genie bowed and said he was glad to be of service.*
help, assistance, aid, use, usefulness, benefit
2 *Their marriage service was held in the local church.*
ceremony, ritual, rite
A service in church is a meeting for *worship*.
3 *Mum says her car needs a service.*
a check-over, maintenance, servicing

service verb
The garage serviced her car.
maintain, check, repair, mend, overhaul

set verb
1 *The removal men set the piano on the floor.*
place, put, stand, position
2 *I helped Dad to set the table.*
arrange, lay, set out
3 *Have they set a date for the wedding yet?*
appoint, specify, name, decide, determine, choose, fix, establish, settle
4 *The jelly will set quicker in the fridge.*
become firm, solidify, harden, stiffen
5 *The sun was just beginning to set.*
do down, sink
to set off
1 *The knights set off on their quest.*
depart, get going, leave, set out, start out
2 *The burnt toast set off the smoke alarm.*
activate, start, trigger
to set something out

The information is clearly **set out** on the page.
lay out, arrange, display, present
to set something up
They're trying to **set up** an after-school club.
establish, create, start, begin, introduce, organize
set noun
1 There is a **set** of measuring spoons in the drawer.
collection, batch, kit
2 Our class painted the **set** for the play.
scenery, setting
setting noun
The house stood in a rural **setting**.
surroundings, location, place, position, site, background
settle verb
1 The brothers tried to **settle** their differences.
resolve, sort out, deal with, end
2 The cat had just **settled** on the sofa.
sit down, relax, rest
3 A robin **settled** on a nearby branch.
land, alight
4 The family is planning to **settle** in Canada.
emigrate (to), move (to), set up home
5 You can see lots of fish when the mud **settles**.
sink to the bottom, clear, subside
6 We'll **settle** the hotel bill in the morning.
pay, clear, square
to settle on
Have you **settled on** a date for the wedding?
agree on, decide on, choose, name, fix
severe adjective
1 The jailer was very **severe** with the prisoners.
harsh, strict, hard, stern
OPPOSITE lenient
2 The traffic warden gave him a **severe** look.
unkind, unsympathetic, disapproving, grim
OPPOSITE kind
3 Ruby has a **severe** case of chickenpox.
bad, serious, acute, grave
OPPOSITE mild
4 The Arctic has a **severe** climate.
extreme, tough, harsh, hostile
A severe frost

is a **sharp** frost.
Severe cold is **intense** cold.
A severe storm is a **violent** storm.
shabby adjective
The witch disguised herself in a **shabby** cloak.
ragged, scruffy, tattered, worn, worn-out, threadbare, frayed, tatty, seedy, dingy
OPPOSITE smart
shade noun
1 They sat in the **shade** of a chestnut tree.
shadow
2 The porch had a **shade** to keep out the sun.
screen, blind, canopy
A type of umbrella used as a sun shade is a **parasol**.
3 The bathroom walls are a pale **shade** of blue.
hue, tinge, tint, tone, colour
shade verb
Wearing a cap will **shade** your eyes from the sun.
shield, screen, protect, hide, mask
shadow noun
Her face was deep in **shadow**.
shade, darkness, gloom
shadow verb
The detective was **shadowing** the suspect.
follow, pursue, tail, stalk, track, trail
shady adjective
1 They found a **shady** spot under a tree.

shaggy

shaded, shadowy, sheltered, dark, sunless
OPPOSITE sunny
2 He took part in some **shady** business deals.
dishonest, disreputable, suspicious, dubious, suspect, untrustworthy (informal) fishy, dodgy
OPPOSITE honest
shaggy adjective
Llamas have long **shaggy** coats.
bushy, woolly, fleecy, hairy, thick
shake verb
1 The hurricane made the whole house **shake**.
quake,

shudder, shiver, rock, sway, totter, wobble, quiver, vibrate, rattle
2 He was so upset that his voice was **shaking**.
tremble, quaver
3 The giant **shook** his fist and growled angrily.
wave, brandish, flourish, wag, waggle, joggle
4 They were **shaken** by the terrible news.
shock, startle, distress, upset, disturb, alarm, frighten
shaky adjective
1 Be careful—the table is rather **shaky**.
unsteady, wobbly, insecure, rickety, flimsy, weak
2 He was so nervous that his hands were **shaky**.
shaking, trembling, quivering
3 He spoke in a **shaky** voice.
quavering, faltering, nervous, tremulous
OPPOSITE steady
shame noun
The guilty man hung his head in **shame**.
disgrace, dishonour, humiliation, embarrassment, guilt
a shame
It's **a shame** that you can't stay for longer.
a pity, unfortunate
shape verb
The potter **shaped** the clay into a tall vase.
form, mould, fashion
To shape something in a mould is to **cast** it.
share noun
Each of the pirates got a **share** of rum.
ration, allowance, portion, quota, helping, division, part (informal) cut
share verb
The robbers **shared** the loot between them.
divide, split, distribute, allot, allocate, deal out, ration out
shatter verb
1 The ball **shattered** a window.
break, smash, destroy, wreck
2 The windscreen **shattered** when a stone hit it.
break, splinter, disintegrate
shed noun
They kept their lawnmower in the garden **shed**.
hut, shack, outhouse
shed verb
A lorry **shed** its load on the motorway.
drop, let fall, spill, scatter
sheer adjective
1 The story he told was **sheer** nonsense.
complete, total, utter,

absolute, pure
2 *Don't try to climb that **sheer** cliff.*
vertical, perpendicular
sheet noun
1 *She started her diary on a fresh **sheet** of paper.*
page, leaf, piece
2 *The pond was covered with a thin **sheet** of ice.*
layer, film, covering, surface
3 *The glazier came to fit a new **sheet** of glass.*
panel, pane, plate
shelf noun
*She put the books back on the **shelf**.*
ledge, rack
*A shelf above a fireplace is a **mantelpiece**.*
shelter noun
*They reached **shelter** just before the storm broke.*
cover, protection, safety, refuge, sanctuary
shelter verb
1 *The hedge **shelters** the garden from the wind.*
protect, screen, shield, guard, defend, safeguard
2 *We **sheltered** from the rain under the trees.*
hide, take refuge
shield noun
*The trees act as an effective wind **shield**.*
screen, barrier, defence, guard, protection
*The part of a helmet that shields your face is the **visor**.*
shield verb
*The mother bear **shielded** her cubs from danger.*
protect, defend, guard, safeguard, keep safe, shelter
shift verb
1 *I need some help to **shift** the furniture.*
move, rearrange, reposition
2 *It was hard work **shifting** the mud off the tyres.*
remove, dislodge, budge
shine verb
1 *A light **shone** from an upstairs window.*
beam, glow, blaze, glare, gleam
2 *He **shines** his shoes every morning.*
polish, rub, brush
shiny adjective
*She polished the mirror until it was **shiny**.*
shining, bright, gleaming, glistening, glossy, polished, burnished, lustrous
OPPOSITE dull
ship noun
*Ships that travel long distances at sea are **ocean-going** or*

seagoing ships.
*People who work on ships at sea are **nautical** or **seafaring** people.*
shiver verb
*Ali waited outside, **shivering** with cold.*
tremble, quiver, shake, shudder, quake
shock noun
1 *The news of his death came as a great **shock**.*
blow, surprise, fright, upset
2 *People felt the **shock** of the explosion miles away.*
bang, impact, jolt
3 *The driver involved in the accident was in a state of **shock**.*
distress, trauma
shock verb
*The whole town was **shocked** by the news.*
horrify, appal, startle, alarm, stun, stagger, shake, astonish, astound, surprise, dismay, upset
*A formal synonym is **traumatize**.*
shoot verb
1 *Robin Hood **shot** an arrow into the air.*
fire, discharge, launch, aim
2 *It is now illegal to hunt and **shoot** tigers.*
fire at, hit, open fire on, gun down
3 *They watched the racing cars **shoot** past.*
race, speed, dash, rush, streak, hurtle, fly, whiz, zoom
4 *Part of the film was **shot** in Canada.*
film, photograph

🕸 WORD WEB

shop noun
VARIOUS TYPES OF SHOP
boutique, corner shop, department store, hypermarket, market, shopping arcade, shopping centre, shopping mall, supermarket
SPECIALIST SHOPS
antique shop, baker, bookshop, butcher, cheesemonger, chemist, clothes shop, confectioner, delicatessen, DIY or do-it-yourself shop, fishmonger, florist, garden centre, greengrocer, grocer, haberdasher, health-food shop, ironmonger, jeweller, music shop, newsagent, off-licence, pharmacy, post office, shoe shop or shoemaker, stationer, toyshop, watchmaker
PEOPLE WHO WORK IN SHOPS
cashier, salesman or saleswoman, shop assistant, shopkeeper or storekeeper

short adjective
1 *They live a **short** distance from the shops.*
little, small
OPPOSITE long
2 *It was a very **short** visit.*
brief, quick, fleeting, hasty, temporary
OPPOSITE long
3 *The troll was very **short** and fat.*
small, tiny, little, squat, dumpy, diminutive, petite
OPPOSITE tall
4 *The supply of water was getting **short**.*
low, meagre, scant, limited, inadequate, insufficient
OPPOSITE plentiful
5 *There is no need to be **short** with me!*
abrupt, rude, sharp, curt, impolite, snappy
OPPOSITE patient, polite
shortage noun
*The **shortage** of water is worrying.*
scarcity, deficiency, lack, want, dearth
*A shortage of water is a **drought**.*
*A shortage of food is a **famine**.*
shorten verb
*She had to **shorten** the essay because it was too long.*
cut down, reduce, cut, trim, abbreviate, abridge, condense, compress, curtail
OPPOSITE lengthen
shot noun
1 *I heard a noise like the **shot** of a pistol.*
bang, blast, crack
2 *The striker had an easy **shot** at the goal.*
hit, strike, kick
3 *The photographer took some unusual **shots**.*
photograph, picture, snap, snapshot
4 *(informal) We each had a **shot** at solving the riddle.*
try, go, attempt
(informal) bash
shout verb
*The ogre was **shouting** and stamping with rage.*
call, cry out, bawl, yell, bellow, roar, howl, yelp, scream, screech, shriek
OPPOSITE whisper

shopping

shove *verb*
*A man ran past and **shoved** me to the side.*
push, thrust, force, barge, elbow, jostle, shoulder

show *verb*
1 *My uncle **showed** us his coin collection.*
present, reveal, display, exhibit
2 *The photo **shows** my grandparents on holiday.*
portray, picture, depict, illustrate, represent
3 *The dance tutor **showed** them what to do.*
explain to, make clear to, instruct, teach, tell
4 *The evidence **shows** that he was right.*
prove, demonstrate
5 *A nurse **showed** them into the waiting room.*
direct, guide, conduct, escort, usher
6 *The signpost **shows** the way.*
indicate, point out
7 *His vest **showed** through his shirt.*
be seen, be visible, appear
to show off
*Walter is always **showing off**.*
boast, brag, crow, gloat, swagger
(*informal*) blow your own trumpet
A person who shows off is a **show-off**.

show *noun*
1 *There is a **show** of artwork at the end of term.*
display, exhibition, presentation
2 *There's a good **show** on at the theatre.*
performance, production, entertainment

shriek *noun, verb*
*'Quick!' **shrieked** Alice. 'Open the door!'*
cry, scream, screech, shout, howl, bawl, squeal, wail, yell

shrill *adjective*
*They heard the **shrill** sound of a whistle.*
high, high-pitched, piercing, sharp, screechy
OPPOSITE low, soft

shrink *verb*
*My jeans have **shrunk** in the wash.*
become smaller, contract
OPPOSITE expand

shrivel *verb*
*The plants **shrivelled** in the heat.*

shrivel

wilt, wither, droop, dry up, wrinkle, shrink

shudder *verb*
*They **shuddered** with fear when they heard the creature roar.*
tremble, quake, quiver, shake, shiver

shuffle *verb*
1 *She **shuffled** along the corridor in her slippers.*
shamble, scuffle, hobble, scrape
2 *Did you remember to **shuffle** the cards?*
mix, mix up, jumble

shut *verb*
*Please **shut** the door behind you.*
close, fasten, seal, secure, lock, bolt, latch
To shut a door with a bang is to **slam** it.
to shut someone up
*He had been **shut up** in a dungeon for five years.*
imprison, confine, detain
shut up
(*informal*) *I wish those people behind us would **shut up**!*
be quiet, be silent, stop talking, hold your tongue

shy *adjective*
*The little girl was too **shy** to say anything.*
bashful, timid, coy, reserved, hesitant, self-conscious, inhibited, modest
OPPOSITE bold

sick *adjective*
1 *Katie is off school because she's **sick**.*
ill, unwell, poorly, sickly, ailing, indisposed, off colour, peaky
OPPOSITE healthy
2 *The sea was rough and the cabin boy felt **sick**.*
nauseous, queasy
to be sick of
*I'm **sick of** this miserable weather!*
be fed up with, be tired of, have had enough of

side *noun*
1 *A cube has six **sides**.*
face, surface
2 *The path runs along the **side** of the field.*
edge, border, boundary, fringe, perimeter
The side of a page is the **margin**.
The side of a road is the **verge**.
3 *I could see both **sides** of the argument.*
point of view, view, angle, aspect
4 *The football club has a strong **side** this year.*
team

sight *noun*
1 *Weasels have sharp **sight** and excellent hearing.*
eyesight, vision
2 *The woods in autumn are a lovely **sight**.*
spectacle, display, show, scene
3 *By the third day, the ship was in **sight** of land.*
view, range
4 *We went to London to see the **sights**.*
attraction, landmark

sign *noun*
1 *A **sign** pointed to the exit.*
notice, placard, poster, signpost
The sign belonging to a particular business or organization is a *logo*.
The sign on a particular brand of goods is a *trademark*.
2 *The witch gave no **sign** that she was angry.*
indication, clue, hint, warning
3 *The guard gave us a **sign** to pass through the gates.*
signal, gesture, cue, reminder

sign *verb*
1 *Please **sign** your name on the form.*
write, inscribe
2 *The club **signed** a new player last week.*
take on, engage, recruit, enrol

signal *noun*
*The spy waited for the **signal** that all was clear.*
sign, indication, prompt, cue
A signal that tells you not to do something is a *warning*.

signal *verb*
*The pilot **signalled** that he was going to descend.*
give a sign or signal, gesture, indicate, motion

significant *adjective*
1 *The book describes the **significant** events of last century.*
important, major, noteworthy, influential
2 *Global warming is having a **significant** effect on wildlife.*
noticeable, considerable, perceptible, striking

silence *noun*
*There was **silence** while we sat the exam.*
quiet, quietness, hush, stillness, calm, peace
OPPOSITE noise

silence *verb*
*He **silenced** the audience by ringing a gong.*
deaden, muffle, quieten, suppress
To silence someone by putting something in or over their mouth is to *gag* them.

silent *adjective*
1 *At night, the desert was cold and silent.*
quiet, noiseless, soundless, still, hushed
Something you can't hear is *inaudible*.
A common simile is *as silent as the grave*.
OPPOSITE noisy
2 *Morris kept silent throughout the meeting.*
quiet, speechless, mute
(*informal*) mum
To be too shy to speak is to be *tongue-tied*.
OPPOSITE talkative

silly *adjective*
It was silly of me to lock myself out of the house.
foolish, stupid, idiotic, senseless, thoughtless, brainless, unwise, unintelligent, half-witted, hare-brained, scatterbrained
(*informal*) daft
OPPOSITE sensible

similar *adjective*
The puppies are similar in appearance.
alike, identical, indistinguishable, matching, the same
OPPOSITE dissimilar, different
similar to
The new book is similar to the previous one.
alike, close to, comparable to
OPPOSITE unlike, different from

similarity *noun*
It's easy to see the similarity between the twins.
likeness, resemblance
OPPOSITE difference

simple *adjective*
1 *Can you answer this simple question?*
easy, elementary, straightforward
OPPOSITE difficult
2 *The help file is written in simple language.*
clear, plain, uncomplicated, understandable, intelligible
OPPOSITE complicated
3 *The girl wore a simple cotton dress.*
plain, undecorated
OPPOSITE elaborate
4 *He enjoys simple pleasures like walking and gardening.*
ordinary, unsophisticated, humble, modest, homely
OPPOSITE sophisticated

sincere *adjective*
Please accept my sincere apologies.
genuine, honest, true, truthful, real, earnest, wholehearted, frank
OPPOSITE insincere

single *adjective*
1 *We saw a single house high on the moors.*
solitary, isolated
When only a single example of something exists, it is *unique*.
2 *Miss Dempster was quite content to stay single.*
unmarried
An unmarried man is a *bachelor*.
An unmarried woman is a *spinster*.

sinister *adjective*
He looked up with a sinister smile on his face.
menacing, threatening, malevolent, evil, disturbing, unsettling, eerie
(*informal*) creepy

sink *verb*
1 *The ship hit the rocks and sank.*
go down, become submerged, founder, capsize
To let water into a ship to sink it deliberately is to *scuttle* it.
2 *The sun began to sink below the horizon.*
drop, fall, descend, subside, dip
When the sun sinks to the horizon it *sets*.

sit *verb*
1 *Rachel sat on the sofa reading a magazine.*
have a seat, settle down, rest, perch
To sit on your heels is to *squat*.
To sit to have your portrait painted is to *pose*.
2 *My brother is sitting his driving test next week.*
take
(*informal*) go in for

site *noun*
This is the site of an ancient burial ground.
location, place, position, situation, setting, plot

situation *noun*
1 *The house is in a pleasant situation.*
location, locality, place, position, setting, site, spot
2 *I found myself in an awkward situation.*
position, circumstances, condition, state of affairs
A bad situation is a *plight* or *predicament*.

size *noun*
1 *What size is the garden?*
dimensions, proportions, area, extent
2 *They were amazed by the sheer size of the pyramids.*
scale, magnitude, immensity

sketch *noun*
1 *She drew a quick sketch of her cat.*
drawing, picture, outline

A sketch you do while you think of other things is a *doodle*.
2 *The actors performed a comic sketch.*
scene, turn, routine

sketch *verb*
He sketched a rough design for the poster
draw, draft, outline, rough out

skid *verb*
The postman skidded on the icy pavement.
slide, slip

skilful *adjective*
Dickens was a skilful writer.
expert, skilled, accomplished, able, capable, talented, brilliant, clever, masterly, deft
If you are skilful at a lot of things, you are *versatile*.
OPPOSITE incompetent

skill *noun*
It takes a lot of skill to build a boat.
expertise, ability, aptitude, capability, competence, accomplishment, talent, proficiency, deftness

skim *verb*
The stone skimmed across the surface of the pond.
glide, slide, skid, slip
to skim through
Luke skimmed through the newspaper.
scan, look through, skip through, flick through

skin *noun*
The cave people were dressed in animal skins.
coat, fur, hide, pelt
The type of skin you have on your face is your *complexion*.
Skin on fruit or vegetables is *peel* or *rind*.
Skin that might form on top of a liquid is a *coating*, *film*, or *membrane*.

skinny *adjective*
A skinny girl in bare feet answered the door.
thin, lean, bony, gaunt, lanky, scrawny, scraggy
OPPOSITE plump

skip *verb*
1 *The children skipped along the pavement.*
hop, jump, leap, bound, caper, dance, prance
2 *I skipped the boring bits in the book.*
pass over, miss out, ignore, omit, leave out

slant *verb*
Her handwriting slants backwards.
lean, slope, tilt, incline, be at an angle

slant *noun*
The floor of the caravan was at a slant.
slope, angle, tilt, incline, gradient
A slant on a damaged ship is a list.
A slanting line joining opposite corners of a square, etc., is a diagonal.
A slanting up to a higher level is a ramp.

slap *verb*
He slapped his hand against his thigh and laughed.
smack, strike, spank, hit, clout (*informal*) whack

slaughter *noun*
The battle ended in terrible slaughter.
bloodshed, killing, massacre, butchery

sleek *adjective*
Otters have sleek coats.
smooth, glossy, shiny, silky, soft, velvety
OPPOSITE coarse

sleep *verb*
The baby is sleeping in the next room.
be asleep, take a nap, doze (*informal*) snooze
To go to sleep is to *drop off* or *nod off*.

sleep *noun*
Mr Khan had a short sleep after lunch.
nap, rest, doze, catnap (*informal*) snooze, forty winks, shut-eye
An afternoon sleep is a *siesta*.
The long sleep some animals have through the winter is *hibernation*.

sleepy *adjective*
The giant was usually sleepy after dinner.
drowsy, tired, weary, heavy-eyed, lethargic, ready to sleep (*informal*) dopey
OPPOSITE wide awake

slender *adjective*
1 *The ballerina had a slender figure.*
slim, lean, slight, graceful, trim, svelte
OPPOSITE fat
2 *The spider dangled on a slender thread.*
thin, fine, fragile, delicate
OPPOSITE thick
3 *They only had a slender chance of winning.*
poor, slight, slim, faint, negligible, remote
OPPOSITE good
4 *The team won by a slender margin.*
narrow, small, slim

slither

OPPOSITE wide
slice *verb*
To slice meat is to *carve* it.

slide *verb*
I like sliding down the chute in the playground.
glide, skid, slip, slither

slight *adjective*
1 *There's a slight problem with the computer.*
minor, unimportant, insignificant, negligible, superficial, trifling, trivial
OPPOSITE important
2 *The fairy was a slight creature, barely two inches tall.*
delicate, fragile, frail, slender, slim, small, spare, thin, tiny
OPPOSITE stout

slim *adjective*
1 *A tall, slim figure appeared out of the fog.*
graceful, lean, slender, spare, thin, trim
OPPOSITE fat
2 *Their chances of winning are slim.*
faint, poor, slight, slender, negligible, remote
OPPOSITE good
3 *They won by a slim margin.*
narrow, small, slender
OPPOSITE wide

slimy *adjective*
The floor of the tunnel was covered with slimy mud.
slippery, slithery, sticky, oozy (*informal*) gooey, icky

sling *verb*
Robin Hood slung his quiver over his shoulder.
throw, cast, fling, hurl, pitch, heave, toss, lob (*informal*) chuck

slink *verb*
The spy slunk away without being seen.
slip, sneak, steal, creep, edge, sidle

slip *verb*
1 *The paper boy slipped on the ice.*
skid, slither, skate
2 *The lifeboat slipped into the water.*
glide, slide
3 *Marion slipped out while everyone was talking.*

sneak, steal, slink, tiptoe, creep, edge, sidle

slippery *adjective*
Take care—the floor is slippery.
slithery, slippy, smooth, glassy
A surface slippery with frost is *icy*.
A surface slippery with grease is *greasy* or *oily*.
A common simile is *as slippery as an eel*.

slit *noun*
The archers shot arrows through the slits in the castle wall.
opening, chink, gap, slot, split, tear, cut

slither *verb*
The rattlesnake slithered through the long grass.
slide, slip, glide, slink, snake

slope *verb*
The beach slopes gently down to the sea.
fall or rise, incline, bank, shelve

slope *noun*
1 *It was hard work pushing my bike up the slope.*
hill, rise, bank, ramp
An upward slope is an *ascent*.
A downward slope is a *descent*.
2 *Rain runs down the roof because of the slope.*
incline, slant, tilt, gradient

sloppy *adjective*
1 *For breakfast, there was a bowl of steaming, sloppy porridge.*
runny, slushy, watery, liquid, wet (*informal*) gloopy
2 *His handwriting is very sloppy.*
untidy, messy, careless, slovenly, slapdash, slipshod

slot *noun*
To use the phone, put a coin into the slot.
slit, chink, hole, opening

slouch *verb*
Enid sat at her desk, slouched over the computer.
hunch, stoop, slump, droop, flop

slow *adjective*
1 *Tortoises move at a slow but steady pace.*
unhurried, leisurely, gradual, plodding, dawdling, sluggish
2 *They took the train to London, followed by a slow bus journey.*

lengthy, prolonged, drawn-out, tedious
3 *The prisoner was* **slow** *to answer.*
hesitant, reluctant, tardy
slow *verb*
to slow down
Slow down—you're driving too fast!
go slower, brake, reduce speed
OPPOSITE **accelerate**
sly *adjective*
The chess player knew several **sly** *moves.*
crafty, cunning, artful, clever, wily, tricky, sneaky, devious, furtive, secretive, stealthy, underhand
A common simile is **as sly as a fox**.
OPPOSITE **straightforward**
smack *verb*
He **smacked** *the other player on the head by accident.*
slap, strike, hit, cuff
(*informal*) whack
small *adjective*
1 *Moles have incredibly* **small** *eyes and ears.*
little, tiny, minute, compact, miniature, microscopic, minuscule, mini, baby
(*informal*) teeny, titchy, dinky
(*Scottish*) wee
OPPOSITE **big, large**
2 *A* **small** *elf was standing on a toadstool.*
little, short, petite, slight, dainty, diminutive
(*informal*) pint-sized
OPPOSITE **big, tall, large**
3 *For breakfast there was stale bread with a* **small** *scraping of butter.*
meagre, inadequate, insufficient, paltry, scanty, stingy, skimpy
(*informal*) measly
OPPOSITE **large, generous, ample**
4 *The writers made some* **small** *changes to the script.*
minor, unimportant, insignificant, trivial, trifling, negligible
OPPOSITE **major, substantial**
smart *adjective*
1 *Everyone looked* **smart** *at the wedding.*
elegant, well-dressed, well-groomed, stylish, spruce, fashionable, chic, neat, trim
To make yourself smart is to **smarten up**.
OPPOSITE **scruffy**
2 *They booked a table in a very* **smart** *restaurant.*
fashionable, high-class, exclusive, fancy
(*informal*) posh

3 *The detective made a very* **smart** *move.*
clever, ingenious, intelligent, shrewd, crafty
OPPOSITE **stupid**
4 *The cyclists set off at a* **smart** *pace.*
fast, quick, rapid, speedy, swift, brisk
OPPOSITE **slow**
smart *verb*
The smoke from the barbecue made our eyes **smart**.
hurt, sting, prick, prickle, tingle
smash *verb*
A vase fell off the table and **smashed** *to pieces on the floor.*
break, crush, shatter, crack
When wood smashes it **splinters**.
To smash something completely is to **demolish** or **destroy** or **wreck** it.
to smash into
A lorry had **smashed into** *the side of a bus.*
crash into, collide with, bang into, bump into
smear *verb*
The chef **smeared** *butter over the cooking dish.*
spread, wipe, plaster, rub, dab, smudge, daub
smell *noun*
1 *The air was filled with the* **smell** *of roses.*
scent, aroma, perfume, fragrance
2 *The* **smell** *of mouldy cheese was unbearable.*
odour, stench, stink, reek, whiff
(*informal*) pong, niff
smell *verb*
1 *I could* **smell** *something baking in the oven.*
scent, sniff
(*informal*) get a whiff of
2 *After walking all day, my feet were beginning to* **smell**.
stink, reek
(*informal*) pong

WRITING TIPS

You can use these words to describe **how something smells**.
TO DESCRIBE SOMETHING WHICH *smells good*
fragrant, aromatic, perfumed, scented, sweet-smelling *The garden was planted with* **sweet-smelling** *herbs.*
TO DESCRIBE SOMETHING WHICH *smells bad*
smelly, stinking, evil-smelling, foul-smelling, musty, odorous, reeking, rotten, fetid, foul
(*informal*) stinky, pongy, whiffy
The witch stirred the **evil-smelling** *brew.*

smile *verb, noun*
The stranger **smiled** *and introduced himself.*
grin, beam
To smile in a silly way is to **simper**.
To smile in a self-satisfied way is to **smirk**.
To smile in an insulting way is to **sneer**.
smoke *noun*
Puffs of green **smoke** *came from the dragon's nostrils.*
fumes, gas, steam, vapour
The smoke given out by a car is **exhaust**.
A mixture of smoke and fog is **smog**.
smooth *adjective*
1 *This part of the road is* **smooth** *and good for cycling.*
flat, even, level
OPPOSITE **uneven**
2 *In the early morning, the lake was perfectly* **smooth**.
calm, still, unruffled, undisturbed, glassy
OPPOSITE **rough**
3 *Otters have* **smooth** *and shiny coats.*
silky, sleek, velvety
OPPOSITE **coarse**
4 *The journey by train is very quick and* **smooth**.
comfortable, steady
OPPOSITE **bumpy**
5 *Stir the cake mixture until it is* **smooth**.
creamy, flowing, runny
OPPOSITE **lumpy**
smooth *verb*
Charlotte stood up and **smoothed** *her dress.*
flatten, level, even out
To smooth cloth you can **iron** or **press** it.
To smooth wood you can **plane** or **sand** it.
smother *verb*
1 *Pythons* **smother** *their prey to death.*
suffocate, choke, stifle
2 *The pudding was* **smothered** *with cream.*
cover, coat
smudge *noun*
There were **smudges** *of ink all over the page.*
smear, blot, streak, stain, mark
smudge *verb*
Don't **smudge** *the icing on the cake!*
smear, blur, streak
snap *verb*
1 *A twig* **snapped** *under one of my boots.*
break, crack
2 *The dog* **snapped** *at the*

a
b
c
d
e
f
g
h
i
j
k
l
m
n
o
p
q
r
s
t
u
v
w
x
y
z

postman's ankles.
bite, nip
3 *Mr Baker was in a bad mood and* ***snapped*** *at everyone.*
snarl, bark
snatch *verb*
The thief ***snatched*** *the jewels and ran off.*
grab, seize, grasp, pluck, wrench away, wrest away
sneak *verb*
I managed to ***sneak*** *in without anyone seeing.*
slip, steal, creep, slink, tiptoe, sidle, skulk
sneaky *adjective*
That was a really ***sneaky*** *trick.*
sly, underhand, cunning, crafty, devious, furtive, untrustworthy
OPPOSITE honest
sneer *verb*
to sneer at
He ***sneered at*** *my first attempts to ice-skate.*
make fun of, mock, ridicule, scoff at, jeer at, deride
snobbish *adjective*
She's too ***snobbish*** *to mix with us.*
arrogant, pompous, superior, haughty
(*informal*) stuck-up, snooty, toffee-nosed
OPPOSITE humble
snoop *verb*
They caught a man ***snooping*** *round the office.*
sneak, pry, poke, rummage, spy
snub *verb*
She ***snubbed*** *the neighbours by not inviting them to the party.*
insult, offend, be rude to, brush off
(*informal*) put down
snug *adjective*
Lucy was tucked up ***snug*** *in bed.*
cosy, comfortable, warm, relaxed
(*informal*) comfy
A common simile is ***as snug as a bug in a rug.***
OPPOSITE uncomfortable
soak *verb*
1 *Days of rain had* ***soaked*** *the cricket pitch.*
wet thoroughly, drench, saturate
2 *Leave the beans to* ***soak*** *in water overnight.*
steep, immerse, submerge
soaking *adjective*
My socks are absolutely ***soaking!***
wet through, drenched, dripping, wringing, saturated, sodden, sopping, soggy
Ground that has been soaked by rain is ***waterlogged***.
soar *verb*
The seagull spread its wings and ***soared*** *into the air.*
climb, rise, ascend, fly, wing

sob *verb*
Tina threw herself on the bed, ***sobbing*** *loudly.*
cry, weep, bawl, blubber, shed tears, snivel
soft *adjective*
1 *The kittens can only eat* ***soft*** *food.*
pulpy, spongy, squashy
(*informal*) squidgy
OPPOSITE hard, dry
2 *My head sank into the* ***soft*** *pillow.*
supple, pliable, springy, yielding, flexible
OPPOSITE firm, rigid
3 *The rabbit's fur felt very* ***soft***.
smooth, silky, sleek, velvety, downy, feathery
OPPOSITE coarse
4 *A* ***soft*** *breeze stirred the leaves.*
gentle, light, mild, delicate
OPPOSITE rough, strong
5 *The smugglers spoke in* ***soft*** *whispers.*
quiet, low, faint
OPPOSITE loud
6 *It was hard to see clearly in the* ***soft*** *light.*
subdued, muted, pale, dim, low
OPPOSITE bright, dazzling
7 *You are being too* ***soft*** *with that puppy.*
lenient, easygoing, tolerant, indulgent
OPPOSITE strict, tough
soggy *adjective*
1 *The pitch was* ***soggy*** *after all the rain.*
wet, drenched, soaked, saturated, sodden, waterlogged
2 *The bread in my sandwich had become* ***soggy***.
moist, soft, pulpy, squelchy
(*informal*) squidgy
solemn *adjective*
1 *The butler always had a* ***solemn*** *expression on his face.*
serious, grave, sober, sombre, unsmiling, glum
OPPOSITE cheerful
2 *The coronation was a* ***solemn*** *occasion.*
formal, dignified, grand, stately, majestic, pompous
OPPOSITE frivolous
solid *adjective*
1 *A cricket ball is* ***solid***.
OPPOSITE hollow
2 *The water turned into* ***solid*** *ice.*
hard, firm, dense, compact, rigid, unyielding
A common simile is ***as solid as a rock***.
OPPOSITE soft

3 *The bars of the climbing frame are quite* ***solid***.
firm, robust, sound, strong, stable, sturdy
OPPOSITE weak, unstable
4 *The crown was made of* ***solid*** *gold.*
pure, genuine
5 *He got* ***solid*** *support from his team-mates.*
firm, reliable, dependable, united, unanimous
OPPOSITE weak, divided
solve *verb*
The professor was trying to ***solve*** *an ancient riddle.*
interpret, explain, answer, work out, find the solution to, unravel, decipher
soothing *adjective*
They played ***soothing*** *music.*
calming, relaxing, restful, peaceful, gentle, pleasant
sore *adjective*
My feet are still ***sore*** *from the walk.*
painful, aching, hurting, smarting, tender, sensitive, inflamed, raw, red
sorrow *noun*
1 *He felt great* ***sorrow*** *at leaving his children behind.*
sadness, unhappiness, misery, woe, grief, anguish, despair, distress, heartache, heartbreak, melancholy, gloom, depression, desolation, wretchedness
Sorrow because of someone's death is ***mourning***.
Sorrow at being away from home is ***homesickness***.
OPPOSITE happiness
2 *She expressed her* ***sorrow*** *for what she had done.*
regret, remorse, repentance, apologies
sorry *adjective*
1 *Scott said he was* ***sorry*** *for losing my football.*
apologetic, regretful, remorseful, ashamed (of), repentant
OPPOSITE unapologetic
2 *We felt* ***sorry*** *for the villagers who had lost their homes.*
sympathetic, pitying, understanding, compassionate
OPPOSITE unsympathetic
sort *noun*
What ***sort*** *of music do you like?*
kind, type, variety, form, nature, style, genre, category, order, class
A sort of animal is a ***breed*** *or* ***species***.
sort *verb*
The books are ***sorted*** *according to their subjects.*
arrange, organize, class, group, categorize, classify, divide
OPPOSITE mix

soft

to sort something out
*They managed to **sort out** their disagreement.*
settle, resolve, clear up, cope with, deal with

WORD WEB

sound noun
*We heard the **sound** of footsteps approaching.*
noise, tone
A loud, harsh sound is a *din* or *racket*.

SOUNDS MADE BY PEOPLE
bawl, bellow, boo, boom, cackle, chortle, clap, croak, cry, gasp, groan, gurgle, hiccup, hiss, howl, hum, moan, murmur, puff, scream, shout, shriek, sigh, sing, sniff, snore, snort, sob, splutter, stammer, stutter, wail, wheeze, whimper, whine, whisper, whistle, whoop, yell, yodel

SOUNDS MADE BY THINGS
bang, blare, beep, bleep, boom, buzz, chime, chink, chug, clang, clank, clash, clatter, click, clink, clunk, crack, crackle, crash, creak, crunch, ding, drone, drum, fizz, grate, grunge, jangle, jingle, patter, peal, ping, plop, pop, purr, putter, rattle, ring, rumble, rustle, scrunch, sizzle, slam, snap, squeak, squelch, swish, throb, thud, thunder, tick, ting, tinkle, twang, whirr, whoosh, whistle, whiz, zoom

---

WRITING TIPS

You can use these words to describe a **sound**.
TO DESCRIBE A *pleasant sound*
dulcet, harmonious, mellifluous, melodious, sweet *I heard the sweet strains of a harp playing.*
TO DESCRIBE AN *unpleasant sound*
grating, harsh, jarring, piercing, rasping, raucous, shrill, thin, tinny *A **raucous** fight was going out outside.*

sound adjective
1 *The walls of the fortress seemed sound.*
firm, solid, stable, safe, secure, intact, undamaged
OPPOSITE unsound, unstable
2 *She gave us some sound advice.*
good, sensible, wise, reasonable, trustworthy
OPPOSITE unwise
3 *The travellers returned safe and sound.*
strong, well, fit, healthy
OPPOSITE weak, unfit

---

sour adjective
1 *These apples are a bit sour.*
tart, bitter, sharp, acid
OPPOSITE sweet
2 *The guard opened the door with a sour look on his face.*
cross, bad-tempered, grumpy, disagreeable, peevish

space noun
1 *There wasn't much space to move about.*
room, freedom, scope
2 *He peered through the tiny space in the curtains.*
gap, hole, opening, break
A space without any air in it is a *vacuum*.
A space of time is an *interval* or *period*.
3 *The astronauts will spend ten days in space.*
outer space

WORD WEB

space noun
Everything that exists in space is the *universe* or *cosmos*.
Distances in space stretch to *infinity*.
Travel to other planets is *interplanetary* travel.
Travel to other stars is *interstellar* travel.
Travel to other galaxies is *intergalactic* travel.
A traveller in space is an *astronaut*.
In stories, beings from other planets are *aliens* or *extraterrestrials*.

NATURAL OBJECTS FOUND IN SPACE
asteroid, black hole, comet, constellation, galaxy, meteor, meteorite, Milky Way, moon, nebula, nova, planet, red dwarf, red giant, shooting star, solar system, star, sun, supernova

WORDS TO DO WITH TRAVEL IN SPACE
blast-off, countdown, launch, mission, orbit, re-entry, rocket, satellite, spacecraft, spaceship, space shuttle, space station, spacesuit, spacewalk *satellite*

A robot spacecraft is a *probe*.
A vehicle which can travel on the surface of a planet is a *buggy* or *rover*.

THINGS YOU MIGHT FIND ON A SPACESHIP
booster rocket, bridge, cargo bay, capsule, computer, docking bay, fuel tank, heat shield, instrument panel, life-support system, module, pod, solar panel

THINGS A SPACESHIP MIGHT DO
blast off, burn up, drift off-course, land, lift off, malfunction, orbit, re-enter the earth's atmosphere, splash down, touch down

---

spare verb
1 *Can you spare any money for a good cause?*
afford, part with, give, provide, do without
2 *Gretel begged the witch to spare her brother.*
show mercy to, pardon, reprieve, let off, release, free

spare adjective
1 *The spare tyre is in the boot.*
additional, extra, reserve, standby
2 *Have you any spare change?*
leftover, surplus, odd, remaining, unused, unwanted

spark noun
There was a spark of light as he struck the match.
flash, gleam, glint, flicker, sparkle

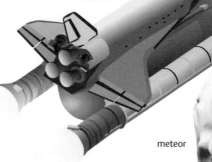
shuttle

meteor

a
b
c
d
e
f
g
h
i
j
k
l

r
s
t
u

sparkle *verb*
*The diamond ring **sparkled** in the sunlight.*
glitter, glisten, glint, twinkle

speak *verb*
*The robot opened its mouth and began to **speak**.*
communicate, express yourself, say something, talk, utter

special *adjective*
1 *Are you keeping the champagne for a **special** occasion?*
important, significant, memorable, noteworthy, momentous, exceptional, extraordinary, out-of-the-ordinary
OPPOSITE ordinary
2 *My granny has her own **special** way of making porridge.*
unique, individual, characteristic, distinctive, different, peculiar
3 *You need a **special** camera to film underwater.*
particular, specific, proper, specialized

speck *noun*
*She brushed a **speck** of dust from her shoes.*
bit, dot, spot, fleck, grain, particle, trace, mark

spectacle *noun*
*The fireworks for Diwali will be a great **spectacle**.*
display, show, performance, exhibition, extravaganza

spectacular *adjective*
1 *The acrobats gave a **spectacular** performance.*
dramatic, exciting, impressive, thrilling, magnificent, sensational
2 *The tulips are **spectacular** at this time of year.*
eye-catching, showy, splendid, breathtaking, colourful

spectator *noun*
The spectators at a show are the *audience*.
The spectators at a football match are the *crowd*.
A person watching TV is a *viewer*.
If you see an accident or a crime you are an *eyewitness* or *witness*.
If you just happen to see something going on you are a *bystander* or *onlooker*.

speech *noun*
1 *His **speech** was slurred and he looked tired.*
speaking, talking, articulation, pronunciation
2 *She was invited to give an after-dinner **speech**.*
talk, address, lecture, oration
A talk in church is a *sermon*.
Speech between actors in a play is *dialogue*.

A speech delivered by a single actor is a *monologue*.

speed *noun*
1 *Could a spaceship travel faster than the **speed** of light?*
pace, rate
A formal synonym is *velocity*.
The speed of a piece of music is its *tempo*.
To increase speed is to *accelerate*.
To reduce speed is to *decelerate*.
2 *They finished clearing up with amazing **speed**.*
quickness, rapidity, swiftness
OPPOSITE slowness

speed *verb*
*The skiers **sped** down the mountain.*
race, rush, dash, dart, hurry, hurtle, career, fly, streak, tear, shoot, zoom, zip

spell *noun*
1 *A magic **spell** had turned the knight into a toad.*
charm, incantation
Making magic spells is *sorcery*, *witchcraft*, or *wizardry*.
2 *We're hoping for a **spell** of dry weather.*
period, interval, time, stretch, run

spend *verb*
1 *Have you **spent** all your pocket money already?*
pay out, use up, get through, exhaust
(*informal*) fork out, shell out
To spend money unwisely is to *fritter* or *squander* it.
2 *She **spends** a lot of time working in the garden.*
pass, occupy, fill
To spend time doing something useless is to *waste* it.

spill *verb*
1 *Katie **spilled** her juice all over the table.*
overturn, upset, tip over
2 *Milk **spilled** onto the floor.*
overflow, pour, slop, slosh, splash
3 *The treasure chest fell open, **spilling** gold coins everywhere.*
shed, tip, scatter, drop

spin *verb*
*The rear wheels of the jeep **spun** round.*
turn, rotate, revolve, whirl, twirl

spine *noun*
1 *Your **spine** runs down the middle of your back.*

backbone, spinal column
The bones in your spine are your *vertebrae*.
2 *A porcupine has sharp **spines**.*
needle, quill, point, spike, bristle

spirit *noun*
1 *He carried a charm to keep evil **spirits** away.*
ghost, ghoul, phantom, spectre, demon
2 *The orchestra played the piece with great **spirit**.*
energy, liveliness, enthusiasm, vigour, zest, zeal, fire
3 *There is a real **spirit** of cooperation in the team.*
feeling, mood, atmosphere

spiteful *adjective*
*He made some really **spiteful** comments.*
malicious, malevolent, ill-natured, hostile, venomous, vicious, nasty, unkind
OPPOSITE kind

splash *verb*
1 *The bus **splashed** water over us.*
shower, spray, spatter, sprinkle, squirt, slop, slosh, spill
(*informal*) splosh
2 *The children **splashed** about in the playing pool.*
paddle, wade, dabble, bathe

splendid *adjective*
1 *There was a **splendid** banquet on the eve of the wedding.*
magnificent, lavish, luxurious, impressive, imposing, grand, great, dazzling, glorious, gorgeous, elegant, rich, stately, majestic
2 *That's a **splendid** idea!*
excellent, first-class, admirable, superb, wonderful, marvellous

splinter *verb*
*The glass **splintered** into pieces.*
shatter, smash, fracture, chip, crack, split

split *verb*
1 *He **split** the log in two.*
chop, cut up, crack open, splinter
2 *He **split** his trousers climbing over the fence.*
rip open, tear
3 *The pirates **split** the gold between them.*
distribute, share out
4 *The path **splits** here.*
branch, fork, separate
to split up
*The search party decided to **split up**.*
break up, part, separate, divide
If a married couple splits up, they may *divorce*.

spell

split *noun*
He had a **split** in the seat of his trousers.
rip, tear, slash, slit

spoil *verb*
1 Bad weather **spoiled** the holiday.
ruin, wreck, upset, mess up, mar, scupper
2 The grafitti **spoils** the look of the new building.
damage, harm, hurt, disfigure, deface
3 His parents have **spoiled** him since he was a baby.
indulge, pamper, make a fuss of

WORD WEB

sport *noun*
I enjoy playing **sport** at the weekend.
exercise, games

TEAM SPORTS INCLUDE
American football, baseball, basketball, bowls, cricket, football or soccer, hockey, lacrosse, netball, polo, rounders, rugby, volleyball, water polo

American football

INDIVIDUAL SPORTS INCLUDE
angling, archery, athletics, badminton, billiards, boxing, bowling, canoeing, climbing, croquet, cross-country running, cycling, darts, diving, fencing, golf, gymnastics, horse racing, jogging, judo, karate, motor racing, mountaineering, orienteering, pool, rowing, sailing, show jumping, snooker, squash, surfing, swimming, table tennis, tae kwon do, tennis, waterskiing, weightlifting, windsurfing, wrestling

WINTER SPORTS INCLUDE
bobsleigh, curling, ice hockey, ice skating, skiing, snowboarding, speed skating, tobogganing

PEOPLE WHO TAKE PART IN SPORT
athlete, coach, competitor, player, sportsman or sportswoman

PLACES WHERE SPORT TAKES PLACE
arena, field, ground, park, pitch, pool, ring, rink, run, slope, stadium, track

boxing

SOME ATHLETIC EVENTS
cross-country, decathlon, discus, heptathlon, high jump, hurdles, javelin, long jump, marathon, pentathlon, pole vault, relay race, running, shot, sprinting, steeplechase, triathlon, triple jump

snowboarding

baseball

basketball

tennis

spot *noun*
1 There were several **spots** of paint on the carpet.
mark, stain, blot, blotch, smudge, dot, fleck, speck
Small brown spots on your skin are *freckles*.
A small dark spot on your skin is a *mole*.
A mark you have had on your skin since you were born is a *birthmark*.
A small round swelling on your skin is a *pimple*.
A lot of spots is a *rash*.
2 We felt a few **spots** of rain.
drop, blob, bead

3 Here's a nice **spot** for a picnic.
place, position, location, site, situation, locality

spot *verb*
1 Nina **spotted** her friend in the crowd.
see, sight, spy, catch sight of, notice, observe, make out, recognize, detect
2 The tyres were **spotted** with mud.
mark, stain, blot, spatter, fleck, speckle, mottle

sprawl *verb*
1 We **sprawled** on the lawn.
flop, lean back, lie, loll, lounge, recline, relax, slouch, slump, spread out, stretch out
2 New houses have started to **sprawl** across the countryside.
spread, stretch

spray *verb*
A passing bus **sprayed** mud over us.
shower, spatter, splash, sprinkle, scatter

spread *verb*
1 I **spread** the map on the table.
lay out, open out, fan out, unfold, unfurl, unroll
2 The milk spilled and **spread** all over the floor.
expand, extend, stretch, broaden, enlarge, swell
3 The school website is a good way of **spreading** news.
communicate, circulate, distribute, transmit, make known, pass on, pass round
4 She **spread** jam on a piece of toast.
smear
5 He **spread** the seeds evenly over the ground.
scatter, strew

spring *verb*
Suddenly a rabbit **sprang** over the fence.
jump, leap, bound, hop, vault
When a cat springs at a mouse, it *pounces*.
to spring up
Weeds **spring up** quickly in damp weather.
appear, develop, emerge, shoot up, sprout

sprinkle *verb*
She **sprinkled** flakes of chocolate over the cake.
scatter, shower, spray, dust, powder

spurt *verb*
Water **spurted** from the hole in the pipe.
gush, spout, shoot out, stream, squirt, jet

a
b
c
d
e
f
g
h
i
j
k
l
m
n
o
p
q
r
s
t
u
v
w
x
y
z

WORD WEB

spy noun
*The **spy** was on a top-secret mission.*
agent, secret agent
The work of a spy is ***spying*** or ***espionage***.
A spy who works for two rival countries or organizations is a ***double agent***.
An informal name for a spy who works undercover is a ***mole***.

THINGS A SPY MIGHT DO
adopt a disguise or cover, assume a secret identity, carry out a secret mission, crack or decipher a code, gather intelligence, keep someone under surveillance, report to headquarters, uncover an enemy agent, work undercover

THINGS A SPY MIGHT USE OR CARRY
coded message, false passport, hidden camera or microphone, listening device, motion detector, night-vision goggles, password, torch, walkie talkie

A SPY'S MISSION MIGHT BE
clandestine, covert, secret, stealthy, surreptitious, top-secret, undercover, informal cloak-and-dagger, hush-hush

---

squabble verb
*The twins are always **squabbling** in the car.*
argue, fight, quarrel, bicker, wrangle

squash verb
1 *My sandwich got **squashed** at the bottom of my schoolbag.*
crush, flatten, press, compress, mangle
To squash food deliberately is to ***mash*** or ***pulp*** or ***purée*** it.
2 *We **squashed** our sleeping bags into our rucksacks.*
squeeze, stuff, force, cram, pack, ram

squat verb
*We **squatted** on the ground to watch the puppet show.*
crouch, sit

squat adjective
*The alien had a **squat** little body on three short legs.*
dumpy, stocky, plump, podgy, portly

squeeze verb
1 *She **squeezed** the water out of the sponge.*
press, wring, compress, crush

2 *Five of us **squeezed** into the back of the car.*
squash, cram, crowd, stuff, push, ram, shove, wedge
3 *Holly **squeezed** her sister affectionately.*
clasp, hug, embrace, cuddle
To squeeze something between your thumb and finger is to ***pinch*** it.

squeeze

squirt verb
*My little brother made the tap water **squirt** all over me.*
spurt, spray, gush, spout, shoot, jet

stab verb
1 *He **stabbed** the sausage with his fork.*
spear, jab, pierce, impale
2 *She **stabbed** a finger at him.*
stick, thrust, push, jab

stab noun
*Jake felt a sudden **stab** of pain in his chest.*
pang, prick, sting

stable adjective
1 *The ladder doesn't look very **stable**.*
steady, secure, firm, fixed, solid, balanced
OPPOSITE **wobbly, shaky**

---

2 *He's been in a **stable** relationship for years.*
steady, established, lasting, durable, strong
OPPOSITE **temporary**

stack noun
*There were **stacks** of books all over the floor.*
pile, heap, mound, tower
Another word for a stack of hay is a ***rick*** or ***hayrick***.

stack verb
***Stack** the papers on the desk.*
gather, assemble, collect, heap up, pile up

staff noun
*There was a party at the hospital for all the **staff**.*
workers, employees, personnel, workforce, team
The staff on a ship or aircraft are the ***crew***.

stage noun
1 *They went up on the **stage** to collect their prizes.*
platform
2 *The final **stage** of the journey was made by coach.*
leg, step, phase, portion, stretch
3 *At this **stage** in her life, she wants to try something new.*
period, point, time, juncture

stagger verb
1 *The wounded knight **staggered** and fell.*
reel, stumble, lurch, totter, sway, falter, waver, wobble
2 *We were **staggered** at the size of the pyramid.*
amaze, astonish, astound, surprise, flabbergast, stupefy, startle, stun

stain noun
*There were several coffee **stains** on the tablecloth.*
mark, spot, blot, blotch, blemish, smear, smudge

stain verb
*Her trainers were **stained** with mud.*
discolour, mark, soil, dirty, blacken, tarnish

stale adjective
*The bread had gone **stale**.*
dry, hard, old, mouldy, musty
OPPOSITE **fresh**

stalk verb
1 *The cheetah **stalked** its prey.*
hunt, pursue, track, trail, follow, shadow, tail
2 *Miss Foster turned and **stalked** out of the room.*
stride, strut

stammer verb
Angela went red and started stammering.
stutter, falter, stumble, splutter

stamp verb
1 *He stamped on the flower by mistake.*
step, tread, trample
2 *The librarian stamped my library book.*
mark, print
To stamp a postmark on a letter is to **frank** it.
To stamp a mark on cattle with a hot iron is to **brand** them.

stand verb
1 *The newborn pup was too weak to stand.*
get to your feet, get up, rise
2 *They stood the ladder against the wall.*
put, place, set, position, station, erect
3 *The offer still stands.*
remain valid, be unchanged, continue
4 *I can't stand the smell any longer.*
bear, abide, endure, put up with, tolerate, suffer
to stand for something
1 *She won't stand for any nonsense.*
put up with, tolerate, accept, allow, permit
2 *What do these initials stand for?*
mean, indicate, signify, represent
to stand out
Among all the photographs, this one really stood out.
catch your eye, stick out, be prominent
to stand up for someone
He always stands up for his friends.
support, defend, side with, speak up for
(informal) stick up for

standard noun
1 *Their writing is of a very high standard.*
grade, level, quality
2 *He considered the book good by any standard.*
guidelines, ideal, measurement, model
3 *The soldiers carried their standard proudly.*
colours, flag, banner

standard adjective
The teacher showed us the standard way to write a letter.
normal, usual, common, conventional, typical, customary, accepted, approved, established, orthodox, regular, traditional
OPPOSITE abnormal

star noun
1 *Astronomers study the stars.*
A word meaning 'to do with stars' is **stellar**.
A night sky in which you can see stars is **starry** or **star-studded**.
A mark in the shape of a star in a piece of writing is an **asterisk**.
2 *Several Hollywood stars attended the premiere of the film.*
celebrity, idol, superstar

stare verb
The guard stared straight ahead, not blinking.
gaze, gape, peer, look
to stare at someone
The wolf was staring hungrily at us.
gaze at, gawp at, goggle at, eye, ogle, scrutinize, watch
To stare angrily at someone is to **glare** at them.

start verb
1 *The new course will start in the autumn.*
begin, commence
(informal) get going, get cracking, kick off
OPPOSITE finish, end
2 *We are planning to start a book club.*
create, set up, establish, found, institute, originate, introduce, initiate, open, launch
OPPOSITE close
3 *The horses started when the gun went off.*
jump, flinch, jerk, twitch, recoil, wince

start noun
1 *Try not to miss the start of the film.*
beginning, opening, introduction, commencement
OPPOSITE end, close, finish
2 *She has been with the theatre company right from the start.*
beginning, outset, creation, inception, birth, dawn, launch
3 *The explosion gave us all a nasty start.*
jump, jolt, shock, surprise

startle verb
The sudden noise startled the deer.
alarm, panic, frighten, scare, make you start, make you jump, surprise, take you by surprise

starving adjective (informal)
What's for dinner? I'm starving!
hungry, famished, ravenous
To be slightly hungry is to be **peckish**.

state noun
1 *The roof of the cottage is in a bad state.*
condition, shape
The state of a person or animal is their **fitness** or **health**.
2 *He gets into a terrible state*

before an exam.
panic, fluster
(informal) flap
3 *The queen is the head of state.*
country, nation

state verb
Her passport states that she is an Australian citizen.
declare, announce, report, say, proclaim, pronounce, communicate

stay verb
1 *Can you stay there while I park the car?*
wait, hang about, remain
OPPOSITE leave, depart
2 *We tried to stay warm by stamping our feet.*
keep, carry on being, continue
3 *Do you plan to stay in America for long?*
live, reside, dwell, lodge, settle, stop

stay noun
Our friends came for a short stay.
visit, stopover, holiday, break

steady adjective
1 *You need a steady hand to be a surgeon.*
stable, balanced, settled, secure, fixed, firm, fast, solid
A common simile is **as steady as a rock**.
OPPOSITE unsteady, shaky
2 *The plants need a steady supply of water.*
continuous, uninterrupted, non-stop, consistent
OPPOSITE intermittent
3 *The runners kept up a steady pace.*
regular, constant, even, smooth, rhythmic, unvarying
OPPOSITE irregular

steal verb
1 *The thieves stole several valuable paintings.*
rob, thieve, take, lift, make off with
(informal) pinch, nick, swipe, snaffle
2 *The children stole quietly upstairs.*
creep, sneak, tiptoe, slip, slink

135

steep *adjective*
*The bus inched its way slowly up the **steep** slope.*
abrupt, sudden, sharp
A cliff or drop which is straight up and down is *sheer* or *vertical*.
OPPOSITE gradual, gentle

steer *verb*
*She **steered** the car into the parking space.*
direct, guide
To steer a vehicle is to *drive* it.
To steer a boat is to *navigate* or *pilot* it.

step *noun*
1 *The baby took her first **steps** yesterday.*
footstep, pace, stride
2 *Be careful not to trip on the **step**.*
doorstep, stair
A set of steps going from one floor of a building to another is a *staircase*.
A folding set of steps is a *stepladder*.
The steps of a ladder are the *rungs*.
3 *The first **step** in making a cake is to weigh the ingredients.*
stage, phase, action

step *verb*
*Don't **step** in the puddle!*
put your foot, tread, walk, stamp, trample
to step something up
*They have **stepped up** security at the airport.*
increase, intensify, strengthen, boost

stern *adjective*
*The coach gave each of the players a **stern** look.*
disapproving, unsmiling, severe, strict, hard, harsh, grim
OPPOSITE lenient

stick
noun
1 *They collected **sticks** to make a fire.*
twig, branch, stalk
2 *The elderly patient walked with a **stick**.*
cane, rod, staff, pole
A stick used by a conductor is a baton.
A stick carried by a police officer is a *truncheon*.
A magic stick used by a witch or fairy is a *wand*.

stick *verb*
1 *He **stuck** his fork into the potato.*
poke, prod, stab, thrust, dig, jab
2 *She tried to **stick** the broken pieces of china together.*
glue, paste, cement, bond, join, fasten
3 *The stamp wouldn't **stick** to the envelope.*
adhere, attach, cling
4 *The wheels of the caravan **stuck** fast in the mud.*
jam, wedge, become trapped
to stick out
*The shelf **sticks out** too far.*
jut out, poke out, project, protrude
to stick up for someone
*(informal) She **stuck up for** him when he was in trouble.*
support, defend, side with, stand up for, speak up for

sticky *adjective*
1 *Someone had left a blob of **sticky** toffee on the chair.*
tacky, gummy, gluey
(informal) gooey, icky
2 *I don't like hot **sticky** weather.*
humid, muggy, clammy, close, steamy, sultry
OPPOSITE dry

stiff *adjective*
1 *Stir the flour and water to a **stiff** paste.*
firm, hard, solid
A common simile is *as stiff as a poker*.
OPPOSITE soft
2 *He mounted the picture on **stiff** card.*
rigid, inflexible, thick
OPPOSITE pliable
3 *Her muscles were **stiff** after the long walk.*
aching, achy, painful, taut, tight
OPPOSITE supple
4 *The team will face **stiff** competition in the final.*
strong, powerful, tough, difficult
OPPOSITE easy
5 *His **stiff** manner made him hard to talk to.*
unfriendly, cold, formal, awkward, wooden
OPPOSITE relaxed
6 *The judge imposed a **stiff** penalty.*
harsh, severe, strict, hard
OPPOSITE lenient
7 *A **stiff** breeze was blowing.*
strong, brisk, fresh
OPPOSITE gentle

stifle *verb*
1 *We were almost **stifled** by the fumes from the exhaust pipe.*
choke, suffocate, smother
To kill someone by stopping their breathing is to *strangle* or *throttle* them.
2 *She tried to **stifle** a yawn.*
suppress, muffle, hold back, repress, restrain

still *adjective*
1 *The prisoner sat **still** and said nothing.*
motionless, unmoving, stationary, static, inert
2 *It was a beautiful **still** evening.*
calm, peaceful, quiet, tranquil, serene, hushed, silent, noiseless, windless

sting *verb*
*The smoke made our eyes **sting**.*
smart, hurt, prick, prickle, tingle

stingy *adjective(informal)*
*He's too **stingy** to give anyone a birthday card.*
mean, miserly, selfish, uncharitable
(informal) tight-fisted, penny-pinching
OPPOSITE generous

stink *verb*
*The dungeon **stank** of unwashed bodies.*
reek, smell

stink *noun*
*The mouldy cheese gave off a dreadful **stink**.*
odour, stench, reek, bad smell

stir *verb*
1 *Stir the mixture until it is smooth.*
mix, beat, blend, whisk
2 *The giant **stirred** in his sleep.*
move slightly, shift, toss, turn
to stir something up
*The bandits were always **stirring up** trouble.*
arouse, encourage, provoke, set off, trigger, whip up

stir *noun*
*The news caused quite a **stir**.*
fuss, commotion, excitement, hullabaloo

stomach *noun*
*He rolled over and lay on his **stomach**.*
belly, gut, paunch
(informal) tummy

steps

a b c d e f g h i j k l m n o p q r **s** t u v w x y z

The part of the body that contains the stomach is the *abdomen*.

stone *noun*
The columns of the temple were carved from **stone**.
A large lump of stone is a *rock*.
A large rounded stone is a *boulder*.
Small rounded stones are *pebbles*.
A mixture of sand and small stones is *gravel*.
Pebbles on the beach are *shingle*.
Round stones used to pave a path are *cobbles*.

stoop *verb*
We had to **stoop** *to go through the tunnel.*
bend, duck, bow, crouch

stop *verb*
1 *I'll go into town when the rain* **stops**.
end, finish, cease, conclude, terminate
OPPOSITE **start**
2 *Can you* **stop** *talking for a minute?*
give up, cease, suspend, quit, leave off, break off
(*informal*) knock off, pack in
OPPOSITE **continue, resume**
3 *Guards,* **stop** *that man!*
hold, detain, seize, catch, capture, restrain
4 *You can't* **stop** *me from going.*
prevent, obstruct, bar, hinder
5 *How do you* **stop** *this machine?*
turn off, immobilize
6 *The bus will* **stop** *at the school gates.*
come to a stop, halt, pull up, draw up
7 *If you tighten the valve, it will* **stop** *the leak.*
close, plug, seal, block up, bung up

stop *noun*
1 *Everything suddenly came to a* **stop**.
end, finish, conclusion, halt, standstill
2 *They drove down through France, with a short* **stop** *in Paris.*
break, pause, stopover, rest

store *verb*
Squirrels need to **store** *food for the winter.*

save, set aside, stow away, hoard, reserve, stockpile
(*informal*) stash

store *noun*
1 *The building is now used as a grain* **store**.
storeroom, storehouse, repository, vault
A store for food is a *larder* or *pantry*.
A store for weapons is an *armoury* or *arsenal*.
2 *He kept a large* **store** *of wine in the cellar.*
hoard, supply, quantity, stock, stockpile, reserve
3 *He's the manager of the local grocery* **store**.

storm *noun*
1 *Crops were damaged in the heavy* **storms**.
squall, blizzard, gale, thunderstorm, hurricane, typhoon
An old word for storm is *tempest*.
When a storm begins to develop it is *brewing*.
2 *Plans to close the library caused a* **storm** *of protest.*
outburst, outcry, uproar, clamour

storm *verb*
The soldiers **stormed** *the castle.*
charge at, rush at

stormy *adjective*
1 *It was a dark,* **stormy** *night.*
blustery, squally, tempestuous, wild, windy, rough, choppy, gusty, raging
OPPOSITE **calm**
2 *Fighting broke out at the end of a* **stormy** *meeting.*
bad-tempered, quarrelsome, turbulent, violent

stout *adjective*
1 *The doctor was a* **stout** *man with grey hair.*
fat, plump, chubby, dumpy, tubby, portly, stocky, beefy, burly
OPPOSITE **thin**
2 *You will need a pair of* **stout** *walking boots.*
strong, sturdy, tough, robust, sound, substantial
OPPOSITE **weak**
3 *The enemy put up a* **stout** *resistance.*
brave, courageous, spirited, plucky, determined, staunch, resolute, firm
OPPOSITE **cowardly**

straight *adjective*
1 *They walked in a* **straight** *line.*
direct, unswerving

A common simile is *as straight as an arrow*.
OPPOSITE **crooked**
2 *It took a long time to get the room* **straight**.
neat, orderly, tidy
OPPOSITE **untidy**
3 *She found it difficult to get a* **straight** *answer from him.*
honest, plain, frank, straightforward
OPPOSITE **indirect, evasive**

strain *verb*
1 *The dog was* **straining** *at its lead.*
pull, tug, stretch, haul
2 *People were* **straining** *to see what was going on.*
struggle, strive, make an effort, try, attempt
3 *Take it easy and don't* **strain** *yourself.*
weaken, exhaust, wear out, tire out, tax

strain *noun*
The **strain** *of her job was making her ill.*
stress, tension, worry, anxiety, pressure

stranded *adjective*
1 *A whale lay* **stranded** *on the beach.*
run aground, beached, marooned
2 *He was* **stranded** *in London without any money.*
abandoned, deserted, helpless, lost, stuck
(*informal*) high and dry

strange *adjective*
1 *A* **strange** *thing happened this morning.*
funny, odd, peculiar, unusual, abnormal, curious, extraordinary, remarkable, singular, uncommon
OPPOSITE **ordinary, everyday**
2 *Did you hear* **strange** *noises in the night?*
mysterious, puzzling, baffling, mystifying, perplexing, bewildering, inexplicable
3 *The professor showed us his* **strange** *inventions.*
weird, eccentric, peculiar, bizarre
(*informal*) oddball, wacky
4 *I find it hard to get to sleep in a* **strange** *bed.*
unfamiliar, unknown, new, alien
OPPOSITE **familiar**

strangle *verb*
The victim had been **strangled**.
throttle

strap *noun*
The trunk was fastened with a leather **strap**.
belt, band

stray *verb*
Some sheep had **strayed** *onto the road.*

a
b
c
d
e
f
g
h
i
j
k
l
m
n
o
p
q
r
s
t
u
v
w
x
y
z

stretch

wander, drift, roam, rove,
straggle, meander, ramble
streak *noun*
1 *The horse had a white **streak** on
his muzzle.*
band, line, stripe, strip, smear,
stain
2 *There is a **streak** of meanness in
his character.*
element, trace
streak *verb*
1 *Rain had begun to **streak** the
window.*
smear, smudge, stain, line
2 *A group of motorbikes **streaked**
past.*
rush, speed, dash, fly, hurtle,
flash, tear, zoom
stream *noun*
1 *The climbers dipped their feet in
a cool mountain **stream**.*
brook, rivulet
(*Scottish*) burn
2 *The raft was carried along with
the **stream**.*
current, flow, tide
3 *A **stream** of water poured
through the hole.*
cataract, flood, gush, jet, rush,
torrent
4 *The museum had a steady
stream of visitors.*
series, string, line, succession
stream *verb*
*Warm sunlight **streamed** through
the window.*
pour, flow, flood, issue, gush,
spill
strength *noun*
1 *Hercules was said to have
enormous **strength**.*
power, might, muscle, brawn,
toughness, force, vigour
2 *The main **strength** of the team is*

in scoring goals.
strong point, asset, advantage
OPPOSITE **weakness**
strengthen *verb*
1 *Regular exercise **strengthens**
your muscles.*
make stronger, build up,
toughen, harden
2 *Concrete was used to **strengthen**
the tunnel.*
fortify, reinforce, bolster, prop up
stress *noun*
1 *The hospital staff were working
under a lot of **stress**.*
strain, pressure, tension, worry,
anxiety
2 *My piano teacher puts great
stress on the need to practise.*
emphasis, importance, weight
stress *verb*
*She **stressed** the need for absolute
secrecy.*
emphasize, draw attention to,
highlight, underline
stretch *verb*
1 *He **stretched** the rubber band
until it snapped.*
expand, extend, draw out, pull
out, elongate, lengthen
2 *She **stretched** her arms wide.*
extend, open out, spread out
3 *The road **stretched** into the
distance.*
continue, extend
stretch *noun*
1 *He had a two-year **stretch** in the
army.*
spell, period, time, stint
2 *There are often accidents on this
stretch of road.*
section, length, piece
3 *It's a beautiful **stretch** of
countryside.*
area, tract, expanse, sweep

strict *adjective*
1 *The club has **strict** rules about
who can join.*
rigid, inflexible
(*informal*) hard and fast
OPPOSITE **flexible**
2 *The sergeant was known for
being **strict** with his men.*
harsh, severe, stern, firm
OPPOSITE **lenient**
3 *He used the word in its **strict**
scientific sense.*
exact, precise, correct
OPPOSITE **loose**
stride *noun*
*The robot took two **strides**
forward.*
pace, step
strike *verb*
1 *Roy **struck** his head on the low
ceiling.*
bang, bump, hit, knock, thump,
collide with
(*informal*) wallop, whack
2 *The enemy could **strike** again at
any time.*
attack
striking *adjective*
*The most **striking** feature of
the mermaid was her iridescent
tail.*
conspicuous, noticeable,
prominent, remarkable,
memorable, extraordinary,
outstanding, impressive
OPPOSITE **inconspicuous**
string *noun*
1 *She tied some **string** round the
parcel.*
rope, cord, twine
2 *They have received a **string** of
complaints.*
series, succession, chain,
sequence

string *verb*
We **strung** the fairy lights on the Christmas tree.
hang, arrange, thread

strip *verb*
1 Lottie **stripped** the paper off her present.
peel, remove
OPPOSITE cover, wrap
2 He **stripped** and got into the bath.
get undressed, undress
OPPOSITE dress

strip *noun*
In front of the house was a narrow **strip** of grass.
band, length, ribbon, piece, bit

stripe *noun*
The tablecloth was white with blue **stripes**.
line, strip, band, bar

stroke *noun*
1 He split the log with a single **stroke**.
blow, hit, action, movement, effort
2 She added a few quick pencil **strokes** to her drawing.
line, mark

stroke *verb*
Jess was curled up on the sofa, **stroking** the cat.
pat, caress, rub, touch, fondle, pet

stroll *verb*
The children **strolled** quietly home.
walk slowly, amble, saunter

strong *adjective*
1 Crocodiles have **strong** jaws
powerful, muscular, mighty, well-built, beefy, brawny, burly, strapping
OPPOSITE weak, puny
2 The tent is made from **strong** material.
robust, sturdy, tough, hard-wearing, durable, stout, substantial
OPPOSITE thin, flimsy
3 The fugitive was caught in the **strong** beam of a searchlight.
bright, brilliant, dazzling, glaring
OPPOSITE weak, pale
4 I smelt the **strong** aroma of roasting coffee.
overpowering, pronounced, pungent, piquant
OPPOSITE faint, slight
5 The police have **strong** evidence of his guilt.
convincing, persuasive, effective, sound, solid, valid
OPPOSITE weak, feeble, flimsy

6 Zelda takes a **strong** interest in fashion.
enthusiastic, keen, passionate, fervent, avid, zealous
OPPOSITE slight

struggle *verb*
1 The captives **struggled** to get free.
strain, strive, wrestle, writhe about, tussle, fight, battle
2 The expedition had to **struggle** through a snowstorm.
stagger, stumble, flounder, labour

struggle *noun*
The rebels surrendered without a **struggle**.
fight, battle, combat, clash, contest

stubborn *adjective*
She's too **stubborn** to admit that she was wrong.
obstinate, pig-headed, strong-willed, uncooperative, inflexible, wilful
A common simile is *as stubborn as a mule*.
OPPOSITE compliant

stuck-up *adjective (informal)*
Nobody likes Ernest—he's so **stuck-up**.
arrogant, conceited, haughty, proud, snobbish, superior (informal) snooty, toffee-nosed
OPPOSITE humble

study *verb*
1 He went to university to **study** medicine.
learn about, read, research into
2 The spy **studied** the document carefully.
examine, inspect, analyse, investigate, look closely at, scrutinize, survey
3 She has to **study** for her exams.
revise, cram (informal) swot

stuff *noun*
1 What's that sticky **stuff** on the carpet?
matter, substance
2 You can put your **stuff** in one of the lockers.
belongings, possessions, things, gear

stuff *verb*
1 We managed to **stuff** everything into the boot of the car.
pack, push, shove, squeeze, ram, compress, force, cram, jam
2 The cushions are **stuffed** with foam rubber.
fill, pad

stuffy *adjective*
1 Open a window—it's **stuffy** in here.

airless, close, muggy, humid, stifling, musty, unventilated
OPPOSITE airy
2 I found the book a bit **stuffy**.
boring, dull, dreary, pompous, stodgy
OPPOSITE lively

stumble *verb*
1 He **stumbled** on a tree root and twisted his ankle.
trip, stagger, totter, flounder, lurch
2 The actress **stumbled** over her words.
stammer, stutter, falter, hesitate
to stumble across something
I **stumbled across** some old photos.
come across, encounter, find, unearth, discover

stun *verb*
1 The pilot was alive but **stunned**.
daze, knock out, knock senseless, make unconscious
2 The whole town was **stunned** by the news.
amaze, astonish, astound, shock, stagger, stupefy, bewilder, dumbfound

stupid *adjective*
1 Trolls are often very **stupid**.
foolish, unintelligent, dense, dim, dim-witted, brainless, dumb, slow, thick, feeble-minded, half-witted, simple, simple-minded, dopey, dull
2 It would be **stupid** to go snowboarding without a helmet.
senseless, mindless, idiotic, unwise, foolhardy, silly, daft, crazy, mad
OPPOSITE intelligent

sturdy *adjective*
1 Shetland ponies are short and **sturdy**.
stocky, strong, robust, athletic, brawny, burly, healthy, hefty, husky, muscular, powerful, vigorous, well-built
OPPOSITE weak
2 She bought some **sturdy** walking boots.
durable, solid, sound, substantial, tough, well made
OPPOSITE flimsy

stutter *verb*
He tends to **stutter** when he's nervous.
stammer, stumble, falter

style *noun*
1 I don't like that **style** of jeans.
design, pattern, fashion
2 The book is written in an informal **style**.
manner, tone, way, wording
3 The actress always dresses with great **style**.
elegance, stylishness, taste, sophistication

strong

subject *noun*
1 *Do you have any strong views on the subject?*
matter, issue, question, point, theme, topic
2 *Her passport shows that she is a British subject.*
citizen, national

subtle *adjective*
1 *There was a subtle smell of roses in the air.*
faint, slight, mild, delicate
2 *His jokes are too subtle for most people.*
ingenious, sophisticated
3 *I tried to give her a subtle hint.*
gentle, tactful, indirect

subtract *verb*
If you subtract 5 from 20, you will have 15 left.
take away, deduct, remove
OPPOSITE **add**

succeed *verb*
1 *You have to work hard if you want to succeed.*
be successful, do well, prosper, flourish, thrive
(*informal*) make it
2 *Everyone hoped that the plan would succeed.*
be effective, produce results, work
(*informal*) catch on
OPPOSITE **fail**
3 *Edward VII succeeded Queen Victoria.*
come after, follow, take over from, replace

success *noun*
1 *She talked about her success as an actress.*
achievement, attainment, fame
2 *They congratulated the team on their success.*
victory, win, triumph
3 *The success of the mission depends on the astronauts.*
effectiveness, successful outcome, completion

successful *adjective*
1 *She owns a very successful chain of restaurants.*
thriving, flourishing, booming, prosperous, profitable, popular
2 *The supporters cheered the successful team.*
winning, victorious, triumphant
OPPOSITE **unsuccessful**

suck *verb*
to suck something up
A sponge will suck up water.
soak up, draw up, absorb

sudden *adjective*
1 *Maria felt a sudden urge to burst into song.*
unexpected, unforeseen, impulsive, rash, quick
OPPOSITE **expected**

2 *The bus came to a sudden halt.*
abrupt, sharp, swift
OPPOSITE **gradual**

suffer *verb*
1 *He suffers terribly with his back.*
feel pain, hurt
2 *He will suffer for his crime.*
be punished, pay
3 *The home team suffered a humiliating defeat.*
experience, undergo, go through, endure, stand, bear, tolerate

suffocate *verb*
The firefighters were nearly suffocated by the fumes.
choke, stifle
To stop someone's breathing by squeezing their throat is to *strangle* or *throttle* them.
To stop someone's breathing by covering their nose and mouth is to *smother* them.

suggest *verb*
1 *Mum suggested going to the zoo.*
propose, advise, advocate, recommend
2 *Her comments suggest that she's not happy.*
imply, hint, indicate, signal

suggestion *noun*
They didn't like his suggestion.
proposal, plan, idea, proposition, recommendation

suit *verb*
1 *Would it suit you to stay here overnight?*
be convenient for, be suitable for, please, satisfy
OPPOSITE **displease**
2 *His new haircut doesn't suit him.*
look good on, become, flatter

suitable *adjective*
1 *Please wear clothes suitable for wet weather.*
appropriate, apt, fitting, suited (to), proper, right
OPPOSITE **unsuitable**
2 *Is this a suitable time to have a chat?*
convenient, acceptable, satisfactory
OPPOSITE **inconvenient**

sulk *verb*
I was sulking because I wasn't allowed to play outside.
be sullen, mope, brood, pout

sulky *adjective*
Ron had turned into a sulky teenager.
moody, sullen, brooding, moping, mopey

summarize *verb*
Can you summarize the main points of the story?
sum up, outline, review
(*informal*) recap

summary *noun*
We each wrote a summary of the poem.
synopsis, précis, outline

summon *verb*
The king summoned his knights from far and wide.
call, send for, order to come, bid to come
To ask someone politely to come is to *invite* them.

sunny *adjective*
It was a beautiful sunny day.
fine, clear, cloudless
OPPOSITE **cloudy**

sunrise *noun*
The magic spell wears off at sunrise.
dawn, daybreak
OPPOSITE **sunset**

sunset *noun*
They arranged to meet in the churchyard at sunset.
sundown, dusk, twilight, evening, nightfall
OPPOSITE **sunrise**

superb *adjective*
Brazil scored another superb goal.
excellent, outstanding, exceptional, remarkable, impressive, magnificent, marvellous, splendid, tremendous, wonderful
(*informal*) brilliant, fantastic, terrific, fabulous, sensational, super

supervise *verb*
Children must be supervised by an adult in the park.
oversee, superintend, watch over, be in charge of, be responsible for, direct, manage
To supervise candidates in an exam is to *invigilate*.

supple *adjective*
The moccasins are made of supple leather.
flexible, pliable, soft
OPPOSITE **stiff, rigid**

supply *verb*
The art shop can supply you with brushes and paints.
provide, equip, furnish

supply *noun*
They had a good supply of fuel for the winter.
quantity, stock, store, reserve
supplies
We bought supplies for the camping trip.
provisions, stores, rations, food, necessities

support *noun*
1 *She thanked them for their support.*
assistance, backing, aid, cooperation, encouragement, help
A support for a shelf is a *bracket*.

a b c d e f g h i j k l m n o p q r **s** t u v w x y z

a
b
c
d
e
f
g
h
i
j
k
l
m
n
o
p
q
r
s
t
u
v
w
x
y
z

A support built against a wall is
a *buttress*.
A support for someone with an
injured leg is a *crutch*.
A bar of wood or metal
supporting a framework is a *strut*.
A support put under a board to
make a table is a *trestle*.
*2 The cinema was reopened
with* **support** *from local
businesses.*
donations, contributions,
sponsorship

support *verb*
1 The rope couldn't **support** *his
weight.*
bear, carry, stand, hold up
2 The beams **support** *the
roof.*
prop up, strengthen, reinforce
3 His friends **supported** *him
when he was in trouble.*
aid, assist, help, back,
encourage, stand by, stand up
for, rally round
4 She had to work to **support**
her family.
maintain, keep, provide for
5 He **supports** *several local
charities.*
donate to, contribute to,
give to
6 Which team did you **support**
in the World Cup?
be a supporter of, follow

supporter *noun*
1 The home **supporters** *cheered
their team.*
fan, follower
2 She is a well-known **supporter**
of animal rights.
champion, advocate, backer,
defender

suppose *verb*
1 I **suppose** *you want to borrow
some money.*
expect, presume, assume,
guess, believe, think
*2 Suppose a spaceship landed
in your garden!*
imagine, pretend, fancy
**to be supposed to do
something**
The bus is **supposed** *to leave
at 9 o'clock.*
be meant to, be due to, be
expected to, ought to

sure *adjective*
1 I'm **sure** *that I'm
right.*
certain, convinced,
confident, definite,
positive
OPPOSITE unsure,
uncertain
2 He's **sure** *to phone
tonight.*
bound, certain
OPPOSITE unlikely

surface *noun*
1 The **surface** *of Mars is barren
and rocky.*
exterior, outside
The surface of something may
be covered with a *crust* or *shell*
or *skin*.
A thin surface of expensive wood
on furniture is a *veneer*.
OPPOSITE centre
*2 A dice has dots on each
surface.*
face, side
OPPOSITE inside
3 Oil floated on the **surface**
of the water.
top
OPPOSITE bottom

surge *verb*
1 Massive waves **surged** *around
the tiny raft.*
rise, roll, swirl, heave,
billow
2 The crowd **surged** *forward.*
rush, push, sweep

surprise *noun*
*The news that Sara was married
came as a* **surprise.***
amazement, astonishment,
revelation, shock, wonder
(*informal*) bombshell

surprise *verb*
1 I was **surprised** *by how well
she could sing.*
amaze, astonish, astound,
stagger, startle, stun, take
aback, take by surprise,
dumbfound
(*informal*) bowl over,
flabbergast
2 He **surprised** *the burglars
as they came through the
window.*
discover, come upon, catch
unawares, catch offguard,
catch red-handed

surprised *adjective*

surprising *adjective*
There are a **surprising** *number
of errors in the book.*
amazing, astonishing,
astounding, extraordinary,
remarkable, incredible,
staggering, startling, stunning,
unexpected
OPPOSITE predictable

surface

SOMEONE WHO *feels surprised*
MIGHT
have eyes bulging out of their
head, have eyes on the end of
stalks, jump out of their skin,
stare wide-eyed
SOMETHING WHICH *surprises you*
MIGHT
knock you for six, knock your
socks off, knock you sideways,
make your eyes pop

surrender *verb*
*1 The band of outlaws refused to
surrender.*
admit defeat, give in, yield,
submit, capitulate
2 Please **surrender** *your ticket
to the driver.*
give, hand over

surround *verb*
1 The garden was **surrounded**
by a stone wall.
enclose, fence in, wall in
2 The pack of wolves **surrounded**
its prey.
encircle, ring, hem in, besiege

surroundings *plural noun*
*The hotel is set in very pleasant
surroundings.*
setting, location, environment

survey *noun*
They did a **survey** *of local leisure
facilities.*
review, investigation, study
A survey to count the
population of an area is
a *census*.

survey *verb*
1 You can **survey** *the whole
valley from the top of the tower.*
view, look over, look at,
observe
2 They **surveyed** *the damage
done by the storm.*
inspect, examine, scrutinize,
study

survive *verb*
1 He managed to **survive** *alone on
the island for six months.*
stay alive, last, live, keep going,
carry on, continue
OPPOSITE die
2 Will the birds **survive** *this cold
weather?*
endure, withstand, live through,
weather

suspect *verb*
1 The police **suspected** *his
motives.*
doubt, mistrust, have suspicions
about
2 I **suspect** *that the shop will be
closed on Sundays.*
expect, imagine, presume, guess,
sense, fancy

suspend verb
1 The meeting was **suspended** until the next day.
adjourn, break off, discontinue, interrupt
2 For the party, we **suspended** balloons from the ceiling.
hang, dangle, swing

suspense noun
The film was a thriller, full of action and **suspense**.
tension, uncertainty, anticipation, expectancy, drama, excitement

suspicion noun
I have a **suspicion** that he is lying.
feeling, hunch, inkling, intuition, impression

suspicious adjective
1 There is something about him which makes me **suspicious**.
doubtful, distrustful, mistrustful, unsure, uneasy, wary
OPPOSITE **trusting**
2 What do you make of his **suspicious** behaviour?
questionable, suspect, dubious, shady
(informal) fishy

swagger verb
The lead actor **swaggered** about on stage.
strut, parade

swarm

swallow verb
The bread was so dry that it was hard to **swallow**.
gulp down
to swallow something up
As it climbed higher, the rocket was **swallowed up** by the clouds.
envelop, engulf, cover over, absorb

swamp verb
A huge wave threatened to **swamp** the ship.
overwhelm, engulf, inundate, flood, submerge

swamp noun
Much of the land near the coast is **swamp**.
marsh, bog, mire, fen, quicksand, quagmire

swap or **swop** verb
We **swapped** seats so I could sit in the aisle.
change, exchange, switch, substitute

swarm verb
Hundreds of people **swarmed** around the film star.
crowd, flock
to swarm with
The garden is **swarming** with ants.
be overrun by, be crawling with, be infested with, teem with

sway verb
The tall grass **swayed** in the breeze.
wave, swing, rock, bend, lean

swear verb
1 The knight **swore** that he would protect the unicorn.
pledge, promise, vow, give your word, take an oath
2 The player **swore** when he bashed his knee.
curse

sweat verb
He **sweats** a lot in hot weather.
perspire

sweep verb
1 She **swept** the floor with an old broom.
brush, clean, dust
2 The bus **swept** past.
shoot, speed, zoom

sweet adjective
1 The pudding is too **sweet** for me.
sickly, sugary, sweetened, syrupy
OPPOSITE **acid** or **bitter** or **savoury**
2 The **sweet** smell of roses filled the room.
fragrant, pleasant
OPPOSITE **foul**
3 Fergus heard the **sweet** sound of a harp.
melodious, pleasant, soothing, tuneful
OPPOSITE **ugly**
4 What a **sweet** little cottage!
attractive, charming, dear, lovely, pretty, quaint
OPPOSITE **unattractive**

swerve verb
The car **swerved** to avoid a hedgehog.
turn aside, veer, dodge, swing

swift adjective
1 They set off at a **swift** pace.
fast, quick, rapid, speedy, brisk, lively
2 She received a **swift** reply to her email.
quick, fast, immediate, instant, prompt, speedy, snappy

swing verb
1 A glass chandelier **swung** from the ceiling.
hang, dangle, sway, flap, wave about
2 She **swung** round when I called her name.
turn, twist, veer, swerve

swirl verb
Clouds of dust **swirled** up in the desert wind.
spin, twirl, whirl, churn

switch verb
1 Please remember to **switch** off the light.
turn

2 The teams will **switch** ends at half-time.
change, swap, exchange, shift

swoop verb
The owl **swooped** and caught the mouse.
dive, drop, plunge, plummet, descend, pounce

symbol noun
The dove is a **symbol** of peace.
sign, emblem, image
The symbols we use in writing are **characters** or **letters**.
The symbols used in ancient Egyptian writing were **hieroglyphics**.
The symbol of a club or school is their **badge**.
The symbol of a firm or organization is their **logo**.

symbol

sympathetic adjective
They were **sympathetic** when my mother was ill.
understanding, compassionate, concerned, caring, comforting, kind, supportive
OPPOSITE **unsympathetic**

sympathize verb
to sympathize with
We **sympathized with** those who had lost their homes.
be sympathetic towards, be sorry for, feel for, commiserate with

sympathy noun
Did you feel any **sympathy** for the characters in the story?
understanding, compassion, pity, fellow-feeling, tenderness

system noun
1 The city has an archaic transport **system**.
organization, structure, network, framework
(informal) set-up
2 Do you understand the new cataloguing **system**?
procedure, process, scheme, arrangement, method, routine

Tt

tactful *adjective*
*She gave him a **tactful** reminder about her birthday.*
subtle, discreet, diplomatic, sensitive, thoughtful
OPPOSITE **tactless**

take *verb*
1 *Naomi **took** her sister's hand.*
clutch, clasp, take hold of, grasp, grip, seize, snatch, grab
2 *The soldiers **took** many prisoners.*
catch, capture, seize, detain
3 *Someone has **taken** my pen.*
steal, remove, make off with
(*informal*) swipe, pinch
4 *The guide will **take** you to the edge of the forest.*
conduct, escort, lead, accompany
5 *The bus **took** us right to the station.*
bring, carry, convey, transport
6 *It'll **take** two people to lift that table.*
need, require
7 *The caravan can **take** six people.*
hold, contain, accommodate, have room for
8 *He couldn't **take** the heat of the midday sun.*
bear, put up with, stand, endure, tolerate, suffer, stomach
9 *He **took** their names and addresses.*
make a note of, record, write down
10 *The magician asked me to **take** a card.*
pick, choose, select
11 *Take 2 from 8 and you get 6.*
subtract, take away, deduct

tame

talent *noun*
*She has a great **talent** for music.*
gift, ability, aptitude, skill, flair, knack
Unusually great talent is *genius*.
talented *adjective*
*He's a very **talented** dancer.*
gifted, able, accomplished,
capable, skilled, skilful, clever, brilliant
If you are talented in several ways, you are *versatile*.

talk *verb*
1 *Doug was trying to teach his parrot to **talk**.*
speak, say things, communicate, express yourself
2 *The two old friends had a lot to **talk** about.*
discuss, converse, chat, chatter, gossip
(*informal*) natter
talk *noun*
1 *I need to have a **talk** with you soon.*
conversation, discussion, chat
The talk between characters in a story is the *dialogue*.
2 *There is a **talk** about Egyptian art at lunchtime.*
lecture, presentation, speech, address
A talk in church is a *sermon*.
talkative *adjective*
*You're not very **talkative** this morning.*
chatty, communicative, vocal, forthcoming, articulate
An informal name for a talkative person is a *chatterbox*.
tall *adjective*
1 *Jasmine is **tall** for her age.*
big
OPPOSITE **short**
2 *Singapore has many **tall** buildings.*
high, lofty, towering, soaring, giant
Buildings with many floors are *high*-rise or *multi-storey* buildings.
OPPOSITE **low**
tame *adjective*
1 *The guinea pigs are **tame** and used to people.*
domesticated, broken in, docile, gentle, obedient, manageable
OPPOSITE **wild**
2 *The film seems very **tame** nowadays.*
dull, boring, tedious, bland, unexciting, uninteresting
OPPOSITE **exciting**
tamper *verb*
to tamper with something
*Someone has been **tampering** with the lock.*
meddle with, tinker with, fiddle about with, interfere with
tap *verb*
*Someone **tapped** three times on the door.*
knock, rap, strike

tape *noun*
*The stack of old letters was tied up with **tape**.*
ribbon, braid, binding
target *noun*
1 *Her **target** was to swim thirty lengths.*
goal, aim, objective, intention, purpose, hope, ambition
2 *She was the **target** of his jokes.*
object, victim, butt
task *noun*
1 *The robot was given a number of **tasks** to do.*
job, chore, exercise, errand
2 *The soldiers' **task** was to capture the hill.*
assignment, mission, duty, undertaking
taste *verb*
1 *Taste the soup to see if it needs salt.*
sample, try, test, sip
2 *The curry **tastes** quite mild.*
taste *noun*
1 *I love the **taste** of ginger.*
flavour
2 *May I have a **taste** of the cheese?*
mouthful, bite, morsel, nibble, bit, piece, sample
3 *Her **taste** in clothes is a bit odd.*
choice, preference, discrimination, judgement
tasteless *adjective*
1 *He apologized for making a **tasteless** remark.*
crude, tactless, indelicate, inappropriate
OPPOSITE **tasteful**
2 *The sprouts were overcooked and **tasteless**.*
flavourless, bland, insipid
OPPOSITE **flavourful**
tasty *adjective*
*That pie was very **tasty**.*
delicious, appetizing
OPPOSITE **unappetizing**
taunt *verb*
*The gladiator **taunted** his opponent.*
barrack, insult, jeer at, laugh at, make fun of, mock, ridicule, sneer at
taut *adjective*
*Make sure the rope is **taut**.*
tight, tense, stretched
OPPOSITE **slack**
teach *verb*
*My dad is **teaching** me to play the guitar.*

taut

a
b
c
d
e
f
g
h
i
j
k
l
m
n
o
p
q
r
s
t
y
z

educate, inform, instruct
To teach people to play a sport
is to *coach* or *train* them.
To teach one person at a time or
a small group is to *tutor* them.

teacher *noun*
We have a new ballet **teacher**.
tutor, instructor, trainer
Someone who teaches you to
play a sport is a *coach*.
In the past, a woman who
taught children in a private
household was a *governess*.

team *noun*
*She's been picked for the junior
hockey* **team**.
side

tear *verb*
1 *The tree branch* **tore** *a hole in
our kite.*
rip, snag, gash, shred, split, slit
2 *He* **tore** *home to watch his
favourite TV programme.*
run, rush, dash, hurry, race,
sprint, speed

tear *noun*
There was a **tear** *in one of the
sails.*
cut, rip, rent, split, gash, hole,
opening, slit, gap

tease *verb*
They **teased** *him about his new
haircut.*
taunt, make fun of, poke fun at,
mock, ridicule, laugh at

tell *verb*
1 **Tell** *us what you can see.*
describe, explain, reveal, report,
say, state
2 **Tell** *me when you are ready.*
let you know, inform, notify,
announce, communicate
3 *He* **told** *them to stop making so
much noise.*
order, command, direct, instruct
4 *We* **told** *each other scary ghost
stories.*
narrate, relate
5 *He* **told** *me he would buy the
tickets.*
assure, promise
6 *She couldn't* **tell** *where she was
in the dark.*
make out, recognize, identify,
perceive
7 *Can you* **tell** *one twin from the
other?*

distinguish, separate
to tell someone off
She **told them off** *for being late.*
scold, reprimand, reproach
(*informal*) tick off

temper *noun*
1 *Mr Black had been in a bad
temper all morning.*
mood, humour, state of mind
2 *The chef is always flying into a
temper.*
rage, fury, fit of anger, tantrum
to lose your temper
When she **loses her temper**, *her
cheeks go red.*
get angry, get annoyed, fly into
a rage

temporary *adjective*
They made a **temporary** *shelter
for the night.*
makeshift, provisional
OPPOSITE permanent

tempt *verb*
Can I **tempt** *you to have more
pudding?*
coax, entice, persuade, attract
To tempt someone by offering
them money is to *bribe* them.
To tempt an animal into a trap is
to *lure* it.

tender *adjective*
1 *Frost may damage* **tender**
plants.
delicate, fragile
OPPOSITE hardy, strong
2 *Cook the meat slowly until it
is* **tender**.
soft, succulent, juicy
OPPOSITE tough
3 *The bruise is still* **tender**.
painful, sensitive, sore
4 *She gave him a* **tender** *smile.*
affectionate, kind, loving,
caring, warm-hearted,
compassionate, sympathetic,
fond
OPPOSITE uncaring

tense *adjective*
1 *The muscles in her shoulders
were* **tense**.
taut, tight, strained, stretched
2 *The crowd were* **tense** *as they
waited to hear the results.*
anxious, nervous, apprehensive,
edgy, on edge, fidgety, jumpy,
jittery
(*informal*) uptight
3 *It was a* **tense** *moment for all
of us.*

nerve-racking, stressful,
worrying
OPPOSITE relaxed

tension *noun*
The **tension** *of waiting was almost
unbearable.*
stress, strain, anxiety,
nervousness, suspense, worry

terrible *adjective*
*We heard there had been a
terrible accident.*
awful, dreadful, horrible,
appalling, shocking, ghastly,
horrific, frightful

terrific *adjective* (*informal*)
1 *The footprint of the yeti was a
terrific size.*
big, huge, immense, enormous,
giant, gigantic, colossal,
massive
2 *She's a* **terrific** *tennis player.*
excellent, first-class, first-rate,
superb, marvellous, wonderful
(*informal*) brilliant, fantastic,
fabulous

terrify *verb*
The dogs were **terrified** *by the
thunder.*
frighten, scare, startle, alarm,
panic, horrify, petrify

terror *noun*
Her eyes filled with **terror** *as she
described the ghost.*
fear, fright, horror, panic, alarm,
dread

test *noun*
How did you do in the maths **test**?
exam, examination, assessment,
appraisal, evaluation
A set of questions you answer
for fun is a *quiz*.
A test for a job as an actor or
singer is an *audition*.
A test to find the truth about
something is an *experiment* or
trial.

test *verb*
1 *I made an appointment to have
my eyes* **tested**.
examine, check, evaluate,
assess, screen
2 *He is* **testing** *a new formula for
invisible ink.*
experiment with, try out, trial

thankful *adjective*
to be thankful for something
The travellers were **thankful for**
her help.
grateful for, appreciative of,
pleased about, relieved about
OPPOSITE ungrateful

tear

thanks *plural noun*
*She sent them a card to show her **thanks**.*
gratitude, appreciation

theme *noun*
*What is the **theme** of the poem?*
subject, topic, idea, gist, argument

theory *noun*
1 *The detective has a **theory** about the case.*
explanation, hypothesis, view, belief, idea, notion, suggestion
2 *She bought a book about musical **theory**.*
laws, principles, rules

thick *adjective*
1 *The Roman wall was about 2 metres **thick**.*
thick
wide, broad
OPPOSITE intelligent
2 *The cabin was made from **thick** logs of wood.*
stout, chunky, heavy, solid, substantial
OPPOSITE thin, slender
OPPOSITE intelligent
3 *The explorers hacked their way through the **thick** jungle.*
dense, close, compact
OPPOSITE intelligent
4 *His boots got stuck in a **thick** layer of mud.*
deep, heavy
OPPOSITE thin, shallow
OPPOSITE intelligent
5 *The guide spoke with a **thick** Polish accent.*
heavy, noticeable
OPPOSITE slight
OPPOSITE intelligent
6 *(informal) Fortunately, the giant was rather **thick**.*
stupid, brainless, foolish
OPPOSITE intelligent

thief *noun*
*The police managed to catch the **thief**.*
robber
Someone who steals from people's homes is a **burglar** or **housebreaker**.
Someone who steals from people in the street is a **pickpocket**.
Someone who steals from shops is a **shoplifter**.
Someone who used to steal from travellers was a **highwayman**.

thin *adjective*
1 *The prisoners were dreadfully **thin**.*
lean, skinny, bony, gaunt, spare, slight, underweight
Someone who is thin and tall is **lanky**.
thin

Someone who is thin but strong is **wiry**.
Someone who is thin but attractive is **slim** or **slender**.
Thin arms or legs are **spindly**.
A common simile is *as thin as a rake*.
OPPOSITE fat
2 *The fairy wore a **thin** cloak of spider's silk.*
fine, light, delicate, flimsy, sheer, wispy
A thin line is a *fine* or *narrow* line.
A thin book is a *slim* book.
OPPOSITE thick
3 *The icing should be **thin** enough to spread.*
runny, watery
OPPOSITE thick

thing *noun*
1 *What's that green **thing** on the floor?*
item, object, article
2 *We had a lot of **things** to talk about.*
matter, affair, detail, point, factor
3 *A lot of **things** had happened since we spoke.*
event, happening, occurrence, incident
4 *I have only one **thing** left to do.*
job, task, act, action
things
*Put your **things** in one of the lockers.*
belongings, possessions, stuff, equipment, gear

think *verb*
1 ***Think** before you do anything rash.*
consider, contemplate, reflect, deliberate, reason
To think hard about something is to *concentrate* on it.
To think quietly and deeply about something is to *meditate*.
To keep thinking anxiously about something is to *brood* on it.
2 *Do you **think** this is a good idea?*
believe, feel, consider, judge, conclude
3 *What do you **think** this ring is worth?*
reckon, suppose, imagine, estimate, guess, expect
to think about something
*I need some more time to **think** about it.*
consider, reflect on, ponder, muse on, mull over
to think something up
*They **thought up** a good plan.*
invent, make up, conceive, concoct, devise

thirsty *adjective*
*They were **thirsty** after their long walk.*
dry, parched
If someone is ill through lack of fluids, they are *dehydrated*.

thorough *adjective*
1 *The doctor gave him a **thorough** examination.*
comprehensive, full, rigorous, careful, methodical, systematic, meticulous, painstaking, conscientious
OPPOSITE superficial
2 *He's made a **thorough** mess of things!*
complete, total, utter, absolute, downright

thought *noun*
1 *She gave a lot of **thought** to the problem.*
consideration, deliberation, study
2 *The detective spent some time in **thought**.*
thinking, contemplation, reflection, meditation
3 *What are your **thoughts** on modern art?*
opinion, belief, idea, notion, conclusion

thoughtful *adjective*
1 *Mr Levi had a **thoughtful** expression on his face.*
pensive, reflective, absorbed, preoccupied
OPPOSITE blank, vacant
2 *She added some **thoughtful** comments in the margin.*
well-thought-out, careful, conscientious, thorough
OPPOSITE careless
3 *It was very **thoughtful** of you to visit me in hospital.*
caring, considerate, kind, friendly, good-natured, unselfish
OPPOSITE thoughtless

thoughtless *adjective*
*It was **thoughtless** of him to mention her dead husband.*
inconsiderate, insensitive, uncaring, unthinking, negligent, ill-considered, rash
OPPOSITE thoughtful

thrash *verb*
1 *The rider **thrashed** and spurred his horse to go faster.*
hit, beat, whip, flog
(informal) whack, wallop
2 *The crocodile **thrashed** its tail in the mud.*
swish, flail, jerk, toss
3 *(informal) The visitors **thrashed** the home side 6–0.*
beat, defeat, trounce

threat *noun*
1 *She made a **threat** about phoning the police.*
warning

2 *Earthquakes are a constant* **threat** *in California.*
danger, menace, hazard, risk

threaten *verb*
1 *The bandits* **threatened** *him when he tried to escape.*
make threats against, menace, intimidate, terrorize, bully, browbeat
2 *The forecast* **threatened** *rain.*
warn of
3 *Wild tigers are* **threatened** *with extinction.*
endanger, put at risk

thrill *noun*
Kim loves the **thrill** *of rock climbing.*
adventure, excitement, sensation, tingle
(*slang*) buzz, kick

thrill *verb*
The thought of seeing a real shark **thrilled** *him no end.*
excite, exhilerate, electrify, rouse, stir, stimulate
OPPOSITE bore

thrilled *adjective*
I was **thrilled** *to be invited to the wedding.*
delighted, pleased, excited, overjoyed, ecstatic

throb *verb*
She could feel the blood **throbbing** *through her veins.*
beat, pound, pulse, pulsate

throw *verb*
1 *I* **threw** *some bread into the pond for the ducks.*
fling, cast, pitch, sling, toss
(*slang*) bung, chuck
To deliver the ball in cricket or rounders is to **bowl**.
To throw the shot in athletics is to **put** the shot.
To throw something high in the air is to **lob** it.
To throw something heavy is to **heave** it.
To throw something with great force is to **hurl** it.
If someone throws a lot of things at you, they **pelt** you
2 *The horse* **threw** *its rider.*

throw off, shake off, dislodge
to throw away
We **threw away** *a pile of old junk.*
get rid of, dispose of, discard, scrap
(*informal*) dump, ditch

thrust *verb*
1 *Drew* **thrust** *his hands into his pockets.*
push, force, shove
2 *The bandit* **thrust** *at him with a dagger.*
lunge, jab, prod, stab, poke

thump *verb*
'Silence!' he rasped, **thumping** *his fist on the table.*
bang, bash, pound, hit, strike, knock, rap
(*informal*) whack, wham

tidy *adjective*
Mr Rackham likes to keep his office **tidy**.
neat, orderly, uncluttered, trim, smart, spruce, straight
OPPOSITE untidy

tie *verb*
1 *Zoe* **tied** *a pink ribbon round the parcel.*
bind, fasten, hitch, knot, loop, secure
To tie up a boat is to **moor** it.
To tie up an animal is to **tether** it.
OPPOSITE untie
2 *The two teams are still* **tied**.
be equal, be level, draw

tight *adjective*
1 *The lid was too* **tight** *for him to unscrew.*
firm, fast, secure
If it is so tight that air cannot get through, it is **airtight**.
If it is so tight that water cannot get through, it is **watertight**.
OPPOSITE loose
2 *They squeezed into the* **tight** *space.*
cramped, compact, small, narrow, poky, snug
OPPOSITE spacious
3 *Make sure that the ropes are* **tight**.
taut, tense, stretched, rigid
A common simile is *as tight as a drum*.
OPPOSITE slack

tighten *verb*
1 *She* **tightened** *her grip on his hand.*
increase, strengthen, tense, stiffen
2 *You need to* **tighten** *the guy ropes.*
make taut, pull tighter, stretch
3 *He tried to* **tighten** *the screw.*
make tighter, screw up
OPPOSITE loosen

tilt *verb*
The caravan **tilted** *to one side.*
lean, incline, tip, slant, slope, angle

When a ship tilts to one side, it **lists**.

time *noun*
1 *Is this a convenient* **time** *to talk?*
moment, occasion, opportunity
2 *Autumn is my favourite* **time** *of the year.*
phase, season
3 *He spent a short* **time** *living in China.*
period, while, term, spell, stretch
4 *Shakespeare lived in the* **time** *of Elizabeth I.*
era, age, days, epoch, period
5 *Please try to keep* **time** *with the music.*
tempo, beat, rhythm
on time
Please try to be **on time**.
punctual, prompt

time

timid *adjective*
At first, the mermaid was too **timid** *to say anything.*
shy, bashful, modest, nervous, fearful, shrinking, retiring, sheepish
A common simile is *as timid as a mouse*.
OPPOSITE brave, confident

tiny *adjective*
The ladybird was so **tiny** *that you could hardly see it.*
little, minute, miniature, microscopic, minuscule
(*informal*) teeny, titchy
OPPOSITE big, large

tip *noun*
1 *The* **tip** *of his nose felt cold.*
end, point
The tip of an ink pen is the **nib**.
2 *The* **tip** *of the mountain was covered in snow.*
cap, peak, top, summit, pinnacle, crown
3 *He gave them some useful* **tips** *on first aid.*
hint, piece of advice, suggestion, clue, pointer
4 *They took a load of rubbish to the* **tip**.
dump, rubbish heap

thrill

tip *verb*
1 *The caravan **tipped** to one side.*
lean, tilt, incline, slope, slant
When a ship tips slightly to one
side, it **lists**.
When a ship tips right over, it
capsizes.
2 *Sophie **tipped** the box of crayons
onto the table.*
empty, turn out, dump, unload
to tip over
*He **tipped** the milk jug **over** by
accident.*
knock over, overturn, topple,
upset

tired *adjective*
*Have a lie down if you're **tired**.*
exhausted, fatigued, weary,
worn out, listless, sleepy,
drowsy
(*informal*) all in
to be tired of something
*I'm **tired of** watching TV.*
bored with, fed up with, sick of
If you are not interested in
anything, you are **apathetic**.

title *noun*
1 *She couldn't think of a **title** for
the story.*
name, heading
The title above a newspaper
story is a **headline**.
A title or brief description next to
a picture is a **caption**.
2 *The form asks you to fill in your
name and **title**.*
form of address, designation,
rank
The ordinary title used before a
man's name is **Mr**.
The ordinary title used before a
woman's name is **Miss** or
Mrs or **Ms**.
A polite way to address someone
whose name you don't know is
sir or **madam**.

tolerant *adjective*
*Molly was very **tolerant** towards
other people.*
understanding, easygoing, open-
minded, sympathetic, charitable,
forgiving, lenient, indulgent,
long-suffering
OPPOSITE intolerant

tolerate *verb*
1 *He won't **tolerate** sloppy
writing.*
accept, permit, put up with
2 *Cactus plants can **tolerate**
extreme heat.*
bear, endure, stand, abide, suffer,
stomach
(*informal*) stick

tomb *noun*
*Inside the **tomb** were several
ancient skeletons.*
burial chamber, crypt, grave,

mausoleum, sepulchre, vault
An underground passage
containing several tombs
is a **catacomb**.
A tomb is often marked by a
tombstone, **gravestone**, or
headstone.

tone *noun*
1 *There was an angry **tone** to
her voice.*
note, sound, quality, intonation,
manner
2 *The room is painted in subtle
tones.*
colour, hue, shade, tint
3 *Eerie music created the right
tone for the film.*
feeling, mood, atmosphere,
spirit, effect

✏ WRITING TIPS

tooth *noun*
You can use these words to
describe **teeth** or **jaws**
jagged, serrated, razor-sharp,
needle-sharp, pincer-like
teeth MAY
bite, chew, grind, munch,
chomp, gnash,
snap, tear,
rip, puncture

---

top *noun*
1 *They climbed to the **top** of the
hill.*
peak, summit, tip, crown, crest,
head
OPPOSITE bottom, base
2 *The desk **top** was covered with
newspapers.*
surface
3 *The **top** of the jar was screwed
on tightly.*
lid, cap, cover, covering

top *adjective*
1 *Their office is on the **top** floor.*
highest, topmost, uppermost,
upper
OPPOSITE bottom, lowest
2 *She got **top** marks in her exam.*
most, best, highest
3 *The skiers set off at **top** speed.*
greatest, maximum
4 *He is one of Europe's **top** chefs.*
best, leading, finest, foremost,

principal, superior
OPPOSITE junior

top *verb*
1 *Mum **topped** the cake with
fudge icing.*
cover, decorate, garnish, crown
2 *The athlete is hoping to **top** her
personal best.*
beat, better, exceed, outdo,
surpass

topic *noun*
*What was the **topic** of the
conversation?*
subject, talking-point, issue,
matter, question

topical *adjective*
*The website often discusses **topical**
issues.*
current, recent, up-to-date

toss *verb*
1 *He **tossed** a coin into the wishing-
well.*
throw, cast, hurl, fling, pitch, sling
(*informal*) chuck
2 *Let's **toss** a coin to see who'll go
first.*
flip, spin
3 *The little boat **tossed** about in the
storm.*
lurch, pitch, roll, heave, rock, bob
4 *She **tossed** and turned, unable to
get to sleep.*
thrash about, flail, writhe, wriggle

total *noun*
*A **total** of 15 million people live in
Tokyo.*
sum, whole, entirety, amount

total *adjective*
1 *The bill shows the **total** amount
due.*
full, complete, whole, entire
2 *The party was a **total** disaster.*
complete, utter, absolute,
thorough, downright, sheer

total *verb*
*The donations **total** almost 300
euros.*
add up to, amount to, come to,
make

touch *verb*
1 *Some animals don't like to be
touched.*
feel, handle, stroke, fondle,
caress, pat, pet
2 *The car just **touched** the gatepost.*
brush, graze, contact
3 *The speed of the racing car
touched 200 miles per hour.*
reach, rise to
4 *I was **touched** by the poem that
she wrote.*
move, affect, stir

touch *noun*
1 *I felt a light **touch** on my arm.*
pat, stroke, tap, caress, contact
2 *There's a **touch** of frost in the air.*
hint, trace, suggestion

touchy *adjective*
Be careful what you say—he's very touchy.
easily offended, sensitive, irritable, quick-tempered

tough *adjective*
1 *You'll need tough shoes for hiking.*
strong, sturdy, robust, durable, stout, hard-wearing, substantial
Common similes are *as tough as nails* and *as tough as old boots*.
OPPOSITE **flimsy**
2 *The meat was very tough.*
chewy, leathery, rubbery
OPPOSITE **tender**
3 *They played against tough opposition.*
strong, stiff, powerful, resistant, determined, stubborn
OPPOSITE **weak, feeble**
4 *The police deal with some tough criminals.*
rough, violent, vicious, hardened
5 *It was a tough job to clean the oven.*
demanding, laborious, strenuous, gruelling, tiring, exhausting
OPPOSITE **easy**
6 *The crossword puzzle was too tough for him.*
difficult, hard, puzzling, baffling, knotty, thorny
OPPOSITE **easy**

tower *noun*
A small tower on a castle or other building is a *turret*.
A church tower is a *steeple*.
The pointed structure on a steeple is a *spire*.
The top part of a steeple with a bell is a *belfry*.
The tall tower of a mosque is a *minaret*.

tower *verb*
to tower above something
The castle towers above the village.
rise above, stand above, dominate, loom over

trace *noun*
1 *The burglar left no trace of his presence.*
evidence, sign, mark,

Eiffel Tower

indication, hint, clue, track, trail
A trace left by an animal might be its *footprint* or *scent* or *spoor*.
2 *They found traces of blood on the carpet.*
tiny amount, drop, spot

trace *verb*
She is trying to trace her distant ancestors.
track down, discover, find, uncover, unearth

track *noun*
1 *A rough track leads past the farm.*
path, pathway, footpath, trail
2 *They followed the deer's tracks for miles.*
footprint, footmark, trail, scent
3 *They are laying the track for a new railway.*
line, rails
4 *The athletes are warming up on the track.*
racetrack, circuit, course

track *verb*
Astronomers are tracking the path of the comet.
follow, trace, pursue, chase, tail, trail, hunt, stalk
to track someone or **something down**
They tracked down the owner of the car.
find, discover, trace, hunt down, sniff out, run to ground

tradition *noun*
It's a tradition to sing 'Auld Lang Syne' on New Year's Eve.
custom, convention, habit, routine, fashion

traditional *adjective*
1 *The African drummers wore traditional costumes.*
national, regional, historical
2 *They chose to have a traditional wedding.*
conventional, customary, established, time-honoured, habitual, typical, usual

tragedy *noun*
The accident at sea was a terrible tragedy.
disaster, catastrophe, calamity, misfortune

tragic *adjective*
He died in a tragic accident.

catastrophic, disastrous, calamitous, terrible, appalling, dreadful, unfortunate, unlucky

trail *noun*
1 *We walked along a trail through the woods.*
path, pathway, track, route
2 *The police were on the trail of the bank robbers.*
track, chase, hunt, pursuit
The trail left in the water by a ship is its *wake*.

trail *verb*
1 *The detective trailed the suspect all day.*
follow, chase, tail, track, pursue, shadow, stalk, hunt
2 *She trailed her suitcase behind her.*
pull, tow, drag, draw, haul
3 *He is already trailing behind the front runners.*
fall behind, lag, straggle, dawdle

train *verb*
1 *He trains the football team every Saturday.*
coach, instruct, teach, tutor
2 *They are training hard for the Commonwealth Games.*
practise, exercise, prepare yourself
(*informal*) work out

tramp *verb*
They tramped across the muddy fields.
march, hike, trek, trudge, plod, stride

trample *verb*
Don't trample the flowers!
crush, flatten, squash, tread on, walk over, stamp on

transfer *verb*
Some paintings have been transferred to the new gallery.
move, remove, shift, relocate, convey, hand over

transform *verb*
They transformed the attic into an office.
change, alter, turn, convert, adapt, modify

transmit *verb*
1 *The spy transmitted her messages in code.*
send, communicate, relay, emit, broadcast
To transmit a programme on radio or TV is to *broadcast* it.
OPPOSITE **receive**
2 *Can the disease be transmitted to humans?*
pass on, spread, carry

transparent *adjective*
The box had a transparent lid.
clear
(*informal*) see-through
Something which is not fully transparent, but allows light to shine through, is *translucent*.

WORD WEB

transport *noun*
TRANSPORT BY AIR
aeroplane, airship, helicopter, hot-air balloon

hot-air balloon

TRANSPORT BY ROAD
bicycle, bus, car, coach, horse, jeep, lorry, minibus, taxi, van

TRANSPORT BY RAIL
monorail, train, tram, underground

TRANSPORT BY WATER
barge, boat, canoe, ferry, punt, raft, ship, yacht

VEHICLES
WHICH CARRY PEOPLE
bus, cab, camper, car or motorcar, caravan, coach, jeep, minibus, minicab, people carrier, rickshaw, taxi, train, tram, trolleybus

bicycle

VEHICLES USED FOR WORK
ambulance, bulldozer, dustcart, fire-engine, hearse, HGV or heavy goods vehicle, horsebox, lorry, milkfloat, removal van, pick-up truck, police car, steamroller, tank, tanker, tractor, truck, van

VEHICLES WHICH TRAVEL
ON SNOW OR ICE
sled or sledge, sleigh, skidoo, snowplough, toboggan

OLD
HORSE-DRAWN
VEHICLES
carriage, cart, chariot, coach, gig, stagecoach, trap, wagon

coach

boat

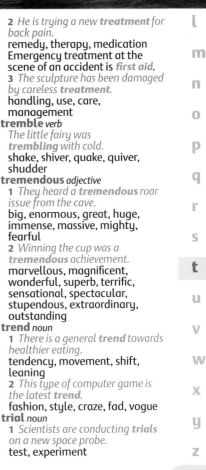

tram

trap *noun*
1 *The animal was caught in a **trap**.*
snare, net, noose, booby trap
2 *The police set up a **trap** to catch the robbers.*
ambush
trap *verb*
*They tried to **trap** the mouse.*
capture, catch, snare, corner
tread *verb*
*Please **tread** carefully.*
step, walk, proceed
to tread on
*Don't **tread on** the wet cement!*
walk on, step on, stamp on, trample, crush, squash
treasure *noun*
*The **treasure** was buried somewhere on the island.*

hoard, riches, wealth, fortune
A hidden store of treasure is a *cache*.
treasure *verb*
*She **treasures** the photograph of her grandmother.*
cherish, prize, value
treat *verb*
1 *The old woman had always **treated** him kindly.*
behave towards, deal with
2 *She is being **treated** for minor injuries.*
give treatment to
To treat a wound is to *dress* it.
To treat an illness or wound successfully is to *cure* or *heal* it.
treatment *noun* **1** *The hospital is for the **treatment** of sick animals.*
care, nursing, healing

2 *He is trying a new **treatment** for back pain.*
remedy, therapy, medication
Emergency treatment at the scene of an accident is *first aid*.
3 *The sculpture has been damaged by careless **treatment**.*
handling, use, care, management
tremble *verb*
*The little fairy was **trembling** with cold.*
shake, shiver, quake, quiver, shudder
tremendous *adjective*
1 *They heard a **tremendous** roar issue from the cave.*
big, enormous, great, huge, immense, massive, mighty, fearful
2 *Winning the cup was a **tremendous** achievement.*
marvellous, magnificent, wonderful, superb, terrific, sensational, spectacular, stupendous, extraordinary, outstanding
trend *noun*
1 *There is a general **trend** towards healthier eating.*
tendency, movement, shift, leaning
2 *This type of computer game is the latest **trend**.*
fashion, style, craze, fad, vogue
trial *noun*
1 *Scientists are conducting **trials** on a new space probe.*
test, experiment

WORD WEB

travel *verb*
*She prefers to **travel** to work by bus.*
go, journey, move along, proceed, progress

VARIOUS WAYS TO TRAVEL
cruise, cycle, drive, fly, go by rail, hike, hitch-hike, motor, pedal, ramble, ride, roam, row, sail, tour, trek, voyage, walk, wander

When birds travel from one country to another they *migrate*.
When people travel to another country to live there they *emigrate*.

PEOPLE WHO TRAVEL AS A WAY OF LIFE
itinerant, nomad, traveller
OTHER PEOPLE WHO TRAVEL
astronaut, commuter, cyclist, driver or motorist, explorer, hitch-hiker, holidaymaker, motorcyclist, passenger, pedestrian, pilot or aviator, rambler or walker, sailor, tourist

A person who travels to a religious place is a *pilgrim*.
A person who travels illegally on a ship or plane is a *stowaway*.
A person who likes travelling round the world is a *globetrotter*.

a
b
c
d
e
l
m
n
o
p
q
r
s
t
u
v
w
x
y
z

2 *The **trial** will be heard in a crown court.*
case, hearing
A military trial is a ***court martial***.

trick *noun*
1 *Stephie played a **trick** on her brother.*
joke, practical joke, prank
Tricks which a magician performs are ***conjuring tricks***.
2 *The Trojans never guessed that the wooden horse was a **trick**.*
deception, pretence, fraud, cheat, hoax
(*informal*) con

trick *verb*
*He **tricked** them into believing he was a police officer.*
deceive, dupe, fool, hoodwink, cheat, swindle
(*informal*) con

trickle *verb*
*Water **trickled** from the tap.*
dribble, drip, leak, seep, ooze
OPPOSITE gush

tricky *adjective*
*There were a couple of **tricky** questions in the exam.*
difficult, complicated, awkward, intricate, involved, ticklish
OPPOSITE straightforward, easy

trip *noun*
*They went on a **trip** to the seaside.*
journey, visit, outing, excursion, jaunt, expedition

trip *verb*
*He **tripped** on the loose carpet.*
catch your foot, stumble, fall, slip, stagger

trivial *adjective*
*Don't bother me with **trivial** details.*
unimportant, minor, insignificant, trifling, negligible, petty, silly, slight, frivolous
OPPOSITE important

trouble *noun*
1 *The family has had a lot of **trouble** recently.*
difficulty, hardship, suffering, unhappiness, distress, misfortune, pain, sadness, sorrow, worry
2 *The police dealt with **trouble** in the crowd.*
disorder, unrest, disturbance, commotion, fighting, violence
3 *The **trouble** with this computer is that it's very slow.*
problem, difficulty, disadvantage, drawback

to take trouble
*He **took trouble** to remember all our names.*
bother, make an effort, take pains

trouble *verb*
1 *What's **troubling** you?*
distress, upset, bother, worry,

concern, pain, torment, vex
2 *I don't want to **trouble** her if she's busy.*
disturb, interrupt, bother, pester
3 *Nobody **troubled** to tidy up the room.*
bother, make an effort, take trouble

true *adjective*
1 *Do you think the newspaper report is **true**?*
accurate, correct, right, factual, authentic, undeniable
OPPOSITE untrue, false
2 *This is a **true** copy of my birth certificate.*
genuine, real, actual, faithful, exact
OPPOSITE false
3 *Esther has always been a **true** friend.*
faithful, loyal, constant, devoted, sincere, steady, trustworthy, dependable, reliable
OPPOSITE unreliable

trust *verb*
*I **trusted** her to keep my identity a secret.*
rely on, depend on, count on, bank on, believe in, be sure of, have confidence in, have faith in

trust *noun*
1 *The director has **trust** in her acting ability.*
belief, confidence, faith
2 *They put their lives in the **trust** of the pilot.*
responsibility, safe-keeping, hands

truth *noun*
1 *The detective doubted the **truth** of her story.*
accuracy, authenticity, correctness, genuineness, reliability, truthfulness, validity
OPPOSITE inaccuracy or falseness
2 *Are you sure you're telling the **truth**?*
facts
OPPOSITE lies

truthful *adjective*
1 *She is normally a **truthful** person.*
honest, frank, sincere, straight, straightforward, reliable, trustworthy
2 *He gave a **truthful** answer.*
accurate, correct, proper, right, true, valid
OPPOSITE dishonest

try *verb*
1 *I'm going to **try** to beat my dad at chess.*
aim, attempt, endeavour, make an effort, strive, struggle
2 *Would you like to **try** a larger size?*
test, try out, evaluate, experiment with

try *noun*
1 *We may not succeed, but it's worth a **try**!*
attempt, effort, go, shot
2 *Would you like a **try** of my mango smoothie?*
trial, test, taste

trying *adjective*
*The way he keeps asking questions is very **trying**.*
tiresome, irritating, annoying, wearing, wearisome

tuck *verb*
*He **tucked** his t-shirt into his jeans.*
push, insert, stuff

tug *verb*
1 *It annoys me when my brother **tugs** my hair.*
pull, yank, jerk, pluck, wrench
2 *We **tugged** the sledge up the hill.*
drag, pull, tow, haul, lug, draw, heave

tune *noun*
*Can you play the **tune** to 'Happy Birthday'?*
melody, song, air, theme

turn *verb*
1 *A wheel **turns** on its axle.*
go round, revolve, rotate, roll, spin, swivel, pivot, twirl, whirl
2 *The van **turned** into a side street.*
change direction, corner
To turn unexpectedly is to ***swerve*** or ***veer*** off course.
If you turn to go back in the direction you came from, you ***do a U-turn***.
If marching soldiers change direction, they ***wheel***.
3 *He **turned** a curious shade of green.*
become, go, grow
4 *They **turned** the attic into a spare bedroom.*
convert, adapt, change, alter, modify, transform, develop

to turn something down
*She **turned down** the offer of a part in the play.*
decline, refuse, reject

to turn something on or **off**
*He **turned on** the radio.*
switch on or off

to turn out
*Everything **turned out** well in the end.*
end up, come out, happen, result

to turn over
*The boat **turned over**.*
capsize, overturn, turn upside down, flip over, keel over

to turn up
*A friend **turned up** unexpectedly.*
arrive, appear, drop in

turn *noun*
1 *She gave the handle a **turn**.*
twist, spin, whirl, twirl
A single turn of wheel is a ***revolution***.

The process of turning is
rotation.
2 *The house is just past the next*
turn *in the road.*
bend, corner, curve, angle,
junction
*A sharp turn in a country road
is a* **hairpin bend**.
3 *It's your* **turn** *to do the washing
up.*
chance, opportunity, occasion,
time, slot, go
4 (*informal*) *Seeing the skeleton
gave her quite a* **turn**.
fright, scare, shock, start,
surprise

twinkle *verb*
The stars **twinkled** *in the
sky.*
sparkle, shine, glitter, glisten,
glimmer, glint

twist *verb*
1 *She* **twisted** *a bandage round
her wrist.*
wind, loop, coil, curl, entwine
2 **Twist** *the handle to open the
door.*
turn, rotate, revolve, swivel
3 *The road* **twists** *through the
hills.*
wind, weave, curve, zigzag
4 *He* **twisted** *and turned in his
sleep.*
toss, writhe, wriggle
5 *I tried to* **twist** *the cap off the
bottle.*
unscrew
6 *Heat can* **twist** *metal out of
shape.*
bend, buckle, warp, crumple,
distort

twisted *adjective*
*The trunk of the olive tree was
twisted with age.*
knarled, warped, buckled,
misshapen, deformed

twitch *verb*
The dog **twitched** *in his sleep.*
jerk, jump, start, tremble

type *noun*
1 *What* **type** *of films do you like
to watch?*
kind, sort, variety, category,
class, genre
2 *The book was printed in large
type.*
print, lettering, letters,
characters

typical *adjective*
1 *The weather is* **typical** *for this
time of year.*
normal, usual, standard,
ordinary, average, predictable,
unsurprising
OPPOSITE **unusual**
2 *The pointed arch is* **typical** *of
Gothic architecture.*
characteristic, representative
OPPOSITE **uncharacteristic**

Uu

ugly *adjective*
1 *The princess had to kiss a fat,
ugly toad.*
grotesque, hideous, unattractive,
repulsive, revolting, monstrous
OPPOSITE **beautiful**
2 *The room was
filled with
ugly furniture.*
unattractive,
unsightly,
displeasing,
tasteless, horrid, nasty
OPPOSITE **beautiful**
3 *The crowd was in an*   ugly
ugly *mood.*
unfriendly, hostile,
menacing, threatening, angry,
dangerous
OPPOSITE **friendly**

unavoidable *adjective*
The accident was **unavoidable**.
inevitable, bound to happen,
certain, destined

unaware *adjective*
unaware of
They were **unaware of** *the dangers
that lay ahead.*
ignorant of, oblivious to,
unconscious of

unbearable *adjective*
*The stench in the cave was
unbearable.*
unendurable, intolerable,
impossible to bear

unbelievable *adjective*
1 *The account of the UFO sighting
was* **unbelievable**.
unconvincing, unlikely, far-
fetched, improbable, incredible
2 *She scored an* **unbelievable**
goal.
amazing, astonishing,
extraordinary, remarkable,
sensational, phenomenal

uncertain *adjective*
1 *I was* **uncertain** *what to do next.*
unsure, doubtful, in two minds,
unclear
2 *They are facing an* **uncertain**
future.
indefinite, unknown, undecided,
unpredictable

uncomfortable *adjective*
1 *She complained that her shoes
were* **uncomfortable**.
restrictive, cramped, hard, stiff,
tight, tight-fitting
2 *He spent an* **uncomfortable**
night sleeping on the floor.
restless, troubled, disagreeable,
uneasy

unconscious *adjective*
1 *The patient had been*

unconscious *for two days.*
*If you are unconscious because
of a hit on the head, you are
knocked out.
If you are unconscious
for an operation, you are
anaesthetized.
If you are unconscious because
of an accident or illness, you are
in a coma.*
2 *She's* **unconscious** *of the effect
she has on other people.*
ignorant, unaware
3 *They laughed at her
unconscious slip of the
tongue.*
accidental, unintended,
unintentional
OPPOSITE **conscious**
unconscious of
He's **unconscious of** *all the trouble
he's caused.*
unaware of, ignorant of,
oblivious to

uncover *verb*
1 *Archaeologists have* **uncovered**
two more skeletons.

dig up, unearth, expose, reveal, show, disclose
To uncover your body is to **strip** or **undress**.
2 *He **uncovered** the truth about his family's past.*
detect, discover, come across
OPPOSITE cover up, hide

understand *verb*
1 *I don't **understand** what you mean.*
comprehend, grasp, follow, see, take in, realize, appreciate, recognize, work out, fathom
2 *Can you **understand** this writing?*
read, interpret, make out, make sense of
To understand something in code is to **decode** or **decipher** it.
3 *I **understand** they're moving to Sydney.*
believe, hear

understanding *noun*
1 *The robot has limited powers of **understanding**.*
intelligence, intellect, sense, judgement
2 *The course will increase your **understanding** of science.*
appreciation, awareness, knowledge, comprehension, grasp
3 *The two sides reached an **understanding**.*
agreement, deal, settlement, arrangement, accord
4 *She treats her patients with **understanding**.*
sympathy, compasssion, consideration

undo *verb*
1 *I'll have to **undo** this row of knitting.*
unfasten, untie, unravel, loosen, release
To undo stitching is to **unpick** it.
2 *Sue **undid** the wrapping on the parcel.*
open, unwrap, unfold, unwind, unroll, unfurl
3 *The good witch tried to **undo** the spell.*
reverse, cancel out, wipe out

unemployed *adjective*
*Since the factory closed, he has been **unemployed**.*
out of work, jobless
(*informal*) on the dole
To be unemployed because there is not enough work to do is to be **redundant**.
OPPOSITE employed, working

uneven *adjective*
1 *The ground was very **uneven** in places.*
rough, bumpy, rutted
OPPOSITE smooth
2 *Their performance has been **uneven** this season.*

uncover

erratic, inconsistent, irregular, variable, unpredictable
OPPOSITE consistent
3 *It was a very **uneven** contest.*
one-sided, unbalanced, unequal, unfair
OPPOSITE balanced

unexpected *adjective*
*Her reaction was totally **unexpected**.*
surprising, unforeseen, unpredictable, unplanned
OPPOSITE expected

unfair *adjective*
1 *Do you think that the umpire's decision was **unfair**?*
unjust, unreasonable, wrong, one-sided, imbalanced, impartial, biased
OPPOSITE fair, just
2 *I felt that her criticism of my work was **unfair**.*
undeserved, unmerited, uncalled-for, unjustified
OPPOSITE fair, deserved

unfamiliar *adjective*
*The astronauts looked on an **unfamiliar** landscape.*
stange, unusual, curious, novel, alien

unfamiliar with
*They were **unfamiliar with** the local customs.*
unaccustomed to, unused to, unaware of

unfortunate *adjective*
1 *The **unfortunate** couple had lost all their possessions.*
unlucky, poor, unhappy, hapless, wretched, ill-fated
2 *The goalkeeper made one **unfortunate** error.*
disastrous, calamitous, unwelcome
OPPOSITE fortunate, lucky
3 *He made an **unfortunate***

remark about her cooking.
regrettable, inappropriate, tactless, unsuitable, untimely

unfriendly *adjective*
*The housekeeper greeted us with an **unfriendly** glare.*
unwelcoming, inhospitable, unsympathetic, unkind, impolite, uncivil, unhelpful, hostile, cold, cool, distant, standoffish, aloof, unsociable, unneighbourly
OPPOSITE friendly, amiable

unhappy *adjective*
*You look **unhappy**—what's the matter?*
brokenhearted, dejected, depressed, desolate, despairing, dismal, distressed
(*informal*) down, downcast, downhearted, forlorn, gloomy, glum, grave, heartbroken, in low spirits, miserable, regretful, sad, sorrowful, sorry, tearful, troubled, upset, wistful, woeful, wretched
OPPOSITE happy

unhealthy *adjective*
1 *One of the calves has been **unhealthy** since birth.*
unwell, ill, sick, diseased, infirm, sickly, poorly, weak, delicate, feeble, frail
OPPOSITE healthy, strong
2 *He eats an **unhealthy** diet of junk food.*
unwholesome, unnatural, harmful, unhygienic
OPPOSITE healthy, wholesome

unhelpful *adjective*
*The shop assistant was most **unhelpful**.*
uncooperative, unfriendly, inconsiderate, reluctant to help
OPPOSITE helpful

unimportant *adjective*
*Don't worry about **unimportant** details.*

a b c d e f g h i j k l m n o p q r s t u v w x y z

insignificant, minor, trivial, trifling, irrelevant, secondary, slight, small, negligible, worthless, petty
OPPOSITE important

unique *adjective*
Each person's fingerprints are unique.
distinctive, different, individual, special, peculiar
(*informal*) one-off

unite *verb*
1 *King Bluetooth united the kingdoms of Denmark and Norway.*
combine, join, merge, link, integrate, unify, amalgamate, bring together
OPPOSITE separate
2 *People of all ages united to celebrate Chinese New Year.*
collaborate, cooperate, join forces
To unite to do something bad is to *conspire*.
OPPOSITE compete

unkind *adjective*
It was a thoughtless and unkind remark.
callous, hard-hearted, cruel, thoughtless, heartless, uncaring, unfeeling, inconsiderate, unsympathetic, unfriendly, uncharitable, harsh, mean, nasty, selfish, spiteful, vicious, malicious
OPPOSITE kind

unknown *adjective*
1 *The letter was in an unknown hand.*
unidentified, unrecognized
OPPOSITE known
2 *The author of the story is unknown.*
anonymous, nameless, unnamed, unspecified
OPPOSITE named
3 *The explorers entered unknown territory.*
unfamiliar, alien, foreign, undiscovered, unexplored, uncharted
OPPOSITE familiar
4 *The part was played by an unknown actor.*
little known, unheard of, obscure
OPPOSITE famous

unlikely *adjective*
No-one believed her unlikely excuse.
unbelievable, unconvincing, improbable, implausible, incredible, far-fetched
OPPOSITE likely

unlucky *adjective*
1 *Some people think that 13 is an unlucky number.*
unfavourable, ill-omened, ill-starred, jinxed

2 *By an unlucky chance, their plan was discovered.*
unfortunate, unwelcome, untimely

unnecessary *adjective*
I'm deleting any unnecessary files from my computer.
inessential, non-essential, uncalled for, unwanted, excessive, superfluous, surplus, extra, redundant
OPPOSITE necessary

unpleasant *adjective*
1 *Mr Smallweed was a thoroughly unpleasant man.*
disagreeable, unfriendly, unkind, bad-tempered, nasty, malicious, spiteful, hateful
2 *Being lost in the jungle had been an unpleasant experience.*
uncomfortable, disagreeable, awful
3 *The smell from the drain was very unpleasant.*
disgusting, foul, repulsive, revolting, horrible, horrid, repellent, offensive, objectionable

unpopular *adjective*
The new manager was unpopular at first.
disliked, hated, despised, unloved
OPPOSITE popular

untidy *adjective*
1 *Our house is the one with the untidy garden.*
messy, disorderly, cluttered, jumbled, tangled, littered, chaotic
(*informal*) higgledy-piggledy, topsy-turvy
2 *His work was untidy and full of mistakes.*
careless, disorganized, slapdash
(*informal*) sloppy
3 *She arrived looking untidy and flustered.*
dishevelled, bedraggled, rumpled, unkempt, scruffy, slovenly

unusual *adjective*
1 *The weather was unusual for the time of year.*
abnormal, out of the ordinary, exceptional, remarkable, extraordinary, odd, peculiar, singular, strange, unexpected, irregular, unconventional, unheard-of
OPPOSITE ordinary
2 *Ebenezer is an unusual name.*
uncommon, rare, unfamiliar
OPPOSITE common

upset *verb*
1 *Something in the letter had upset her.*
distress, trouble, disturb, displease, unsettle, offend, dismay, grieve, fluster, perturb

2 *Bad weather upset the train timetable.*
disrupt, interfere with, interrupt, affect, throw out
3 *The baby upset a whole bowl of cereal.*
knock over, spill, tip over, topple
4 *A fallen tree branch upset the canoe.*
overturn, capsize

urge *verb*
He urged her to reconsider her decision.
advise, counsel, appeal to, beg, implore, plead with, press
To urge someone to do something is also to *advocate* or *recommend* it.
OPPOSITE discourage

urge *noun*
I had a sudden urge to burst into song.
impulse, compulsion, longing, wish, yearning, desire, itch
(*informal*) yen

urgent *adjective*
1 *She had urgent business in New York.*
pressing, immediate, essential, important, top-priority
OPPOSITE unimportant
2 *He spoke in an urgent whisper.*
anxious, insistent, earnest

use *verb*
1 *She used a calculator to add up the figures.*
make use of, employ, utilize
To use your knowledge is to *apply* it.
To use your muscles is to *exercise* them.
To use a musical instrument is to *play* it.
To use an axe or sword is to *wield* it.
To use people or things selfishly is to *exploit* them.
2 *Can you show me how to use the photocopier?*
operate, work, handle, manage
3 *You've used all the hot water.*
use up, go through, consume, exhaust, spend

use *noun*
1 *Would these books be any use to you?*
help, benefit, advantage, profit, value
2 *A sonic screwdriver has many uses.*
function, purpose, point

useful *adjective*
1 *A flask is useful for keeping food warm.*
convenient, handy, effective, efficient, practical
2 *The website offers some useful advice.*

good, helpful, valuable, worthwhile, constructive, invaluable
OPPOSITE **useless**

useless *adjective*
1 *This old vacuum cleaner is* **useless**.
ineffective, inefficient, impractical, unusable
OPPOSITE **useful, effective**
2 *Her advice was completely* **useless**.
worthless, unhelpful, pointless, futile, unprofitable, fruitless
OPPOSITE **useful**
3 (*informal*) *I'm* **useless** *at drawing.*
bad, poor, incompetent (*informal*) rubbish, hopeless
OPPOSITE **good**

usual *adjective*
1 *I'll meet you at the* **usual** *time.*
normal, customary, familiar, habitual, regular, standard
2 *It's* **usual** *to knock before entering.*
common, accepted, conventional, traditional

Vv

vacant *adjective*
1 *The house over the road is still* **vacant**.
unoccupied, uninhabited, deserted
OPPOSITE **occupied**
2 *The receptionist gave me a* **vacant** *stare.*
blank, expressionless, mindless, absent-minded, deadpan
OPPOSITE **alert**

vague *adjective*
1 *The directions she gave me were rather* **vague**.

view

indefinite, imprecise, broad, general, ill-defined, unclear, woolly
OPPOSITE **exact, detailed**
2 *A* **vague** *shape could be seen through the mist.*
blurred, indistinct, obscure, dim, hazy, shadowy
OPPOSITE **definite**

vain *adjective*
1 *The duchess was* **vain** *about her appearance.*
arrogant, proud, conceited, haughty, self-satisfied
OPPOSITE **modest**
2 *He made a* **vain** *attempt to tidy the room.*
unsuccessful, ineffective, useless, worthless, fruitless, futile, pointless
OPPOSITE **successful**

valuable *adjective*
1 *Apparently the painting is very* **valuable**.
expensive, costly, dear, precious, priceless
2 *He gave her some* **valuable** *advice.*
useful, helpful, constructive, good, worthwhile, invaluable
OPPOSITE **worthless** Notice that invaluable is not the opposite of **valuable**.

value *noun*
1 *The house has recently increased in* **value**.
price, cost, worth
2 *He stressed the* **value** *of taking regular exercise.*
advantage, benefit, merit, use, usefulness, importance

value *verb*
1 *He had always* **valued** *her advice.*
appreciate, respect, esteem, have a high opinion of, set great store by

To value something highly is to **prize** or **treasure** it.
2 *A surveyor was sent to* **value** *the house.*
price, cost, rate, evaluate, assess

vanish *verb*
With a flick of his wand, the wizard **vanished** *into thin air.*
disappear, go away, fade, dissolve, disperse
OPPOSITE **appear**

vanity *noun*
His **vanity** *is such that he never admits he's wrong.*
arrogance, pride, conceit, self-esteem, self-importance

variety *noun*
1 *The centre offers a* **variety** *of leisure activities.*
assortment, mixture, array
2 *The supermarket has over thirty* **varieties** *of pasta.*
kind, sort, type, make, brand
A variety of animal is a **breed** or **species**.
3 *There is not much* **variety** *in her choice of words.*
variation, change, difference, diversity

vast *adjective*
1 *The miser accumulated a* **vast** *fortune.*
large, huge, enormous, great, immense, massive
2 *A* **vast** *stretch of water lay between them and dry land.*
broad, wide, extensive, sweeping

version *noun*
1 *The two newspapers gave different* **versions** *of the accident.*
account, description, story, report
2 *It's an English* **version** *of a French play.*
adaptation, interpretation
A version of something which was originally in another

language is a *translation*.
3 *A new version of the computer game will be released in May.*
design, model, form, variation

very *adverb*
Carl is a very talented juggler.
extremely, highly, enormously, exceedingly, truly, intensely, especially, particularly, remarkably, unusually, uncommonly, outstandingly, really
(*informal*) terribly
OPPOSITE slightly

vibrate *verb*
I pulled a lever and the whole engine began to vibrate.
shake, shudder, tremble, throb, judder, quake, quiver, rattle

vicious *adjective*
1 *This was once the scene of a vicious murder.*
brutal, barbaric, violent, bloodthirsty, cruel, merciless, pitiless, ruthless, callous, inhuman, malicious, sadistic, atrocious, barbarous, murderous, villainous, wicked
2 *Male baboons can be vicious if provoked.*
fierce, ferocious, violent, savage, wild

victory *noun*
Hannibal won several victories over the Romans.
win, success, triumph
OPPOSITE defeat

view *noun*
1 *There's a good view from the top of the hill.*
outlook, prospect, scene, panorama, scenery
2 *What are your views on animal testing?*
opinion, thought, attitude, belief, conviction, idea, notion

view *verb*
1 *Thousand of tourists come to view Niagara Falls each year.*
look at, see, watch, observe, regard, contemplate, gaze at, inspect, survey, examine, eye
2 *Wanda viewed her cousin with extreme dislike.*
think of, consider, regard

vile *adjective*
1 *The professor gave us a vile concoction to drink.*
disgusting, repulsive, revolting, foul, horrible, loathsome, offensive, repellent, sickening, nauseating
OPPOSITE pleasant
2 *Murder is a vile crime.*
dreadful, despicable, appalling, contemptible, wicked, evil

villain *noun*
Detectives are on the trail of an infamous villain.

criminal, offender, rogue, wrongdoer
An informal word for the villain in a story is baddy.
OPPOSITE hero

violence *noun*
1 *The marchers protested against the use of violence.*
fighting, might, war, brute force, barbarity, brutality, cruelty, savagery
OPPOSITE non-violence, pacifism
2 *The violence of the storm uprooted trees.*
force, power, strength, severity, intensity, ferocity, fierceness, fury, rage
OPPOSITE gentleness, mildness

violent *adjective*
1 *There were violent clashes in the streets.*
aggressive, forceful, rough, fierce, frenzied, vicious, brutal
OPPOSITE gentle, mild
2 *The bridge was washed away in a violent storm.*
severe, strong, powerful, forceful, raging, tempestuous, turbulent, wild
OPPOSITE weak, feeble

visible *adjective*
There were no visible signs that the door had been forced.
noticeable, obvious, conspicuous, clear, distinct, evident, apparent, perceptible, recognizable, detectable
OPPOSITE invisible

visit *verb*
They're visiting friends in Toronto for a few days.
call on, come to see, drop in on, go to see, pay a call on, stay with

visit *noun*
1 *My grandmother is coming for a visit.*
call, stay
2 *We are planning a short visit to Paris.*
trip, excursion, outing

visitor *noun*
1 *They've got some Polish visitors staying with them.*
guest, caller
2 *Rome welcomes millions of visitors every year.*
tourist, holidaymaker, sightseer, traveller

vivid *adjective*
1 *Gaugin often painted in vivid colours.*
bright, colourful, strong, intense, vibrant, dazzling, brilliant, glowing, striking, showy
2 *He gave a vivid description of his travels in Mexico.*

lively, clear, powerful, evocative, imaginative, dramatic, lifelike, realistic, graphic
OPPOSITE dull

voice *noun*
The robot spoke with a slow, metallic voice.
speech, tone, way of speaking

> ✎ **WRITING TIPS**
>
> You can use these words to describe a **voice**:
> croaky, droning, gruff, high-pitched, husky, low, shrill, soft-spoken, squeaky, throaty
> *A gruff voice cried, 'Who dares to enter my cave?'*

voluntary *adjective*
She does voluntary work for a charity.
optional, unpaid
OPPOSITE compulsory

vomit *verb*
The seasickness made him want to vomit.
be sick, heave, retch
(*informal*) throw up

vote *verb*
Everyone has a right to vote in the election.
cast your vote
to vote for someone or **something**
I haven't decided who to vote for.
choose, opt for, nominate, elect

vote

vote *noun*
The results of the vote will be known tomorrow.
ballot, election, poll, referendum

vulgar *adjective*
1 *The new colour scheme just looks vulgar to me.*
tasteless, unsophisticated, cheap, tawdry
(*informal*) tacky
OPPOSITE tasteful
2 *The book sometimes uses vulgar language.*
indecent, offensive, rude, coarse
OPPOSITE decent

Ww

wail *verb*
Upstairs, the baby began to wail.
cry, howl, bawl, cry, moan, shriek

wait *verb*
Please wait here until I get back.
remain where you are, stay, stop, rest, pause, linger
(*informal*) hang about or around, hold on

wait *noun*
There was a long wait before the show began.
interval, pause, delay, hold-up

wake, waken *verbs*
1 *Hagor the giant woke from a deep sleep.*
awake, awaken, become conscious, come round, rise, arise, stir, wake up
2 *The alarm clock woke me at 6 a.m.*
rouse, arouse, awaken, disturb

walk *verb*
1 *I walked down the lane, humming a tune.*
amble, crawl, creep, dodder, pace, plod, saunter, step, stroll, wander
2 *A squat little troll walked towards the forest.*
hobble, limp, lope, lurch, shamble, shuffle, stagger, stumble, toddle, totter, waddle
3 *The robot walked its way up the stairs.*
clump, pound, stamp, traipse, tramp, trudge, wade
4 *The burglar walked away into the shadows.*
mince, pad, patter, prowl, slink, stalk, steal, tiptoe
5 *Captain Flint walked on board the ship.*
march, parade, stride, strut, swagger, trot
6 *They are planning to walk across the Himalayas.*
hike, trek, ramble
7 *The children walked into the classroom.*
file, troop

walk *noun*
1 *We went for a walk in the country.*
stroll, saunter, ramble, hike, trek, tramp, trudge
2 *There are some lovely walks through the forest.*
path, route

wander *verb*
1 *Sheep wandered about the hills.*
stray, roam, rove, range, ramble, meander, travel, walk

2 *We must have wandered off the path.*
stray, turn, veer, swerve

want *verb*
1 *He desperately wants to win a medal.*
wish, desire, long, hope
2 *Gayle had always wanted a pony of her own.*
wish for, desire, fancy, crave, long for, yearn for, hanker after, pine for, set your heart on, hunger for, thirst for
3 *That floor wants a good scrub.*
need, require

war *noun*
The war between the two countries lasted many years.
fighting, warfare, conflict, strife, hostilities

warm *adjective*
1 *It was a warm September evening.*
Weather which is unpleasantly warm is *close* or *sultry*.
Water or food which is only just warm is *lukewarm* or *tepid*.
A common simile is *as warm as toast*.
OPPOSITE cold
2 *Sandy put on a warm jumper.*
cosy, thick, woolly
OPPOSITE thin
3 *The fans gave the singer a warm welcome.*
friendly, warm-hearted, welcoming, kind, affectionate, genial, amiable, loving, sympathetic
OPPOSITE unfriendly

warm *verb*
She sat by the fire, warming her hands and feet.
heat, make warmer, thaw out
OPPOSITE chill

warn *verb*
The guide warned us to keep to the path.
advise, caution, alert, remind
To warn people of danger is to *raise the alarm*.

warning *noun*
1 *There was no warning of the danger ahead.*
sign, signal, indication, advance notice
2 *The traffic warden let him off with a warning.*
caution, reprimand

wash *verb*
1 *It took Rapunzel a long time to wash her hair.*
clean
To wash something with a cloth is to *mop*, *sponge*, or *wipe* it.
To wash something with a brush is to *scrub* it.
To wash something in clean water is to *rinse*, *sluice*, or *swill* it.

To wash yourself all over is to *bath* or *shower*.
2 *Waves washed over the beach.*
flow, splash

waste *verb*
Let's not waste any more time.
squander, misuse, throw away, fritter away
OPPOSITE save

waste *noun*
A lot of household waste can be recycled.
rubbish, refuse, trash, garbage, junk, litter
Waste food is *leftovers*.
Waste metal is *scrap*.

wasteful *adjective*
It's wasteful to cook more food than you need.
extravagant, uneconomical, prodigal, lavish, spendthrift
OPPOSITE economical, thrifty

watch *verb*
1 *I could sit and watch the sea for hours.*
gaze at, look at, stare at, view, contemplate
2 *Watch how the batsman holds the bat.*
observe, take notice of, keep your eyes on, pay attention to, attend to, heed, note
3 *Could you watch my bag for a few minutes?*
keep an eye on, keep watch over, guard, mind, look after, safeguard, supervise, tend

---

✎ WRITING TIPS

water *noun*
You can use these words to describe **how water moves**: bubble, cascade, dribble, drip, flood, flow, froth, gurgle, gush, jet, ooze, overflow, ripple, roll, run, seep, shower, spill, spatter, splash, spout, spray, sprinkle, spurt, squirt, stream, surge, sweep, swirl, swish, trickle, well up

---

wave *verb*
1 *The tall grass waved in the breeze.*
move to and fro, sway, swing, flap, flutter
2 *I tried to get their attention by waving a newspaper.*
shake, brandish, flourish, twirl, wag, waggle, wiggle

wave *noun*
1 *We watched the waves break on the shore.*
breaker, roller, billow
A very small wave is a *ripple*.
A huge wave caused by an earthquake is a *tidal wave* or *tsunami*.

A number of white waves following each other is *surf*. The top of a wave is the *crest* or *ridge*.

2 *A **wave** of anger spread through the crowd.*
surge, outbreak

wavy *adjective*
*The mermaid combed her long **wavy** hair.*
curly, curling, rippling, winding, zigzag
OPPOSITE **straight**

way *noun*
1 *Can you show me the **way** to the bus station?*
direction, route, road, path
2 *Is your house a long **way** from here?*
distance, journey
3 *This is the best **way** to make porridge.*
method, procedure, process, system, technique
4 *What a childish **way** to behave!*
manner, fashion, style
5 *In some **ways**, the brothers are very alike.*
respect, particular, feature, detail, aspect
6 *Things are in a bad **way**.*
state, condition

weak *adjective*
1 *The footbridge was old and **weak** in places.*
fragile, flimsy, rickety, shaky, unsound, unsteady, unsafe, decrepit
2 *The patient was too **weak** to walk very far.*
feeble, frail, ill, sickly, infirm, delicate, puny
3 *The nobles plotted against the **weak** king.*
timid, spineless, ineffective, powerless, useless
4 *The film was fun, but the plot was a bit **weak**.*
feeble, lame, unsatisfactory, unconvincing
5 *He asked for a mug of **weak** tea.*
watery, diluted, tasteless, thin (*informal*) wishy-washy
OPPOSITE **strong**

weakness *noun*
1 *He pointed out the **weakness** in their plan.*
fault, flaw, defect, imperfection, weak point
2 *Eve has a **weakness** for toffee apples.*
liking, fondness (*informal*) soft spot

wealthy *adjective*
*They say that he comes from a very **wealthy** family.*
rich, well-off, affluent, prosperous, moneyed, well-to-do (*informal*) flush, loaded

OPPOSITE **poor**

wear *verb*
1 *Can I **wear** my new dress to the party?*
dress in, be dressed in, have on
2 *The rug in the hallway is starting to **wear**.*
fray, wear away, wear out
3 *Those tyres have **worn** well.*
last, endure, survive

weather *noun see panel*

weird *adjective*
1 ***Weird** noises have been heard in the tower at midnight.*
eerie, ghostly, unearthly, mysterious, uncanny, unnatural (*informal*) spooky, creepy
OPPOSITE **ordinary, natural**
2 *My big sister has a **weird** taste in music.*
strange, odd, peculiar, bizarre, curious, quirky, eccentric, outlandish, unconventional, unusual
(*informal*) wacky, way-out
OPPOSITE **conventional**

welcome *noun*
*The landlady gave us a friendly **welcome**.*
greeting, reception

welcome *adjective*
1 *A cup of tea would be very **welcome**.*
pleasant, pleasing, agreeable, appreciated, desirable, acceptable
OPPOSITE **unacceptable**
2 *You're **welcome** to use my bike.*
allowed, permitted, free
OPPOSITE **forbidden**

welcome *verb*
*An elderly butler **welcomed** us at the door.*
greet, receive, meet, hail

well *adverb*
1 *The whole team played **well** on Saturday.*
ably, skilfully, expertly, effectively, efficiently, admirably, marvellously, wonderfully
OPPOSITE **badly**
2 *It's cold outside, so you'd better wrap up **well**.*
properly, suitably, correctly, thoroughly, carefully
3 *I know her brother **well**.*
closely, intimately, personally

well *adjective*
*Mrs Orr looks surprisingly **well** for her age.*
healthy, fit, strong, sound, robust, vigorous, lively, hearty
OPPOSITE **ill**

well-known *adjective*
*A **well-known** athlete will open the new sports shop.*
famous, celebrated, prominent, notable, renowned,

WORD WEB

weather *noun*
The typical weather in a particular area is the *climate*.
A person who studies and forecasts the weather is a *meteorologist*.

SOME TYPES OF WEATHER
fog: mist, (*Scottish*) haar, haze, smog; ice and snow: blizzard, frost, hail, ice, sleet, snowstorm light rain: drizzle, shower heavy rain: cloudburst, deluge, downpour, monsoon, torrent sun: drought, heatwave, sunshine storm: squall, tempest light wind: breeze, gust strong wind: cyclone, gale, hurricane, tornado, typhoon, whirlwind

WRITING TIPS

You can use these words to describe weather.
TO DESCRIBE *cloudy weather*
dull, grey, overcast, sunless
TO DESCRIBE *cold weather*
arctic, bitter, chilly, frosty, icy, nippy, perishing, raw, snowy, wintry
TO DESCRIBE *snow*
crisp, powdery, slushy
4 TO DESCRIBE hot weather:
baking, humid, melting, roasting, sizzling, sticky, sultry, sweltering
TO DESCRIBE *stormy weather*
rough, squally, tempestuous, turbulent, violent, wild
6 thunder MAY:
boom, crash, resound, roar, rumble
TO DESCRIBE *sunny weather*
bright, cloudless, fair, fine, springlike, summery, sunny, sunshiny
TO DESCRIBE *wet weather*
damp, drizzly, raining cats and dogs, showery, spitting, torrential
rain MAY
lash or pelt down, pour, teem (*informal*) bucket, tip down
TO DESCRIBE *windy weather*
biting, blowy, blustery, breezy, gusty
wind MAY
batter, blast, buffet, howl, moan, wail

d
e
f
g
h
i
n
o
p
q
r
s
t
u
v
w
x
y
z

distinguished, eminent
OPPOSITE **unknown, obscure**

wet *adjective*
1 *Archie took off his **wet** clothes and had a hot bath.*
damp, soaked, soaking, drenched, dripping, sopping, wringing wet
2 *The pitch was too **wet** to play on.*
waterlogged, saturated, sodden, soggy, dewy, muddy, boggy
3 *Take care—the paint is still **wet**.*
runny, sticky, tacky
4 *It was cold and **wet** all afternoon.*
rainy, showery, pouring, drizzly, misty

whip *verb*
1 *The jockey **whipped** his horse to make it go faster.*
beat, hit, lash, flog, thrash
2 *Whip the cream until it is thick.*
beat, whisk

whirl *verb*
*The snowflakes **whirled** in the icy wind.*
turn, twirl, spin, twist, circle, spiral, reel, pirouette, revolve, rotate

whisper *verb*
*What are you two **whispering** about?*
murmur, mutter, mumble
OPPOSITE **shout**

whole *adjective*
1 *I haven't read the **whole** book yet.*
complete, entire, full, total, unabbreviated
OPPOSITE **incomplete**
2 *The dinosaur skeleton appears to be **whole**.*
in one piece, intact, unbroken, undamaged, perfect
OPPOSITE **broken, in pieces**

wicked *adjective*
1 *Cinderella had a **wicked** stepmother.*
evil, cruel, vicious, villainous, detestable, mean, corrupt, immoral, sinful, foul, vile
OPPOSITE **good, virtuous**
2 *They hatched a **wicked** scheme to take over the world.*
evil, fiendish, malicious, malevolent, diabolical, monstrous, deplorable, dreadful, shameful
3 *The goblin had a **wicked** grin on his face.*
mischievous, playful, impish, naughty

wide *adjective*
1 *The hotel is close to a **wide** sandy beach.*
broad, expansive, extensive, large, spacious
OPPOSITE **narrow**
2 *She has a **wide** knowledge of*

classical music.
comprehensive, vast, wide-ranging, encyclopedic
OPPOSITE **limited**

wield *verb*
*The lumberjack was **wielding** his axe.*
brandish, flourish, hold, use

wild *adjective*
1 *I don't like seeing **wild** animals in captivity.*
undomesticated, untamed
OPPOSITE **tame**
2 *The hedgerow was full of **wild** flowers.*
natural, uncultivated
OPPOSITE **cultivated**
3 *To the west is a **wild** and mountainous region.*
rough, rugged, uncultivated, uninhabited, desolate
OPPOSITE cultivated
4 *The crowd were **wild** with excitement.*
riotous, rowdy, disorderly, unruly, boisterous, excited, noisy, uncontrollable, hysterical
OPPOSITE **calm, restrained**
5 *The weather looked **wild** outside.*
blustery, windy, gusty, stormy, turbulent, tempestuous
OPPOSITE **calm**

willing *adjective*
1 *She is always **willing** to help.*
eager, happy, pleased, ready, prepared
2 *I need a couple of **willing** volunteers.*
enthusiastic, helpful, cooperative, obliging
OPPOSITE **unwilling**

wilt *verb*
*The flowers **wilted** in the heat.*
become limp, droop, flop, sag, fade, shrivel, wither
OPPOSITE **flourish**

win *verb*
1 *Who do you think will **win**?*
come first, be victorious, succeed, triumph, prevail
To win against someone is also to *beat*, *conquer*, *defeat* or *overcome* them.
OPPOSITE **lose**
2 *She **won** first prize in the poetry competition.*
get, receive, gain, obtain, secure
(*informal*) pick up, walk away with

wind *verb*
1 *She **wound** the wool into a ball.*
coil, loop, roll, turn, curl

2 *The road **winds** up the hill.*
bend, curve, twist and turn, zigzag, meander

wilt

windy *adjective*
*It was a cold, **windy** day.*
breezy, blustery, gusty, squally, stormy
OPPOSITE **calm**

wink *verb*
*The lights **winked** on and off.*
flash, flicker, sparkle, twinkle

winner *noun*
*The **winner** was presented with a silver cup.*
victor, prizewinner, champion, conqueror
OPPOSITE **loser**

wipe *verb*
*I **wiped** the table with a cloth.*
rub, clean, polish, mop, swab, sponge

to wipe something out
*Pompeii was **wiped out** by the eruption of Mount Vesuvius.*
destroy, annihilate, exterminate, get rid of

wire *noun*
*Several **wires** protruded from the robot's head.*
cable, lead, flex
*A system of wires is **wiring**.*

wise *adjective*
1 *The soothsayer was very old and **wise**.*
sensible, reasonable, intelligent, perceptive, knowledgeable, rational, thoughtful
2 *I think you made a **wise** decision.*
good, right, proper, sound, fair, just, appropriate
OPPOSITE **foolish**

wish *noun*
*Her dearest **wish** was to travel to the Amazon.*
desire, want, longing, yearning, hankering, craving, urge, fancy, hope, ambition
(*informal*) yen

wish *verb*
*I **wish** that everyone would sit still for a minute!*
If you wish something would happen, you can say that you *want* or *would like* it to happen.

wither *verb*
*The flowers had **withered** and died.*
shrivel, dry up, shrink, wilt, droop, sag, flop
OPPOSITE **flourish**

witness *noun*
*A **witness** said that the car was*

wink

going too fast.
bystander, observer, onlooker, eyewitness, spectator

witty *adjective*
*He gave a **witty** account of his schooldays.*
humorous, amusing, comic, funny
OPPOSITE **dull**

wizard *noun*
1 *The **wizard** cast a spell over the whole palace.*
magician, sorcerer, enchanter
2 *My sister is a **wizard** with computers.*
expert, specialist, genius
(*informal*) whizz

wobble *verb*
1 *The cyclist **wobbled** all over the road.*
sway, totter, tetter, waver, rock
2 *The jelly **wobbled** as I carried the plate.*
shake, tremble, quake, quiver, vibrate

wobbly *adjective*
1 *The baby giraffe was a bit **wobbly** on its legs.*
shaky, tottering, unsteady
2 *This chair is a bit **wobbly**.*
loose, rickety, rocky, unstable, unsafe

woman *noun*
A polite word for a woman is ***lady**.*
A married woman is a ***wife**.*
A woman who has children is a ***mother**.*
An unmarried woman is a ***spinster**.*
A woman whose husband has died is a ***widow**.*
A woman on her wedding day is a ***bride**.*
A woman who is engaged to be married is a ***fiancée**.*
Words for a young woman are ***girl** and **lass**.*
Old words for a young woman are ***maid** and **maiden**.*

wonder *noun*
*The sight of the Taj Mahal filled them with **wonder**.*
admiration, awe, reverence, amazement, astonishment

wonder *verb*
*I **wonder** why she left in such a hurry.*
be curious about, ask yourself, ponder, think about

wonderful *adjective*
1 *It's **wonderful** what computers can do these days.*
amazing, astonishing, astounding, incredible, remarkable, extraordinary, marvellous, miraculous, phenomenal
2 *We had a **wonderful** time at the party.*

excellent, splendid, great, superb, delightful
(*informal*) brilliant, fantastic, terrific, fabulous, super
OPPOSITE **ordinary**

wood *noun*
1 *All the furniture in the room was made of **wood**.*
timber, lumber, planks, logs
2 *We followed a nature trail through the **wood**.*
woodland, woods, forest, trees

word *noun*
1 *What's the French **word** for 'birthday'?*
expression, term
All the words you know are your ***vocabulary**.*
2 *You gave me your **word**.*
promise, assurance, guarantee, pledge, vow
3 *There has been no **word** from him for several weeks.*
news, message, information

work *noun*
1 *Digging the garden involves a lot of hard **work**.*
effort, labour, toil, exertion
2 *Do you have any **work** to do this weekend?*
task, assignment, chore, job, homework, housework
3 *What kind of **work** does she do?*
occupation, employment, job, profession, business, trade, vocation

work *verb*
1 *She's been **working** in the garden all day.*
be busy, exert yourself, labour, toil, slave
2 *He **works** in the bookshop on Saturdays.*
be employed, have a job, go to work
3 *My watch isn't **working**.*
function, go, operate
4 *Is the DVD player easy to **work**?*
operate, run, use, control, handle

world *noun*
1 *Antarctica is a remote part of the **world**.*
earth, globe
2 *Scientists are searching for life on other **worlds**.*
planet

worried *adjective*
*You look **worried**. Is something the matter?*
anxious, troubled, uneasy, distressed, disturbed, upset, apprehensive, concerned, bothered, tense, strained, nervous
OPPOSITE **relaxed**

world

worry *verb*
1 *There's no need to **worry**.*
be anxious, be troubled, be disturbed, brood, fret
2 *It **worried** her that he hadn't replied to her letter.*
trouble, distress, upset, concern, disturb

worry *noun*
1 *He's been a constant source of **worry** to her.*
anxiety, distress, uneasiness, vexation
2 *I don't want to add to your **worries**.*
trouble, concern, burden, care, problem

worthwhile *adjective*
*It may be **worthwhile** to get a second opinion.*
helpful, useful, valuable, beneficial, profitable
OPPOSITE **useless**

wound *noun*
*He is being treated in hospital for a head **wound**.*
injury, cut, gash, graze, scratch, sore

wound *verb*
*The fox was **wounded** in the leg and bleeding.*
injure, hurt, harm

wrap *verb*
1 *She **wrapped** the presents in shiny gold paper.*
cover, pack, enclose, enfold, swathe
To wrap water pipes is to ***insulate** or **lag** them.*
2 *The mountain was **wrapped** in mist.*
cloak, envelop, shroud, surround, hide, conceal

a
b
i
j
k
l
m
n
o
p
q
r
s
t
u
v
w
x
y
z

159

wreck *verb*
1 *His bicycle was* **wrecked** *in the accident.*
demolish, destroy, crush, smash, shatter, crumple
2 *The injury* **wrecked** *her chances becoming a dancer.*
ruin, spoil

wreckage *noun*
Divers have discovered the **wreckage** *of an old ship.*
debris, fragments, pieces, remains
The wreckage of a building is *rubble* or *ruins*.

wriggle *verb*
The prisoner managed to **wriggle** *out of his bonds.*
twist, writhe, squirm, worm your way

wrinkle *noun*
The old hag's face was covered in **wrinkles**.
crease, fold, furrow, line, ridge, crinkle, pucker, pleat
A small hollow on someone's skin is a *dimple*.

wrinkle *verb*
The creature **wrinkled** *its nose and sniffed.*
pucker up, crease, crinkle, crumple, fold
OPPOSITE smooth

write *verb*
1 *My granny* **wrote** *a diary when she was a girl.*
compile, compose, draw up, set down, pen
To write letters or emails to people is to *correspond* with them.
To write a rough version of a story is to *draft* it.
2 *He* **wrote** *his address on the back of an envelope.*
jot down, note, print,

scrawl, scribble
To write on a document or surface is to *inscribe* it.
To write your signature on something is to *autograph* it.

writer *noun*
A person who writes books is an *author*.
A person who writes novels is a *novelist*.
A person who writes plays is a *dramatist* or *playwright*.
A person who writes scripts for films or television is a *scriptwriter* or *screenwriter*.
A person who writes poetry is a *poet*.
A person who writes about someone else's life is a *biographer*.
A person who writes for newspapers is a *correspondent*, *journalist*, or *reporter*.
A person who writes music is a *composer*.

writing *noun*
1 *Can you read the* **writing** *on the envelope?*
handwriting
Untidy writing is a *scrawl* or *scribble*.
The art of beautiful handwriting is *calligraphy*.
2 *The* **writing** *on the stone was very faint.*
inscription
3 *(often plural) She introduced me to the* **writings** *of Roald Dahl.*
literature, works

✦ WORD WEB

writing *noun*
VARIOUS FORMS OF WRITING AND LITERATURE
autobiography, biography, children's literature, comedy, crime or detective story, diary, drama or play, essay, fable, fairy story or fairy tale, fantasy, fiction, film or TV script, folk tale, ghost story, historical fiction, history, journalism, legend, letters or correspondence, lyrics, myth, newspaper article, non-fiction, novel, parody, philosophy, poetry or verse, prose, romance, satire, science fiction or sci-fi, spy story, thriller, tragedy, travel writing, western

---

wrong *adjective*
1 *It was* **wrong** *to take the book without asking.*
bad, dishonest, irresponsible, immoral, sinful, wicked, criminal, unfair, unjust
2 *His calculations were all* **wrong**.
incorrect, mistaken, inaccurate

3 *Did I say the* **wrong** *thing?*
inappropriate, unsuitable, improper
4 *There's something* **wrong** *with the TV.*
faulty, defective, not working, out of order
OPPOSITE right
to go wrong
The professor's plan began to **go wrong**.
fail, backfire
(informal) flop, go pear-shaped
OPPOSITE succeed

Yy

yell *verb*
I **yelled** *to attract their attention.*
call out, cry out, shout, bawl, bellow

young *adjective*
1 *A lot of* **young** *people went to the concert.*
youthful, juvenile
OPPOSITE older, mature
2 *I think this book is a bit* **young** *for you.*
childish, babyish, immature, infantile
OPPOSITE adult, grown-up
A young person is a *child* or *youngster*.
A young adult is an *adolescent* or *youth*.
A very young child is a *baby* or *infant*.
A young bird is a *chick*, *fledgling*, or *nestling*.
Young fish are *fry*.
A young plant is a *cutting* or *seedling*.
A young tree is a *sapling*.

young *plural noun*
The mother bird returned to feed her **young**.
offspring, children, young ones, family
A family of young birds is a *brood*.
A family of young cats or dogs is a *litter*.

Zz

zero *noun*
Four minus four makes **zero**.
nothing, nought
A score of zero in football is *nil*; in cricket it is a *duck*, and in tennis it is *love*.